THE GREENWOOD ENCYCLOPEDIA OF
ROCK HISTORY

The Greenwood Encyclopedia of Rock History

Volume 1
The Early Years, 1951–1959
Lisa Scrivani-Tidd

Volume 2
Folk, Pop, Mods, and Rockers, 1960–1966
Rhonda Markowitz

Volume 3
The Rise of Album Rock, 1967–1973
Chris Smith

Volume 4
From Arenas to the Underground, 1974–1980
Chris Smith with John Borgmeyer, Richard Skanse, and Rob Patterson

Volume 5
The Video Generation, 1981–1990
MaryAnn Janosik

Volume 6
The Grunge and Post-Grunge Years, 1991–2005
Bob Gulla

THE GREENWOOD ENCYCLOPEDIA OF
ROCK HISTORY

From Arenas to the Underground,
1974–1980

CHRIS SMITH with
JOHN BORGMEYER,
RICHARD SKANSE, and
ROB PATTERSON

GREENWOOD PRESS
Westport, Connecticut • London

Library of Congress Cataloging-in-Publication Data

The Greenwood encyclopedia of rock history.
    p. cm.
  Includes bibliographical references and index.
  ISBN 0–313–32937–0 ((set) : alk. paper)—ISBN 0–313–32938–9 ((vol. 1) : alk. paper)—ISBN
0–313–32960–5 ((vol. 2) : alk. paper)—ISBN 0–313–32966–4 ((vol. 3) : alk. paper)—ISBN
0–313–33611–3 ((vol. 4) : alk. paper)—ISBN 0–313–32943–5 ((vol. 5) : alk. paper)—ISBN
0–313–32981–8 ((vol. 6) : alk. paper) 1. Rock music—History and criticism.
  ML3534.G754 2006
  781.66'09—dc22   2005023475

British Library Cataloguing in Publication Data is available.

This book is included in the *African American Experience* database from Greenwood Electronic
Media. For more information, visit www.africanamericanexperience.com.

Library of Congress Catalog Card Number: 2005023475

ISBN 0–313–32937–0 (set)
    0–313–32938–9 (vol. 1)
    0–313–32960–5 (vol. 2)
    0–313–32966–4 (vol. 3)
    0–313–33611–3 (vol. 4)
    0–313–32943–5 (vol. 5)
    0–313–32981–8 (vol. 6)

First published in 2006

Greenwood Press, 88 Post Road West, Westport, CT 06881
An imprint of Greenwood Publishing Group, Inc.
www.greenwood.com

Printed in the United States of America

The paper used in this book complies with the
Permanent Paper Standard issued by the National
Information Standards Organization (Z39.48–1984).

10 9 8 7 6 5 4 3 2 1

CONTENTS

# SET FOREWORD

Rock 'n' roll, man, it changed my life. It was like the Voice of America, the real America, coming to your home.

—Bruce Springsteen[1]

The term *rock 'n' roll* has a mysterious origin. Many have credited legendary disc jockey Alan Freed for coining the term. Some claim that it was actually a blues euphemism for sexual intercourse, while others even see the term rock as having gospel origin, with worshippers "rocking" with the Lord. In 1947, DeLuxe Records released "Good Rocking Tonight," a blues-inspired romp by Roy Brown, which touched off a number of R&B artists in the late-1940s providing their own take on "rocking." But many music historians point to the 1951 Chess single "Rocket 88" as the first rock record. Produced by Sam Phillips and performed by Jackie Brenston and Ike Turner's Kings of Rhythm (though released under the name Jackie Brenston & His Delta Cats), the record established the archetype of early rock and roll: "practically indecipherable lyrics about cars, booze, and women; [a] booting tenor sax, and a churning, beat-heavy rhythmic bottom."[2]

Although its true origins are debatable, what is certain is that rock 'n' roll grew into a musical form that, in many ways, defined American culture in the second half of the twentieth century. Today, however, "rock 'n' roll" is used with less and less frequency in reference to the musical genre. The phrase seems to linger as a quaint cliché co-opted by mass media—something that a *Top Gun* pilot once said in voicing high-speed, mid-air glee. Watching MTV these days, one would be hard-pressed to find a reference to "rock 'n' roll," but the term *rock* survives, though often modified by prefixes used to denote the growing hybridization of the genre: There is alternative rock, blues rock, chick rock, classic rock, folk rock, funk rock, garage rock, glam rock, grunge rock, hard rock, psychedelic rock, punk rock, roots rock, and countless other sub-genres of rock music. It seems that musicians found more and more ways to rock but, for some reason, stopped rolling—or to paraphrase Led Zeppelin's "Stairway to Heaven," the music world opted to rock, but not to roll.

Call it what you will, rock music has never existed within a vacuum; it has always reflected aspects of our society, whether it be the statement of youth culture or rebellion against adult society; an expression of love found, lost, or never had; the portrayal of gritty street life or the affirmation of traditional American values; the heady pondering of space-age metaphysics or the giddy nonsense of a one-hit wonder, rock music has been an enduring voice of the people for over five decades. *The Greenwood Encyclopedia of Rock History* records not only the countless manifestations of rock music in our society, but also the many ways in which rock music has shaped, and been shaped by, American culture.

Testifying to the enduring popularity of rock music are the many publications devoted to covering rock music. These range from countless single-volume record guides providing critics' subjective ratings to the multi-volume sets that lump all forms of popular music together, discussing the jazz-rock duo Steely Dan in the same breath as Stravinsky, or indie-rock group Pavement with Pavarotti. To be sure, such references have their value, but we felt that there was no authoritative work that gives rock music history the thorough, detailed examination that it merits. For this reason, our six-volume encyclopedia focuses closely on the rock music genre. While many different forms of rock music are examined, including the *influences* of related genres such as folk, jazz, soul, or hip-hop, we do not try to squeeze in discussions of other genres of music. For example, a volume includes the influences of country music on rock—such as folk rock or "alt.country"—but it does not examine country music itself. Thus, *rock music* is not treated here as synonymous with *popular music*, as our parents (or our parents' parents) might have done, equating whatever forms of music were on the charts, whatever the "young kids" were listening to, as basically all the same, with only a few differences, an outsiders' view of rock, one that viewed the genre fearfully and from a distance. Instead, we present a six-volume set—one that is both "meaty" and methodical—from the perspective of the rock music historians who provide narrative chapters on the many different stories during more than five decades of rock music history.

The Greenwood Encyclopedia of Rock History comprises six information-packed volumes covering the dizzying evolution of this exciting form of music. The volumes are divided by historical era: *Volume 1: The Early Years, 1951–1959*, spans from the year "Rocket 88" (arguably the first rock single) was released to the year of the infamous "Day the Music Died," the fatal airplane crash that took the lives of Buddy Holly, Ritchie Valens, and J. P. Richardson (a.k.a. The Big Bopper). *Volume 2: Folk, Pop, Mods, and Rockers, 1960–1966,* covers the period when the British Invasion irrevocably changed the world, while such American rock scenes as Motown and surf rock held their own. In *Volume 3: The Rise of Album Rock, 1967–1973*, Chris Smith chronicles the growing experimentation during the psychedelic era of rock, from *Sgt. Pepper* to *Dark Side of the Moon* and everything in between. In *Volume 4: From Arenas to the Underground, 1974–1980*, Smith et al., record how rock became big business while also spawning hybrid forms and underground movements. *Volume 5: The Video Generation, 1981–1990* starts with the year of MTV's debut and captures the era when video threatened to kill the radio star. Finally, in *Volume 6: The Grunge and Post-Grunge Years, 1991–2005*, Bob Gulla captures the many innovations of millennial rock music and culture. Within each volume, the narrative chapters are supplemented by a timeline, discography, bibliography, and a glossary of encyclopedia entries for quick reference.

We hope that librarians, researchers, and fans alike will find endless nuggets of information within this reference. And because we are talking about rock, we hope you will find that reading *The Greenwood Encyclopedia of Rock History* will be a whole lot of fun, too.

Rock on.

Rob Kirkpatrick
Greenwood Publishing Group

NOTES

1. Rock and Roll Hall of Fame and Museum home page, http://www.rockhall.com.
2. All Music Guide entry for Jackie Brenston, http://www.allmusic.com.

 **PREFACE**

The 1970s were a confusing and contradictory decade for rock music. Some of the most significant figures toiled away in dank basements and on beer-soaked pub stages, while some of the most historically inconsequential sold out stadiums around the country. Some musicians were celebrated as the new Bob Dylan and quickly forgotten; others died in obscurity, only to be appreciated by a later generation as artists ahead of their time. Progressive rockers took posturing to new heights and punk rockers took celebrity to new lows; corporate rockers broke sales records and singer-songwriters broke hearts; fusion artists got people to jump up and dance, soft rockers got them to sit back and relax, and new wavers somehow got them to do both.

Like 1970s rock, this volume, *From Arenas to the Underground, 1974–1980*, is also fractured, authored by four music critics who bring more than fifty years of combined experience to these pages in an attempt to discover where the rock genre begins and ends in this turbulent decade. Between us, we have written for nearly every major rock publication in the United States—*Creem*, *Billboard*, *Rolling Stone*, *Circus*, *Musician*, *No Depression*, *Performing Songwriter*, *Harp*, *Tracks*, *Sing Out!*, *Spin*, and *Crawdaddy!*, just to name a few—and have contributed to texts such as *The Rolling Stone Record Guide*, *The Rolling Stone Encyclopedia of Rock & Roll*, and *The New Rolling Stone Album Guide*. Currently, Richard Skanse is working as the editor of *Texas Music* in Austin, Texas; Rob Patterson is an Austin-based freelance writer; John Borgmeyer is senior staff writer at *C-ville* in Charlottesville, Virginia; and Chris Smith is a freelance writer in Vancouver, Canada, and author of Volume 3 of this series.

The focus of *The Greenwood Encyclopedia of Rock History* is on rock music in the United States. The 1970s in particular saw enormous contributions to American rock from countries such as Australia, Canada, Germany, and Great Britain. Without these influences, rock through the 1970s and beyond would have taken a much different shape—from Britain came a number of new-wave and punk artists who brought rock back to its basic three-chord structure; from Germany came the sound of electronica that would later influence new wave, disco, rave music, and techno; from Canada came both soft-rock and hard-rock bands that would help shape the important California scene; and from Australia came an eclectic mix of sounds, including the heavy-metal strains of AC/DC, the soothing vocals of Olivia Newton-John, and, by way of the United Kingdom, the funk-inspired disco grooves of the Bee Gees. As much as these other countries influenced American rock, we have attempted here to gloss over the early careers of these rockers in favor of focusing on their impact in the United States.

All data concerning album rankings and gold/platinum status come from the Recording Industry Association of America (http://www.riaa.com) and Joel Whitburn's archives of the *Billboard* charts, widely acknowledged to be the authoritative source:

> Whitburn, Joel, ed. *The Billboard Book of Top 40 Albums*. New York: Billboard, 1987.
>
> Whitburn, Joel, ed. *The Billboard Book of Top 40 Albums, 1955–1992*. New York: Billboard, 1993.
>
> Whitburn, Joel, ed. *The Billboard Book of Top 40 Hits*. New York: Billboard, 1996.
>
> Whitburn, Joel, ed. *Joel Whitburn Presents a Century of Pop Music*. New York: Billboard, 1999.

It should be noted here that in addition to numerous print sources, the authors of this volume also utilized online databases of periodical content from 1970s music journalism. While this has aided in obtaining first-hand accounts that would have otherwise been difficult to come by, some journalism databases did not list details such as article titles, authors, and page numbers, leading to incomplete endnotes in some chapters. Despite these incomplete citations, we are confident of the sources' validity, and enough citation information is provided should an eager reader wish to track down a particular article. Countless primary and secondary sources were used in researching this material as well, as is detailed in this volume's Reference Guide. Although historical reporting is inherently subjective—particularly in the arts—the authors have made every attempt to properly cite specific reactions or commentary on the music of this period, as often critical observations differed wildly from popular reaction. Such was the bizarre split personality of 1970s rock.

Like the other volumes in *The Greenwood Encyclopedia of Rock History*, *From Arenas to the Underground, 1974–1980* includes lively narrative chapters describing the prominent performers, composers, trends, and genres of the era, as well as an A-to-Z chapter that briefly defines the key elements of this time period, including important performers, albums, managers, genres, and more. Other useful features of the book include a timeline of important events in rock history from 1974 through 1980, a list of the top-ranking albums of the period, a list of the most significant rock albums of the period, and a reference guide to useful books, articles, Web sites, museums or special collections, and films. A comprehensive index provides access to the volume's contents.

INTRODUCTION

Once upon a time, rock and roll was simple. A handful of adventurous artists took elements of blues, skiffle, folk, rhythm and blues (R&B), jazz, gospel, and country and western, gave it a strong backbeat and energetic tempo, and played it for enthralled rhythm and blues audiences. In 1951, Cleveland disc jockey Alan Freed began broadcasting this "race music"—so-called for the large number of black artists and fans—to a mainstream white audience and called it rock and roll.

This is, of course, a gross generalization of its origins, but for its first decade or so, rock and roll was considered a single genre. Despite its many influences, the music—and its early subgenres such as surf music and rockabilly—was easily recognizable as falling under the rubric of rock and roll.

As a genre born from such widely varied sources, rock and roll could not help but quickly expand and evolve. By its second decade, regional differences in the United States and influences from countries such as England, Canada, and Australia began to move rock and roll—which now took on the more encompassing title of "rock music"—into new directions. Particularly crucial to this expansion was Minnesota folkie Bob Dylan, who emphasized rock's acoustic roots, and the British Invasion bands, especially the Liverpool quartet the Beatles. Though Dylan and the Beatles started from opposite ends of rock's (at the time somewhat limited) spectrum, they influenced each other enormously, leading to a swarm of imitators and rock's golden age of experimentation in the mid-1960s.

By the late 1960s, rock was a potpourri of styles, tempos, rhythms, melodies, instruments, and personalities. Largely fueled by the psychedelic scene in San Francisco, rock became a dominant entertainment industry, leading to greater album sales, rock festivals, and a large variety of styles such as glam rock, southern rock, heavy metal, folk rock, and progressive music, all vying for mainstream acceptance. The important thing to note about this period of the late 1960s and early 1970s—particularly in the way it relates to this volume—is that even as rock music was expanding, it was still recognizably rock. In the exotic guitar work of Jimi Hendrix, Duane Allman, and Eric Clapton; in the powerful vocals of Janis Joplin, Robert Plant, and Ozzy Osbourne; in the thick seriousness of Robert Fripp, Iron Butterfly, and Bob Dylan; in the odd experiments of Sly Stone, David Bowie, and Pink Floyd, it was not terribly difficult to distinguish rock from other types of music on the radio.

The defining characteristic of the transition that rock underwent between 1974 and 1980 is this ability to recognize rock as a single genre. As rock continued to develop different personalities, these subgenres began to compete with each other. Where rock had recently been about incorporating other styles of music into its fold, artists now wished to expand their individual subgenres to create entirely new types of music that would be less identifiable as rock, or at least would carry among their defining traits a negative association with other rock styles.

The result was a fracturing of rock styles in the 1970s. As the commercial market for rock grew exponentially in the 1960s and 1970s, more bands left their garages for the stage, and with more acts flooding the market, artists sought to find a distinctive voice, exploring territory further and further from the rock mainstream, creating new genres and subgenres in their wake. One consequence of this phenomenon was a growing schizophrenia within rock and its subgenres. Musical styles became inherently contradictory, often grasping certain rock elements with one hand and pushing away those same elements with another.

One of the most obvious examples of this contradiction comes from one of the few 1960s subgenres to remain popular in the 1970s: progressive rock. As progressive rock grew from a mellotron-infused hard-rock style of the late 1960s into overproduced, self-important posturing (sometimes with full-orchestra accompaniment) in the 1970s, progressive bands became more pretentious and distant from their fans, with acts like Yes, Jethro Tull, and Emerson, Lake & Palmer selling out arenas and stadiums, using increasingly advanced recording and amplification technology to fill every nook and cranny of the venue with sound and attitude. Other progressive acts, like Kraftwerk and Brian Eno, embraced the same technology to chart an opposite course, creating minimalist electronic works that used very few, if any, live instrumentation, leading Eno to create ambient music in the later 1970s.

The singer-songwriter movement of the early decade also sought a minimalist approach—usually an individual musician playing and singing his or her own material on an acoustic guitar or piano—but lacked progressive's dependence on technology and impersonal themes. As America's divorce rate skyrocketed and the "me" decade began, a confessional brand of relationship-centered music launched artists such as James Taylor and Carly Simon to prominence. At the same time, artists such as Gordon Lightfoot, Billy Joel, and Bruce Springsteen brought rock music a more literary, narrative focus.

Meanwhile, heavy metal, a subgenre that emphasized volume over literary pretension, turned in several distinct directions as well. In some respects, metal grew angrier and faster, with antiauthority acts like Judas Priest and Black Sabbath using dark imagery and heavy guitars to frighten parents and create legions of teenage fans, giving rise to later metal forms such as speed metal and goth. More glitzy metal acts such as KISS and Alice Cooper appealed to a slightly younger teen audience, turning metal into entertaining theater with makeup, fantasy-inspired costumes and scenery, and less threatening (i.e., cheesier) lyrics—turning anticorporate music into a corporate industry with long lines of branded products. This not-so-heavy metal would later develop into the enormously popular hair metal and power pop of the 1980s. Beyond the heavy and the light sat two of the genre's greatest bands—Led Zeppelin and Queen—who incorporated such unusual styles as metal, folk, raga, and even opera into their music, sometimes in the same song (Zep's "Stairway to Heaven" and Queen's "Bohemian Rhapsody").

Hard-rock bands such as the Rolling Stones and the Who survived the turn of the decade to continue as top acts in the 1970s, creating the privileged rock-star persona and influencing a string of imitators such as Aerosmith, Bad Company, and Ted Nugent. On the opposite end of the spectrum, funk and jazz-fusion were reworked into the more danceable form of disco, in which the artists were faceless and the audience (i.e., the dancers) became the stars of the show. The enormous and sudden popularity of disco would then lead the aforementioned rock stars to incorporate disco beats into their own music to keep up with the times.

In reaction to the mega-celebrity stardom of hard rock, the excessive pretensions of progressive rock, and the bloated fashion show of disco, garage bands ceased emulating rock gods and began reveling in their proletarian amateurism, creating the phenomenon of punk rock in New York and London. By the middle of the decade, rock had become simultaneously grand and sleazy, proud and humble, virtuous and decadent, speedy and measured. Where was there left to go but ironic? Enter new wave, which took the antiestablishment themes of punk rock, added art-school flourishes and poppy grooves, and created a highly marketable form of rock that reveled in and commodified an affected boredom with its own genre.

Beyond the expanding and fracturing rock genres, changes in the music industry also played a part in rock's development. By the dawn of the 1970s, rock music had become a large and swiftly growing business, quickly outpacing movies and sports as the dominant form of entertainment. Music retailing moved from the department stores and mom-and-pop record shops where music had been sold in the past into ever-larger record-store chains, giving consumers greater access to recorded music. Despite the struggling American economy and the growing separation between rich and poor, overall Americans saw a growth in their disposable income, and with record sales hitting the $2 billion-a-year mark in 1974 (80 percent of it rock music), more and more of it was being spent on rock albums.

For most of the 1970s, the music industry—particularly rock-music outlets—saw significant growth. At the beginning of the decade, it was the rare hit album that would earn gold album status (for sales of 500,000 copies). But as increasingly diverse artists created increasing hordes of fans, rock acts were able to sell albums in higher volume, leading the Recording Industry Association of America (RIAA) to introduce platinum status for albums that sold 1 million units. By the end of the decade, top acts were enjoying multimillion sales, and even one-hit wonders sometimes earned gold albums.

Similarly, rock concerts grew out of the theaters and smaller arenas they played in the 1960s into larger sports arenas and stadiums in the 1970s. These massive concerts came to be known as "arena rock"—an ironic development that led to a return to the one-way-street style of performance (in which audience members were passive recipients) rather than the audience being part of the show as in the mid-1960s San Francisco festival scene from which rock concerts grew. All but gone was the element of audience/performer interactivity of festivals, replaced by heavily produced shows for major acts with tightly controlled sets.

Many of rock's greatest leaps over the years had been brought about by advances in technology, and in the 1970s this was as true about the industry's economic growth as it was about its aesthetic development. Though the cumbersome 8-track was never as popular as the album format, the smaller cassette tapes began a slow march toward popularity when they were introduced in 1963, eventually edging out home reel-to-reel systems. In the 1970s cassette sales skyrocketed as combination radio receivers and cassette players were installed in automobiles, making it easy to play one's music at home and in the car. After Sony introduced the Walkman in 1979 (originally called the Soundabout), allowing people to carry their music with them, cassettes continued to become a dominant medium that eventually outgrew album sales, only to be replaced by compact discs in the 1980s.

Also contributing to the increasing popularization of rock music was the telecommunications revolution of the 1970s that saw the advent of cable television and a marked increase in global telecommunications transmissions. The relatively new phenomenon of the music video took root, eventually leading to the MTV network in 1981. Advances such as digital technology found their way into recording studios—in the form of multitrack recorders, synthesizers, effects devices, drum machines, and tape delay looping, to name a few—and music lovers could hear these sounds more clearly than ever with high-fidelity record players and headphones. But even these advances could not keep fans away from the arenas, as this technology was also used to create increasingly theatrical concerts with digital sound effects, laser-light shows, and walls of music.

The music industry was also undergoing sweeping change at its highest levels. An Arab oil embargo made petroleum-based products (including records) so expensive that some small labels folded, leading to a consolidation of record companies into large, multinational corporations. By the end of the decade, six labels controlled the vast majority of music released in the United States, a trend that continued until the independent label resurgence in the 1990s. Larger labels meant bigger contracts for the top-selling artists in the 1970s, as the labels relied on profits from these artists' massive sales to underwrite other, less-profitable acts. Between 1970 and 1972 Stevie Wonder successfully fought Motown for a substantially greater degree of control over his music, which was unheard of in rock, and in 1974 Elton John negotiated a whopping (at the time) $8 million contract with MCA.

By 1980, rock music was almost unrecognizable when compared to the beginning of the period covered in this volume. In 1974 progressive music ruled the arenas and rock's softer acts ruled the charts and the airwaves, with the occasional hard-rock 1960s monster—Led Zeppelin, the Who, the Rolling Stones—surfacing to snatch the headlines. Only six years later rock seemed worn out by its own success, with punk revolting against progressive pomp, corporate rock creating superstar acts with no superstars in them, rap and hip-hop emerging from funk and fusion to move rock in an entirely new direction, and new wave borrowing from world-music sounds to take rock to more pop-oriented places. Though rock music in the 1970s was decidedly contradictory, its internal personality battles gave rise to a new sense of ownership in which the artists were invested in their material, leading to a font of inventiveness among American musicians and a constantly expanding diaspora of rock into myriad forms in the 1980s and beyond.

TIMELINE: 1974–1980

1974

March:	Punk-rock instigators the Ramones form in Queens, New York.
March 31:	Television is the first punk band to play at New York's CBGB, the birthplace of the American punk movement.
April 6:	Some 350,000 gather at the California Jam Festival at Ontario Speedway to hear Deep Purple, Black Sabbath, the Eagles, and Emerson, Lake & Palmer.
May 8:	Blues/rock organist Graham Bond, leader of Cream forerunner the Graham Bond Organization, throws himself under a subway train in London.
May 10:	Led Zeppelin form their own record label, Swan Song.
May 24:	Famed bandleader Duke Ellington dies of lung cancer and pneumonia.
July 29:	Cass Elliot ("Mama Cass"), of the Mamas and the Papas, dies of a heart attack in London.
September 14:	After nearly ten years of rock god-dom, Eric Clapton finally reaches the No. 1 chart spot with Bob Marley's "I Shot the Sheriff."
October:	Robert Fripp announces that his founding progressive and heavy-metal band King Crimson "is over for ever and ever," beginning the slow decline of progressive rock's popularity.

October 13:   Ed Sullivan, who had helped introduce Elvis Presley, the Beatles, the Rolling Stones, and the Doors to a national audience with his variety show, dies of cancer.

November 16:   John Lennon has his first post-Beatles No. 1 with "Whatever Gets You Thru the Night."

November 25:   British folkie Nick Drake, who would later acquire a large cult following in the United States, overdoses on antidepressants.

November 28:   John Lennon performs three songs with Elton John during an Elton concert at Madison Square Garden; it would be the last time Lennon performed in the United States.

1975

January 8:   Led Zeppelin sell out three shows at Madison Square Garden in a record four hours, solidifying their reputation as the most popular rock band in the world.

January 17:   Bob Dylan makes a remarkable critical comeback with the release of *Blood on the Tracks*, one of his most acclaimed albums.

February 3–10: While touring to support their album *War Child*, Jethro Tull break attendance records at the Los Angeles Forum, drawing 93,000 spectators to five shows.

March: Patti Smith and Television begin their legendary seven-week run at New York's CBGB, for many marking the beginning of the punk rock and new wave movements.

March 1:   The Eagles have their first chart-topper with "Best of My Love," beginning a streak of hit albums that would make them one of the most popular acts of the decade.

March 16:   Texas blues legend T-Bone Walker dies of pneumonia.

March 19:   The rock musical film *Tommy* is released in the United States.

May: Elton John's *Captain Fantastic and the Brown Dirt Cowboy* becomes the first album ever to debut at No. 1 on the *Billboard* charts.

June: Peter Gabriel leaves Genesis for a solo career; drummer Phil Collins takes his place as lead singer.

June 3:   Ralph Gleason, co-founder and editor of *Rolling Stone* magazine, dies of a heart attack.

June 29:   Folk artist Tim Buckley dies of a heroin overdose.

August: John Lydon shows up at Malcolm McLaren's shop in London wearing an "I Hate Pink Floyd" T-shirt. Lydon changes his name to Johnny Rotten, and the Sex Pistols are born.

August 4: Led Zeppelin lead singer Robert Plant is seriously injured in an automobile accident in Greece.

August 25: Bruce Springsteen releases his critically acclaimed album *Born to Run*, launching him into the American spotlight.

September 20: David Bowie scores his first No. 1 in the United States, "Fame," co-written by John Lennon.

October 9: Sean Lennon is born to John Lennon and Yoko Ono, marking the beginning of John's five-year hiatus from music.

October 30: Bob Dylan kicks off his Rolling Thunder Revue in Plymouth, Massachusetts.

November: Patti Smith releases her debut record *Horses*, widely considered one of punk rock's foundation albums.

November 6: The Sex Pistols play their first show in London.

1976

January 10: Chester "Howlin' Wolf" Burnett, a major blues influence on 1960s British and American rockers, dies of kidney failure.

February 7: Paul Simon has his first post–Simon and Garfunkel No. 1 with "50 Ways to Leave Your Lover."

February 17: The Eagles release *Their Greatest Hits 1971–1975*, the first album to be certified platinum under the RIAA's revised ranking system, which awards platinum status for 1 million units sold. The album would retain tremendous staying power, averaging almost a million copies sold a year well beyond the end of the century, ultimately becoming the best-selling album in history.

March 19: Free guitarist Paul Kossoff dies of a heart attack brought on by excessive drug abuse.

April 9: Folkie and protest music legend Phil Ochs hangs himself after years of battling clinical depression.

April 23: The Ramones release their self-titled debut album.

April 29: During a stop in Memphis on his Born to Run tour, Bruce Springsteen jumps the fence at Graceland to meet Elvis Presley. The King was not home.

July 4: The Ramones play at the Roundhouse in London, galvanizing the UK punk scene.

October 16: Stevie Wonder's seminal pop/soul/rock album *Songs in the Key of Life* debuts on the charts at No. 1—only the third album in history to do so.

November 24: The Band play their final performance in a farewell concert at San Francisco's Winterland. The concert is filmed by Martin Scorsese for the documentary film *The Last Waltz*.

December 8: The Eagles release their magnum opus *Hotel California*, which debuts at No. 1.

1977

February 15: Sid Vicious joins the Sex Pistols, replacing bassist Glen Matlock, who was reportedly fired for being too talented.

February 26: Fleetwood Mac's album *Rumours* debuts on the charts (after being released on February 4), where it sits at No. 1 for an astonishing thirty-one weeks—at the time the highest charting in rock history.

May 25: *Star Wars* is released in theaters.

August 16: The King of Rock 'n' Roll, Elvis Presley, dies of a heart attack at his Graceland mansion.

September 16: Glam-rocker Marc Bolan, leader of the band T. Rex, dies in a car crash in London.

Seminal new wave band Talking Heads release their debut, *Talking Heads: 77*.

October 20: Lynyrd Skynyrd guitarist Steve Gaines, singer Cassie Gaines, singer Ronnie Van Zant, road manager Dean Kilpatrick, and two pilots are killed during a tour as their private plane crashes into a Mississippi swamp.

October 28: The Sex Pistols release their only official studio album, *Never Mind the Bollocks, Here's the Sex Pistols*, generating a storm of controversy over profanity and the album's disrespectful representation of the British monarchy.

December 14: The smash disco drama *Saturday Night Fever* premieres in New York City.

1978

January 14: The Sex Pistols end their famously disastrous two-week tour of the United States with a show at San Francisco's Winterland Ballroom, where lead singer Johnny Rotten quits the band onstage after asking the audience, "Ever get the feeling you've been cheated?"

January 25: Bob Dylan's artsy semi-documentary *Renaldo and Clara* is released in U.S. theaters.

April 26:	The rockumentary concert film *The Last Waltz* premieres in the United States.
June 16:	The hit musical *Grease* premieres in U.S. movie theaters.
July 21:	The film version of *Sgt. Pepper's Lonely Hearts Club Band* debuts in New York City.
September 7:	The Who drummer Keith Moon dies in his sleep from an accidental overdose of antiseizure medication.
October 12:	Nancy Spungen—girlfriend of the Sex Pistols' Sid Vicious—is found stabbed to death in a New York City hotel room. Vicious is arrested for murder.
October 23:	Maybelle Carter, one of the twentieth century's most important music figures, dies. As a member of the Carter Family and Mother Maybelle and the Carter Sisters, she was enormously influential on later country, bluegrass, folk, and rock.

1979

January 1:	Bill Graham closes San Francisco's legendary Winterland Ballroom.
January 15:	MCA Records buys ABC Records and dissolves the ABC label.
February 2:	Sex Pistols bassist Sid Vicious is found dead of a heroin overdose.
February 7:	The Clash kick off their first American tour at Berkeley Community Theatre outside of San Francisco.
February 23:	Dire Straits begin their first American tour in Boston.
March 27:	Eric Clapton marries Pattie Boyd, ex-wife of Clapton friend George Harrison and subject of Clapton's opus "Layla."
June 26:	Robert Plant's son Karac dies of a stomach infection, forcing Led Zeppelin to cut short their massive U.S. tour.
June 29:	Little Feat guitarist/singer Lowell George dies of a heart attack.
July 1:	Sony introduces the Walkman portable stereo (originally called the Soundabout in the United States).
July 12:	A "disco demolition" night—involving the mass destruction of disco albums—at Comiskey Park in Chicago results in a riot and the cancellation of a White Sox game.
August 25:	The Knack hit "My Sharona" spends six weeks at the top of the singles charts, a sign for many that disco—which had dominated the charts for the previous two years—was finally dying. Though the Knack were hailed as the next Beatles, the group quickly faded into obscurity.

September: The Sugarhill Gang's single "Rapper's Delight" becomes the first hip-hop song to break the Top 40, marking the beginning of hip-hop's commercial acceptance.

December 3:   Eleven fans are trampled to death at a Who concert in Cincinnati, Ohio.

December 8:   Pink Floyd release *The Wall* in the United States, which would spend fifteen weeks at No. 1 and become one of the best-selling albums of all time.

1980

January: The Clash release their masterpiece *London Calling* in the United States.

January 30:   Famed New Orleans jazz pianist Professor Longhair dies of a heart attack.

February 19:   Bon Scott, singer for Australian heavy-metal band AC/DC, chokes to death after a night of heavy drinking.

March 1:   Punk heroes Patti Smith and Fred Sonic Smith of MC5 wed.

April 28:   Tommy Caldwell of the Marshall Tucker Band dies in a car accident.

May 18:   Joy Division singer Ian Curtis hangs himself the night before the band's first U.S. tour. The remaining band re-forms under the name New Order.

September 25:   Led Zeppelin drummer John Bonham dies of asphyxiation after a night of heavy drinking, resulting in the band's breakup three months later.

December: Led Zeppelin officially break up.

December 7:   Darby Crash, singer for the hardcore punk band the Germs, commits suicide by heroin overdose, leaving a sign taped above him reading: "Here Lies Darby Crash."

December 8:   John Lennon is gunned down by deranged fan Mark David Chapman in front of Lennon's Upper West Side apartment.

December 27:   Three weeks after John Lennon's death, the tragically ironic single "(Just Like) Starting Over" hits No. 1. The album *Double Fantasy*—which spent eight weeks in the top spot—was to mark a return to music for Lennon, who had been absent five years.

FUNK, JAZZ-ROCK, AND FUSION: THE RHYTHM REVOLUTION

John Borgmeyer

In 1974, public life in America felt like the end of a party. That year Richard Nixon became the first U.S. president to resign office after the protracted spectacle of Watergate. The country was still tangled in Vietnam, yet a survey of army generals in Southeast Asia revealed that a mere 14 percent of the respondents believed that the war was "worth the effort."[1] People endured an oil shortage and the worst economic recession since the Great Depression. In American music, though, the party was just getting started. After all, what better way to blow off steam and forget anxiety than a long night of dancing?

Funk, jazz-rock, and fusion swept into rock with the experimental spirit of the late 1960s. Artists such as James Brown and Miles Davis introduced new rhythms eagerly embraced by an American rock audience who were tuning into new styles of popular music. The artists described in this chapter came to prominence in the years after black Americans had organized like never before to fight for greater social integration. In this atmosphere, black artists felt free to proudly proclaim their racial identity and to swirl diverse influences (jazz, soul, rock, as well as traditional music from Africa, Latin America, and India) into new kinds of popular music. Funk, jazz-rock, and fusion grew out of black soul music, but groundbreakers like Sly Stone and George Clinton drew from psychedelic rock as well; thus their fan base included the multiracial menagerie of American counterculture.

The new fans came to dance. The rhythm revolution, especially disco, can be seen as a reaction to the rock bombast of bands like Pink Floyd and Led Zeppelin. In the mid-'70s, major rock bands focused on elaborate stage shows, complex musical arrangements, and virtuosic performances, but they did not demand much from the audience. When George Clinton exhorted the crowd to "free your mind . . . let your ass follow," he was telling people exactly what they wanted to hear. Disco, meanwhile, decentralized celebrity altogether, so that performers disappeared from the scene, replaced by disc jockeys who spun extended dance tracks by mostly faceless artists. The dancers themselves were the real stars of the discothèque.

This chapter explores the genesis and evolution of this rhythm revolution, with special attention to the ways this music drew from, responded to, and influenced rock. Funk, jazz-rock, and fusion rhythms found their way into progressive and experimental rock of the late 1970s and in new wave bands like Talking Heads. The cross-pollination continues—disco culture survives in the techno "rave" scene, funk developed into hip-hop, while bands like the Beastie Boys, the Red Hot Chili Peppers, and Beck have kept the rhythm revolution alive in modern rock.

FUNK

The Godfather Opens His "Brand New Bag"

A James Brown performance was a force of nature. Brown strutted onstage like a nuclear reaction barely contained within a shiny, skin-tight jumpsuit, spinning, sliding, shaking, sweating, grabbing the microphone for an explosive "Good Gawd" as his band burned up on a vamping one-chord jam. Nobody could move a crowd like James Brown, the Godfather of Soul, and his sex-machine rhythms set the beat for the funky '70s.

Brown sang in church throughout his life, and gospel formed the backbone of his musical influence. "The preacher really got down," Brown related in *The Godfather of Soul*, his 1986 autobiography written with Bruce Tucker.

> He was just screaming and yelling and stomping his foot and then he dropped to his knees. The people got into it with him, answering him and shouting and clapping time. . . . I watched the preachers real close. Then I'd go home and imitate them because *I* wanted to preach.
>
> Audience participation in church is something the darker race of people has going because of a lot of trials and tribulations, because of the things that we understand about human nature. It's not something I can explain, but I can bring it out of people. I'm not the only person who has the ability, but I *work* at it.[2]

Brown's prodigious ambition and drive earned him a reputation as "the hardest working man in show business." The work ethic that made him wildly successful also made him notoriously difficult to work with. For example, during incessant touring in the early 1960s with his first group, the Furious Flames, Brown reportedly fined his musicians for flubbing notes. It paid off, though, as the group that would become the James Brown Revue developed a superlative reputation. The band was tighter, tougher, and louder; Brown was the flashiest dresser and the most spectacular dancer, with each performance orchestrated down to the last second.

Under his leadership, the James Brown Revue helped instigate the rhythm revolution with a new beat articulated in their 1965 hit "Papa's Got a Brand New Bag." The new beat is best understood by hearing a drummer's high hat. In the 1940s and 1950s, R&B drummers double-timed their counts—*da dat, da dat, da dat, da dat*—to create a skipping rhythm derived from jazz swing. Brown's "new bag" was an even, driving high hat—*dat dat dat dat*—that created a stomping beat with holes of anticipation and rhythmic tension. Brown's guitarist Jimmy Nolan played chords by choking the guitar neck so hard that the strings emitted a muffled, percussive *chicka-chicka* sound. The horns accented the rhythm with sharp, declamatory bursts. The bass played dramatically off-beat staccato lines over the drummer's cross-rhythms tinged by Latin and African influences. Cutting through it all was the voice of James Brown, singing repetitive phrases in a semi-improvised melody, with a sanctified fervor that sounded like a chainsaw touched by the Holy Spirit.

This hard-charging music would come to be known as "funk." It expressed the attitudes of blacks caught up in a social revolution and a new freedom to express their animosity toward white society. Funk's usurpation of shuffle was significant because

> segregation had determined that blacks never stand tall, look whites in the eye, or talk back—just shuffle along, head down, with their dignity gone. The symbolism of the shuffle was one of many negatives of "Negroness" that were done away with in the 1960s: Just like the civil rights marching song said, "Ain't gonna shuffle no more."[3]

Brown put six singles in the Top 10 between 1965 and his zenith in 1968, when he was preaching sermons like "I Can't Stand Myself " and "Say It Loud—I'm Black and I'm Proud." As the 1970s progressed, Brown continued to chart with socially conscious hits like "Talking Loud and Saying Nothing," "King Heroin," and "The Payback." Although he was an immense star, Brown's personal life suffered. In 1973 his son died in a car accident, and the Internal Revenue Service accused Brown of owing $4.5 million in taxes. Because of his celebrity and wealth, Brown's credibility was already questioned by militant black activists; his inexplicable endorsement of Richard Nixon for president did not help his reputation. In the mid-1970s, Brown's music seemed like a fossilized relic beside the likes of Parliament/Funkadelic (P-Funk) and Stevie Wonder, who made millions in the pop market with souped-up versions of Brown's music, while Brown himself slipped into obscurity. He failed to score another hit until "Living in America," a 1986 tune featured in the film *Rocky IV.*

In 1988, Brown was arrested after a high-speed car chase. He was convicted of assault and weapons charges, and during his four-year stint in jail, he no doubt heard dozens of rap songs built from samples of his early records. After his release in 1991, Brown proved his setbacks had not dampened the work ethic that made him famous. He reassembled his band and played new gigs, proving to a new generation that at fifty-eight the Godfather was still "superbad."

Going Higher: Sly and the Family Stone

Sly and the Family Stone dominated pop music between 1968 and 1970 with a sound that fused James Brown's groovy funk with the guitar screams and outrageous style of psychedelic rock. In a few short years, though, the group disintegrated, invisible except for an influence that continues to permeate rock, jazz-rock, pop, and funk.

Born in Texas in 1944, Sylvester Stewart grew up as a street tough in the factory town of Vallejo, California. He played in high school bands, then went to radio school. As a DJ he spun an eclectic playlist mixing the Beatles and Bob Dylan in with Otis Redding and Isaac Hayes, while Sly and his band played bars at night. Originally named the Stoners, the band eventually included his brother Freddie; Jerry Martini and his cousin, drummer Greg Errico; Sly's sister Rose; Cynthia Robinson; and groundbreaking bassist Larry Graham. Blooming from the flower-power scene in San Francisco, Sly and the Family Stone expressed the wildness of a rock band, the technical discipline of a soul band, and a utopian vision of musical, racial, and sexual integration.

At the time, soul music was stuck in the rut of its own commercial hit-factory formulas, while some of the joy of rock was being sucked out by progressive and avant-garde pretensions to High Art. Sly and the Family Stone broke through this morass with their 1967 debut *A Whole New Thing*. Here was a band who could perform in both rock and soul venues, anywhere, from Harlem's Apollo to rock clubs like the Avalon. In 1969 the band released the album that some consider their artistic peak, *Stand!*, which featured the dance funk of "Sing a Simple Song," the ecstatic rock of "I Want to Take You Higher," the pop hit "Everyday People," and the arch black pride anthem "Don't Call Me Nigger, Whitey." It was the first true funk album.

That year Sly and the Family Stone ascended the summit of rock, playing Woodstock and getting called back for an encore by half a million people. To the whites and blacks in his fan base, Sly was a philosopher who reflected the hopes of both the counterculture and the ghetto. "Everyday People" coined the phrase "different strokes for different folks," a powerful ideology that, for a while, offered racial integration as a promise of rock music.

As quickly as Sly skyrocketed, however, he fell off. He started to miss gigs or offer blasé performances. His eccentricity was obvious, and rumors of drug abuse persisted as he continued to cancel shows and fail to release records. The "whole new thing" lost its luster, even as Stone's influence could be heard in the Motown sound of the Jackson 5 and the Temptations, as well as the

Philadelphia production team of Gamble and Huff (discussed later in this chapter).

In November 1971, Sly and a reconstituted Family Stone released an album that surprised old fans—and scared them. *There's a Riot Goin' On* offered a vision not of a harmonious interracial utopia but the harsh realities of black American experience. Sly threw his rock success back in the face of a white audience that dug black music's grooves but had little appetite for a direct look at urban life; he expressed his disdain by remaking his old hit "Thank You Falettinme Be Mice Elf Agin" as "Thank You for Talkin' to Me Africa."

Riot's follow-up, 1973's *Fresh*, was by some accounts a more upbeat album, but by then the fans had stopped showing up. The release of *Small Talk* in 1974 was obscured by popular funk bands like Earth, Wind and Fire and the Ohio Players, who recast Sly's funk-rock without the unpleasant imagery. The Family Stone fractured, and the only way Sly could sell out Madison Square Garden anymore was by getting married onstage in 1975.

A 1977 disco remix of "Dance to the Music" cemented the image of Sly as over the hill. He made some live appearances with his closest funk disciples, George Clinton and his band Parliament/Funkadelic, but the relationship broke off after the two were arrested together for possession of cocaine in 1981. By that time, Talking Heads were incorporating Stone's music into their groove-based version of new wave. His influence is heard in the '80s soul of Prince and the samples of countless rap songs, not to mention almost every funk-rock hybrid from the likes of Frank Zappa, the Beastie Boys, the Red Hot Chili Peppers, and Living Colour. Perhaps the idea of integration through music is not dead after all. As one writer put it, "The Godfather broke the door open, but Sly let everyone in."[4]

One Nation under a Groove: The Funky '70s

Funk is more than just a style of music. Rickey Vincent writes that funk "is a nasty vibe, and a sweet sexy feeling; Funk is funkiness, a natural release of the essence within." In his 1996 book *Funk: The Music, the People, and the Rhythm of the One*, Vincent goes on to quote Barry Walters: "Trying to put that thang called funk into words is like trying to write down your orgasm. Both thrive in that gap in time when words fall away, leaving nothing but sensation."[5]

In musical terms, the roots of funk extend to Africa. Traditional West African music emphasized rhythm as a spiritual vehicle—waves of drumbeats washing around a single center induced trances and were often accompanied by ritualistic dances. Funk developed from ancient African rhythms that flowed into American pop via black churches, something funk has in common with blues, jazz, and R&B.

Funk's spiritual history was obvious in pioneers such as James Brown, Sly Stone, and George Clinton. In their bands, the beat was the thing. Each instrument functioned as a kind of drum, and thus funk bands harnessed the trance-inducing quality of complex, layered rhythms to provoke outbursts of dancing in an audience that came to shows ready to move. The rest of this section follows the evolution of funk through bands that contributed significantly to rock music.

Stax and the Memphis Sound

The Memphis-based record company Stax was an important catalyst of the evolution of rhythm and blues into funk. Stax Records was the home of Otis Redding, Booker T & the MGs, the Mar-Keys, Rufus Thomas, Isaac Hayes, Johnnie Taylor, Albert King, and others, comprising a musical empire that produced southern-fried blues, rock, and soul records rivaling Motown in total sales. Siblings Jim Stewart and Estelle Axton founded Stax in the late 1950s with an easygoing attitude that allowed artists the freedom to experiment—a freedom that gave birth to funk.

The 1967 song "Tramp" by Otis Redding and Carla Thomas was a notable proto-funk foray, with its clipped drumbeats and deep bass grooves, while Johnnie Taylor's 1968 hit, the risqué "Who's Making Love," addressed a seedier side of life that, until that time, had not been celebrated in popular black music. Taylor survived the demise of Stax in 1975 on the popularity of sexually explicit music like that heard on his 1976 album *Eargasm*, which toed the line of decency that was constantly being redrawn in the mid-'70s.

The Meters and the New Orleans Sound

The Meters' lineup of R&B veterans—guitarist Leo Nocentelli, keyboardist Art Neville, bassist George Porter Jr., and drummer Zigaboo Modeliste—defined the New Orleans scene in the early 1970s with songs like "Sophisticated Cissy," "Cissy Strut," "Cardova," "Stretch Your Rubber Band," "Doodle Oop," and "Chicken Strut."

Beginning with 1969's *The Meters*, the group released a series of albums that were underrated at the time but have since been extensively reissued in many different forms. The band made a bid for commercial acceptance with a disco effort, 1976's *Trick Bag*. When the album failed to hit, the group disbanded, although their sound would reemerge in the 1980s when Art joined his brother Aaron in their group the Neville Brothers.

The Meters were part of a New Orleans rock tradition that stretches back to the legendary Professor Longhair, a 1940s R&B pianist who helped innovate the rock rhythm. Fittingly, his playing style was born on whorehouse pianos that were never properly repaired or tuned; Longhair and others learned to mash the keys with their fists to get a good sound. The combination of propulsive tension and carefree feeling expressed in the bass-heavy rhythms is the defining feature of the New Orleans sound, and it was a significant influence on both rhythm and blues and rock.

Within the scope of this chapter, it is important to note Professor Longhair's psychedelic successor: Dr. John, The Night Tripper. In the late '60s Dr. John found inspiration for self-conscious weirdness in the voodoo rites of New Orleans folklore. With the 1972 album *Dr. John's Gumbo* and hits like "Right Place, Wrong Time" and "Such a Night," Dr. John updated the New Orleans sound for the funky '70s.

Kool and the Gang

On the East Coast, there was fun-loving Kool and the Gang, a group that James Brown himself referred to as "the second-baddest out there."[6] In fact, some critics cite Kool and the Gang as the first important funk band of the 1970s. Indeed, no hip party at the time was complete without the Gang's jazz-influenced instrumentals, featuring loud horn blasts and band members hooting with delight in the background. Kool and the Gang epitomized the spirit of boogie, and their string of hits took funk to the top of the charts, where it would reside through the 1970s.

The group formed out of the New Jersey public housing projects in the mid-1960s, led by Ronald Bell (who would later change his name to Khalis Bayyan) and his brother Robert (Kool) on bass. They signed a record contract as Kool and the Flames in 1969, then changed their name to avoid confusion with James Brown's group, the Furious Flames. Some of the members converted to the Nation of Islam in 1972, inspiring the Afrocentric themes articulated on albums such as 1976's *Open Sesame*. In 1973, Kool and the Gang set new standards of groove with "Funky Stuff," which hit No. 29 on the charts; the follow-up "Jungle Boogie" went gold, reaching No. 4 on both the pop and R&B charts. Kool and the Gang would chart twenty singles in the Top 40, including six gold singles and one, "Celebration," that went platinum in 1980.

Following in the wake of Kool and the Gang's breakthrough, two bands emerged who would take funk from party music to a distinct genre in the rock spectrum and impart on funk its own spiritual-political doctrines that both drew from and influenced rock in profound ways—Earth, Wind and Fire and George Clinton's Parliament/Funkadelic.

Earth, Wind and Fire

The most optimistic Afrocentric expressions of the 1970s could be heard in the uplifting funk of Earth, Wind and Fire. Founder Maurice White already had a solid pedigree as a session drummer for Chess Records and part of the groundbreaking pop-jazz Ramsey Lewis Trio when he decided to form a new band that would mix the new funk sound with mainstream jazz, straight-ahead soul, and African folk rhythms. White and his brothers Verdine, on bass, and (later) Fred, on drums, formed the core of Earth, Wind and Fire in Los Angeles in 1970. Over the next decade, some of the best musicians in funk rotated in and out of the group as it became one of the most popular bands in the world.

Earth, Wind and Fire during a 1975 performance. Courtesy of Photofest.

In the early '70s, White and his band—generally eight to ten members—honed a wide-ranging sound that shifted from tender ballads to deep tribal funk, laced with poetic lyrics. Their breakthrough came in 1975, when Earth, Wind and Fire performed the score to Sig Shore's *That's the Way of the World*, the now-obscure follow-up to *Superfly*. The album produced "Shining Star," a perfect statement of the band's optimistic idealism and musical skill that went to No. 1. The record has been hailed as a production masterpiece, with its tango rhythms and Latin beats fueling hard-driving funk vamps that swell and swoop under White's guidance.

The popularity of *That's the Way of the World* brought a live tour, captured in the 1975 double-album *Gratitude*, "a gospel experience that was an existential hosanna guaranteed to heal your ills."[7] Earth, Wind and Fire's elegant grooves and increasing complexity can be heard on songs like "Sun Goddess" and "New World Symphony," and on stage band members boasted a wild wardrobe to complement their prodigious chops. Their colorful skin-tight suits, platform shoes, sequins, and bell-bottoms rivaled Sly Stone, and they adopted stage props to match the most outlandish progressive rock bands of the time, like contraptions to spin the drum kit in the air and lift group members to the ceiling.

White took his band on the road every year between 1975 and 1979 as they traded hit records with the other dominant funk group of the era, George Clinton's Parliament/Funkadelic. Earth, Wind and Fire's polished sheen would prove a target for Clinton's notorious barbs (he called the band "Earth, Hot Air and No Fire"), which could be seen as a testament to Earth, Wind and Fire's position, along with Clinton, at the top of the '70s funk heap. Indeed, by the late '70s a host of imitators appeared on the scene, as funk showed up in the work of jazz artists such as Herbie Hancock and filtered into avant-garde rock and new wave.

Earth, Wind and Fire cracked the Top 40 twice in the 1980s, with "Let's Groove" peaking at No. 3 in 1981, then two years later with "Fall in Love With Me," which hit No. 17. In 2000, Earth, Wind and Fire were inducted into the Rock and Roll Hall of Fame, an appropriate tribute to a band that remains the standard for brilliant dance music.

George Clinton, King of the Groove Nation

On the other end of the spectrum from Earth, Wind and Fire's shimmering pop-funk was George Clinton's wicked psychedelic roar. As James Brown did with the Flames, Clinton transformed his band, the Parliaments, from a soul band of sharkskin-clad crooners into dance-inducing funkateers. In creating Funkadelic, Clinton drew not only from soul and R&B but from the acid rock of Sly Stone, Jimi Hendrix, and Frank Zappa to create a freewheeling group with a sound and a philosophy that heavily influenced later funk-rock hybrids.

The name "Funkadelic" was partly a business necessity, since Clinton recorded with both Parliament and Funkadelic for two different record labels. The new moniker also had stylistic meaning, as Funkadelic's groundbreaking albums *Funkadelic* (1970), *Free Your Mind* (1970), and *Maggot Brain* (1971) created a whole new kind of psychedelic rock with a dance groove. Later, Clinton resurrected Parliament to play a funk that was less psychedelic and more in line with the James Brown soul tradition. The groups included many of the same musicians and merged into a menagerie called Parliament/ Funkadelic, or P-Funk, which at times included as many as 100 different musicians.

Born in an outhouse in Kannapolis, North Carolina, in 1940, Clinton eventually settled in New Jersey with

Funkadelic during their 1978 incarnation. Courtesy of Photofest.

his mother and eight siblings. Here Clinton honed his prodigious talking skills in a barbershop, specializing in "conking" hair, a process of melting curly hair straight with heat and chemicals. He formed the doo-wopping Parliaments, who bounced around the Motown scene before putting their song "I Wanna Testify" in the R&B Top 5 in 1967. The group foundered when their record label, Revilot, went under; but the resilient Clinton reinvented his backing band by giving them big, loud amplifiers and a license to "do their thing" with the wide-open spirit of rock 'n' roll.

After *Funkadelic*, Clinton brought the classically trained keyboardist Bernie Worrell, whom Clinton called "DaVinci," into the fold. In a development that reflects the general rise of classical influence and new technology of progressive rock in the early '70s, Worrell brought European influences and a mind-bending array of electronic organ effects to Funkadelic. *Maggot Brain* is a rock performance that rivals the guitar wizardry of Jimi Hendrix. The record is a dark treatise on the nature of fear and transcendence, based on writings from an obscure religious cult called the Process Church of Final Judgment. The album's liner notes proclaim, "As long as human beings fail to see THEIR fear reflected in these and a hundred other manifestations of fear, then they will fail to see their part in the relentless tide of hatred, violence, destruction, and devastation that sweeps the earth."[8] This was more than just good-time dance music.

The double-album follow-up, 1972's *America Eats Its Young*, expanded this theme and the Funkadelic mystique. The band's fifth album, 1973's *Cosmic Slop*, includes a repertoire of much shorter songs, while 1974's *Standing on the Verge of Getting It On* shows Clinton's talent for blasting his funk competitors. As a whole, Funkadelic represents a powerful synthesis of funk and rock that is "not always pretty or appealing, but perhaps the truest representation of urban life offered in black music."[9]

In 1974, Clinton resurrected Parliament as Funkadelic's more accessible alter ego. The new Parliament emerged when Clinton met two important influences—in 1972 he hooked up with bass player Bootsy Collins, who had led James Brown's group, the JBs, at the tender age of eighteen; in 1973 he signed with Casablanca Records, led by president Neil Bogart. The alliances would rocket P-Funk to the heights of stardom.

Their first two albums, 1974's *Up for the Down Stroke* and 1976's *Chocolate City*, were not well received at the time, although now both are considered classics. Pop stardom came with the success of 1975's *Mothership Connection*, in which Clinton articulated a half-serious funk mythology and his vision of a groove nation that one critic called "a Space Age Mardi Gras."[10] With a new cast of musicians on board to replace the often drug-addled original Funkadelic members, *Mothership* contained no ballads—one of the first all-funk albums.

Clinton's P-Funk whirlwind spun out a flurry of new records including Funkadelic's 1978 opus *One Nation Under a Groove*. In 1976, Parliament, Funkadelic, and Bootsy Collins all released separate albums. The P-Funk spun off more acts—female singers Lynn Mabry and Dawn Silva released two albums as the Brides of Funkenstein; guitarist Eddie Hazel made *Games, Dames and Guitar Thangs* in 1978; Bernie Worrell recorded *All the Woo in the World*. In 1976 P-Funk kicked off their Earth Tour with a $275,000 budget—the largest for any black act to date—and the help of Jules Fischer, stage designer for bands like KISS and the Rolling Stones. Just as rock had mythological characters like the Who's "Tommy," Clinton and P-Funk used elaborate stage props to tell the tales of funk adventurers "Sir Nose D'Voidoffunk," "Mr. Wiggles," and "Gloryhallastupid."

In 1979, Clinton embarked on a series of small-venue gigs he called an "anti-tour." At a show in Washington, D.C. (which Clinton had dubbed "a Chocolate City encircled by Vanilla Suburbs"), he played a five-hour show. Wearing a red beret and fatigues, Clinton pumped up the audience with "get funky . . . get loose . . . free your mind . . . let your ass follow . . . let your booty do its duty." Clinton's role in the band was to lay down the rap atop the explosive sounds and deep funk rhythms.

Yet as P-Funk reached the heights of its stardom, it was clear that the "groove nation" was just imagery for the stage. The reality was the more familiar rock story of fair-weather friends, legal disputes, and strong drugs. Departing P-Funk members lashed out at Clinton's ego, while new members often went unpaid. Clinton announced his retirement in 1980, yet he continued to build bands and make funk music throughout the decade. During these years, a collaboration with Clinton was not the sure-fire hit it might have been in the late '70s—critics say Clinton's work with the likes of Sly Stone and James Brown in the 1980s constituted low points for everyone involved. Clinton did make a short-lived comeback with the song "Atomic Dog" in 1982, which would become one of the most oft-sampled beats in all of hip-hop music.

Still, Clinton and P-Funk should be remembered for creating a musical world that inspired an almost religious devotion. In the process, P-Funk brought black music into the electronics age and created a new landscape for the imagination of black Americans. Clinton put it this way:

> All this shit is connected. . . . Ain't no one mafunker can do this shit. And no one species . . . no one state . . . no one nothin'. 'Cause it's all the One. I mean I am not one. I am *part* of one. We are all part of one. . . . At base the funk is rhythmic, and being in the pocket is a rhythmic concept analogous to the classical idea of swing. Once time is in the pocket, the funk is ready to roll.[11]

Perhaps more than any other funkster, Clinton has enjoyed enduring popularity among rock listeners; he produced the 1985 Red Hot Chili Peppers album *Freaky Styley* and also appeared on the bill of the Lollapalooza art-rock festival in 1994.

The Ohio Players

Middle America's answer to Parliament/Funkadelic, the Ohio Players were an obscure R&B group until 1973, when "Funky Worm" hit the radio. The gold single would be eclipsed by their later hits, but "Funky Worm" is important because its shrill, squiggling keyboard lines would be resurrected in 1990s hip-hop to express the tensions of urban Los Angeles.

The Players covered a wide range of musical territory—stomping blues, tender ballads, explosive funk-rock, and dance anthems—but the band was perhaps just as famous for a string of sexy album covers designed by *Playboy* photographer Richard Fegley. The audacious cover for 1975's *Honey* featured *Playboy* centerfold Ester Cordet nude, lapping up honey, and it created quite a stir. The sheer audacity of the image drew clucking from moralists, and as a result, it piqued the interest of rock fans. Controversy grew around the Ohio Players when rumors floated that Cordet had been murdered during the taping of the song "Love Rollercoaster," and her final screams could be heard in the background. Untrue, of course, but it sent the songs "Fire" and "Love Rollercoaster" both to No. 1 in 1975 and 1976.

Average White Band and the Racial Backdrop of Funk

Funk was generally seen as black music, but in fact the groove was open to everyone. Scotland produced the Average White Band, which had a No. 1 hit in 1975 with the funky instrumental "Pick Up the Pieces." The energy, melodies, and propulsive rhythms of their second album, 1974's *AWB*, had established the band as more than a gimmick or George Clinton rip-off, of which there were many in the mid-1970s. When drummer Robbie McIntosh died of an accidental drug overdose in 1974, however, much of the band's energy seemed to die with him. The four singles AWB put into the *Billboard* Top 40 after that had a more monotonous disco flavor.

For funk historians like Rickey Vincent, white funk bands raise questions about "authenticity." In his view, Grand Funk Railroad had a "funky attitude," but in musical terms they did not play "The Funk." By contrast, the white-led K.C. and the Sunshine Band "literally passed for a black band playing dance funk," putting a string of hits into the Top 40 in the late '70s, including five No. 1 hits—"Get Down Tonight" (1975), "That's the Way (I Like It)" (1975), "(Shake, Shake, Shake) Shake Your Booty" (1976), "I'm Your Boogie Man" (1977), and "Please Don't Go" (1979). Vincent has less tolerance for Wild Cherry, whose "Play That Funky Music" hit No. 1 on both pop and R&B charts in 1976. Their follow-up a year later, "Baby Don't You Know," confirmed his doubts about Wild Cherry's authenticity.[12]

Funk attracted fans of different races, and rock and funk influenced each other in many ways; still, Vincent argues that the music industry keeps rock and funk segregated, apparent in the fact that AWB's "Pick Up the Pieces" is one of the very few funk songs played on contemporary classic rock radio stations.

Stevie Wonder

In a career that began at the tender age of thirteen, Stevie Wonder blended funk, jazz, reggae, rock, rhythms from Africa and Latin America, and electronic experiments, all bound together by well-crafted pop songwriting. His first hits rolled off Berry Gordy's Motown assembly line in Detroit, but after his twenty-first birthday in 1971, Wonder used his newfound creative freedom

Stevie Wonder, 1976. Courtesy of Photofest.

to create a string of hit albums that, like Sly Stone, captured new white listeners without alienating his African American fan base.

Raised Steveland Morris in Detroit, the soon-to-be "Little Stevie Wonder" was a musical wunderkind. Blind since infancy, his singing talent and proficiency on various instruments developed so early that he was only ten when he was introduced to Gordy, who changed his surname to "Wonder." His first hit was "Fingertips—Pt. 2," and it went all the way to No. 1 in 1963. Wonder spent his teenage years cranking out Motown songs that did well on the pop and R&B charts, and it is important to note that his audience was integrated from the very beginning. In 1964, his opening act was the Rolling Stones; in 1966, his cover of Bob Dylan's "Blowin' in the Wind" reached No. 9.

Wonder put nineteen songs in the Top 40 between 1963 and 1971, the year that marked a turning point in his career. Until then, he was a product of the Motown organization. The company wrote and arranged most of his songs, engineered the recording sessions, and oversaw his business affairs. Motown held Wonder's money in a trust and paid him an allowance ($2.50 a week when he was thirteen). Then, in 1971, Wonder turned twenty-one and took control of his $1 million trust fund. He negotiated an unprecedented 120-page contract with Motown that granted him complete artistic freedom, control over his publishing enterprise, and a healthy royalty check.

His first release under the new terms, 1971's *Where I'm Coming From*, only hints at Wonder's potential. In a 1973 interview, Wonder called that record "a little premature. . . . It's nothing like the things I write now. I love getting into just as much weird shit as possible."[13] Indeed, his next albums—*Music of My Mind* (1972), *Talking Book* (1972), *Innervisions* (1973), *Fulfillingness' First Finale* (1974), and *Songs in the Key of Life* (1976)—reflected his artistic maturity and established Wonder as one of the most popular musicians of the mid-'70s. An opening slot for the Rolling Stones during their 1972 American tour also cemented Wonder's appeal to white, counterculture rock fans.

Wonder claimed his songwriting was partially influenced by the Beatles, that he was inspired by their use of vocal echoes and other electronic flourishes, as well as their innovative songwriting. "Why can't I?" Wonder asked himself. His artistic freedom manifested itself in lyrics that were far more political, social, and spiritual than the more sentimental Motown fare. Additionally, Wonder and his producers during this period—Robert Margouleff and Malcolm Cecil—took advantage of the new technology of the modern recording studio. Overdubbing, for example, allowed Wonder to play most of the instruments on his albums. His experiments with synthesizers, clavinets, and electric pianos created a sense of rock urgency in tunes like "Higher Ground," which reached No. 4 in 1973.

The most significant hallmark of Wonder's adult music is that it grew beyond the three-minute confines of conventional pop. He charted twenty-five songs in the Top 40 between 1971 and 1987, including seven No. 1 hits; nevertheless, Wonder's genius shone most clearly onstage, in front of a live audience. In 1973, he was nearly killed while on tour in North Carolina—he was riding in a car when a log fell from a truck and smashed through the windshield, hitting him in the forehead. He lost his sense of smell but emerged otherwise unscathed. In his first major U.S. performance after the accident, a March 1974 gig at Madison Square Garden, he acknowledged the influence of Sly Stone and James Brown by performing long, ecstatic vamps and extended improvisations on songs like "Living for the City." Critics suggest the live versions of his up-tempo hits surpass anything Wonder has done in the recording studio.

While his studio albums continued to produce hits throughout the 1980s, critics have lamented that too many sappy ballads and generic pop lyrics intrude on his solid songwriting craftsmanship, and after the mid-'70s he failed to produce much of anything new. His post-'70s high points include 1980's *Hotter Than July* and 1991's *Jungle Fever*, the soundtrack to a film by director Spike Lee. Neither record surpasses 1974's "Living for the City," but he continues to make music with his unique style that, as one critic put it, "is probably too original for guaranteed, comfortable acceptance. Which, of course, constitutes his ultimate strength."[14]

JAZZ-ROCK AND FUSION

Jazz has always influenced rock, and (much to the dismay of some jazz aficionados) vice versa. Many early rock musicians first played in jazz groups, and jazz artists wasted little time incorporating rock tunes into their work. In 1966 Duke Ellington recorded the Beatles' "I Wanna Hold Your Hand" and Count Basie released the album *Basie's Beatle Bag*. The next year, the cover of the jazz magazine *Down Beat* declared that "Jazz As We Know It Is Dead" and from then on included rock music in its coverage.[15]

Jazz-rock was more than just jazz musicians playing rock tunes, however. Jazz-rock emerged as a distinct genre, according to rock critic Robert Palmer in *The Rolling Stone History of Rock & Roll*, when bands like Chicago, Electric Flag, and Blood, Sweat & Tears incorporated jazz-style horns into conventional pop arrangements.

Electric Flag pioneered the idea of a rock band with horns. Guitarist Michael Bloomfield, singer Nick Gravenites, drummer/vocalist Buddy Miles, and bassist Harvey Brooks all play in top form on their 1968 debut *A Long Time Comin'*, featuring horns in the style of jazz and blues bands from the 1940s and 1950s.

Al Kooper formed Blood, Sweat & Tears in 1968, but recorded only one album with them. Their 1968 debut, *Child Is Father to the Man*, is historically important because Kooper's ambitious horn arrangements and artful song constructions expanded the possibilities for blending jazz with rock. The band hit its commercial peak with the 1969 album *Blood, Sweat & Tears*, which produced three gold singles blending rock with big-band jazz. "You've Made Me So Very Happy," "Spinning Wheel," and "And When I Die" all reached No. 2 that year. After that, the band had trouble retaining a singer and failed to produce music surpassing their early work.

The horn arrangements on Chicago's 1969 debut, *Chicago Transit Authority*, leaned more toward middle-of-the-road pop than jazz, and it proved that a rock band could play with a funk groove. Their first album was the last time Chicago would break any new ground, though. None of Chicago's subsequent albums offered much that was new, but the band was hugely successful. Between 1970 and 1991, Chicago put thirty-five songs into the Top 40.

The term "jazz" applies very loosely to these three bands, however, since the horns generally played prearranged patterns and rarely, if ever, improvised. They were, after all, rock bands. It was not until Miles Davis put electric instruments in the hands of bona fide jazz musicians that the genre of jazz-rock fully developed.

Miles Davis

Davis's 1970 album *Bitches Brew* is considered to be the first jazz-rock crossover. Davis had a long career in jazz before then, and many fans of his earlier work disliked the abrupt rhythm shifts, harsh tones, and muddy textures of *Bitches Brew*. But it sold well among rock listeners, as did a 1970 live double-album recorded at the Fillmore East. The dance beats on *Bitches Brew* reflected Sly Stone; the wild improvisations drew from Hendrix and sounded far out compared to even the most experimental psychedelic or progressive rock of the era.

Before he died in 1991, Davis was asked what he thought he had accomplished. "Well," Davis replied, "I've changed music five or six times."[16] Indeed, there is not enough room in this history of rock to even summarize Davis's long and groundbreaking jazz career. After *Bitches Brew*, Davis explored jazz fusions more fully with the rock compositions of 1971's *A Tribute to Jack Johnson* and 1972's *On the Corner*. He took a six-year break from recording and performing in 1975, returning in the '80s to more accessible, R&B-based jazz-funk. For our purposes in this volume, it is sufficient to note that Davis is the father of jazz-rock. He set the formula for how to blend jazz and rock styles, and most of the musicians who would go on to define and perfect jazz-rock got their start playing with Davis.

John McLaughlin and the Mahavishnu Orchestra

British guitarist John McLaughlin was a jazz guitarist who knew how to rock. Whereas most psychedelic guitarists noodled solos out of conventional blues scales, McLaughlin's searing lines on *Bitches Brew* are jazz melodies played loud and distorted. In 1971 he formed the Mahavishnu Orchestra, a band that would prove more influential than Davis in defining jazz-rock as it became a

pop phenomenon in the mid-1970s. *Bitches Brew* is a groundbreaking album, but in places the jazz ensemble fails to master the challenges posed by the new technology. On the Mahavishnu Orchestra's 1972 debut, *The Inner Mounting Flame*, McLaughlin and his crew set the standard for jazz music adapted to the roaring volumes and sonic possibilities of increasingly sophisticated electric technology.

Like guitarists in San Francisco's acid rock scene or those playing progressive rock in London clubs, McLaughlin used state-of-the-art amplifiers to create "walls of sound." What set McLaughlin apart was his command of jazz. By the early '70s, rock listeners were used to long guitar solos, but the harmonic and melodic sophistication of *The Inner Mounting Flame* was something new.

McLaughlin's drummer, Billy Cobham, recognized that playing jazz-style drums amidst a wall of rock sound was like trying to slice steak with a butter knife. The conventional jazz technique of keeping time with the high-hat cymbal is lost in electric music, so Cobham kept time with the bass

John McLaughlin, 1976. Courtesy of Photofest.

drum and snare, the way a rock drummer might. He kept the backbeat interesting with the addition of skittering compound rhythms he learned from Indian drummers.

The Mahavishnu Orchestra also knew how to solve the instrumental clut-
tering that plagued some sections of *Bitches Brew*. McLaughlin used the jazz
convention of "trading fours," where players take turns trading four-bar musical
statements, to balance multiple soloists. He also employed the jazz concept of
grounding improvisations with prewritten and well-rehearsed refrains that give
his jams a sense of cohesiveness. The Mahavishnu Orchestra set the standard
for the jazz-rock that often provoked harsh criticism from jazz purists but nevertheless brought jazz many new listeners from the world of rock.

The success of albums by Miles Davis and the Mahavishnu Orchestra, as
well as Herbie Hancock's 1973 funk-jazz album *Head Hunters*, brought jazz-
rock into popular consciousness. It prompted record companies to adjust their
marketing and promoting strategies to gather the rock audience. As a result,
many established jazz artists took ill-advised plunges into jazz-rock fusion without fully understanding the nuances of electric instruments. Except for
Weather Report, most of the mid-1970s jazz-rock groups disbanded within a
few years. In the late '70s, a new generation of groups took a softer version of
jazz fusions into the mid-'80s, including Pat Metheny, Spyro Gyra, and the Jeff
Lorber Fusion (featuring saxophonist Kenny Gorelick, soon to be known as the
oft-maligned Kenny G).

The Davis Offspring: Herbie Hancock, Chick Corea, and Weather Report

Besides the Mahavishnu Orchestra, other members of Miles Davis's ensemble
on *Bitches Brew* created the defining jazz-rock of the mid-1970s. Josef Zawinul
and Wayne Shorter, who formed Weather Report, were both former sidemen for
Davis. Their 1971 debut *Weather Report* resembles Davis's music, with an emphasis on group mood over individual solos. *I Sing the Body Electric* (1972) features one side recorded live in Tokyo, exemplifying the kind of energy Weather
Report generated in concert. One of the few jazz-rock fusion bands to enjoy
critical acclaim over a long career, Weather Report continued making well-
received albums geared toward funk and rock listeners into the mid-1980s.

Herbie Hancock dabbled in electronics as a member of the Miles Davis
Quintet in the late 1960s. He listened to James Brown and Sly Stone and collected a band called the Headhunters, a group of funk musicians who knew
how to play jazz. Their 1973 debut, *Head Hunters*, outsold all previous jazz-rock
records and produced the hit single "Chameleon." Its success invited more
mainstream attention to jazz-rock, and as a result the genre would become
more blatantly commercial. Hancock, meanwhile, delved more deeply into
jazz-funk fusions with his next albums, *Thrust* (1974), *Man-Child* (1975), and
Secrets (1976).

With his band Return to Forever and their eponymous 1972 debut album, Chick Corea developed a brand of loud but lyrical music more akin to West Coast rock. "My own personal ideal," Corea told *Rolling Stone* in 1974, "is combining all the most beautiful forms of music, classical, rock and jazz into a really present time experience that doesn't go over people's heads, and doesn't go under their heads and denigrate them either."[17] As the 1970s progressed, however, Corea's music ceased to break ground as critics decried it as cute and pretentious.

While not a product of Davis sidemen, the jazz-funk rock of Oakland's Tower of Power drew from the same audience as the bands mentioned above, with more mainstream success. The band's five-piece horn section powered three tunes into the Top 40 in the early 1970s—"You're Still a Young Man" (1972), "So Very Hard to Go" (1973), and "Don't Change Horses (In the Middle of a Stream)" (1974). Yet it was the energy of their funk-infused live shows that earned Tower of Power a reputation on the jazz-rock scene. The group's sound matured around vocalist Lenny Williams on their third album *Tower of Power* (1973), and the following year they released three albums—*Funkland*, *Back to Oakland*, and *Urban Renewal*—that constitute a perfect example of the tight, complex music popular in the late 1970s.

Mainstream Jazz-Rock: Joni Mitchell, Steely Dan, and the Doobie Brothers

Although best known as a folk musician, singer-songwriter Joni Mitchell began to display signs of jazz influence with complex chord structures, as well as piano and woodwind sounds, on her 1972 album *For the Roses*. With her 1974 follow-up, *Court and Spark*, Mitchell hit her commercial highpoint with orchestral arrangements and a full-band, jazz-oriented sound. That album produced her biggest hit, "Help Me," which peaked at No. 7.

She would continue in the jazz-pop vein for the rest of the 1970s, with varying results. Her 1974 live album *Miles of Aisles* featured her earlier songs reworked into jazzier tunes by her backing band, the L.A. Express. She experimented with African influences on 1975's *The Hissing of Summer Lawns*, while 1976's *Hejira* was more subdued, with most tracks just guitar, drums, and the bass playing of jazz-rocker Jaco Pastorius. On 1977's *Don Juan's Reckless Daughter*, she experimented with Latin rhythms, but by then even die-hard fans started to question her artistic direction. Her collaboration with jazz great Charles Mingus for the 1979 album *Mingus* testified to the aimlessness of much late 1970s jazz-fusion, as does Pat Metheny's noodling solos on 1980's *Shadows and Light*. She continued to experiment with various styles, from folk rock to synth pop and jazz, including collaborations with former Davis sidemen Wayne Shorter and Herbie Hancock, but critics say her recent work lacks the inspiration of her mid-1970s releases.

Steely Dan was the musical vehicle for songwriting duo Donald Fagen and Walter Becker. The two took their group name from the novel *Naked Lunch* by

William Burroughs, and their music reflected a similarly dark comic sensibility. After their 1972 debut *Can't Buy a Thrill*, Steely Dan ventured into jazz-rock with the 1973 follow-up *Countdown to Ecstasy*, on which guitarists Denny Dias and Jeff Baxter display their virtuosity on longer solos. On 1974's *Pretzel Logic*, the band contained their technical abilities in conventional three-minute pop songs. That album produced their biggest hit, "Rikki Don't Lose That Number," which reached No. 4 in 1974. Steely Dan released five successful albums between 1974 and 1980, all of which charted hits. The near-perfect musicianship and substantial production (the cast on 1977's *Aja*, for example, included seven guitarists, six drummers, six keyboard players, and at least eight different saxophone players) started to sound bland to some critics, however. In 1981, Becker and Fagen split up. Fagen released a solo album, *The Nightfly*, in 1982, but the duo reunited for new Steely Dan albums in 1995, 2000, and 2003.

After playing with Steely Dan, Jeff Baxter brought his virtuosic jazz-rock guitar playing to another California band, the Doobie Brothers, in the mid-'70s. In the early 1970s, the Doobie Brothers created a successful sound by combining the folksy finger-picking of guitarist Pat Simmons with the rock riffs of Tom Johnston. The Doobies' 1971 eponymous debut was widely panned; the band's breakthrough came with their 1972 follow-up, *Toulouse Street*, which produced the No. 11 single "Listen to the Music" and "Jesus Is Just Alright," which hit No. 35.

Album reviewers at the time described the group's songs as somewhat shallow but irresistibly catchy—a well-proven formula for commercial success in the early '70s. The Doobie Brothers established themselves as a formidable rock act and concert draw with the release of *The Captain and Me* in 1973—spawning the now-classic rock single "China Grove"—and the 1974 follow-up *What Were Once Vices Are Now Habits*. The single "Black Water" from that album became the band's first No. 1 hit.

Baxter joined the group after the release of *Stampede* in 1975, and he soon recruited another Steely Dan veteran, Michael McDonald, to join the Doobies as well. Their presence was felt on the jazz-influenced effect of *Takin' It to the Streets* in 1976. The album went platinum on the success of the title track single, which hit No. 13. With McDonald as lead songwriter, the Doobies continued to chart hits like "What a Fool Believes" (the band's second No. 1) and "Minute by Minute," both included on the album *Minute by Minute* in 1978. The following year the Doobies appeared at the Musicians United for Safe Energy (MUSE) concert, along with Bruce Springsteen and Jackson Browne.

Baxter left the group before the Doobies won four Grammy Awards in 1980—three for "What a Fool Believes" and one for "Minute by Minute." By this time the Doobie Brothers were more or less the backing band for Michael McDonald. The group broke up in 1982, reforming once a year for a concert to benefit the Lucille Salter Packard Children's Hospital near their hometown of San Jose.

Fusion

"Fusion" is a broad term, referring not only to jazz-rock but also to bands that blended aspects of rock with various influences. Some of the most successful fusion acts of the 1970s drew from Indian, African, and Latin rhythms and instruments.

One of the most successful of these fusion groups was John McLaughlin's Shakti. McLaughlin had always been interested in the way Indian music intertwined with Hindu spirituality, and while he was playing with the Mahavishnu Orchestra, he took up a structured study of Indian religion at Wesleyan University in Connecticut. There he met Indian violinist L. Shankar, and after a few jam sessions in McLaughlin's apartment, the two formed the Indo-jazz acoustic group Shakti (named for a Hindu goddess). The Mahavishnu Orchestra disbanded in 1975 so McLaughlin could focus on his new group. Shakti released three records—*Shakti* (1975), *A Handful of Beauty* (1976), and *Natural Elements* (1977). McLaughlin recruited percussionist T. H. "Vikku" Vinayakram for a tour of the United States and Europe in 1978, but the group disbanded in 1978 when Vinayakram returned to India.

The propulsive rhythms of Latin America inspired the southern California band War, which enjoyed pop success in the early 1970s with hits like 1975's "Low Rider," one of the all-time great cruising songs. A more explosive combination of rock and Latin sounds came from the San Francisco band Santana, led by the soaring guitar solos of Carlos Santana. Producer Bill Graham secured Santana a gig at Woodstock, and within three months the group had a contract with Columbia Records and released their first album, 1969's *Santana*, which sold more than a million copies. The band put a long string of hits in the Top 40 between 1970 and 1982 (although Carlos Santana would not reach the top until his 1999 album *Supernatural* produced two No. 1 hits— "Smooth" in 1999 and "Maria Maria" in 2000). Nevertheless, Santana truly shined onstage. Carlos Santana considered music a profoundly spiritual experience, and his ability to express those deep emotions through his playing made him an innovator of jazz-rock fusion and one of the greatest rock guitar players of all time.

PHILADELPHIA SOUL AND THE DISCO REVOLUTION

MFSB and the Sound of Philadelphia

Kenny Gamble, Leon Huff, and Thom Bell wrote more than a thousand songs together. During the 1970s, their work included twenty-eight gold or platinum albums and thirty-one gold or platinum singles. Bell was an independent producer, while Gamble and Huff formed the Philadelphia International record label; together they created the "Philadelphia sound" that made the town the most influential source of black music in the early 1970s. Their songs served as a model for disco, which broke into the American mainstream in 1974.

Harold Melvin and the Blue Notes, the O'Jays, Teddy Pendergrass, the Spinners, and the Stylistics all emerged from Philadelphia and became stars. Indeed the Philadelphia International record company was the last great "hit factory" in popular music, turning out glossy R&B defined by string sections, deep basslines, and propulsive rhythm sections.

The scene dominated by Gamble, Huff, and Bell emerged from the television show *American Bandstand*, which Dick Clark hosted from Philadelphia in the early 1960s. The session musicians who played for Chubby Checker and Frankie Avalon during the day would gather for nighttime jams at local jazz clubs. Gamble, Huff, and Bell made their names as songwriters and performers in the mostly white *Bandstand* scene before they teamed up to produce their own records. Their signature sound coalesced in sessions with Jerry Butler, a Chicago soul singer whose career was waning before he moved to Philadelphia. Butler's string of 1969 hits, "Only the Strong Survive," "Moody Woman," and "What's the Use of Breaking Up," exemplified the mature Philadelphia sound generated by the band MFSB (which stands for Mothers, Fathers, Sisters, Brothers). MFSB became the house band for Philadelphia International when the company formed in 1971.

Marketing through black radio stations and media, Gamble and Huff made the label an instant success. Hits in 1972 like "Me and Mrs. Jones" by Billy Paul and "If You Don't Know Me By Now" by Harold Melvin and the Blue Notes bore the sweet string melodies and lively grooves that marked MFSB. In 1974, the Philadelphia sound saw the peak of its fame and the beginning of its decline. That year the three producers were big winners in *Billboard*'s end-of-the-year awards for singles with the most sales and airplay—Bell charted eleven hit singles in 1974, while the Gamble-Huff team charted ten.

Early in 1974, MFSB recorded the mostly instrumental hit "TSOP (The Sound of Philadelphia)," which hit No. 1 on the charts and offered the musical blueprint for disco—lush string orchestrations and a driving, almost mechanical beat. A few months later, disco exploded on the scene with beats that were actually mechanical. The flowery strings and bass-heavy rhythms of Philadelphia became disco conventions, at the same time rendering the productions of Bell, Gamble, and Huff, in the words of one writer, "about as fresh as the jingles for Wrigley's Doublemint gum."[18] The Philadelphia sound made a direct contribution to rock through the music of David Bowie, who produced his 1975 tribute to the Philadelphia sound, *Young Americans*, in Philly's Sigma Sound recording studio.

By then, though, the trio was embattled by legal troubles. In 1975, the first indictments in a payola investigation became public. Gamble and Huff were both implicated; a year later the charges against Huff were dismissed, but Gamble was found guilty and fined $2,500. When the popularity of disco faded in the 1980s, Gamble, Huff, and Bell mostly retired, having distinguished themselves as innovators of a new dance music and the dominant soul producers of the 1970s.

Disco—Everyone's a Superstar

In the mid-1970s, rock's excesses were obvious. Rock stars were fabulously wealthy and as famous as the biggest movie stars. Bands like the Who or Yes had become so self-consciously "artistic" that some musicians felt compelled to explain their songs to the audience before playing them. Fun seemed to be disappearing from the rock equation. Pink Floyd epitomized the wall separating superstar rockers from the audiences that paid to bask in their success, and they directly addressed the feeling that something was amiss in their 1979 album *The Wall*.

By then it was a moot point, as the disco craze had come and mostly gone by 1979. Along with punk rock, disco swept away the progressive bombast that dominated rock in the early 1970s; but whereas punk wanted to tear down the wall and smash every trace of rock excess, disco sought to embrace both the profound and the inane in rock and put it all to a pulsing dance beat. With its DJs spinning extended dance mixes by mostly faceless musicians, disco was seen as a response to the performer-centered theater of rock.

Yet disco was born more out of necessity than a conscious reaction to the state of rock. The scene generally took root in gay dance clubs like the Loft and the 10th Floor in Manhattan. The owners hired DJs to spin records because many bands refused to play gay clubs, since homosexuality was not well accepted at the time. As it spread to the mainstream culture, disco, for most enthusiasts, was more about communal dance ecstasy than anything else.

Within the confines of the disco, the collective spirit of the late 1960s mingled with the new post-Watergate self-absorption of the 1970s in a scene that mixed a physical workout with drug-induced highs and a spark of sexual electricity. It was a jolt of excitement that popular music in the mid-'70s seemed to desperately need. Writer Tom Smucker offers his own personal story of how a rock fan ended up in the discothèque:

> In particular I remember a hippie Halloween party at the beginning of the Seventies where we all sat around on the floor in stoned silence listening to what would later be called classic rock. A few years earlier those sessions, punctuated by "oh wows," had been fun. Now they were a dead end.[19]

For some, it seemed that being a rock fan meant sitting in silence, listening as other people—the stars—enjoyed all the fun. Disco was a way to break that silence.

Disco was not a very complicated style, mostly smooth, black urban danceable pop based on the Philadelphia sound. But the quirky tastes of clubgoers meant that a song could be a hit at the disco but never heard outside the disco or could go on to mainstream success.

For example, Manu Dibango's "Soul Makossa" was recorded in Paris by an African. It was first imported to American discos, then released as a single. When "Soul Makossa" appeared in the Top 40 in 1973, it signaled the beginning of the era of disco in popular American culture. A year later, disco hits regularly broke through to the pop mainstream. The mid-'70s became the era of the "disco version," as DJs created disco tracks by adding propulsive 4/4 dance rhythms to any song they could—show-biz standards, rock and soul oldies, gospel, even classical music. Original songs, much longer than the three-minute pop convention, were being composed as well. Actress Donna Summer, for example, became one of the few recognizable performers in the disco scene when she panted and moaned scandalously on the sixteen-minute "Love to Love You Baby," which reached No. 2 on the charts in 1975.

Disco's culture and music really hit the mainstream with the release of the film *Saturday Night Fever* in 1977, giving people outside the disco subculture their first glimpse into the scene. The film's soundtrack, released the same year, made superstars out of the Bee Gees, a trio of brothers from Manchester, England. The Bee Gees were already an established rock group, having put twenty-one singles into the Top 40 between 1969 and 1977, but *Saturday Night Fever* made them disco kings. Three of the songs from that record—"How Deep Is Your Love," "Stayin' Alive," and "Night Fever"—all hit No. 1 in 1977 and 1978. (See Chapter 8, "Rock on the Big Screen.")

Like a lit match or a bout with the flu, disco went as quickly as it came. In 1978, as one writer put it,

> [I]n a disco-mad city like New York, you could walk down the street and *every* radio in a passing car, on a stoop, in a store, out an apartment window, carried down the street by a teen, would be tuned to the same radio station—WKTU. . . . Disco had gone from an underground taste to the sound of everything from elevator music to the Rolling Stones.[20]

Although rock bands like the Stones incorporated the sound of disco (even the hard-rock band KISS delved into disco beats with "I Was Made for Lovin' You," the first single off their 1979 album *Dynasty*), most rock fans greeted the disco fad with revulsion. "Disco sucks" became common graffiti in New York, but the most dramatic death knell came in violent fashion in 1979. During a baseball game at Comiskey Park, Chicago rock DJ Steve Dahl held an anti-disco rally, setting fire to thousands of disco records and prompting a full-scale riot that canceled the game. A peace of sorts was called between disco and rock when Michael Jackson's 1982 hit "Beat It" featured a guitar solo by heavy-metal guitar hero Eddie Van Halen; the backlash was more formally resolved when traditional rocker Bruce Springsteen released "Dancing in the Dark" in 1984, accompanied by a dance remix.

Tom Smucker claims that homophobia, racism, and sexism were undercurrents of the virulent disco backlash. No music was so openly reflective of gay culture, and the predominately female vocals lacked the more aggressive aesthetic of the male voice. And except for crossover acts like Sly Stone, George Clinton, and Stevie Wonder, rock was mostly marketed toward a white audience. By the 1980s, disco's optimism ran into the materialist "yuppie" culture, the conservative politics of Ronald Reagan, and the fear of AIDS. Still scorned by rock fans, disco at its best represented a "city street," Smucker writes—

> A place where strangers could interact with one another if they wanted to without having to become just like one another. It reminded us that cities aren't just places where people get mugged. If the vibes are right, they're places where people can be stimulated, lots of happy accidents can happen, and even strangers can fall in love.[21]

NOTES

1. Hendler 1983, 167.
2. Brackett 2005, 152.
3. Vincent 1996, 62.
4. Ibid., 99.
5. Ibid., 3.
6. Ibid., 183.
7. Marsh 1979, 118.
8. *Maggot Brain* liner notes, 1971.
9. DeCurtis et al. 1992, 142.
10. Ibid., 523.
11. Brackett 2005, 262.
12. Vincent 1996, 189.
13. Brackett 2005, 257.
14. DeCurtis et al. 1992, 297.
15. Whitburn 2004, 129.
16. DeCurtis et al. 1992, 503.
17. Ibid.
18. Ibid., 519.
19. Ibid., 562.
20. Ibid., 565.
21. Ibid., 572.

2

PROGRESSIVE ROCK IN THE 1970s: BUT IS IT ART?

John Borgmeyer

In 1974, guitarist Robert Fripp dissolved his band King Crimson. It was a significant moment in the evolution of progressive rock, since King Crimson's 1969 debut, *In the Court of the Crimson King*, is often cited by fans and critics as the foundation of progressive rock as a distinct genre. By 1974, the brand of classically influenced rock that King Crimson helped define topped the American charts, even though critics lamented a dearth of new ideas.

"King Crimson ceased to exist in September 1974, which was when all English bands in that genre should have ceased to exist," Fripp said later. "But since the rock and roll dinosaur likes anything which has gone before, most of them are still churning away, repeating what they did years ago without going off in any new direction."[1] Still, many of the bands that established, along with King Crimson, the style that came to be known as progressive rock (the Moody Blues; Yes; Jethro Tull; Emerson, Lake & Palmer) persevered and continued to perform as nostalgia acts through the 1980s—Fripp, too, reunited King Crimson several times and continued to perform throughout the 1990s.

Meanwhile, during the mid-1970s America embraced an array of eclectic avant-garde bands. Influenced by experimental modern composers, their sounds prefigured some of the biggest bands of the 1980s. Fripp stood on the cutting edge here, too, in his work with avant-garde pop pioneer Brian Eno. This chapter covers progressive rock between 1974 and 1980, as the genre expanded and fragmented, evolving into new genres before disappearing as a commercially viable style. Talented musicians will always find an audience, however, and progressive rock reappeared in the late 1990s in the music of popular bands such as Phish, Radiohead, and Wilco.

THE EVOLUTION OF PROGRESSIVE ROCK

As described in Volume 3, Chapter 6, progressive rock (also known as "prog," "art," "symphonic," or "classical" rock) emerged from British clubs in the late 1960s. Young English musicians drew on San Francisco's psychedelic movement, American jazz, and experimental classical artists such as Edgard Varèse, Igor Stravinsky, and John Cage to create rock as a form of "high art." American audiences had already followed artists like the Beatles, the Who, and Jimi Hendrix into strange new musical territory; in the mid-1970s, the progressive bands that followed in their wake would become some of the biggest acts "over there," as the British music press dubbed the vast and lucrative American market.

Because eclecticism is a hallmark of progressive rock, it is difficult to define precisely. The chapter on progressive rock in Volume 3 of this series traces its origins through such bands as the Moody Blues—their 1967 album *Days of Future Passed* became one of the first commercially successful examples of a symphony orchestra in a rock context. Bands like Frank Zappa and the Mothers of Invention, along with King Crimson, created multimovement pieces on their albums, marked by a wild contrast of sounds, from soft whispers to crashing cacophonies. The Who's 1969 "concept" album *Tommy* helped establish the idea of the album as a sustained narrative, an oft-imitated theme in progressive rock. In the late 1960s and early 1970s, Pink Floyd and the Velvet Underground broke ground for avant-garde artists who conducted wild musical experiments with rock and technology. These characteristics defined progressive rock.

While fans will disagree as to exactly which bands fall under the progressive rock umbrella, it is broadly defined in Jerry Lucky's book *The Progressive Rock Files* as music that incorporates:

- Predominantly long songs that are structured, not improvised.
- Dynamic arrangements that mix loud and soft passages with musical crescendos.
- The use of a live symphony orchestra backing, or the use of a mellotron or synthesizer to simulate strings.
- Extended instrumental solos, often showcasing the skill of individual musicians.
- Blending of acoustic, electric, and electronic elements to translate the emotion of a composition containing multiple moods.
- Multimovement compositions that may be created from unrelated parts and may or may not return to a unifying theme.

The importance of technology in the development of progressive rock cannot be overstated. Technology became a familiar part of American life in the 1970s—people witnessed the first portable electronic calculator (1970), the first video game (1972), and the first space station (1973). Technology changed the way music was created, performed, and experienced by listeners; as a style of music that looked to the future, progressive rock embraced emerging technology with special enthusiasm.

On a practical level, technology provided artists with new ways to make music. The mellotron and other sound-sampling devices, or synthesizers, that defined early progressive sounds were mass-produced in the 1970s. Synthesizers cost anywhere from a few hundred dollars to $20,000 for professional models; they gave a whole generation of musicians the ability to compose with a literally unlimited array of sounds. A wide range of other musical equipment hit the market in the mid-1970s. Numerous albums displayed the sounds of guitar effects pedals—"fuzz" boxes (especially the Big Muff), wah-wahs, whooshing phase shifters, and frequency modifiers produced captivating sounds and tones. Electric drum machine pads allowed bands like Kraftwerk to compose entire albums without acoustic instruments. Equipment that was once found only in professional recording studios now appeared in the basements of amateur musicians.

Another important invention was the time-lag tape-delay system, developed by composer Terry Riley in the 1960s. His device was essentially two Revox tape recorders into which he fed traditional instruments, like an organ or saxophone. The two-tape system takes a musical phrase and repeats it into infinity, layering the phrase on top of itself over and over again to create an entirely new sound. Brian Eno would become the pop master of this tape-delay looping in the 1970s, using the technology to create pieces that put human performers in the background and sound as if the song is writing itself.

Technology also changed the listening experience. Albums were recorded to be played on the high-fidelity record players and headphones that were part of every serious music fan's living room. New concert technology also allowed progressive bands to reproduce the rich sounds of an album in a live setting, in front of thousands of listeners. Bands like Pink Floyd incorporated the latest lighting (which included lasers by 1976) and film technology into their concerts.

In a more abstract way, technology was part of the progressive rock aesthetic. Spaceships and handheld gizmos permeated Western culture, so it seems natural that progressive music would embrace technology and ponder its implications. Futuristic images graced many a progressive album cover; a famous example is the man-machine painting on Emerson, Lake & Palmer's 1973 record *Brain Salad Surgery*. The Electric Light Orchestra kicked off their 1977 concerts by emerging from a giant flying saucer. The music of Tangerine Dream and Kraftwerk predicted a future when man and machine would become indistinguishable, while Eno designed "ambient" music to help people cope with the stress of a fast-paced urban lifestyle.

Progressive bands carved a niche in the expanding American music market. By 1974, the $2 billion-a-year record industry stood nearly as tall in American culture as movies ($1.6 billion) and professional sports ($600,000) combined.[2]

The industry flourished despite a vinyl shortage and an overall economic downturn that caused a shakeout in the concert business, which progressive rock seemed to weather quite comfortably. "Progressive music is what's happening," said Clive Davis, founder of Arista Records, in 1975. "Artists without singles doing strong, progressive music are doing better than ever."[3]

Because progressive rock generally takes the form of long, complex compositions, even at its zenith the style never produced many hit singles in America. Thus progressive rock ascended in American culture along with the FM radio stations that played album-length cuts and introduced the generally British-born progressive acts to American listeners. FM airplay helped progressive endure the fierce competition for radio airplay as many AM stations cut their playlists from Top 40 down to Top 20—some as low as Top 12—in the mid-1970s.

This chapter organizes the era's major progressive bands into three categories, roughly corresponding to the grouping described in *The Rolling Stone Illustrated History of Rock & Roll*. The first category includes chart-topping classically influenced rock (the Moody Blues, ELP, Yes). The second category is much more broad, covering the wide range of eclectic experimentalist acts that appeared between 1974 and 1980. The final section treats the technology-driven work of avant-garde artists like Brian Eno and Kraftwerk, whose music would prefigure styles that dominated American music throughout the 1980s. As has been repeated often throughout these volumes, few bands fit neatly into any category; these classifications are not perfect, but neither are they completely random.

CHART-TOPPING CLASSICAL BOMBAST

This style of progressive rock reached its peak in 1974. As the decade progressed, the complex music and elaborate stage displays of bands like Yes would provide easy targets for the punk artists (and the critics that embraced them).

Before the punk revolution, however, progressive rock topped the charts; bands outside the progressive genre incorporated classical elements in a bid for artistic respectability. The most famous of these efforts was Led Zeppelin's 1975 double-album *Physical Graffiti*, released during Zeppelin's reign as the biggest hard-rock band in the world. The record covers Zeppelin's blues and hard-rock sounds but also features the Marrakech Symphony Orchestra on the hit "Kashmir." The album went gold and hit No. 1 in America.

Also in this era, new bands emerged with a sound derived from the groundbreaking progressive acts described in more detail below. Kansas, for example, emerged from the American Midwest with their eponymous 1974 debut. The progressive sound was driven by Robby Steinhardt's lead violin work and the soaring vocals of keyboardist Steve Walsh. Over a series of follow-up albums like *Song for America* and *Masque* (both 1975), which spawned numerous hit singles, the band blended their prog influences with a straight-up hard-rock sound. With 1976's *Leftoverture*, Kansas sounded like a lighter version of Led Zeppelin, fitting squarely into a genre known as "arena rock" rather than progressive rock.

Another American band, Styx, emerged out of Chicago as a more teen-friendly version of Yes. The group displayed enough guitar wizardry and arty album covers to impress younger fans who came to progressive rock at the height of its popularity.

The Canadian power trio Rush fits here with music that melded progressive with hard-rock styles. After a self-titled 1974 debut, Rush toured America incessantly, then finally broke into the American market two years later with *2112*. The album featured Rush's hallmarks—the science-fiction themes and furious drumming of Neil Peart, Alex Lifeson's blazing guitar, and bassist Geddy Lee's high-pitched wail. Their 1977 release *A Farewell to Kings* broke the Top 40 in both America and Britain and included the hit "Closer to the Heart." The band enjoyed continued success throughout the 1980s and 1990s, albeit with shorter, less epic songs.

The Moody Blues

A 1974 review of the Moody Blues at the Los Angeles Forum put the Moody Blues alongside the Who as one of the few rock bands to survive into the mid-'70s with most of their original members intact. The lineup of guitarist Justin Hayward, bassist John Lodge, keyboard player Michael Pinder, flautist and singer Ray Thomas, and drummer Graeme Edge produced seven successful original albums between their 1967 *Days of Future Passed*, which stayed on the *Billboard* charts for two years, and 1972's *Seventh Sojourn*, which reached No. 1 on both American and British album charts. Stylistically, though, the band repeated the same mellotron-infused orchestral rock sound that had catapulted them to stardom.

The strain of steady touring took its toll on the band, however, a condition that would affect many of the progressive bands that rose to stardom in the early 1970s. In 1973 the band broke up following a long world tour. The Moody Blues remained in the public eye, however, with the release of the 1974 album *This Is the Moody Blues*, a collection of their hits between 1968 and 1972. Hayward and Lodge released a duet album, *Blue Jays*, in 1975, but it offered little departure from the typical Moody Blues sound. A live album, *Caught Live + 5*, appeared in 1977, and all five members released solo albums before the band reunited to record *Octave* in 1978.

Unhappy with *Octave*, Pinder left the band, to be replaced by Patrick Moraz, who had recently left Yes. The Moody Blues continued to release albums and tour as a nostalgia act throughout the 1980s and 1990s, but the band would never again be anywhere near the cutting edge of music.

Emerson, Lake & Palmer (from left) Keith Emerson, Greg Lake, and Carl Palmer, 1976. Courtesy of Photofest.

Emerson, Lake & Palmer

In the mid-'70s, the supergroup Emerson, Lake & Palmer stood as the heaviest band in rock—literally. During their 1974 tour the group traveled with thirty-six tons of equipment. The tour climaxed as ELP performed for 350,000 people, as well as an ABC television audience, at the California Jam festival in April, with keyboardist Keith Emerson playing his grand piano as it lifted thirty feet off the stage and rotated end over end.

The tour supported the band's 1973 album *Brain Salad Surgery*, which reached No. 11 in America. By the mid-'70s ELP had established themselves as perhaps the most "classical" of the major progressive bands. During the 1974 tour critics described them as "one of rock and roll's premier concert attractions, a blend of technical virtuosity, visceral power and ethereally majestic stage presence."[4] But the seriousness with which ELP, especially Emerson, approached their music also drew fierce criticism, most famously from the keyboard of *Creem* writer Lester Bangs, who called the band "the utter befoulment of all that was gutter pure in rock."[5]

After the 1974 tour, ELP released a triple album, *Welcome Back My Friends to the Show That Never Ends*, which went platinum and hit No. 4 on the U.S. charts. The band took a long vacation as Emerson worked on a piano concerto with the London Philharmonic. The rocker found the classical musicians would not take his vision seriously. "They couldn't give a damn about this new piece of music," said Emerson in an interview on the band's official Web site. "The brass section at the back would be reading porney magazines."

ELP reemerged in 1977 with the release of *Works, Volume 1*, a double album that featured the unusual format of three sides of solo material and one side of original ELP recordings. The ensuing tour was overly ambitious—a full symphony orchestra, an entourage of 130 people, and a daily payroll of $20,000. After two weeks, the band was on track to lose $3 million, so ELP dropped the orchestra and finished the tour as a trio. In November 1977, they released *Works, Volume 2*.

After the band's final show in March 1978, ELP tried to take a break. Atlantic Records, however, would not let the band out of its contract. So to fulfill their obligations, in late 1978 the band released *Love Beach*, a disjointed, uninspired collection of songs and the end of ELP for twelve years. Emerson would spend the early 1980s writing film scores, while drummer Carl Palmer would join the pop supergroup Asia. In 1986 Emerson and bassist Greg Lake reunited with Whitesnake drummer Cozy Powell for an album and a tour; after Palmer left Asia, ELP would play together off and on through the 1990s.

Yes

In 1973, the busiest and most successful year for Yes, cracks began to appear that would doom Yes and other classically infused rock bands. That year Yes keyboardist Rick Wakeman released his first solo album, a series of vignettes called *The Six Wives of Henry VIII* that hit No. 30 in America. As Yes toured the world, they released a triple live album, *Yessongs*, that would hit No. 12 on the American charts. In November, Yes released *Tales from Topographic Oceans*.

Written mostly by guitarist Steve Howe and singer Jon Anderson, the double album was supposed to be a crowning artistic achievement for Yes. Instead, it would prompt critics and fans to turn their backs on the band. Reviews of the album were almost universally bad: "Brilliant in patches but often taking far too long to make various points and curiously lacking in warmth or personal expression . . . the music is more a test of endurance than a transport of delight."[6]

The album was by no means a commercial flop, reaching No. 6 on the American charts, but fans that came to performances hoping for hits from 1972's *Fragile* and *Close to the Edge* reacted coldly to new pieces like "The Revealing Science of God." Yes did not help lighten the vibe with announcements that informed fans: "It is essential that all ticket holders be seated prior to the time of performance. Nobody will be admitted after the start of the performance."[7] It was stricture like this that would prompt attack from the punk movement, just beginning to well up in London.

One of *TFTO*'s most vocal critics was Wakeman, who left the band in May 1974. He went on to produce *Myths and Legends of King Arthur* and perform the theme album as an ice show with a full symphony and vocal group. Yes replaced

Wakeman with Patrick Moraz for their next album, *Relayer*, which exhibited a harder, more vital sound. Their 1977 tour was particularly lucrative, with Yes riding from city to city in a private Gulfstream jet. When Yes returned to England, they found the Sex Pistols dominating headlines in the music press. Wakeman would return to play on Yes's tenth and eleventh albums, 1977's *Going for the One* and 1978's *Tormato*. Yes continued to make albums after Anderson left in 1979, while Steve Howe joined ELP drummer Carl Palmer in the band Asia. Anderson would return to sing on Yes's 1983 album *90125*, which included "Owner of a Lonely Heart," the band's first single to hit No. 1 on the American charts.

Jethro Tull

In 1975, Jethro Tull toured America to support their album *War Child*, released the previous year. The band broke attendance records at the Los Angeles Forum, drawing 93,000 people over five nights. The tour was so large that the band traveled with two separate stage sets and crews staggered from city to city, so that one crew could travel ahead of the band to set up the elaborate stage before the group arrived.

The band had learned a lesson about taking itself too seriously. During their supporting tour for 1973's *A Passion Play*, even dedicated Tull fans criticized the music as too slow and obscure. The band adopted a lighter mood for the *War Child* tour—flautist and bandleader Ian Anderson had his flute delivered by scantily clad women, and bassist Jeff Hammond-Hammond juggled tennis balls "laid" by a fake zebra.

Critics proclaimed Tull's next album, 1975's *Minstrel in the Gallery*, as Anderson's most successful fusion of Elizabethan and rock structures. The band released a compilation of their hits in 1976, followed by an original album that year called *Too Old to Rock 'n' Roll: Too Young to Die!*—an all-too-appropriate title. "I'm 30 now and this just isn't really decent," Anderson said in 1978. Rock stardom "is still marginally acceptable at the age of 30."[8]

Jethro Tull survived the punk era. Employing more than a dozen different lineups, Anderson and guitarist Martin Barre continued to front Tull as it released albums and toured well into the 1990s. Tull had sold 28 million albums by 1988, and although Anderson had become a successful salmon farmer, Tull (with their thirteenth lineup) continued to perform. The music was so out of fashion that even the notoriously ill-tempered Anderson had to get in on the joke—the stage backdrop to one of the band's late '80s concerts proclaimed: "Oh No! Not Another 20 Years of Jethro Tull!"[9]

The Electric Light Orchestra

Progressive rock rarely sent songs to the singles charts, but a notable exception is the Electric Light Orchestra. Twenty ELO singles and nine albums

The Electric Light Orchestra during a 1978 performance. © Corbis.

broke the *Billboard* Top 40 between 1975 and 1986, qualifying the band as one of the rock era's top 100 chart artists.

The band evolved from the Move, a successful British pop act formed by Roy Wood. Along with drummer Bev Bevan, Wood joined with up-and-coming songwriter Jeff Lynne to form ELO in 1969. The band was different than other orchestral rock bands. Whereas the Moody Blues hired orchestras to sit in on recording sessions and, later, used the mellotron to simulate strings, ELO was one of the few acts to recruit classical musicians—a French horn player, a violinist, and three cellists—into the group itself.

Performing live rock shows with classical instruments proved difficult at first. After releasing their 1971 debut album, *No Answer*, the band embarked on its first tour—and sounded awful. Amplifying the acoustic cellos proved difficult, and their sound was often inaudible to the rest of the band. Wood left the band shortly after its debut album, leaving Lynne as ELO's sole songwriter.

By the time ELO released their next album, *Electric Light Orchestra II*, in 1973, progressive rock was a commercially lucrative genre. The album only reached No. 62 on the American charts, but tunes like "Roll Over Beethoven," a melding of Chuck Berry's tune with Beethoven's Fifth and Ninth Symphonies, became a staple on American FM radio. The band had also solved its technical problems with the advent of a new type of pickup for acoustic instruments, freeing the cellist to dance around the stage during concerts. For Lynne, fame was accompanied by close critical scrutiny; reviewers noted the songwriter's debt to the Beatles, with some accusing him of blatantly pilfering the group's ideas.

British listeners snubbed ELO, but American listeners continued to warm up to the band after 1973's *On the Third Day*, which used automatic double-tracking to give the vocals a more powerful edge and multitrack recording to make ELO's classical instruments sound like a full orchestra. Lynne actually brought in a twenty-piece orchestra for 1974's *Eldorado*. The album launched ELO to stardom in America, reaching No. 16, earning a gold record, and producing the band's first Top 10 single, "Can't Get It Out of My Head."

The band's next album, 1975's *Face the Music*, outsold *Eldorado* and marked a transition as the band began moving toward disco and away from progressive rock. The record produced two hit singles—"Evil Woman" reached No. 10 and "Strange Magic" hit No. 14—and Lynne's high-pitched falsetto drew comparisons to a disco band, the Bee Gees.

Then *A New World Record* in 1976 continued along the same path, producing a string of three carefully crafted hit singles (including "Do Ya," ELO's rerecording of an old Move hit) on its way to becoming a platinum album. It spent a year on the American charts, falling out of the Top 40 before ELO released the record that would mark their commercial zenith, *Out of the Blue*.

With a cover painting inspired by space movies like *Star Wars* and *Close Encounters of the Third Kind* (both released in 1977) and two sides of the lush, state-of-the-art sound that made ELO famous, *Out of the Blue* would sell 5 million copies worldwide. The album also spawned an ambitious forty-four-date American tour during which the band emerged onstage from a giant flying saucer. It would be ELO's last live appearances for three years.

The 1979 album *Discovery* went platinum and spawned a pair of Top 10 singles ("Shine a Little Love" and "Don't Bring Me Down," the first ELO song to abandon strings). With its ballads, dance tracks, and few cello sounds, the album was more disco than progressive rock. In 1980 ELO performed the soundtrack for Olivia Newton-John's film *Xanadu*, which perhaps showed how far ELO had strayed from cutting-edge rock music. The band's last Top 10 single came in 1981 with "Hold on Tight," off the album *Time*. The group effectively ceased to exist amid several lawsuits initiated by and against it in 1983. ELO reunited in 1986 for their contractually obligated final record, the brief *Balance of Power*. As an aging rock superstar, Lynne became friends with former Beatle George Harrison. Together Harrison and Lynne formed the all-star Traveling Wilburys with Bob Dylan, Tom Petty, and Roy Orbison.

ECLECTIC EXPERIMENTALISM

In the mid-1970s, American ears were receptive to a wide variety of experimental music—what might have been dubbed "weird" a few years earlier was now embraced by the pop mainstream.

Frank Zappa, along with his band the Mothers of Invention, stood as the most influential figure in this group—Paul McCartney claimed that Zappa's

1966 debut album *Freak Out!* inspired the classic Beatles album *Sgt. Pepper's Lonely Hearts Club Band*, the album that opened the door to commercially successful experimental rock.

This chapter details the most popular experimental acts in America between 1974 and 1980. During this period, Zappa's music evolved—or, some critics would say, devolved—into a style that won him many new fans and a Grammy nomination even as it disappointed his original listeners. Genesis rose to fame playing progressive rock influenced by the cinema but attained even greater album sales in the 1980s by abandoning progressive rock for a more streamlined pop sound. Pink Floyd, meanwhile, continued to produce its trademark "space rock" throughout the decade.

Other bands did not attain such commercial success in America, but they deserve mention here. Ron and Russell Mael moved their band Sparks from California to England in search of commercial success in 1974. They were darlings of the UK press but failed to hit it big in America, although that year the band's 1974 album *Kimono My House* became a staple of FM radio in America, and *Creem* magazine readers ranked it as one of the year's Top 20 albums. Like Sparks, the British band 10cc drew critical acclaim for a string of albums that combined art-rock sounds with pop structure.

Occasionally experimental bands would score a surprise hit, as the Dutch band Golden Earring did in 1974 with "Radar Love." However, most of these bands, such as Gentle Giant and Crack the Sky, never attained rock star heights, but as the progressive audience became larger and more fragmented, they were able to enjoy some success by drawing loyal cult followings.

The British band Gentle Giant, for example, released ten critically acclaimed albums—eight in the United States—throughout the decade but never developed more than a small American fan base devoted to the band's highly innovative song structures, superb musicianship, and diverse styles drawn from classical, jazz, and progressive rock, as heard on albums like *Interview* (1976), *Playing the Fool* (1977), and *The Missing Piece* (1977).

John Palumbo's Ohio band Crack the Sky enjoyed more popularity in America with its menacing modal harmonies and epic orchestral arrangements. The band released three albums, with 1976's *Animal Notes* standing as perhaps their most mature, focused work.

Genesis

Genesis took the scenic route to rock stardom. Founded by teenagers Peter Gabriel and Tony Banks in 1967, the band would release five obscure albums of solid progressive rock before breaking into the American music scene in the mid-'70s, only to lose their founding member and abandon their conceptual roots for a pop sound that would make them superstars.

Their 1969 debut *From Genesis to Revelation* is engineered with orchestral accompaniment that recalls the Moody Blues. In 1970, drummer and former child actor Phil Collins joined the band, along with guitarist Steve Hackett. The two added a tougher rock sound to Banks' classically inspired keyboard arrangements. The band's progressive sound developed over four albums of original material between 1970 and 1973: *Trespass*, *Nursery Cryme*, *Foxtrot*, and *Selling England by the Pound*. Meanwhile, singer and flautist Peter Gabriel began incorporating masks, makeup, and props into the live act as the band developed a reputation among its fans as one of the best live bands in the world.

But Genesis had a tough time breaking into the American market; bored concertgoers sometimes hurled beer cans or shouted "Boogie!" as Genesis tried to build the mood with quiet interludes.[10] "I can now understand why so many English bands break up after American tours," Banks said during this period. "You're in England, secure and doing well then once in the States it feels like you're getting nowhere. That situation can be quite a bring-down, smashed egos and all."[11]

In 1974 Genesis released what the band would regard as its progressive rock masterpiece, *The Lamb Lies Down on Broadway*. Over a double album of muscular rock, Gabriel spins the tale of a counterculture hero named Rael. The record would meet with criticism for being dense and overblown, which by now had become a familiar greeting to most new progressive albums. Still, *The Lamb Lies Down on Broadway* showcased Gabriel's fractured lyricism and marked the high point of Genesis' commercial success to date. The band's cinematic 1974 tour featured props, masks, explosions, elaborate costumes, and 3,000 slides projecting images to help tell Rael's story; between songs Gabriel heightened the fantasy mood with poetic monologues. Throughout the performances, Gabriel donned gowns with a fox-head mask; a yellow-orange, three-foot-wide flower headdress; bats wings; and an inflatable phallus.

Gabriel's theatrics were so identified with Genesis that when he quit the band in 1975, most rock journalists wondered how the band could possibly continue without him. Yet carry on they did, with Phil Collins trading his drum sticks for the microphone stand. The first album without Gabriel, 1976's *A Trick of the Tail*, hit No. 31 on the American charts. It was Genesis' best showing on the charts so far. The group followed up that album with *Wind and Wuthering* in 1977 and a double live album that year, *Seconds Out*, which was bolstered by the drumming of Bill Bruford, formerly of Yes.

When *Seconds Out* was released, Hackett announced he was out of the band. His departure would mark the end of Genesis as a progressive rock band; their next album, 1978's *And Then There Were Three*, embraced a softer, less ambitious pop sound. This more commercially viable version of Genesis lacked the aggressive edge many loyal fans had come to identify with the band, but the sound would translate into a string of big-selling albums in America: *Duke* (1980), *Abacab* (1981), *Genesis* (1983), and the multiplatinum *Invisible Touch* (1986). Genesis is nothing if not durable. Although Phil Collins left the band for good in 1991, the group continues to write music with new singer Ray Wilson.

Gabriel, meanwhile, went on to success as a solo artist. He released a pair of critically acclaimed records in 1977 and 1978—both titled *Peter Gabriel*. The first album is a hard-rock record infused with Gabriel's witty lyrics; the second album, produced by former King Crimson guitarist Robert Fripp, is less commercial, harkening back to Genesis' art-rock. Gabriel scored his first Top 40 hit with "Shock the Monkey" in 1982, and his 1986 album *So* attained multiplatinum status with a series of groundbreaking videos and the No. 1 hit "Sledgehammer."

Pink Floyd

Volume 3's chapter on progressive rock covers the early avant-garde stages of Pink Floyd in detail; by the mid-'70s, the band had become superstars in America in the wake of their 1973 masterpiece, *Dark Side of the Moon*, which would hit No. 1 on the U.S. charts and remain on the *Billboard* Top 200 for a record-setting fourteen years. Between 1974 and 1980, however, critics observe that Pink Floyd suffered a decline in creativity, even as the band reached the heights of their popularity—an affliction affecting many of progressive rock's major bands during this period.

In 1975, Pink Floyd released *Wish You Were Here*, a tribute to former band-leader Syd Barrett, who left the group in 1968 after he had succumbed to drug abuse and emotional stress. The album continues in the majestic vein of *Dark Side of the Moon*, but it also incorporates older elements of Pink Floyd's sound, such as faster rock songs and dramatic musical violence. More than 900,000

Pink Floyd (from left) Nick Mason, David Gilmour, Roger Waters, and Rick Wright, 1970s. Courtesy of Photofest.

fans preordered *Wish You Were Here*, one of the largest preorders in Columbia Records history.[12]

No discussion of Pink Floyd (or mid-'70s progressive rock in general) is complete without mentioning hallucinogenic drugs—marijuana, psilocybin mushrooms, and especially LSD. Many elements of the progressive aesthetic—everything from album art, sprawling compositions, and elaborate stage-shows—appealed to the psychedelic influence. At this time Pink Floyd was known for delivering the lush sound and light displays that appealed to fans of the music-drug interaction. As such Pink Floyd also drew unwanted attention from law enforcement agencies that, in the mid-'70s, began to take more seriously the intersection of drugs and rock music. When Pink Floyd spent five nights performing at the Los Angeles Sports Arena in 1975, Los Angeles police chief Ed Davies arrested 511 people and promised to continue a crackdown on the large rock concerts he called "dope festivals."[13] The incident prompted indignation from concert promoters, who threatened to boycott cities where police had set up sting operations at rock concerts.

On *Wish* and Floyd's next album, 1977's *Animals*, guitarist David Gilmour emerged as the band's premier instrumentalist, while keyboardist Rick Wright sank deeper into the background to provide Floyd's characteristic "space rock" sound. The lyrics of bassist and songwriter Roger Waters cast a grim, pessimistic hue over Pink Floyd's music. As one critic put it, "[I]ts joyless methodicalness embodied rather than protested repression."[14] Indeed, Pink Floyd exemplified the seriousness and shimmering excess the emerging punks longed to tear down. When John Lydon was photographed walking into Malcolm McLaren's SEX shop wearing an "I Hate Pink Floyd" T-shirt in 1975, it signaled for many the beginning of the punk revolution.

Frank Zappa

While progressive and art-rock was predominantly a British phenomenon, America did produce one legendary genius in this genre: the irrepressible Frank Zappa.

In 1974, Zappa marked the tenth anniversary of his band, the Mothers of Invention (their early history is detailed in Volume 3) with the release of his sixteenth album, *Apostrophe*. Zappa had already produced more music than most bands, and his career was not even halfway over.

Zappa's famous work ethic drove his prodigious output. In the mid-'70s he reportedly spent sixteen to eighteen hours a day writing music, typing, and working on films. When he recorded music, he spent ten to fourteen hours a day in the studio. "What else are you gonna do?" said Zappa. "Work in a gas station?"[15] Although his eclectic sound and zany songs would be strongly linked to the popularity of drugs in American youth culture, Zappa often pronounced himself a strict teetotaler. A journalist noted that his band practice "resembled a symphony rehearsal more than the usual loose rock session, with nary a beer bottle or joint to be seen."[16] Indeed, one of Zappa's great strengths was as a bandleader. Ruth Underwood, Zappa's conservatory-trained percussionist in the mid-'70s, put it this way: "He was a remarkable referee. He knew how to synthesize people's talents. He wasn't just a conductor standing there waving his arms; he was playing us as people!"[17]

In 1973 Zappa scored his first gold record with *Over-Nite Sensation*, which hit No. 32 on the *Billboard* album charts. *Apostrophe* pushed into the Top 10 with the comic hit "Don't Eat the Yellow Snow," a song that perfectly captured Zappa's penchant for combining dumbed-down humor and complex playing. On other albums in this period—*One Size Fits All* (1975), *Bongo Fury* (1975), *Zoot Allures* (1976), *Zappa in New York* (1978), and *Studio Tan* (1978)—Zappa departed from the jazz-influenced compositional experiments that marked his earlier music. The songs are more conventional in structure, yet they retain Zappa's affinity for odd rhythms and blazing guitar solos. The records are most notable, perhaps, for the numerous scatological and sexually explicit jokes. His favorite gag was slapping shocking titles on delicate pieces of music. Zappa often complained his compositions were not recognized outside rock, but classical music fans were not likely to embrace tunes such as "I Promise Not to Come in Your Mouth," despite its gentle melody and sophisticated orchestration.

In his biting satire it was never clear whether Zappa was laughing with or at his fans; in live performances during this period, Zappa was known to lecture and, in some cases, vilify his audience. At a 1977 concert in Louisville, for example, he told the crowd: "What we're going to do now is sing a song with real easy-to-understand lyrics, real stupid chords, and a real simple beat. That way we can reach you people."[18]

With 1979's *Joe's Garage*, Zappa told the semiautobiographical story of a musician in a society who regards music as a social ill. The story would play out for real when the song "Jewish Princess," off Zappa's 1979 album *Sheik Yerbouti*, hit the airwaves. The song prompted the Anti-Defamation League (ADL—a Jewish advocacy group) to file a protest with the Federal Communications Commission, asking that the song be banned from airplay. Ironically, the song did not get much notice until the ADL's uproar.

Sheik Yerbouti marked some Zappa milestones. With its deft employment of smutty lyrics, parodies, and brilliant music, the album reached No. 21 on the *Billboard* charts, and the song "Dancin' Fool" reached No. 23. The record earned Zappa his first Grammy nominations: Best Rock Vocal Performance (Male) for "Dancin' Fool" and Best Rock Instrumental for "Rat Tomago." While the album sold well, it also marked the decline of Zappa's live audience. In the late 1970s he generated new legions of younger fans, but many of the people who started listening to Zappa in the late '60s did not stay with him. Zappa blamed his waning popularity on the rise of punk, but unlike other artists he never tailored his music to fit commercial expectations. His CBS press release for the 1981 double album *Tinseltown Rebellion* featured this note:

> Over the years it has become fashionable to despise what I do. Well, folks,
> I am not going to go away . . . and neither will the various works of art

which regularly get disapproved of. It might not be PUNK . . . it might not be NEW WAVE . . . it might not be whatever trend you are worshiping at the moment, but it is good stuff nonetheless, so, check it out.[19]

AVANT-GARDE COMPOSERS WHO INSPIRED MODERN ROCK

John Cage (1912–1992): American composer John Cage stood as the father figure to the avant-garde rock scene. His main contribution is the idea that any object can be a musical instrument, and any sound (even noise) can be music—thinking that had a profound impact on both modern jazz and rock.

Cage was radically ahead of his time with his *Imaginary Landscape No. 1*, a 1939 composition for frequency recordings, piano and cymbal, and two turntables that blended recorded music with acoustic instruments. In 1951, Cage drew both praise and derision for his most famous composition, 4'33", which called for a performer to sit at his instrument for 4 minutes and 33 seconds without playing. It enabled the audience to focus on the "chance music" around them—humming of lights, honking of cars outside, squeaking of chairs. Throughout the 1950s Cage's chance music performances grew increasingly bizarre and inspired the Fluxus art movement, which included experimental composer La Monte Young, Yoko Ono, and Al Hansen (grandfather of the pop star Beck).

Cage's influence can be heard in the ambient sounds of Eno's *Music for Airports* (1978); more broadly, though, Cage championed ideas that influenced the work of many progressive and avant-garde musicians for decades. Like Andy Warhol, Cage believed that art is not necessarily the product of some artistic genius who works through mystical processes far removed from everyday life; he believed that anybody can be an artist by living their life with a creative spirit and an eye for the beauty all around them.

La Monte Young (1935–): Young began his career as an experimental jazz saxophonist

Throughout Zappa's long career, he waged an unyielding war on conformity of any kind, even appearing before the U.S. Senate in the mid-1980s to testify against the Parents Music Resource Center (PMRC), a powerful interest group that lobbied to print warning labels on albums the group deemed offensive. Zappa continued to make music until his death from prostate cancer in 1993.

BRIAN ENO AND THE ELECTRONIC AVANT-GARDE

There was a great deal of interest in electronica among practitioners of psychedelic music in the late 1960s, and electronic experimentation was very much in vogue by 1974. In simple terms, the electronic avant-garde were more interested in tone and the ability of sound to create mood, more so than in melody, harmony, or rhythm. Drawing on the influence of avant-garde composers (see Avant-garde Composers Who Inspired Modern Rock), these artists constructed music by generating sounds electronically or by using electronics to alter conventional instruments. The resulting pulses, whooshes, and buzzes would not be considered "musical" by traditional Western standards; instead, composers layered sounds on top of one another to create collages designed to envelop the listener.

As discussed in Volume 3's chapter on progressive rock, one of the first bands to incorporate this sort of electronic experimentalism in their act was Pink Floyd and especially Floyd's keyboardist Rick Wright. By the early '70s, however, Pink Floyd and other progressive bands relegated electronics to the margins of their work. After 1970, electronic experimentalism developed in Germany, where bands like Kraftwerk and Tangerine Dream dispensed with drums and acoustic instruments altogether and imagined a future where man was indistinguishable from machine. The most important avant-garde figure in American music, however, was Brian Eno. By using the recording studio itself as an instrument and embracing musical "accidents," Eno would establish himself as a pioneer of ambient rock, New Age music, and later, new wave.

Roxy Music

"Roxy Music is the only music that says anything new or reflects the spirit of '74 with any accurate passion," wrote critic Lester Bangs for *Creem* magazine in October 1974. "If you still haven't bought *Stranded* GO GET THE GODDAMN THING."

When the band debuted with *Roxy Music* in 1972, the group and its songwriter Bryan Ferry became overnight stars in their native Britain. Critics and fans fell in love with Ferry's mannered singing and his affected boredom, not to mention the band's sizzling rock music. The band was always Ferry's project, but the press soon became enamored with its keyboard player, the flamboyant and articulate Brian Eno. He and Ferry clashed, and Eno left the band after their second album, *For Your Pleasure*, in 1973.

Perhaps it was for the best. The band hit their high point and broke into the American scene with their third album, *Stranded*, in 1974. Roxy's roaring, metallic sound was propelled by guitarist Phil Manzanera, saxophonist Andrew Mackay, the drumming

 AVANT-GARDE COMPOSERS WHO INSPIRED MODERN ROCK *(continued)*

in Los Angeles in the early 1950s, where he discovered the work of fellow Californian John Cage. Under his influence Young dabbled in the Fluxus movement, a playful group of musicians, actors, and visual artists.

Young's musical work in the Fluxus movement involved instruments playing long, sustained notes to create a droning chord that produced intricate harmonic effects. Between 1962 and 1966 he collaborated with fellow minimalist composers Tony Conrad and John Cale in a project called the Theater of Eternal Music that used alternate tuning systems, sustained notes, and a limited number of pitches to produce long, transcendental compositions.

After the group disbanded, Cale, Conrad, and drummer Angus MacLise went on to form the Velvet Underground. In that group, Young's influence can be heard in the hypnotic drones that turned Lou Reed's pop songs into psychedelic anthems.

Philip Glass (1937–): Born in Baltimore, Glass differed from other composers in that he deliberately tried to make himself a part of the rock scene. After studying at New York's Juilliard School, Glass went to Paris in the late 1960s, where he worked transcribing the music of Ravi Shankar (an Indian composer who would inspire the Beatles) into Western notation. Upon returning to New York in the early '70s, he founded the Philip Glass Ensemble and played galleries and rock clubs in the city's underground scene.

Along with other minimalists like Terry Riley (who invented the tape-delay loop) and Steve Reich, Glass made music that repeated similar patterns of notes over and over to create floating, trance-inducing compositions that would influence Brian Eno and, later, Talking Heads.

Roxy Music (left to right) Phil Manzanera, Paul Thompson, Dave Skinner, Bryan Ferry, Gary Tibbs, and Andy Mackay, 1980. Courtesy of Photofest.

of Paul Thompson, and a rotating cast of bassists, most often King Crimson veteran John Wetton.

Roxy Music released four more albums before breaking up in 1977—*Country Life* and *Siren*, along with a live album and a greatest hits collection—all of which displayed Ferry's compelling attitude, his witty lyrics, and glamorous rock 'n' roll.

Ferry liked to play rock's iconoclast. On his debut solo album, 1973's *These Foolish Things*, Ferry "covered" conventional rock hits. The Rolling Stones hit "Sympathy for the Devil" was reworked with an electronic big band, for example, and Ferry sung the Bob Dylan classic "A Hard Rain's a-Gonna Fall" from the top of his throat, with an overly British accent. Along with his solo follow-up, 1974's *Another Time, Another Place*, Ferry created pop pastiches that layered Elvis, the Beach Boys, Motown, '40s big band music, pop, and avant-garde. As Stephen Holden put it in *Rolling Stone*: "The first impulse is to dismiss it as a bad joke," but Ferry, along with Bowie and Elton John,

> are ushering in "rock mannerism," where the elements of style that informed the 64–70 era are polished to a high surface gloss and refined into sound artifacts whose humanism is distorted or opaque, whose eroticism is narcissistic, whose iconography is refracted into a multiplicity of aesthetic and moral contradictions. . . . [I]t both fascinates and repels, and there is no denying its significance.[20]

Krautrock: Kraftwerk, Tangerine Dream, and "the Cybernetic Inevitable"

In post–World War II Germany, a generation of students set out to reestablish their culture after it had been brutalized by the Nazi movement. Artists sought to break with the past and establish a new vision of the future; thus the rock music produced in Germany in the late 1960s and early '70s was rooted in progressive and avant-garde traditions. In a time when technology was a growing influence on life, the music known as "kosmiche" (cosmic) music in Germany—it was dubbed "krautrock" by U.S. and British press—set out to create a soundtrack for the modern age.

Kraftwerk is the most influential in terms of American culture, thanks to their 1974 hit album *Autobahn*, which uses pulsating electronic rhythms and

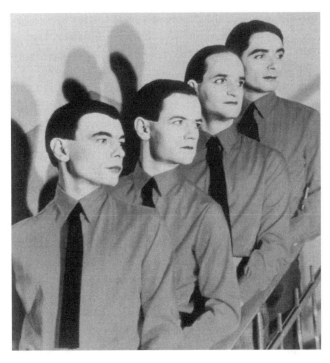

Kraftwerk (left to right) Karl Bartos, Ralf Hütter, Florian Schneider, and Wolfgang Flür, 1978. © Bettmann / Corbis.

synthesized swooshes to render a musical vision of a drive along the famous German highway. And you can dance to it. Except for a flute and a guitar, *Autobahn* is completely electronic, all programmed into drum machines and synthesizers by Ralf Hütter and Florian Schneider. They were classmates at Düsseldorf Conservatory in the late '60s, where they heard the music of Karlheinz Stockhausen. Their debut came as members of a quintet called the Organization, with a 1970 album *Tone Float*.

That year, Hütter and Schneider stuck together and formed Kraftwerk (or "power station"). They recorded the first Kraftwerk album at their own Kling-Klang studio, with percussionists Klaus Dinger and Thomas Hohman. When guitarist Michael Rother replaced Hohman, the group's sound began to explore guitar-groove territory; Hütter, though, found the music so repulsive he quit the group for a while in 1971. The trio lasted only six months before Hütter returned, and Hohman and Dinger left to form Neu! Gone but not forgotten, their rhythmic influence remained with Kraftwerk's albums *Kraftwerk 2* (1972) and *Ralf and Florian* (1973).

In shortened form, the twenty-two-minute "Autobahn" became an international hit; it was a Top 5 album and Top 40 single in the United States. It is "more than just a record," wrote Lester Bangs, "it is an indictment. An indictment of all those who would resist the bloodless iron will and order of the ineluctable dawn of the Machine Age." In the same essay, Bangs said Kraftwerk's music presented a question: The beauty of Chuck Berry's guitar lines is that "any idiot" can play them. "But if any idiot can play them, why not eliminate such genetic mistakes altogether, punch 'Johnny B. Goode' into a computer printout and let the machines do it in total passive acquiescence to the Cybernetic Inevitable?"[21]

Kraftwerk performed wearing matching suits, standing stock still in front of identical synthesizer machines. With an anti-image that took their individual personalities out of the performance, Hütter and Schneider became the only German art-rock band to cross into the American mainstream in the 1970s. Other German progressive bands (Can, Faust, Neu!) found only cult followings in America, but their music influenced later generations of American rockers.

Can is considered by some fans to be the kings of krautrock.

> Can's music is so influential it can be said to have transcended its ghet-toization as krautrock and joined the ranks of rock's most important work, like the Velvet Underground. Can was a primary meeting ground between music traditionally defined as high and music deemed low, and in its ability to make experimental sound groovy—and dance music intricate.[22]

Can released nineteen albums in America, plus a tribute "remix" album recorded in 1997, when Sonic Youth, the Orb, and Brian Eno reconceived their music. *Ege Bamyasi* (1972) is Can's most accessible album, and it became something of a commercial success. "I found *Ege Bamyasi* in the 49-cents bin at Woolworth's," said Thurston Moore of Sonic Youth. "I didn't know anything about them except this okra can on the cover, which seemed completely bizarro. I finally picked that record up, and I completely wore it out. It was so alluring. . . . It was unlike anything else I was hearing at the time."[23]

Faust was the creation of journalist Uwe Nettelbeck, who formed the band in 1970 with backing from a German record label. He recruited musicians from Hamburg bands and named the group for the literary character (the word also means "fist" in German). The group's core members—Werner Diermaier, Jean-Hervé Perón, and Rudolf Sosna—built some of their own instruments and made the most experimental music of any German band in this era.

The band's 1971 debut album, *Faust*, came in a unique package—clear vinyl inside a clear jacket with an x-ray image of a fist on it. The music consisted of an absurd jumble of fragments and styles, jumping from radio static to sampled bits of the Beatles to acid rock to classical piano to marching horns. Faust designed 1972's *So Far* as their debut's polar opposite: packaged in black, offering music more recognizable as rock. After recording 1973's *Outside the Dream Syndicate* with minimalist composer Tony Conrad, Faust broke up in 1975, although the group would reunite twenty years later.

After leaving Kraftwerk in 1971, guitarist Michael Rother and drummer Klaus Dinger formed Neu! (pronounced "noy," translated as "new"). With nothing more than a drum set, a guitar, and an array of effects pedals, Neu! created minimalist, groove-based soundscapes on their self-titled 1972 debut, a critically acclaimed work with Kraftwerk producer Conrad Plank. The sparse cover art—the word "Neu!" in bold red against a solid white background—reflected the minimalist sound of the mostly instrumental music. The next album, *Neu! 2*, featured the same stark cover art and rock that alternates between hypnotic grooves and raging punk. Rother and Dinger's budget ran out during recording, however, and they split up after the album's release in 1973. The two set out on solo projects, reuniting to make one last record and end the band on a high note. Rother and Dinger accomplished that goal with *Neu! 75*.

Along with Kraftwerk, Tangerine Dream was one of the few German experimental bands to get popular notice in America. The band originated in 1967 as a fairly conventional Berlin rock outfit. After releasing two albums—*Electronic Meditation* (1970) and *Alpha Centauri* (1971)—Tangerine Dream fully embraced electronics with 1972's *Zeit*, a drumless sound-shape double album, and with *Phaedra* in 1974. "They sound like silt seeping on the ocean floor," said one reviewer.[24] Like Kraftwerk, Tangerine Dream eliminated personality from their stage show. The band never spoke to the audience, and members obscured themselves behind three huge Moog organs and about fifty synthesizers. This is the future toward which krautrock pointed—a time when technology dominated every aspect of human life, with man as the servant, not the master, of his machines.

Brian Eno

"I can't play any instruments in any technically viable sense at all," confessed Brian Eno. "And it's one of my strengths, I think, actually."[25]

Of all the artists to emerge from progressive rock's avant-garde scene in the mid-1970s, few made such a lasting impact on American music as Brian Peter George St. John le Baptiste de la Salle Eno. His career is as impressive as his name. As a musician and producer, Eno left an enormous body of work that figured prominently in the development of art-rock, ambient, new wave, no wave, New Age,

Brian Eno, 1980. Courtesy of Photofest.

trance-dance, and mannered pop and shaped the sound of some of rock's most influential bands.

Eno grew up in Suffolk, England, where he heard early rock, doo-wop, and pop on American radio broadcasts from the nearby U.S. Air Force base. In the late '50s a new invention captured young Eno's imagination—the tape recorder. He could not play any instruments, but he mastered the tape recorder's possibilities, in a sense becoming the machine's first pop virtuoso.

In the mid-1960s Eno entered art school at Ipwich and, later, Winchester. He studied painting and sculpture, absorbing ideas about self-expression and conceptual doodling that would influence his later work as a musician.

"It wasn't a big move from art to music," Eno told *Creem* magazine in July 1975.

> They both concentrate on systems. I had reached a stage in painting where I was actually making a score which I would then carry out in the same way that a musician might. I mean, a score is only a behavior pattern. It says if you do this, this and this, you'll come out with a result of some kind. So it wasn't unnatural to make a transition into music.

Bryan Ferry enlisted Eno to play keyboards in Roxy Music in 1971. Eno never made any pretensions of being an accomplished keyboardist—he did not so much play music as he used technology to sculpt sounds, helping create the group's pre-glam style.

After two years, the relationship between Eno and Roxy bandleader Bryan Ferry began to fray. Eno's eccentric keyboard work never seemed to fit with Ferry's more straightforward songs. The conflict, however, was more than musical. Even though Ferry was the principal songwriter behind Roxy Music, it was Eno—with his wild costumes and willingness to talk with reporters for hours—who drew much of the media attention. Eno left to pursue solo work in 1973.

His first work was a collaboration with King Crimson's founding guitarist, Robert Fripp. Eno used a technique called tape looping to delay, loop, and layer Fripp's classical guitar lines into mesmerizing aural landscapes, much the same way a painter might add layers of color to build up a rich texture on canvas. Instead of using the recording studio simply as a place to capture music, Eno was using new recording technology to create music from scratch. Fripp would later perform solo concerts with the tape loop, which he called "Frippertronics."

Also in 1973, Eno produced an album by the Portsmouth Sinfonia, a fifty-piece orchestra comprising entirely nonmusicians. Although the album, *Portsmouth Sinfonia Plays the Popular Classics*, has been declared "perhaps the worst record ever made,"[26] it illustrated Eno's concept that accidents could have value in music. Eno also recorded a pair of rock albums—*Here Come the Warm Jets* (1973) and *Taking Tiger Mountain (By Strategy)* (1974). Both were rock albums that established Eno as an inspired lyricist and, at times, seemed to prefigure both punk rock and synth-pop.

A watershed year for Eno came in 1975, when he and artist Peter Schmidt created Oblique Strategies, a set of cards with instructions and suggestions that might be applied to a variety of creative situations. While in the recording studio, Eno would place the cards face down around the room. When a creative problem presented itself, he would consult 1 of the more than 100 cards, which offered a variety of suggestions—"Give way to your worst impulse"; "Emphasize the flaws"; "Use 'unqualified people'"; "The most important thing is the thing most easily forgotten."[27]

Also that year, Eno was crossing the street on a rainy day when he was knocked over by a taxicab. While he was lying in bed, heavily medicated, a friend brought him a record of harp music. But one of the record player's speakers was broken, and the other pointed away from him. The wind and rain outside mixed with the harp sounds, but Eno was too weak to get out of bed and turn up the volume.

At first he was frustrated. But then he relaxed, then surrendered. "I drifted into this kind of fitful sleep, a mixture of painkillers and tiredness," Eno said.

> And I started hearing this music as if I'd never heard music before. It was a really beautiful experience. I got the feelings of icebergs. I would occasionally just hear the loudest parts of the music, get a little flurry of notes coming out above the sound of the rain . . . and then it would drift away again.[28]

With *Discreet Music* in 1975, Eno designed music to be both heard and ignored at the same time. The record included two parts. The first part involved a pair of synthesizer melodies processed through a system of tape-delay loops; the second part recast Pachelbel's *Canon* in D Major (a popular classical piece) by shifting the tempo of certain instruments. The results proved so calming they were played in hospitals during childbirth.

Eno called the music "ambient," and he continued along that path with 1978's *Ambient 1/Music for Airports*, which was broadcast at LaGuardia Airport, and 1982's *Ambient 4/On Land*. Thus Eno must accept the blame for the "New Age" music that would proliferate in the 1980s; the music would also inspire the style of "ambient techno" dance music that would become popular across America and Europe in the 1990s.

Eno's groundbreaking experimental work drew critical acclaim but never yielded hit singles. He would, however, become the producer of choice for "new wave" bands of the late '70s and early '80s, where his playful and adventurous outlook would inspire superstar acts like Talking Heads and U2. "Some bands went to art school," said Bono, U2's lead singer. "We went to Brian Eno."[29]

NOTES

1. Macan 1997, 179.
2. Hendler 1983, 165.
3. *Rolling Stone*, May 22, 1975.
4. *Rolling Stone*, January 3, 1974.
5. Macan 1997, 169.
6. Welch 1999, 138.
7. Ibid.
8. *Creem*, June 1978.
9. *Q*, September 1988.
10. *Circus*, March 1975.
11. *New Musical Express*, August 25, 1973.
12. *Rolling Stone*, November 5, 1975.
13. *Rolling Stone*, June 5, 1975.
14. DeCurtis et al. 1992, 425.
15. *Rolling Stone*, July 4, 1974.
16. Ibid.
17. Miles 2004, 240.
18. Ibid., 264.
19. Ibid., 283–284.
20. *Rolling Stone*, January 2, 1975.
21. Bangs 2003, 154.
22. Sarig 1998, 108.
23. Ibid., 111.
24. Bangs 2003, 209.
25. *Creem*, July 1975.
26. Marsh 1979, 300.
27. Morley 2005, 165.
28. Ibid., 166.
29. Sarig 1998, 128.

3

CORPORATE AND MAINSTREAM SOUNDS: ROCK IS DEAD, LONG LIVE ROCK!

Richard Skanse

Few lines in rock and roll have ever captured the original, thrilling rush of the genre better than Pete Townshend's immortal "Hope I die before I get old" from the Who's iconic 1965 single "My Generation." Delivered by frontman Roger Daltrey in a contemptuous snarl that bridged the gap between James Dean in *Rebel without a Cause* and the Sex Pistols' Johnny Rotten, "Hope I die before I get old" was the ultimate "us versus them" battle cry, even more so than the same song's ferocious taunt of "Why don't you just f-f-f-fade away." For the British "mods" and the rest of the '60s counterculture generation, "old" represented the Establishment and was thus not to be trusted—let alone *joined*—under any circumstances. But even as it drew a line in the sand, "My Generation" was an anthem of unity, a rallying cry and pledge of allegiance between band and fans.

Had fate but called Townshend's bluff, or had "My Generation" proven to be the Who's only hit, that "Hope I die . . ." line would have made a fine epitaph. Instead, it became—much like the Who's phenomenally successful 1969 rock opera *Tommy*—something of an albatross for Townshend. In 1975, ten years after "My Generation" stormed its way to No. 2 on the British charts, the Who were still very much alive—and one of the three biggest rock bands in the world (alongside the Rolling Stones and Led Zeppelin). But the landscape had changed immeasurably in the interim. Rock music—for years regarded as an unsavory and hopefully passing fad by the stodgy suits calling the shots in the entertainment industry—was now big business. The old guard may have been stubborn, but it was not stupid, and little counterculture hootenannies like Woodstock proved devastatingly effective (if unintentional) wake-up calls. Once rock became priority number one at the major record labels, the "revolution" was officially commodified; by the end of 1968, "But the Man can't bust our music" was not a bad song lyric—it was the slogan for a Columbia Records print ad.[1]

With bigger and bigger profits from rock music now on the corporate agenda, the top draws—both '60s holdovers like the Who and a whole new crop of '70s superstars—were ushered out of the ballrooms and theaters of the '60s and into bigger and bigger sports arenas. Rock crowds in the tens and hundreds of thousands—formerly seen only at major "event" festivals like Woodstock and Altamont—became more and more the norm, as tours became events in and of themselves. And the bigger the audiences got, the more rock shows began to place as much emphasis on spectacle—from Alice Cooper's onstage guillotine gimmick to Ted Nugent's trapeze stunts to pretty much everything KISS ever did—as on music.[2]

Not that Townshend himself was particularly averse to spectacle. The Who's reputation as one of the '60s' most exciting live bands was built not only on their larger-than-life anthems and the band members' kinetic stage presence but also their propensity for wreaking all manner of violent destruction on their instruments by show's end. And in 1976, the Who became the first band to incorporate lasers into their performances. But as the Who evolved from scrappy spokesband for the British mod scene into stadium-packing monsters of rock, Townshend—who turned thirty in 1975—was all too keenly aware that he "was now a generation older than the fans he had initially spoken for."[3] But even more troubling to the guitarist/songwriter than his own advancing age was the realization that the line between the counterculture "us" and the Establishment "them" really no longer existed. Worst of all, lost in translation as rock went from underground to mainstream was the sense of intimate connection between artists and fans that had imbued songs like "My Generation" with such cultural relevance in the first place. Though "My Generation" remained a staple in the band's live set, it had long since outlived its original relevancy; the not-so-long-ago battle cry had for all intents and purposes become just another greatest hit. Townshend, onetime spokesman for a generation turned elder statesman of rock, could relate.

Of course, many of the Who's '60s contemporaries—from the Rolling Stones and the Kinks to Beatles-gone-solo and guitar gods like Eric Clapton and fellow former-Yardbird Jimmy Page—were also still stalking the earth as rock music rolled (some would say *lumbered*) out of its heady, rebellious youth and anything-can-happen adolescence and closer to the big 3-0 itself. But out of all of his peers, only Townshend seemed to really be losing any sleep over the matter. John Lennon readily declared that the "dream" was over, dismissing the past with his infamous "I don't believe in Beatles" admission in his 1970 song "God." Paul McCartney traipsed happily through the new decade singing "Silly Love Songs" with his new outfit Wings. The Kinks' Ray Davies further indulged his love of vaudeville and English music hall as he pined for the "young and innocent days" of a bygone era that was old when rock was in its infancy. Clapton, who helped *invent* hard rock with both the Yardbirds and the power trio Cream in the '60s, settled comfortably into a decidedly more easygoing, MOR-friendly groove typified by his 1974 solo breakthrough *461 Ocean Boulevard*. Meanwhile, Page and the rest of his post-Yardbirds band, Led Zeppelin—whose members ranged in age from twenty-seven to thirty-one upon the release of 1975's titanic, four-sided *Physical Graffiti*—seemed to relish every bit of the fame and fortune laid at their feet by arena after arena full of stoned teenagers, most of whom likely had no clue about the Yardbirds, let alone the American blues and English folk traditions from which the mighty Zep raided without prejudice.

And as for the Rolling Stones, those former street-fighting men long since turned triumphant conquerors (and millionaires several times over) with apparently nothing left to prove? Well, *they* were not sweating middle age. The title of their 1974 album spoke volumes: "Hey," one could imagine the infamous tax exiles shrugging between champagne toasts on the Riviera, "it's *only* rock 'n' roll."

But Townshend, arguably more so than any other rocker of *his* generation, was an artist who had always believed in the power of rock music as a catalyst for both positive change (societal, cultural, and political) and, on a deeper level—courtesy of his interest in the teachings of Eastern mystic Meher Baba—personal enlightenment and connection with others. Not for nothing did he make *Tommy*'s most powerful theme the repeating motif of "see me, feel me, touch me, heal me." Shortly after completing that career milestone, Townshend immersed himself, Don Quixote–like, in a doomed project called *Lifehouse*—a proposed film and double record concept album centered around the concept of an ultimate rock concert that would not only liberate the audience from the shackles of an oppressive Orwellian society but also, as each listener connected on a deeply personal level with the musical vibrations from the band, elevate everyone in attendance to a permanent state of nirvana. "What *Lifehouse* was about, at its root, was to reaffirm that what's important is that music reflects its audience as absolutely and completely as possible,"[4] Townshend would later explain, essentially casting the ambitious *Lifehouse*, with its theme of music joining people together, as "My Generation" writ large. But *Lifehouse* never got off the ground, and the whole project was ultimately pared down to a single, straight-ahead rock record, 1971's *Who's next*.

Townshend was devastated by his inability to make his Big Statement, and much of the Who's output for the rest of the '70s reflected his troubled faith in himself, his peers, his audience, and the present state of rock in general, wherein commercialism had all but trampled idealism into a vast "teenage wasteland." If the Who's 1973's *Quadrophenia*, yet another concept album, seemed a bittersweet farewell to the mod generation, 1975's deceptively low-key *The Who by Numbers* all but seethed with loathing both inward and outward. Even the band's famously unflappable bassist John Entwistle weighed in on the state of affairs with the cautionary tale "Success Story," wryly singing, "Back in the studio, to make our latest number 1 / Take 276, you know this used to be *fun*."

Such disillusionment was seconded by many a rock journalist at the time. In a 1976 *New Musical Express* editorial, writer Mick Farren decried "the absorption of rock and roll into the turgid masterstream of traditional establishment show biz,"[5] while the notorious critic Lester Bangs held nothing back in his scathing reviews of any number of his former rock idols gone soft or, even worse, pointless. "There is a sadness about the Stones now," Bangs wrote in *Creem* magazine in 1973, reviewing the band's *Goats Head Soup* album, "because they amount to such an enormous 'So what?' The sadness comes when you measure not just one album, but the whole sense they're putting across now against what they once meant."[6] For Bangs and others all too ready to heap the Stones and their aging contemporaries on the funeral pyre and burn them for growing obsolete, the concurrent burgeoning rise of punk only added fuel to the fire.

And yet should any of this give the impression that traditional-based hard rock literally breathed its last gasp somewhere between 1973 and 1975 (or, as comic Dave Foley put it in a memorable skit on the subject in an episode of the '90s sketch comedy series *The Kids in the Hall*, "1974, the year the first Bad Company album was released"), there was no shortage of evidence to the contrary. How else to explain, in the midst of a depressing economy, the biggest boom period for the record industry in its history? By 1975, an unprecedented 80 percent of all music sales were for rock records.[7]

Commoditized into the mainstream or not, rock and roll was still very much alive in the '70s and into the '80s, and it certainly was not just '60s holdovers like the Who, the Stones, and Zeppelin selling out all those concert halls and arenas. Crisscrossing the U.S. touring circuit at the same time was a scruffy, unapologetically raunchy hard-rock troupe from Boston called Aerosmith, who by mid-decade had established themselves as America's foremost answer to the Stones. Southern rock, with Lynyrd Skynyrd and Texas boogie-blues kings ZZ Top in the vanguard, continued its rise, while Black Sabbath spawned a successful solo career for frontman Ozzy Osbourne. And the aforementioned Bad Company—a "supergroup" composed of former members of Free, Mott the Hoople, and King Crimson—racked up hit after hit on FM rock radio but still left plenty of room for the varied likes of Blue Öyster Cult, Queen, Styx, Ted Nugent, and especially KISS to build sizable audiences of their own. And all of this, mind, *before* the unprecedented commercial success of 1976's *Frampton Comes Alive!*, the self-titled, multiplatinum debuts of Boston and Foreigner, the evolution of seasoned journeymen outfits REO Speedwagon and Journey from B-listers into seemingly unstoppable hit factories, and the "eruption" of party metal heroes Van Halen, forerunners of the coming reign of "hair metal" in the '80s.

For the cynically inclined, many of the above acts fit neatly under the umbrella of "corporate rock": mass-produced, interchangeable, soulless, overly calculated, safe, and ultimately disposable music that was more product than art. But that was just the critics (and the punks) talking. For the average, denim-clad, concert-ticket-buying teenager in the '70s, it was all just rock 'n' roll, as relevant a soundtrack to their own day-to-day lives during the Ford and Carter administrations as "My Generation" and "(I Can't Get No) Satisfaction" had been to kids in the '60s. And far from being disposable, much of the rock music that emerged in the '70s proved as durable as anything produced in rock's first two decades; for evidence, one need look no farther than the nearest "classic rock" station on the FM (or satellite) radio dial today.

True, by 1974, the counterculture as it had existed in the '60s had long since f-f-f-faded away: There was no more Vietnam War to rally in protest against, and the utopian dream of peace and love that ostensibly united the unwashed masses at Woodstock had been left for dead on the bloody field of Altamont. But more than ever before, rock still offered fans the same thing it always had, beneath all of that other stuff: in a word—fittingly adopted by Journey as the title to their 1981 breakthrough album—"escape." The scale was larger not only because the venues had grown larger but because, arguably for the first time in the genre's life span, rock was not just offering escape to *kids* but to the entire baby-boom generation who grew up with rock in the late '50s and through the '60s. "The reason that rock is still around," offered Townshend in a 1974 *Creem* interview, "is that it's not youth's music—it's the music of the frustrated and the dissatisfied looking for some sort of musical panacea."[8] Or, as he put it four years later to *Trouser Press*, "[Rock] . . . clicks your social conscience—makes you think about the world, makes you think about life—and then makes you dance to forget about it."[9]

In the '70s, rock and roll in all its varied forms allowed listeners to temporarily forget about unpleasant realities like a worrisome economy and the decade's infamous gas crisis. It offered refuge from the cloying Debby Boone and Carpenters singles logjamming AM radio and the even more sinister onslaught of disco. It offered escape from the drudgery of school, work, or general teenage angst via the thrill of scoring concert tickets to the latest Aerosmith or KISS tour or, as teen-aged rock scribe-turned-filmmaker Cameron Crowe wrote in the liner notes to Zeppelin's 1993 box set *The Complete Studio Recordings*, "a good set of headphones and a decent copy of *Led Zeppelin II*."[10] And for rock fans pushing closer to or just beyond thirty, a nostalgic escape back to their not-so-distant youth by hearing the latest Who or Stones single on the radio for the first time—or fellow thirty-something Bob Seger's reassurance that, however far removed one felt from their wild youth, "rock and roll never forgets."

Fittingly, it was Townshend, tortured by his own self-perceived disconnect with his audience but still enough of a true believer at heart to know that rock itself would somehow survive for generations to come, who summed up the state of rock in the '70s the best. His original, working title for *Quadrophenia*: "Rock Is Dead—Long Live Rock."

MEET THE NEW BOSS, SAME AS THE OLD BOSS: THE ONWARD MARCH OF THE DINOSAURS

For all the new faces on the hard rock/mainstream rock scene of the '70s, the surviving titans of the preceding decade still cast an indomitable shadow. The aforementioned Who and Rolling Stones proved the most dominating, but they were not the only two bands from the '60s with gas still in the tank. The Kinks, relegated to smaller theaters for most of the decade as group leader Ray Davies focused on increasingly eccentric concept albums, closed out the '70s as born-again arena rock gods following a belated return to more straight-ahead, guitar-driven rock anthems. On the front end of the decade, a rough and tumble group of '60s vets called the Faces—Rod Stewart and Ron Wood from the Jeff Beck Group and Ronnie Lane, Kenney Jones, and Ian McLagan from the Small Faces—gave the Stones a serious run for their money as the period's most rock 'n' roll rock and roll band. In fact, when Stones guitarist Mick Taylor left the band following 1974's *It's Only Rock 'N Roll*, Faces guitarist Wood joined the Stones on tour in '75 and became an official member the following year (by which point the Faces had broken up). Three years later, Faces drummer Jones joined the Who, replacing the late Keith Moon. Stewart, meanwhile, had long since graduated to solo stardom (see Chapter 4, "The Softer Side of Rock").

The '70s also brought considerable success—both commercial and critical—to Buffalo Springfield/Crosby, Stills, Nash & Young alum Neil Young. Though his solo career is covered primarily in Chapter 5 ("Singer-Songwriters: Rock Grows Up"), Young's live and studio work (like 1975's *Tonight's the Night* and *Zuma*) with his band Crazy Horse in the '70s, featuring his epic, feedback-drenched guitar solos, yielded some of the decade's most passionate and trenchant hard rock. His impact and influence on the grunge movement of the early '90s (most notably Pearl Jam) cannot be overstated. And while Eric Clapton—the most celebrated rock guitarist to come out of the '60s, next to the late Jimi Hendrix—charted far mellower waters in the '70s than he did with Cream the previous decade, his hugely successful stadium tours and the occasional new anthem like "Cocaine" (off of 1977's platinum-selling *Slowhand*) proved he had lost none of his legendary firepower on his signature Fender Stratocaster.

The Rolling Stones

But even as the rock royalty of the '60s continued to pack concert venues and maintain a sizable share of the FM radio airwaves deep into the '70s, the barbarians were at the gate. Besieged by punk on one flank and disco on the other—with no shortage of younger, hungrier hard rockers like Aerosmith attacking straight up the middle—a band like the Rolling Stones rested on its laurels and took its own relevancy for granted at great risk. Lester Bangs was not the only critic ready to declare the emperors naked, stripped of their former fire as much by their own apparent complacency and success as by the competition. In a review of the 1974 concert film *Ladies and Gentlemen: The Rolling Stones*

The Rolling Stones (left to right) Keith Richards, Ron Wood, Mick Jagger, and Charlie Watts, 1980. Courtesy of Photofest.

(filmed during the band's *Exile on Main St.* tour two years earlier), *Phonograph Record*'s Ron Ross deemed the Stones "too rich to rock." "The Stones' 1972 show formularized and made mundane everything that had ever been special about them," noted Ross, "so that they came off like just another rock and roll band, instead of *the* rock and roll band."[11]

On a somewhat more charitable note, in the same review Ross admitted that Mick Jagger did not "look *that* old." But the fact that age was addressed at all at that point in the band's career speaks volumes. In 1972, Jagger (born July 26, 1943) was twenty-nine—a mere pup compared to the sixty-three-year-old Jagger still actively touring with the Stones into the twenty-first century. But even though rock music as a genre had already proven itself not to be the passing fad its early detractors hoped for, the concept of maturing but still artistically and commercially viable rock *stars* was still relatively foreign in the '70s. When the Stones released *Exile* in '72, the band had been together for ten years—two years longer than the Beatles' entire career. In 1968, the year Elvis Presley performed his much-lauded "comeback" special, he was all of thirty-three years old. And by the time he died at a mere forty-two on August 16, 1977, it had been years since "The King of Rock 'n' Roll" had genuinely *rocked*. So if the Stones, the Who, and the rest of their surviving contemporaries were not *literally* over the hill a decade into their careers, in the context of the time they were certainly viewed by many to be dangerously close. Critics and fans alike generally greeted each new Stones album in the '70s looking not for new revelations but rather telltale signs of wear, tear, and ennui.

And yet in spite of—or perhaps spurred by—the accumulative weight of such diminishing expectations stacked against them, many of these grizzled, thirty-something "geezers" produced some of their most enduring (and commercially successful) music in the '70s. Every studio album the Stones released between 1971 and 1981—*Sticky Fingers, Exile on Main St., Goats Head Soup, It's Only Rock 'N Roll, Black and Blue, Some Girls, Emotional Rescue,* and *Tattoo You*—topped the U.S. album chart and yielded at least one Top 10 or 20 single. The band's 1978 chart-topping single "Miss You" and the title track to 1980's *Emotional Rescue* tackled the disco movement head-on by proving the Stones could stir up a dance floor as easily as a stadium full of rock fans, while both '78's *Some Girls* and especially *Exile on Main St.* are generally regarded today as high-water marks of the band's career (with *Exile* ranking No. 7—higher than any other Stones album—in *Rolling Stone* magazine's list of the "500 Greatest Albums of All Time," as determined by a poll of 273 musicians, critics, and music industry executives).[12] Time, to loosely quote one of the band's early '60s hits, seemed to definitely be on their side after all. "When *Exile on Main Street* [*sic*] was unleashed, many people questioned the album's merit," Barbara Charone wrote in *Sounds* in 1976. "Now, four years later, it is considered a classic."[13] By decade's end, the Rolling Stones were no longer just rock survivors: they were an institution. Or, as Keith Richards quipped to Charone in another 1976 feature (this one for *Creem*): "When bands have been around this long, they should be dead and buried. But we're still here and you have to live with us."[14]

The Who from the 1979 film *The Kids Are Alright* (left to right) Roger Daltrey, John Entwistle, Keith Moon, and Pete Townshend. Courtesy of Photofest.

The Who

Meanwhile, over in Whoville, Pete Townshend's frustrations over his failed *Lifehouse* project and the growing generation gap between the band and their fans only seemed to make the Who stronger. *Live at Leeds*, released in 1970, has long been hailed by many as one of rock's greatest live albums (if not *the* greatest), while the following year's *Who's next*—which spawned the evergreen "classic rock" radio staples "Behind Blue Eyes," "Baba O'Riley," and "Won't Get Fooled Again"—and 1973's ambitious No. 2 album *Quadrophenia* made it clear that there was life yet left in the band after *Tommy*. 1975's *The Who by Numbers*, featuring Townshend's most personal batch of songs to date, was marked by a decidedly quieter tone than the band's previous albums, but the subsequent tour—the band's last with original drummer Keith Moon—was anything but mellow. A critical and commercial triumph, the Who's 1975–1976 tour was considered by many fans to be the Who's greatest run of shows ever. It was certainly among the band's biggest, flashiest, and *loudest*: It was in 1976 that the Who made rock history as the first band to incorporate lasers into their live show, and the band's May 31, 1976, gig in Charlton, South London, landed in the *Guinness Book of World Records* as the loudest concert ever played—a jet-engine-rivaling 120 decibels.

Twelve years into their career, the Who were bigger than ever, and their profile shot even higher with the late 1978 release of the No. 2 *Who Are You* album and the 1979 premiere of the feature-length *Quadrophenia* movie (the second film based on the band's music, following 1975's Ken Russell–directed *Tommy*). But the end of the '70s also came with tragedy for the Who. On September 7—four weeks after *Who Are You* hit stores—Moon died of an accidental drug overdose. The rest of the band pressed on with new drummer Kenney Jones and a fifth member, keyboardist John "Rabbit" Bundrick, but further tragedy struck the band when eleven fans were crushed to death at a December 3, 1979, gig at the Riverfront Coliseum in Cincinnati, Ohio. The incident happened before the Who even took the stage, as the crowd rushed inside the venue for prime "general admission" spots, and it was not until after the performance that the band members were informed of the deaths. Once again, the Who soldiered on, but not for long. After two more studio albums, 1981's *Face Dances* and '82's *It's Hard* (both of which made the American Top 10), the group disbanded at the end of 1982. (There would be numerous reunions throughout the '90s and into the first decade of the new century—even after bassist John Entwistle's death at the age of fifty-seven on June 27, 2002.)

The Kinks

While the dominance of the Stones and the Who on the rock scene throughout the '70s represented an enduring status quo, the mainstream embrace of perennial underdogs the Kinks late in the decade was a genuine surprise even to the band's biggest fans. After a string of seminal rock/pop hits in the mid-'60s, beginning with the hard-rock cornerstone "You Really Got Me," the Kinks slipped quietly into cult-band status while many of their contemporaries (and followers) zipped by on the way to massive success. Part of this was due to the band's three-year (1966–1969) ban from American performance by the American Federation of Musicians (the result of an ill-fated appearance on the U.S. TV show *Hullabaloo*), though it undoubtedly also had much to do with songwriter Ray Davies's willful resistance to trends like psychedelic rock and the whole conceit of a youth-led cultural revolution.

Davies's pop songs by and large tended to take a wistful-if-bittersweet look back to simpler times. But with "Lola," a No. 9 hit single from 1970's *Lola versus Powerman and the Moneygoround, Part One* (the band's first Top 40 album since 1966's *The Kinks Greatest Hits*), the band slowly began to regain ground on American shores. Subsequent 1971–1975 Kinks albums—*Muswell Hillbillies* and the "theatrical" concept albums *Preservation* (*Act 1* and *2*), *Soap Opera*, and *Schoolboys in Disgrace*—failed to muster up hits on either side of the Atlantic, but a late '70s return to a more straight-ahead rock sound reminiscent of their early '60s roots, with Ray's brother Dave Davies reasserting his presence on lead guitar, brought a dramatic change in fortune for the band. 1977's No. 21 *Sleepwalker* and '78's No. 40 *Misfits* set the stage, with 1979's No. 11 *Low Budget* and a pair of timely Kinks covers by hot up-and-comers the Pretenders ("Stop Your Sobbing") and Van Halen ("You Really Got Me") officially cinching the band's ascension to arena-worthy headliner status.

Though some disgruntled fans and critics at the time cried "sell-out," the Kinks' output during this period arguably holds up with some of their very best: the muscular, aggressive attack was as much punk in its attitude and immediacy as it was stadium-pleasing hard rock, while Davies' lyrics remained as wryly sardonic as ever (best evidenced on 1981's "Give the People What They Want" and '83's "Young Conservatives"). *Low Budget*, with its songs about the gas crisis ("Gallon of Gas") and the flailing U.S. economy (the title track and "Catch Me Now I'm Falling"), was certainly the band's most topical record, perhaps the most topical in all of rock music in the late '70s. As veteran rock writer Fred Schruers observed in the liner notes to the album's 1999 CD reissue, "*Low Budget* was a clarion statement that the Kinks could meet whatever challenge punk and disco might lay down, and successfully enough to have their largest-selling record ever."[15]

After *Low Budget*, the Kinks had three more successive Top 20 albums—1980's live *One for the Road*, 1981's *Give the People What They Want*, and 1983's *State of Confusion*. Although the band only charted one Top 10 single during this period (1983's No. 6 "Come Dancing"), songs like the elegiac "Rock 'N' Roll Fantasy," the disco-infused "(Wish I Could Fly Like) Superman," and the hard rocker "Destroyer" all fared strongly on the FM dial. By the mid-'80s, the Kinks were already slipping quietly back into "kultdom," but their come-from-behind 1977–1983 winning streak still ranks—alongside the washed-up Aerosmith's dramatic second coming in the '90s—as one of the most impressive comebacks in rock history: irrefutable proof that even "old" rock dogs could still pull off a surprise new trick or two.

DAZED AND CONFUSED WITH THE GODS OF THUNDER: THE REIGN OF METAL

Led Zeppelin

If it never occurred to Pete Townshend that he might still be playing "My Generation" past middle age, it likewise probably never occurred to Who drummer Keith Moon that the little band he (allegedly) predicted would "go down like a lead zeppelin" would actually impact the rock world like an atomic bomb. While the Who and the Stones thrived throughout the '70s, *the* band of the decade was undoubtedly the mighty Zeppelin. By the end of the decade, Led Zeppelin's catalogue (eight studio albums and the soundtrack to the live concert film *The Song Remains the Same*) had collectively amassed 718 weeks on the *Billboard* Top LPs chart, with all but three of the records going to No. 1. More signifi-

Jimmy Page and Robert Plant from Led Zeppelin performing in 1973. Courtesy of Photofest.

cantly, and a testament to the band's lasting influence, the catalogue still sells, massively: To date, more than 100 million Led Zeppelin albums have been sold in the U.S. alone.

There were, of course, plenty of challengers to Zeppelin's throne. Had either Black Sabbath or Alice Cooper (see Volume 3, Chapter 2, "Hard-Rock Lightning, Heavy-Metal Thunder") been able to maintain their early '70s momentum through the rest of the decade, the mighty Zeppelin might not have flown quite as high for so long. But in the wake of Sabbath and Cooper's slow slip from relevance by mid-decade, it was three relative newcomers who came closest. By combination of sheer flash and in-your-face heavy exposure, KISS, at times, certainly *seemed* bigger than Zeppelin—and surely legions of KISS Army diehards would argue that the painted foursome trampled Jimmy Page and Co. under platform-heeled foot. Likewise, both America's Aerosmith and England's Queen would outlive Zeppelin and find fame of such magnitude later down the line that, in retrospect, it is hard to imagine them ever playing second or third string behind *anyone*.

But Led Zeppelin were not just "anyone"; between the 1971 release of Zeppelin's untitled, breakthrough fourth album and their 1979 swan song, *In Through the Out Door*, guitarist Jimmy Page, vocalist Robert Plant, bassist/keyboardist John Paul Jones, and drummer John Bonham reigned over the heavy-metal universe like veritable gods. It was *their* world, and everyone else just lived in it. "Zeppelin make more noise, has more guitar gimmickry, more sexuality, more flash, and generates more violence than any of their competitors, so that they are more than mere musicians, simple superstars," wrote Jaan Uhelzki in *Creem* upon the 1975 release of the band's No. 1 *Physical Graffiti*. "They have become the longest-lasting model for those culturally bankrupt 'trendies' to follow. Underage masses walk, talk, dress, and dope like Zep. They have become a necessary trapping for the terminally hip, as well as providing the audial backdrop for any social gathering."[16]

That "audial backdrop" was the Rosetta stone of hard rock throughout the '70s, and, arguably, remains so to the present day. Though without question the decade's archetypal "heavy-metal" band by merit of its thunderous rhythm section, Page's arena-sized riffs and epic solos, and Plant's banshee scream (not to mention a certain air of dark mystery stemming from Page's avowed interest in notorious occultist Aleister Crowley), Led Zeppelin's music also drew heavily from the American blues and acoustic English folk traditions. And though the lyrics often traded in themes of myth and fantasy (with no shortage of sex, to boot), Zeppelin's metal was unabashedly—often, noted critics, *portentously*—serious in both tone and musical proficiency: a marked contrast to the cartoon party anthem approach of KISS and the decadent, bloozy swagger of Aerosmith (or for that matter, the Rolling Stones).

Like many of the "monsters of rock" that emerged in the early '70s, Zeppelin's fame was earned first and foremost through relentless touring—a marked contrast to the hit-singles-propelled careers of most major rock bands in the '60s. But unlike the aforementioned KISS and Aerosmith, both of whom worked the road for several years before seeing a payoff in album sales, Zeppelin's success was not long in coming. It took the band's debut album, 1969's *Led Zeppelin*, only two months to climb into the Top 10; later that same year, *Led Zeppelin II* would reach No. 1 in the same amount of time. By 1973's tour in support of their fifth album, *Houses of the Holy*, the band was breaking concert box-office records previously set by the Beatles.

Led Zeppelin's popularity and fortunes would continue to escalate through the end of the decade. But a series of tragic events would interrupt each of the band's remaining tours. After a year off from the road in '74 (which found the Zeppelin empire still growing, via the formation of their own label, Swan Song, and the out-of-the-gate success of one its first signings, Bad Company), the band kicked off 1975 with the release of its sprawling double album, *Physical Graffiti*. But the ensuing tour—which grossed more than $5 million in its first two and a half months in America alone—was cut short after singer Robert Plant and his wife were seriously injured in a car crash in Greece.[17] It would be two years before the band hit the road again, in support of 1976's No. 1 *Presence*, but that tour would also be cut short: this time, following the death of Plant's six-year-old son from a viral infection. The concert movie *The Song Remains the Same* (filmed during the '73 tour) was released to help fill the void, but by 1979, Led Zeppelin was primed for a comeback. Over two weekends that August (the month the band's eighth and final studio album, *In Through the Out Door*, was released), Zeppelin performed for more than a quarter-million fans at the 1979 Knebworth Festival in the United Kingdom (it was their first appearance in their homeland in four years). The summer of 1980 found Zeppelin on a successful fourteen-date tour of Europe, with a U.S. leg scheduled for the fall. But on September 25, 1980, drummer Bonham died in his sleep of asphyxiation (choking on his own vomit after a night of heavy drinking).

Unlike the Who, Zeppelin would not fly on with a new member: Page, Plant, and Jones announced the official breakup of the band on December 4, 1980. Though Page and Plant would record and tour together in the '90s (as Page and Plant), all three surviving members would perform in public (not counting Jones's wedding) under the Led Zeppelin name only three more times: at Live Aid in 1985, at Atlantic Records' 40th Anniversary Party in 1988, and during the all-star jam at Zeppelin's 1995 induction into the Rock and Roll Hall of Fame.

KISS

If Led Zeppelin, architects of "Stairway to Heaven" and the equally epic "Kashmir," represented '70s heavy metal at its most self-consciously majestic and "sophisticated" (just shy, at times, of "prog-rock"), a quartet of opportunistic New York rockers calling themselves KISS made out like gangbusters by stripping the music down to its basest animal instincts and dressing it up in kabuki makeup, studded leather, chain mail S&M gear, and seven-inch-high platform boots. At their commercial peak in the second half of the decade— perhaps not coincidentally, around the same time that Zeppelin was off the road—KISS carried themselves off rather convincingly as the biggest rock band in the world. Or at the very least, the most overexposed: Thirty years later, the band's signature double-lightning-bolt logo and painted faces still evoke the '70s as vividly as the decade's iconic "Have a Nice Day" yellow smiley face.

Visually, KISS took its cues from both Alice Cooper and the New York Dolls, but the band's music lacked the creative flair and wit of the former and the raw, punkish energy of the latter. Critically, KISS took a beating that made Zeppelin's icy early reception by the music press seem positively fawning by comparison. But the quartet of singer/guitarist Paul Stanley (whose face paint designated him "The Starchild"), bassist/singer Gene Simmons ("The Demon"), guitarist Ace Frehley ("The Spaceman"), and drummer Peter Criss ("The Catman")—armed to the fake-blood-stained teeth with bombastic, no-brainer party anthems like "Strutter," "Cold Gin," "Detroit Rock City," "Love Gun," and of course, "Rock and Roll All Nite"—had no problem connecting with hormone-charged teens (and eventually, teenyboppers and preteens, too). The band's "keep it simple, stupid" songcraft (to quote Stanley himself) translated

KISS in concert (left to right) Gene Simmons, Peter Criss, Paul Stanley, and Ace Frehley, c. 1970s. Courtesy of Photofest.

especially well to live performance, where they were accompanied by all manner of theatrical bells and whistles ranging from Simmons's famous, serpentine tongue-waggling and fire breathing and Criss's levitating drum kit to elaborate stage backdrops and a generous supply of pyrotechnics.[18]

Though far too flashy and image conscious to ever strictly be lumped in with the burgeoning "corporate rock" brigade (that term, at least in the beginning, was generally reserved for rock "stars" who were ostensibly so interchangeable and nondescript that they could walk down the street unrecognized, even with major hits on the radio), KISS for all intents and purposes was—and remains—*the* most corporate-minded rock band in history. By decade's end, KISS was as much a brand name as a band, with officially sanctioned merchandise running the gamut from comic books and action figures to trashcans and lunchboxes. Years later (2001), the band even introduced its own full-sized, autographed "KISS Kasket."

Of course, KISS sold records and concert tickets, too—though initially far more of the latter than the former. Signed to the fledgling Casablanca records in late 1973 (two weeks after TV producer Bill Aucoin discovered the band and offered up his services as manager), KISS's self-titled debut album was released in February 1974 to little fanfare. Two more studio albums (*Hotter Than Hell* and *Dressed to Kill*) followed in quick succession with similar lackluster sales, though the band's outlandish stage show was earning them a reputation as a formidable opening act and a headliner in their own right. Fittingly, it was the band's first live album—1975's *Alive!*—that catapulted KISS to superstardom. The double album—which climbed to No. 9 on the charts and spawned a No. 12 hit with its live version of "Rock and Roll All Nite"—went gold in two weeks and platinum by early '76, ultimately selling 4 million copies in the United States alone. The band's biggest hit, an atypical ballad sung by drummer Criss called "Beth," peaked at No. 7 and propelled KISS's fourth studio album, 1976's *Destroyer*, to No. 11. *Rock and Roll Over*—released eight months later—also reached No. 11, while 1977's *Love Gun* and a second live album (*Alive II*) went to No. 4 and No. 7, respectively. KISS were nothing if not prolific, and they were rewarded with the distinction of being the first band in rock history to simultaneously have four albums (*Alive!* through *Love Gun*) on the charts.

Inevitably, the band's seemingly endless outpouring of product—from toys to bubblegum cards to *four* individual solo albums (all released on the same day in 1978)—eventually oversaturated the market. Although KISS would continue to record and tour steadily through the next two decades, 1979's disco-flavored *Dynasty* would be the band's last Top 10 album for thirteen years. By 1983's No. 24 *Lick It Up*—which ushered in a minor comeback thanks to a much-publicized "no-more-makeup" makeover—KISS were reduced to two original members (Stanley and Simmons). But any doubts as to the band's lasting impact on an entire generation of teens growing up in the '70s were laid to rest when the original lineup reapplied their makeup for a hugely successful reunion tour in 1996.

Between the polar extremes of Led Zeppelin and KISS, the mid- to late '70s hard rock and heavy-metal scene was a deafening battle ground of grizzled veterans and rock legends in waiting, showcasing a diverse range of styles from meat-and-potatoes blues rock to screaming guitar head-banger fare to, courtesy of England's Queen, full-on rock (mock?) opera. Following is a rundown of some of the other key players who rocked the arena circuit of the day, ranked in order of contemporary (1974–1980) impact if not lasting influence.

Aerosmith

While KISS, thanks in no small part to its merchandising *blitzkrieg*, may have been the most ubiquitous American rock band of the '70s, Boston's Aerosmith were arguably its most decadent. Although their eponymous debut albums were released within a year of each other (*Aerosmith* in 1973, *KISS* in '74), by the time both bands were running at full speed in '76, Aerosmith's knack for punching out fast and greasy, riff-driven rockers with equal measures of punkish élan and Stones-inspired grit and swagger made them the band of choice for America's "cooler" older brothers (and sisters). By comparison, KISS, lunchboxes and comic books in tow, was for kids.

Formed in 1970, Aerosmith (the original lineup of frontman Steven Tyler, guitarists Joe Perry and Brad Whitford, bassist Tom Hamilton, and drummer Joey Kramer has been intact for thirty-five years, bar a brief, early '80s departure of Perry and Whitford) watched their first two albums sell only modestly before finally hitting pay dirt with 1975's No. 11 *Toys in the Attic*, which spawned both their first Top 40 hit (the No. 36 "Sweet Emotion") and the concert favorite "Walk This Way." A rerelease of the "Stairway to Heaven"–esque power ballad "Dream On," from the 1973 debut, climbed all the way to No. 6 in 1976. That same year, Aerosmith's fourth long-player, *Rocks*, hit No. 3 on the album charts (a feat KISS would not match until their 1998 reunion album, *Psycho Circus*). Aerosmith was soon selling out not just arenas but stadiums as a festival headliner.

But the band's crash came fast and hard. While 1977's *Draw the Line* and 1978's *Live! Bootleg* both cracked the Top 20, substance abuse and internal friction derailed the band by the end of the decade. Perry left the band during the making of 1979's *Night in the Ruts* (No. 14), recording three albums with his new band, the Joe Perry Project, while the rest of Aerosmith (with new guitarist Jim Crespo) stumbled on through 1982's *Rock in a Hard Place* while public interest in the band plummeted. Salvation came in 1986 in the unlikely form of the rap group Run-D.M.C., which invited a reunited Aerosmith to guest on a cover of "Walk This Way." Fueled by a popular MTV video featuring both groups, the remake went to No. 4 and paved the way for Aerosmith's unprecedented commercial (and critical) comeback. From 1987's *Permanent Vacation* through 2004's *Honkin' on Bobo*, Aerosmith racked up nine Top 20 albums, including three chart toppers. To date, the band's worldwide album sales exceed 100 million.

Queen

To call Queen one of the most bizarre rock bands in history—not to mention one of the biggest—is a royal understatement. Formed in England in 1971, the band was three parts Led Zeppelin (guitarist Brian May, drummer Roger Taylor, and bassist John Deacon) and one heaping part Liza Minnelli (frontman extraordinaire Freddie Mercury). Together, they created a singular sound that owed as much to opera (via Broadway) and occasionally even vaudeville as it did to heavy metal. Most surprising of all, this seemingly incongruous cocktail not only paved the way to massive success for the band in the '70s but ultimately secured their standing as Great Britain's No. 2 most popular band of all time—right behind the Beatles.

Queen's first big U.S. hit, the No. 12 "Killer Queen" (from the band's third album, 1974's *Sheer Heart Attack*), introduced many a mainstream rock fan to Queen's characteristic knack for camp, bombast, and studio savvy, with May's guitars and Mercury's vocals multitracked seemingly ad infinitum. But it was the following year's mini-epic "Bohemian Rhapsody," from the No. 4 *A Night at the Opera*, that really heralded Queen's arrival. The song reached No. 2 in America and spent a record-breaking nine weeks at No. 1 in England. Successive hit singles demonstrated a stylistic mélange ranging from chest-thumping bravado (1977's eternal sports arena double-hitter "We Will Rock You" and "We Are the Champions," from the No. 3 *News of the World*) to pseudo-rockabilly and disco-ready funk-rock ("Crazy Little Thing Called Love" and "Another One Bites the Dust," respectively— both No. 1 singles from 1980's chart-topping *The Game*). Live, Queen reveled in larger-than-life productions that lived up to the pomp and circumstance suggested by their name, while Mercury's "half-martial, half-coy preening" played up the moniker's homosexual connotations as well.[19]

Mercury, who announced his affliction with AIDS only two days before his death from the disease on Novem-

Freddie Mercury performing during a Queen concert in 1980. Courtesy of Photofest.

ber 24, 1991, was for years rock's most ambiguously gay superstar—never quite coming "out of the closet" but always seemingly leaving the door wide open. Somewhat curiously, given the prevailing macho/heterosexual attitudinal status quo of the heavy-metal scene, the mainstream rock audiences of the '70s did not seem put off in the least by this. Critics, however, were another matter entirely. While some of Queen's many detractors in the rock press were content to merely dismiss the band as "ersatz" Zeppelin clones, snide and arguably borderline-homophobic digs at Mercury's "flamboyant posturings" were not uncommon.[20] The band's propensity to grow even more bombastic as their fame and fortune increased through the decade did not exactly win them many press converts, either. In an oft-quoted, scathing review of Queen's 1978 album *Jazz*, *Rolling Stone*'s Dave Marsh called them "arrogant brats," "creeps," and most memorably, "the first truly fascist rock band." But not *all* critics were so quick to overlook the band's ambition, talent, and perhaps most unique of all in the rock scene of the day, sense of humor. "The great thing about Queen," noted England's *Melody Maker*, "is that they make one's critical barbs thoroughly redundant, so hell-bent are they on self-parody."[21] Or as Bud Scoppa effectively summed it up in a review of *Sheer Heart Attack* for *Rolling Stone*: "If it's hard to love, it's hard not to admire: This band is skilled, after all, and it dares."[22]

Bad Company (left to right) Mick Ralphs, Simon Kirke, Paul Rodgers, and Boz Burrell, c. 1978. Courtesy of Photofest.

Bad Company

In the wake of 1973's *Houses of the Holy*, everything Led Zeppelin touched seemed to turn to gold. That included Bad Company, the first band signed to Zeppelin's own Atlantic Records imprint, Swan Song. Though the band would only score two Top 10 singles in the '70s, Bad Company's first five albums all made strong showings in the Top 20, with their self-titled, 1974 debut peaking at No. 1. While the Zeppelin touch (in particular, the hand of Zeppelin/Bad Co. manager Peter Grant) certainly helped open doors for the band, the four members of Bad Company more than pulled their own weight, drawing on years of previous experience on rock's frontlines.

Powerhouse vocalist Paul Rodgers and drummer Simon Kirke were both veterans of the recently disbanded British blues rock band Free, whose crunchy 1970 No. 4 hit "All Right Now" set the template not only for Bad Company but also countless other album-oriented rock (AOR) acts to come (Foreigner's 1978 hit "Hot Blooded" being one obvious descendant). Bassist Boz Burrell served time in the prog-rock court of King Crimson, and guitarist Mick Ralphs was hot out of Mott the Hoople (of "All the Young Dudes" fame). "Can't Get Enough," a Ralphs song originally written for (but unused by) Mott the Hoople gave Bad Company their first and biggest (No. 5) hit in 1974, followed in quick succession by future classic rock radio staples like "Bad Company," "Ready for Love" (both from the debut), "Feel Like Making Love," "Shooting Star" (from 1975's No. 3 *Straight Shooter*), and "Rock 'N' Roll Fantasy" (from 1979's No. 3

Desolation Angels). Following 1982's No. 26 *Rough Diamonds*, Rodgers left the band for a solo career and to record two albums with former Zeppelin guitarist Jimmy Page as the Firm, while the remaining members, joined by new singer Brian Howe, carried on the Bad Company name with modest mainstream rock success through the mid-'90s. The original lineup re-formed for a one-off reunion tour in 1999.

Blue Öyster Cult

Formed in Long Island, New York, in 1969, Blue Öyster Cult (BÖC) were a living, breathing oxymoron: a commercially successful heavy-metal band that were actually *embraced*, rather than pilloried, by critics. It might have helped that BÖC was initially conceived by two rock critics (longtime Cult producer/visionary Sandy Pearlman and Richard Meltzer, whose role in the band by the time of their self-titled 1972 debut was strictly behind the scenes, contributing on songwriting), and that critics' darling/punk poetess Patti Smith, who dated the band's keyboard player Allen Lanier in the mid-'70s, occasionally pitched in, too (co-writing, with drummer Albert Bouchard, the band's defacto theme song, 1974's "Career of Evil"). But the potent songwriting and musical proficiency of the band itself—rounded out by guitarists/singers Donald "Buck Dharma" Roeser and Eric Bloom and bassist Joe Bouchard—contributed mightily to BÖC's critical/popular appeal as well.

Beneath a veneer of pseudo-Satanic biker-gang menace, the band's first three albums—1972's *Blue Öyster Cult*, '73's *Tyranny and Mutation*, and '74's *Secret Treaties*—seethed with a cunning intelligence. Moreover, BÖC fast earned a reputation for a pummeling live show, with lasers and flash pots used not as a distracting scrim to hide behind so much as exclamation points to the group's trademark "stun" guitar attack—which on occasion found all five members playing guitars at once. The 1975 double live album *On Your Feet or On Your Knees* proved to be the highest-charting (No. 22) album of their career, but BÖC's legacy would be unveiled on the following year's No. 29 *Agents of Fortune*: the No. 12 classic single "(Don't Fear) the Reaper." There would be more (minor) FM rock hits to come—most notably "Godzilla," from 1977's *Spectres*, and the No. 40 "Burnin' for You," from 1981's *Fire of Unknown Origin*, the band's last gold album. *Fire* also featured another Patti Smith co-write (the title track) and "Veteran of the Psychic Wars," which was co-written by Bloom and science-fiction/fantasy writer Michael Moorcock and prominently featured in the animated cult film *Heavy Metal*.

Ozzy Osbourne

Although Black Sabbath—Led Zeppelin's closest contemporary on the early metal scene (both British bands formed within a year of each other in the late '60s)—maintained a firm grip on the metal scene as a touring act through most of the '70s, by 1975 its run of million-selling records sputtered to a halt. Though the No. 48 1976 greatest hits collection, *We Sold Our Soul for Rock 'N' Roll*, did go platinum, 1975's *Sabotage*, '76's *Technical Ecstasy*, and '78's *Never Say Die!* all stopped short of gold. The first two years of the '80s did bring a brief commercial comeback (with 1980's *Heaven and Hell* hitting platinum and No. 28), but by then it was no longer the classic Sabbath of "Paranoid" and "War Pigs" fame. At the beginning of 1979, founding member and original frontman Ozzy Osbourne was fired from the group and replaced with former Rainbow singer Ronnie James Dio. Dio himself would not last but two years in the group, and one by one the rest of Sabbath dropped out for various reasons until, by 1986, only guitarist Tony Iommi remained from the original Birmingham foursome. His former bandmate Osbourne, meanwhile, was by then the biggest name in '80s heavy metal.

Following his dismissal from Sabbath in 1979, Osbourne wound up in Los Angeles, strung out on booze and drugs and at the end of his rope. "I thought it was all over," he has said of that period, admitting that he was terrified to try starting again on his own.[23] But pushed and prodded by his manager (and soon to be wife), Sharon, he pulled himself together enough to assemble a new band, starting with twenty-three-year-old guitar wunderkind Randy Rhoads. Osbourne's solo debut, 1980's *Blizzard of Ozz* (released in '81 in America), was an out-of-the-gate success, climbing to No. 21 in the wake of the mainstream rock hit "Crazy Train" and eventually certified quadruple platinum. The following year's *Diary of a Madman* was just as successful, with Osbourne's notoriety at an all-time high, thanks to controversial stunts like his biting the head off a live dove during a meeting with Columbia record executives and later doing the same to a live bat at a concert. On March 19, 1982, during a tour stop in Florida, Rhoads was killed in a plane crash (the guitarist, a hairdresser, and the band's bus driver were "joy riding" in Osbourne's small tour plane, which crashed into the band's bus. All three on board the plane died.) Osbourne would later honor Rhoads with the 1987 release of the No. 6 *Tribute*, a live album recorded with Rhoads in 1981.

Throughout the 1980s, Osbourne was a frequent target of parental and religious groups decrying the corruptive, evil influence of heavy metal and was even sued three times by parents who claimed his song "Suicide Solution" (from his debut) led their children to kill themselves. (Osbourne insisted that the song was about the perils of alcoholism). A decade later, after launching the huge annual, multiartist *Ozzfest* tour and reuniting with Black Sabbath for a Grammy-winning live album (1998's No. 11 *Reunion*), Osbourne, his wife Sharon, and their two teen-aged kids became household names as the stars of a wildly successful MTV reality series, *The Osbournes*, which showed rock's self-proclaimed "Prince of Darkness" and onetime parents' worst nightmare comically fumbling his way around the domestic arena.

Ted Nugent

Although he would ultimately be known primarily as rock music's most outspoken right-wing conservative and bow-hunting outdoorsman, in the late '70s Detroit-born guitarist Ted Nugent was a multiplatinum-selling recording artist and the top-grossing touring act from 1977 through 1979. After finding only modest success with his first real band, the Amboy Dukes (which scored a No. 16 hit with the 1968 psychedelic garage rocker "Journey to the Center of the Mind"), Nugent hit the big time with his self-titled 1975 solo debut. Working his "Motor City Madman" persona to the brink of absurdity even by showy '70s rock 'n' roll standards (swinging onto stages Tarzan-style, wearing nothing but his guitar and a loincloth), Nugent's wild showmanship helped make him one of the decade's most popular and consistently entertaining live acts. His records sold impressively, too: Between 1975 and 1980, he charted seven albums in the Top 20, with 1975's *Ted Nugent*, 1976's *Free-For-All*, and 1977's *Cat Scratch Fever* all going double platinum ('78's *Double Live Gonzo!* also came close). It would all dry up by the early '80s, though Nugent continued to tour and record when not stalking game or tending to deputy sheriff, radio host, and hunting magazine publishing duties, eventually landing a short comeback in the early '90s as part of the supergroup (with Styx and Night Ranger alums) Damn Yankees.

Judas Priest

The line between basic "hard rock" and "heavy metal" was often hard to discern in the '70s. But Judas Priest, ensconced in black leather and propelled by the twin guitars of Glenn Tipton and K. K. Downing and the fearsome screamage of frontman Rob Halford (often riding onstage astride a Harley Davidson), was metal to the core. Judas Priest's music was loud, *fast*, and surprisingly melodic—qualities that would make the band a formative influence on both latter-day, hardcore speed-metal bands and more mainstream-friendly "pop metal" acts like Def Leppard. Formed by Downing and bassist Ian Hill in Birmingham (Black Sabbath's hometown) in 1969, with Halford, Tipton, and the first of many drummers signing on shortly thereafter, the band toured heavily throughout the United Kingdom and Europe in the first half of the decade, which did little to spur sales of their first two independent records but did, ultimately, win them enough of a following to land a major-label deal and a ticket to the American market. Judas Priest's 1977 Columbia Records debut *Sin after Sin*, followed by '78's *Stained Class* and '79's *Hell Bent for Leather*, placed the band in the vanguard of the burgeoning "New Wave of British Heavy Metal" movement (which would also spawn '80s metal titans Iron Maiden), but it would take a live album, 1979's platinum-selling *Unleashed in the East*, to break the band in America. After that, Judas Priest saw eight consecutive albums make the U.S. Top 40, with 1982's *Screaming for Vengeance*, '84's *Defenders of the Faith*, and '86's *Turbo* selling platinum and the rest of its studio catalogue through 1990 going at least gold.

AC/DC

If heavy metal ever had its very own Ramones, surely it was AC/DC. By the time 1979's *Highway to Hell* clawed its way to No. 17 on the American album charts, the Sydney, Australia-formed AC/DC were already one of their homeland's top-selling rock bands. The trademark AC/DC sound—gleefully juvenile anthems marked by crunchy, blues-based riffs, a thunderous rhythm section, and the blood-curdling, demented demonic growl of frontman Bon Scott—had been honed to a jagged edge across their first four albums, *T.N.T.*, *High Voltage*, *Let There Be Rock*, and *Powerage*, but the introduction of producer Robert John "Mutt" Lange's soon-to-be-famous magic touch to the mix made *Highway to Hell* the band's expressway to worldwide fame. And then, on February 19, 1980, Scott died—choking on his vomit following a drinking binge, just as Zeppelin's John Bonham would seven months later. The rest of the band—Scottish-born guitarist brothers Angus and Malcolm Young, drummer Phil Rudd, and bassist Cliff Williams—carried on, recruiting new singer Brian Johnson, who remarkably possessed a throaty scream nearly twice as rough as Scott's. The Johnson-fronted lineup promptly recorded and released 1980's *Back in Black* as a tribute to Scott. Again helmed by Lange, the record went to No. 4 and has since gone on to be one of the best-selling (and hardest) hard-rock albums of all time, certified platinum twenty times over. The record also gave AC/DC—which would remain a popular touring and recording act into the new century—the first of their two career Top 40 pop hits, the No. 35 "You Shook Me All Night Long."

Van Halen

Had Van Halen's self-titled debut arrived any earlier in the decade than February 1978, the landscape of '70s rock—or at least the pecking order—very likely would have been markedly different. But with two years left to make their mark on the decade, the Pasadena, California, foursome made up for lost time with a vengeance. *Van Halen* rose to No. 19 and was certified gold within three months of its release and platinum by October. Both 1979's *Van Halen II* and 1980's *Women and Children First*—both reaching No. 6—sold just as quickly, setting a pattern in which every one of the eleven albums the band released up until 1998's *Van Halen III* sold at least 2 million copies in America alone, with the debut and 1984's *1984* both eventually selling 10 million apiece.

But it was not sales figures that set Van Halen apart from the crowd. It was Eddie Van Halen, arguably one of the most prodigiously gifted and original guitar stylists in rock since Jimi Hendrix. Eschewing traditional blues-based riffs in favor of a more virtuoso, almost classical-sounding style achieved through a self-taught technique involving "hammer-ons, pull-offs, two-handed tapping, and any combination thereof,"[24] his tone was instantly recognizable: fat and fuzzy but unfailingly melodic—and quite unlike any other guitarist in heavy metal at the time. Soon enough, however, the '80s metal scene would be full of guitar-"shredding" Van Halen imitators. Beginning in 1978, Eddie was named *Guitar Player Magazine*'s "Best Guitarist of the Year" for five straight years.

Talented as he was, though, Van Halen was not a one-man show. The guitarist's technical flash was matched song for song by frontman David Lee Roth. Roth was an effortlessly charismatic (and acrobatic) showman whose over-the-top, irreverent (and witty) personality infused Van Halen's music and image with a sense of *fun* that was as fresh and new to the era's rock scene as his bandmate's guitar sound. Roth was far from the world's greatest singer, but he was a world-class *entertainer*. The band was rounded out by Van Halen's brother Alex on drums and bassist Michael Anthony.

By the turn of the decade, with Aerosmith on the rocks and KISS and Ted Nugent both past their sell-by dates, Van Halen were seasoned stadium headliners and the biggest hard-rock band in America. Proof of their uncontested popularity was made absolute when 1984's "Jump" became the band's first No. 1 single, even though it prominently featured Eddie Van Halen playing keyboards instead of his signature guitar. Even Roth's departure from the band in 1985 could not stop the group's momentum: 1986's *5150*, which introduced new frontman Sammy Hagar (a veteran '70s arena rocker as a solo artist), was the band's first No. 1 album. Three more consecutive "Van Hagar" studio albums through the mid-'90s would also top the charts.

Rush, Cheap Trick, and Deep Purple

While each of the aforementioned "spotlight" artists distinguished themselves as heavy-metal heavyweights of their day, the list is far from complete. Honorable mention must also be made of Canadian prog-metal power trio Rush—whose 1976 concept album *2112* began a twenty-year streak of gold and platinum records—and Chicago's power-pop-chopped Cheap Trick, for years the MVP of opening acts on the American arena circuit until the triple-platinum success of their 1979 live album *At Budokan* (recorded in Japan) hit No. 4 and made the band headliners in their own right. And, of course, we can't forget British geezers Deep Purple (see Volume 3, Chapter 2, "Hard-Rock Lightning, Heavy-Metal Thunder"), which begat Ritchie Blackmore's Rainbow, Whitesnake, and perhaps most memorably—with equal credit owed to Uriah Heep—Spinal Tap.

Still missing from this subsidiary roundup, however, are a host of phenomenally successful '70s arena rockers who, justly or not, will forever be corralled not into the wider hard-rock and heavy-metal pool but rather a critically maligned (and defined, however loosely) subgenre: corporate rock.

Rush (left to right) Geddy Lee, Neil Peart, and Alex Lifeson, c. 1975. Courtesy of Photofest.

JUKEBOX HEROES: CORPORATE ROCK

"Foreigner, Boston, Journey, Styx . . ." Ask the average rock critic/snob/historian to define the term "corporate rock," and you will most likely be answered with a list of band names rather than a concrete explanation. The reason for this is that there is no clear definition of "corporate rock," as it was never a *true* genre so much as a catchall term for any and all artists deemed by critics and/or the punk crowd as essentially too successful to possibly be *good*. Corporate rock was the name given to the phantom menace of "the Man" distilling, via carefully studied market research, the safest elements of rock music that appealed most to the mass market, then churning out product that promised only maximum profit returns. This result, ostensibly, was the rock equivalent of fast food: McMusic, designed not for art's sake but to serve millions and billions of gullible consumers who did not know better.

A wide-angle view of rock and pop history does, of course, reveal a few concrete examples of the corporate rock theory in actual practice—from the Monkees in the '60s to the wildly successful teen pop "boy bands" of the late '90s. But by and large, "corporate rock" in the '70s and '80s was just a fancy term the rock cognoscenti of the day used to describe pretty much anything that appealed to an audience big enough to fill a sports arena and generate platinum or even gold sales. In the '60s, the Beatles' critical and popular approval grew in tandem with their record sales, but by the middle of the '70s, commercial success was practically considered anathema by the guardians of taste and the anarchist rebels of the punk movement. By the end of the '70s, everyone from usual suspects Foreigner and Boston to the Eagles and Fleetwood Mac to warhorses like Zeppelin, the Stones, Pink Floyd, the Who, Eric Clapton, and Rod Stewart were deemed, at one point or other, "corporate." By the mid-'80s, not even early critics darlings Bruce Springsteen and Tom Petty were safe from the tag.

The corporate rock field is narrowed considerably with the introduction of the "faceless" factor: a not completely unfounded charge that many of the "main offenders" most readily grouped under the corporate banner—the aforementioned Foreigner, Boston, Journey, and Styx—all lacked that certain "star quality" of larger-than-life charisma or even mere showbiz pizzazz that made legends out of artists like Mick Jagger and Keith Richards and KISS, who were, at the very least, mildly amusing. By contrast, the millions and millions of rock fans buying all those Foreigner and Boston records would likely have a hard time picking their "jukebox heroes" out of a lineup; years later, they might still know the words to every Foreigner and Journey song on classic rock radio by heart but not necessarily which songs were Foreigner's and which ones were Journey's—or was that Supertramp?

Still, the implication—however exaggerated—that all of the above acts were conceived in a boardroom was never much more than cultural elitism. Boston's immaculately produced and hook-filled 1976 debut (*Boston*)—which became the fastest-selling debut album of all time until Whitney Houston's debut ten years later—was recorded primarily in group mastermind Tom Scholz's basement before he even had a record deal. Peter Frampton had labored in the minor leagues for years before his 1976 double live album *Frampton Comes Alive!* made him an "overnight" superstar. Ditto San Francisco's Journey and Chicago's REO Speedwagon, both hard touring through most of the decade before finding anything resembling a mainstream hit. Foreigner *was* assembled from scratch, by journeyman, down-on-his-luck British guitarist Mick Jones; but apart from second guitarist/horn player Ian McDonald, a veteran of the original lineup of prog-rock giants King Crimson, the band Jones put together was made up mostly of relative unknowns. Their demo was shopped to and passed on by every major label, until Atlantic Records reconsidered and signed the band. Within three years of the band's formation, Foreigner would sell more than 12 million albums in America alone—making them Atlantic's best-selling rock band, ahead of both Led Zeppelin and the Rolling Stones.[25] And like Zeppelin before them, Foreigner's success came without help from the critics.

"Obviously, the critics felt they hadn't nurtured us," reflected Jones in 2000.

> In fact, they knew nothing about us, and suddenly, there we were, very successful, and they felt that they hadn't had a part to play in our success.

I think they were just annoyed at us for selling millions of records. . . . The press in the '70s were very much into "discovering" bands, and they kind of gave the OK for public acceptance.[26]

Of course, quite *unlike* Zeppelin and the rest of the early metal brigade, Foreigner and company were not shy when it came to releasing radio-ready singles. Crafted with a keen attention to studio finesse and consummate musicianship, songs like Boston's "More Than a Feeling," Foreigner's "Feels Like the First Time," and Supertramp's "Give a Little Bit" were a far cry from the patience-testing jam excuse "Dazed and Confused," not to mention the naked, raw aggression of the Sex Pistols. And with Frampton's "Baby, I Love Your Way" lighting the way, the invariably sappy "power ballad" would in time become every "corporate rock" band's golden ticket to *truly* mainstream success, bridging the gap between hard rock and Top 40 pop. Unlike the bulk of the "soft rock" artists of the '70s, the Foreigners and Journeys still loaded their albums and sold-out arena and stadium shows with plenty of rock anthems ("Juke Box Hero," "Separate Ways"), but it was the ballads ("Waiting for a Girl Like You," "Open Arms," etc.) that set the charts on fire and got concert crowds to wave their cigarette lighters in the air.

By the mid- to late '80s, this hybrid model of rockers and ballads would pay off just as handsomely for a new generation of MTV-era metal bands, from Whitesnake, Def Leppard, and Bon Jovi to even Guns N' Roses and the resurrected Aerosmith. Following are brief biographical sketches of some of the mainstream-approved "faceless" rockers who, to loosely quote Frampton, showed them the way.

Boston

Formed by MIT grad, Polaroid senior product designer, and closet studio whiz Tom Scholz, Boston, the band, came together after Scholz had already landed a record deal with his homemade (on a 12-track recorder) demo tapes. Said demos were embellished and polished only slightly in the studio, with Scholz on guitar and keyboards, singer/guitarist Brad Delp, guitarist Barry Goudreau, bassist Fran Sheehan, and drummer Sib Hashian (all local Boston musicians), with the results yielding 1976's 17 million–selling (to date) *Boston*, a No. 3 hit. Boston's sound, as exemplified by the album's three Top 40 singles—"More Than a Feeling" at No. 5, "Long Time" at No. 22, and "Peace of Mind" at No. 38—was built around soaring guitars, tight vocal harmonies, and *huge* hooks, all of which made Boston an instant arena draw. So successful was Boston's first album, in fact, that Scholz—an avowed perfectionist—bowed to label pressure to rush out a follow-up, 1978's *Don't Look Back*. The sophomore effort topped the charts and spawned the No. 4 single with the title track, but much to his label's consternation, Scholz took his leisurely time—*eight* years—before finishing 1986's *Third Stage*, which spent four weeks on top. That album swiftly sold 4 million copies and yielded Boston's first No. 1 single, "Amanda," and two more Top 20 tracks; but by the time Boston's fourth album, *Walk On*, made it to stores in 1994, Boston's commercial heyday had long since expired.

Foreigner

With Boston's multimillion-selling debut setting a previously unheard of precedent for out-of-nowhere success, the blockbuster performance of *Foreigner* a year later made it official: Selling platinum (or multiplatinum) was the new gold, and playing sold-out theaters and arenas on your maiden tour became the new slugging-it-out-for-years-on-the-club-circuit.

But for founding member Mick Jones, the overnight success was a long time coming. Prior to forming Foreigner in 1976 (recruiting fellow English-men Ian McDonald and Dennis Elliott on sax and drums, respectively, and Americans Lou Gramm [vocals], Al Greenwood [keyboards], and Ed Gagliardi [bass]), the thirty-

Foreigner, 1979. Courtesy of Photofest.

two-year-old Jones had spent years as a hired gun, playing guitar for French pop star Johnny Hallyday, English hard rockers Spooky Tooth, and Leslie West of Mountain. He was squeaking out a living on Hallyday royalties when he began writing songs like "Cold as Ice" and "Feels Like the First Time," which sparked his interest in finally trying to start his *own* band.

The key ingredient was Gramm, a powerful singer with some recording and songwriting experience of his own from an upstate New York band called Black Sheep. Gramm's muscular vocals and Jones's knack for meaty guitar riffs, keyboard flourishes, and seemingly effortless melodic hooks paid off immediately. Buoyed by the first three of many Foreigner Top 20 hits ("Feels Like the First Time," "Long, Long Way From Home," and "Cold as Ice"), *Foreigner* peaked at

No. 4 and was certified platinum within five months of its release. *Double Vision* (1978), *Head Games* (1979), and *4* (1981) followed in quick succession, all landing in the Top 5 and catapulting Foreigner to the head of the arena rock class.

With *4* (which featured Motown legend Jr. Walker blowing sax on the No. 4 single "Urgent"), Foreigner even managed to win the begrudging respect of the stubborn rock press: "Foreigner Gets Good" teased a headline on the cover of the October 15, 1981 issue of *Rolling Stone*. The band's first and only No. 1 single, 1984's gospel-rock ballad "I Want to Know What Love Is" (from the No. 4 *Agent Provocateur*), also received critical kudos. But growing creative friction between Gramm and Jones—stoked in part by the success of Gramm's 1987 solo debut, *Ready or Not* and its No. 5 hit single "Midnight Blue"—resulted in the singer's departure from Foreigner following the same year's *Inside Information*. By the time Gramm and Jones reunited in 1992, Foreigner's chart days were behind them, though the band continued to perform and tour on the festival and smaller theater scene through the rest of the decade. Between Foreigner albums, Jones established a name for himself as a producer—beginning auspiciously with Van Halen's chart-topping first album with Sammy Hagar, 1986's *5150*.

Peter Frampton

Peter Frampton started the '70s as a former (minor) British teen pop idol and was well on his way toward building a reputation as a serious guitar hero alongside former Small Faces frontman Steve Marriott in the hard-rock outfit Humble Pie. After that band hit No. 21 on the charts with 1971's live *Performance—Rockin' the Fillmore*, Frampton left for a solo career and high-profile session work on albums like George Harrison's *All Things Must Pass* and Harry Nilsson's *Son of Schmilsson*. Despite heavy touring and constant recording, by mid-decade his solo projects had netted him only one gold record, 1975's No. 32 *Frampton*. Then came 1976's blockbuster double album *Frampton Comes Alive!* which topped the charts, spawned three hit singles ("Baby, I Love Your Way," "Do You Feel Like We Do," and "Show Me the Way") and became, at the time, one of the best-selling albums in history, selling more than 6 million in the United States and 18 million worldwide. The following year's *I'm in You* made it to No. 2 on the charts, but its sales were nowhere near the level of *Alive!*; as quickly as Frampton became one of the '70s greatest success stories, he became an equally trenchant cautionary tale. Like KISS, market saturation—spurred on by Frampton's overzealous manager—proved his undoing: "Rather than practicing restraint," wrote Fred Goodman in *The Mansion on the Hill*, "Frampton was frequently performing seven nights a week, and virtually all publicity opportunities were accepted indiscriminately." A shirtless cover shot for *Rolling Stone* and a starring role in the infamously horrific *Sgt. Pepper's Lonely Hearts Club Band* movie in 1978

Peter Frampton in concert at JFK Stadium in Philadelphia, Pennsylvania, 1977. Courtesy of Photofest.

did not help.[27] Five years after *Frampton Comes Alive!* Frampton was dropped by his label, A&M.

Heart

Led by sisters Ann and Nancy Wilson (lead vocals and guitar, respectively), the co-ed band Heart was a refreshing anomaly on the male-dominated hard-rock scene of the '70s. In the mid-'80s, a string of "comeback" hits branded them queens of the MTV-driven power ballad (1986's "These Dreams" and '87's "Alone" both topped the singles chart); but the '70s found Heart charting with harder-edged fare like the 1976 No. 35 "Crazy on You" and '77's No. 11 "Barracuda." Formed in Seattle in the early 1970s, the band honed their chops on the Vancouver, Canada, club scene. Their first album, 1976's *Dreamboat Annie*, was released on a Canadian independent label and eventually went platinum (and to No. 7 on the charts) in America. Subsequent releases like 1977's *Little Queen*, '78's *Magazine*, '78's *Dog & Butterfly*, and '80's *Bebe Le Strange* and *Greatest Hits/Live* all went Top 20. Heart closed out the decade as a solidly successful touring act but slipped from prominence in the first half of the '80s—only to bounce back with the No. 1 quintuple platinum *Heart* in 1985.

Heart (left to right) Howard Leese, Nancy Wilson, Michael Derosier, Ann Wilson, and Steve Fossen, 1979. Courtesy of Photofest.

Journey

At the beginning of the '70s, Neal Schon was a sixteen-year-old, California-born guitar prodigy who reportedly turned down an offer to join Eric Clapton's Derek and the Dominos, choosing to join Carlos Santana's band Santana instead. That was where he first played with singer/keyboardist Gregg Rolie, with whom Schon would co-found Journey in 1973. The Santana factor and San Francisco–area buzz netted them a major-label deal, but the band's jam-intensive progressive rock failed to generate significant sales or radio attention. But with the introduction of singer-songwriter Steve Perry into the mix in time for the band's fourth album, 1978's No. 21 *Infinity*, Journey was cleared for take-off. Perry's voice—something of a hybrid of Rod Stewart and Sam Cooke—was one of the most distinctive in rock from the late '70s through the mid-'80s, and Journey's mix of soaring anthems (penned mostly by Schon, Perry, and keyboardist Jonathan Cain) proved remarkably effective on the charts. During the Perry-era (1978–1986), Journey produced eight multiplatinum albums, with 1981's *Escape* and '83's *Frontiers* collectively selling 15 million copies domestically and 1988's *Greatest Hits* eventually certified ten-times platinum. Perry left for a solo career after 1986's No. 4 *Raised on Radio* but returned long enough for one more album (the No. 3 *Trial by Fire*) in 1996.

The Steve Miller Band

Milwaukee-born, Dallas-raised guitarist Steve Miller was a major player on the San Francisco rock scene of the late '60s, but it was his transformation from psychedelic blues rocker to slick, up-tempo pop artist on 1973's No. 2 *The Joker* that paved his way toward becoming one of the decade's top-selling artists—the follow-up, 1976's No. 3 *Fly Like an Eagle*, stayed on the charts for nearly two years. Miller's mid-'70s hits like "The Joker," "Fly Like an Eagle," "Take the Money and Run," and "Rock'n Me"—all collected on 1978's 8 million–selling

Greatest Hits 1974–78—were the epitome of mainstream pop in the '70s: bouncy, fun, impeccably played and produced, and mercilessly catchy. The 1982 chart-topping "Abracadabra" continued in this vein, but the end of the '80s found Miller stepping out of the mainstream to return to more jazz- and blues-oriented pursuits.

REO Speedwagon/Styx

Although their styles were markedly different (basic rock 'n' roll versus pseudo-arty prog-rock), REO Speedwagon and Styx are lumped handily together by merit of their shared roots (both were formed in Illinois and spent years touring behind modest-selling albums to build up a core following in the Midwest) and eventual breakthrough as uncontested masters of the high-school prom theme ballad. Two decades after their commercial peak in the early '80s, the remnants of both bands would frequently tour together as a popular double-bill on the nostalgia circuit, even cutting a live album together (2000's *Arch Allies: Live at Riverport*). REO Speedwagon, formed in Champaign, Illinois, in 1968, were eight records into their career before scoring their first Top 40 album with 1978's million-selling *You Can Tune a Piano, But You Can't Tuna Fish*. With 1980's chart-topping *Hi Infidelity*, the band officially became one of the biggest names in mainstream rock, as the album's four Top 10 singles (including the No. 1 power ballad "Keep on Loving You") pushed its sales past the 7 million mark. The band would have several more Top 10 singles through the '80s but would never come close to repeating *Hi Infidelity*'s remarkable success.

While Styx never had a blockbuster record quite on the same level as *Hi Infidelity*, the long-running (formed in 1963), Chicago-based group fared better on an album-to-album basis: Between 1977's *The Grand Illusion* and '83's *Kilroy Was Here*, Styx charted five Top 10 albums, all of them selling at least platinum. In 1978, Styx was deemed America's most popular rock band among kids aged thirteen to eighteen in a Gallup poll, and their popularity continued to swell through 1981's 3 million–selling No. 1 album *Paradise Theater*. The band sported three distinctive songwriters and co-frontmen: guitarists James Young and Tommy Shaw and keyboard player Dennis DeYoung. Styx's sound was somewhat mockingly (but accurately) described as "pomp rock." Young and Shaw brought the rock, but it was DeYoung's arch-pomp—characterized by the smash ballads "Lady," "Come Sail Away," and "Babe"—that brought the group its greatest fame—and, inevitably, critical disdain.

Supertramp

Co-founded in 1969 by songwriters Richard Davies and Roger Hodgson, England's Supertramp was the rare "corporate rock" band that did, in fact, start its existence with something of a silver spoon in its mouth. But the band's financial backing was private, not corporate: It came from Dutch millionaire and rock fan Stanley August Misesegaes, who offered Davies the opportunity and monetary support to put together his dream band. With Hodgson on board as co-frontman, Supertramp released their self-titled debut to little fanfare in 1970. The 1973 follow-up, *Extremes*, fared little better, but 1974's *Crime of the Century* topped the British charts and made a promising, if not spectacular, impact on American radio. But the band's idiosyncratic, progressive but tightly melodic pop sound was by then slowly winning over more than just a cult audience Stateside, as evidenced when 1977's *Even in the Quietest Moments . . .* went to No. 16 and featured the band's first Top 20 U.S. hit, the No. 15 "Give a Little Bit." Record buyers gave a little bit and more when Supertramp released 1979's *Breakfast in America*: the album went to No. 1 and yielded three hit singles (the highest being the No. 6 "The Logical Song"), ultimately selling more than 18 million copies worldwide. The double live album *Paris,* released in 1980, went to No. 8, and 1982's prophetically titled . . . *Famous last words* peaked at No. 5, but Hodgson's departure in 1983 for an unsuccessful solo career marked the end of Supertramp's chart reign.

Bachman-Turner Overdrive

The story goes that guitarist Randy Bachman left his first major band, the Guess Who, shortly after its 1970 No. 1 breakthrough hit, "American Woman," because the band's hedonistic ways conflicted with his recent conversion to Mormonism. Precisely what it was that the Guess Who did that he found objectionable is open to interpretation, but it certainly was not the pursuit of the "devil's music." Immediately following his exit from the Guess Who, Bachman dived right into a solo album, a new band (the short-lived Brave Belt) with fellow former Guess Who-er Chad Allan and, by 1972, the project that made his name all but synonymous with workmanlike '70s classic rock: Bachman-Turner Overdrive. The original lineup featured Bachman on lead guitar and vocals, his brothers Tim and Robbie on guitar and drums, respectively, and bassist/vocalist Fred Turner—all four members hailing from Canada.

The BTO approach to rock 'n' roll is perfectly summarized in the title of the band's best known hit, "Takin' Care of Business." That song (from 1974's *Bachman-Turner Overdrive II*), along with the same year's "Let It Ride" and the No. 1 "You Ain't Seen Nothing Yet," seemed devoid of any pretensions to "art" or meaning beyond the visceral thrill of hearing crunchy guitar chords blasting out of car-radio speakers or bouncing off the walls of a hockey arena. The same could of course be said for any number of BTO's contemporaries; but unlike, say, KISS, BTO's anthems did not pander to kids or even seem overly concerned with sex. They were just meat-and-potatoes rock 'n' roll songs, saying little and threatening even less but saying it all with hooks and punchy choruses as big as the band's homeland. The result: more than 7 million album sales in America during the band's heyday, which ended with 1977's *Freeways* album. Randy Bachman left the group later that same year (preceded by his brother Tim in 1975). BTO kept on trucking for another couple of years before breaking up and subsequently reforming numerous times over the next two decades in various combinations—albeit never with as much success.

Meat Loaf

Marvin Lee Aday and Jim Steinman were never household names, but together—along with producer Todd Rundgren—they created one of the best-selling albums of the '70s. Steinman wrote the songs—epic, unabashedly bombastic teenage symphonies, many lifted from a Peter Pan musical he had penned called *Never Land*. Rundgren's production, a savvy mix of metal, opera, and Broadway-show tune overtures, made the songs even bigger. And Aday, alias Meat Loaf, sang them all with a fearless passion and over-the-top verve evoking a bizarre hybrid of Bruce Springsteen and Luciano Pavarotti. The album? 1977's *Bat Out of Hell*, which spawned three Top 40 singles: "Paradise by the Dashboard Light," "Two Out of Three Ain't Bad," and "You Took the Words Right Out of My Mouth."

The album itself peaked at No. 14 but ultimately sold 17 million copies worldwide. From seemingly out of nowhere, Meat Loaf—previously best (if barely) known for a small role in *The Rocky Horror Picture Show* and for singing on Ted Nugent's *Free-For-All* album—was one of the biggest superstars in rock (or, at 250-plus pounds, *the* biggest). But in the wake of *Bat Out of Hell*, he quickly fell back into obscurity. The album's follow-up, 1981's *Dead Ringer*, peaked at No. 45, and subsequent releases sank without a trace. Then, in 1993, Meat Loaf and Steinman reunited for *Bat Out of Hell II: Back Into Hell*. From out of nowhere, again, Meat Loaf was huge; the album topped the charts, sold 10 million copies worldwide, and won Loaf a Grammy (Best Male Rock Vocal Performance) for the No. 1 single, "I'd Do Anything for Love (But I Won't Do That)."

Kansas

How it was that Kansas—by any measure, America's most ambitious progressive rock band in the '70s (not to be confused with the dozens of such acts hailing from the United Kingdom at the time)—ultimately wound up in the "corporate rock" bin is no great mystery. Simply put, despite their best efforts to be arty, Kansas wrote catchy songs. There were far too many members in the band for the public to keep track of: guitarist/keyboardist Kerry Livgren wrote most of the songs, Robby Steinhardt provided the band's unique calling card (electric violin), and Steve Walsh handled the vocals, but none of them stood out as rock stars any more so than, well, the other three guys in the band. After building a reputation (and a small Midwestern following) for mixing progressive overtures reminiscent of British prog-rockers like Emerson, Lake & Palmer (dense arrangements, tricky time signatures, and twelve-minute songs with titles like "Incomudro—Hymn to the Atman") with American arena-rock boogie, the Topeka, Kansas-formed sextet stumbled into the mainstream in 1976 with the No. 11 hit single, "Carry On Wayward Son," which spurred the band's fourth album, *Leftoverture*, to No. 5 and sales of 3 million.

With the following year's aptly titled *Point of Know Return* reaching No. 4, Kansas' fate as a classic rock radio warhorse was sealed. The album's anthemic title track was a Top 40 hit and the fatalistic ballad "Dust in the Wind" reached No. 6. A platinum live album (1978's *Two for the Show*) and two gold-sellers (1979's No. 10 *Monolith* and 1980's No. 26 *Audio-Visions*) helped the band continue to pack arenas into the early '80s, but the hits dried up soon after. Later-day albums hinted at a conscious effort to reinforce their prog roots, but Kansas' legacy, for better or worse, begins and ends with those three breakout hits from the mid-'70s. Everything else—epic in scope or not—is just . . . dust in the wind.

WORKING-CLASS HEROES: AMERICAN HEARTLAND ROCK

From Aerosmith to late-model Who, heavy metal and classic hard rock maintained an unavoidable presence on the '70s rock scene. But the headbangers were not alone. Leaving the California country-rockers and punks to their own respective chapters—and the filling of that giant, Bruce Springsteen–sized hole to the songwriters chapter—a sweeping overview of "mainstream rock" of the era would still be incomplete without mention of what might be called, to adopt an admittedly generic, catchall term as hazily defined as the aforementioned "corporate rock," "American Heartland Rock." Or, failing all else, "Where Does One Put Bob Seger, ZZ Top, and the J. Geils Band?"

The answer, of course, is right here. As odd as it may seem to cover bread-and-butter blue-collar rockers like Detroit's Seger and soul shouters like Boston's (the city, not the band) Peter Wolf (of the J. Geils Band) in the same space as KISS, back in the '70s, they were all sharing the same theaters, arenas, and stadiums. Seger, in a 1977 *Creem* interview, talked about shared concert dates with KISS—a seemingly incongruous paring that no doubt made sound financial sense to promoters at the time, above and beyond the mere fact that KISS had "Cat Man" Peter Criss and Seger sang "Katmandu." And in 1975, the biggest rock tour of the year—or, for that matter, the biggest tour *ever* at that point in rock history—was not by the Stones, the Who, or Led Zeppelin: It was ZZ Top's year-and-a-half-long "Worldwide Texas Tour," which found the Texas trio playing to 2 million people across the United States and Europe and grossing $20 million. ZZ Top's opening acts on the tour? Up-and-comers Aerosmith and Lynyrd Skynyrd. Two years earlier, Skynyrd had opened for the Who on the *Quadrophenia* tour, a fortuitous trek that effectively put the southern rock newcomers on the map as one of the '70s greatest live bands.

Lynyrd Skynyrd (from left, standing) Leon Wilkeson, Artimus Pyle, Allen Collins, Leslie Hawkins, Gary Rossington, Ronnie Van Zant, Steve Gaines, Jo Billingsley; (seated) Billy Powell and Cassie Gaines, c. 1977. Courtesy of Photofest.

Lynyrd Skynyrd's remarkable—and remarkably tragic—career is covered in detail in Volume 3, Chapter 4 ("The South Rises Again"). But the group merits brief mention here again in part because the bulk of their success came between 1974 (the year their multiplatinum second album, *Second Helping*— with the immortal No. 8 southern pride anthem "Sweet Home Alabama"—was released) and 1977 (the year frontman Ronnie Van Zant, guitarist Steve Gaines, and backup singer Cassie Gaines all died in a plane crash at the height of the band's fame). But a reminder of Skynyrd's (and southern rock's) prominence in the mid-'70s also underscores the extent that the mainstream rock audiences of the day were receptive to more than just metal, reheated glam, and bands with one-word names and nifty logos. And the success of Seger, the J. Geils Band, and ZZ Top proved that the public's appetite for nonmetallic rock extended beyond dueling guitar jams and songs about the Southland: Sometimes it just wanted some of "that old time rock 'n' roll," served straight-up and fuss-free, dished out like a funky old-school "Houseparty," or slathered in deep Texas blues and barbeque sauce.

Bob Seger and the Silver Bullet Band

If Bruce Springsteen was the uncontested (and critically endorsed) "Boss" of working-class rock, Bob Seger was surely the senior vice president of the

Bob Seger in concert, 1976. Courtesy of Photofest.

Midwest and heartland division. Seger was already a six-year veteran of the Detroit club scene when he scored his first regional hit, 1966's "East Side Story." He signed to Capitol Records two years later and briefly tasted national fame with the No. 17 title track off his major-label debut, *Ramblin' Gamblin' Man* (1969). Subsequent releases through the rest of the '60s and early '70s (including a handful on his own label, Palladium, before a return to Capitol in 1975), supported by constant touring, firmly established Seger's standing as a regional powerhouse. His breakthrough, in prime '70s fashion, came with a double live album, 1976's Top 40 *Live Bullet*. Beginning with *Night Moves* later that year, Seger had six consecutive Top 10 albums, all selling platinum or better.

Seger's specialty, as exemplified on *Night Moves*, 1978's No. 4 *Stranger in Town*, and 1980's No. 1 *Against the Wind*, was a crowd-pleasing mix of exemplary bar band garage rock and soulful ballads, many marked by a bittersweet sense of nostalgia and middle-aged angst: themes (and music) that *grown-ups* could ostensibly identify with more readily than teen party anthems. Seger was thirty-one when *Night Moves* was released, and, just like Pete Townshend, he was well aware that his own generation was not always out en force rocking quite like it used to. The *Night Moves* single "Rock and Roll Never Forgets" was an open invitation to everyone his age and older to get out of the house and find their rock 'n' roll thrill again. Seger, in fact, made it his mission to reach these latent rock fans, much as bands like KISS tirelessly targeted a much younger demographic. "Whenever we go to a concert, we see mostly young people," admitted Seger at the time. "I wanted to bring back people my own age, write a song for them. In Detroit we get a crowd mixed between young and old, and I wanted to see that everywhere."[28]

The J. Geils Band

Boston's J. Geils Band targeted a slightly older crowd than the average metal band, too—or at least a crowd hip enough to rock's roots to dig the band's spirited evocation of the classic R&B and soul that *they* grew up on as teens in the late '50s and early '60s. The J. Geils Band drew from the same deep well of soul and blues as the Rolling Stones, but they skipped the dark, sleazy path that characterized much of the Stones' late '60s and '70s work and just let the good times roll. Named after guitarist Jerome Geils and fronted by charismatic, jive-talking showman Peter Wolf (a popular Beantown DJ during the dawn of free-form FM radio), the J. Geils Band made party music that catered both to obsessive soul and blues fans and a broader mainstream crowd of young-at-heart adults who never surrendered to middle-of-the-road and easy listening fare. Although the group would not hit the top of the album and singles charts until MTV helped push both 1981's *Freeze-Frame* and its catchy single, "Centerfold," to No. 1, the J. Geils Band maintained a steady popular and critical buzz throughout the '70s with constant touring (packing theaters and arenas nationwide) and the occasional Top 40 hit (like 1971's No. 39 "Looking for a Love" and '74's No. 12 "Must of Got Lost").

ZZ Top

While ZZ Top did not become a household name until the '80s—when the Texas trio seized on the marketing goldmine that was MTV and reinvented itself as one of the most recognizable bands of the music video age—it was in the '70s that the "Lil' Ol' Band from Texas" built its reputation as America's foremost proponents of stadium-sized boogie and blues. The band's 1970 debut *First Album* failed to chart and '72's *Rio Grande Mud* peaked at No. 104, but beginning with 1973's No. 8 *Tres Hombres*, every studio album of fuzz-toned Texas blues rock that guitarist Billy Gibbons, bassist Dusty Hill, and drummer Frank Beard released over the next twenty-three years would hit the Top 40, with all but two going Top 20 and *all* selling gold or platinum. Among the landmarks: *Tres Hombres*, home of the John Lee Hooker/Texas whore house–inspired "La Grange"; 1975's half-live, half-studio *Fandango!*—notable both for the band's first Top 20 single (the No. 20 "Tush") and for spawning the aforementioned Texas-sized Worldwide Texas Tour (the first and surely only rock tour to feature live cattle as stage props); 1979's streamlined *Deguello* with its immortal salute to "Cheap Sunglasses"; and 1983's Top 10 blockbuster *Eliminator*, which brought ZZ Top roaring into the MTV era with an updated sound (synthesizers now featured prominently in the instrumental mix) and three iconic smash videos for "Gimme All Your Lovin'," "Sharp Dressed Man," and fittingly, the thirteen-year-old band's biggest hit ever, "Legs," at No. 8.

NOTES

1. Goodman 1997, 78.
2. Breithaupt and Breithaupt 2000, 116.

3. George-Warren and Romanowski 2001, 1063.

4. *Lifehouse Chronicles* album liner notes, 2000.

5. Mick Farren, "The Titanic Sails at Dawn," *New Musical Express*, June 19, 1976.

6. Bangs 2002, 154.

7. Breithaupt and Breithaupt 2000, 118.

8. Charles Shaar Murray, "The Who: Exorcising the Ghost of Mod," *Creem*, January 1974.

9. Dave Schulps, "In Which Pete Townshend Gets Personal," *Trouser Press*, May 1978.

10. *Led Zeppelin: The Complete Studio Recording* album liner notes, 1993.

11. Ron Ross, "Rolling Stones: Are They Too Rich to Rock?" *Phonograph Record*, May 1974.

12. "The 500 Greatest Albums of All Time," *Rolling Stone*, April 21, 2005.

13. Barbara Charone, "Rolling Stones: We're Nearly Famous," *Sounds*, August 21, 1976.

14. Barbara Charone, "Keith Richards: The Pusher Behind the Stones," *Creem*, October 1976.

15. *Low Budget* album liner notes, 1999.

16. Jaan Uhelszki, "Led Zeppelin: Rock's Best Body English," *Creem*, May 1975.

17. Cameron Crowe, "Led Zep Conquers States, 'Beast' Prowls to the Din of Hordes," *Rolling Stone*, May 22, 1975.

18. *KISS Box Set* album liner notes, 2001.

19. George-Warren and Romanowski 2001, 794.

20. Logan and Woffinden 1977, 189.

21. Steve Lake, "Queen's Gambit," *Melody Maker*, September 22, 1984.

22. Bud Scoppa, "Queen: *Sheer Heart Attack*," *Rolling Stone*, May 8, 1975.

23. *Blizzard of Ozz* album liner notes, 2002.

24. George-Warren and Romanowski 2001, 1028.

25. David Fricke, "Foreigner Plays Its Head Games Fair, But Plays to Win," *Circus*, December 25, 1979.

26. *Foreigner Anthology: Jukebox Heroes* album liner notes, 2000.

27. Goodman 1997, 313–315.

28. John Morthland, "Bob Seger Conquers the World (and About Time!)," *Creem*, July 1977.

THE SOFTER SIDE OF ROCK

Rob Patterson

By 1974, rock and roll music had endured for two decades and was entering adulthood. So it is only natural that the music followed suit by maturing into a more grown-up sound with adult lyrical concerns—hence the rise of soft rock. And the epicenter for soft rock became southern California, from where such antecedents as the Beach Boys, the Byrds, Buffalo Springfield, and Crosby, Stills, Nash & (sometimes) Young had emerged earlier.

California was the setting for the archetypal modern American dream, thanks to the movies and TV shows created there as well as the sounds from the Golden State. "The music that has resulted from all this has generally spoken to the heart-stream of American tastes," noted critic John Rockwell in *The Rolling Stone Illustrated History of Rock & Roll.* "Los Angeles pop-rock tended to be bright, buoyant and upbeat. It was white music for white audiences and was generally polished in sound."[1]

Softer rock acts also emanated from England, which during the British invasion years of the 1960s had been a consistent source of pop-rock hits on the American charts. And this more song- and pop-oriented trend toward adult music also came to include country-rock acts and everything from former psychedelic bluesman Steve Miller to the jazz-rock of Steely Dan.

Developments in radio gave soft-rock sounds wide access to the airwaves. The initially free-form FM album-rock format became more tightly programmed as it transformed into "album-oriented rock" (AOR) in the early 1970s. The concentration was on shorter songs and sounds that were familiar and pleasing to mass listeners as burgeoning radio programming research techniques suggested stations avoid music that caused listeners to "tune out." And this served soft rockers well. The maturing and splintering of the pop and rock audience also resulted in the rise of "adult contemporary" (AC) and "middle-of-the-road" (MOR) radio formats for which soft rock acts were also ideal. And all of those formats provided launching grounds for acts to find an audience from which their songs could then leapfrog onto the pop charts. The result was that soft rock became a staple of a number of radio formats throughout the 1970s.

With the end of the Vietnam War and the subsiding of the social changes and occasional chaos of the 1960s, American music audiences were ripe for music that was relaxing and reassuring. Soft rock provided an ideal antidote with its personal and largely apolitical themes and musical accents on melody, harmony, and gentler rhythms. The prevalence of roots-music styles within country and folk also influenced soft rock and added to its sentimental sound.

The 1970s was the decade when rock music became mainstream culture in America. Music radio provided the soundtrack for the lives of millions, and record shopping and attending concerts became common recreational activities for teens as well as young and even older adults. Soft rock was a more palatable alternative to harder rock sounds for many music listeners, and the rock audience had begun to mature. Hence it became one of the dominant rock paradigms of the period. As a result, soft-rock acts like the Eagles, the Bee Gees, Fleetwood Mac, and Elton John became some of the most popular musical artists of the decade.

THE CALIFORNIA SOUND

"There's people out there turnin' music into gold," sang singer-songwriter John Stewart on his 1979 No. 5 hit song "Gold," a wry look at the California music business. Indeed, the mid- to late '70s were golden times for soft rockers and purveyors of the California sound. And Stewart's hit itself provides a telling example. A member of the Kingston Trio during the 1960s folk boom, he had since toiled as a fringe folk-rock artist whose albums never went beyond the lower reaches of the Top 200. The album that yielded "Gold," *Bombs Away Dream Babies*, featured guests Lindsey Buckingham and Stevie Nicks from the newly minted superstar band Fleetwood Mac. It reached No. 10 on the charts thanks to "Gold," giving Stewart his greatest career success. Indeed, the California sound was commercial magic.

It was a sound so appealing that it launched two of the best-selling rock groups of all time: the Eagles and Fleetwood Mac. It frequently mixed the catchy California pop sensibility that Brian Wilson had developed with the Beach Boys with the folk- and country-influenced styles of the Byrds and Buffalo Springfield that came later in the 1960s. Similarly, soul and blues also fed into the poppy soft-rock sounds from California during the mid- to late 1970s. Catchy songs, proficient musicianship, and an accent on vocal harmonies were prime characteristics that most California-sound acts shared, and it was a formula that made them ripe for radio play and moved millions of records and concert tickets.

Crosby, Stills, Nash & Young

In various configurations as well as through solo efforts, Stephen Stills and Neil Young from Buffalo Springfield, David Crosby from the Byrds, and Graham Nash from the Hollies were soft-rock and California-sound superstars during the years from 1974 to 1980. And this was with only releasing one album of new material by Crosby, Stills & Nash during that time, which is a testament to the lasting impact this supergroup made at the dawn of the decade.

Debuting as Crosby, Stills & Nash in 1969 and adding Young for the No. 1 1970 album *Déjà vu*, the union broke up soon after hitting No. 1 again in 1971 with a live album, *4 Way Street*. Yet when the foursome reunited in 1974, they toured stadiums and hit No. 1 with a best-of album, *So Far*, that eventually sold 6 million copies. Crosby, Stills & Nash also reunited in 1977 for the album *CSN*, which reached No. 2 and quickly went platinum.

During most of the 1970s, CSN&Y were subject to speculation as to whether they might get together again. Yet the music they created as a three-some and foursome became a staple of FM album radio while the members recorded and toured as solo artists as well as in the duos of Crosby and Nash and, briefly in 1976, the Stills-Young Band. It was Neil Young who enjoyed the most consistent artistic achievements as a solo artist during this period, though his work ranged from softer sounds to such raw rocking that he was actually one of the few dinosaur-rock-star acts who was admired by punk rockers.

The foursome in all their permutations were certainly pioneers of the soft-rock style as well as demigods within the California sound. They laid groundwork for both in the music they made, bringing an accent to vocal harmonies, high-quality songs and musicianship, and a mellower rock sound that drew from folk and country to create a new breed of American pop-rock.

The Eagles

In American rock and roll, the Eagles ruled the roost in the 1970s. They took the California sound tradition, country-rock, and good old rock 'n' roll and fashioned it all into a commercial juggernaut that would result in two of the best-selling albums in recorded music history: *Hotel California*   The Eagles in concert, 1979. Courtesy of Photofest.

(1976) and *Their Greatest Hits 1971–1975* (1976). And the band had it all musically: superbly crafted songs, expert musicianship, beautiful harmonies, and red-hot guitar playing. No act better defined the post-1960s American rock and roll sound than this Los Angeles–based band.

Although the Eagles were the quintessential California rock band, the band's two main singers and songwriters hailed from opposite poles in the American heartland. Drummer Don Henley came from a small town in Texas, while guitarist Glenn Frey grew up in urban industrial Detroit. Although it was the allure of California that drew them both to Los Angeles in the late 1960s, the sheer Americanism of their band no doubt stemmed from their middle-American backgrounds.

The four founding members of the Eagles first played together in 1971, backing up Linda Ronstadt. Guitarist and banjo player Bernie Leadon had been in the pivotal country-rock band the Flying Burrito Brothers, and bassist Randy Meisner had played on the first album by country-rockers Poco. By the end of the year, they had signed a deal with impresario David Geffen's Asylum Records, and in early '72 the band traveled to London to record their debut album with top rock producer Glyn Johns, who had worked with the Rolling Stones and the Who.

The band's ambitions soared as high as the bird that provided their name. "We didn't want to be just another L.A. band," said Frey.[2] *Eagles*, released in June 1972, caught public attention with its first single, "Take It Easy," a song co-written by Frey and Jackson Browne that hit No. 12 on the charts. "Witchy Woman" then cracked the Top 10, and "Peaceful Easy Feeling" reached No. 22. On the strength of the singles the album topped out at No. 22 and eventually went gold.

For their next album, the Eagles undertook an ambitious scheme for a new and not yet established band. *Desperado*, released in April 1973, was a concept album that equated life in a rock band with the Old West Doolin' Dalton outlaw gang. Though the album did not result in any Top 40 singles, it reached No. 41 on the charts and in time became the band's second gold album. *Desperado* also featured two songs that would become standards in the Eagles canon: the title tune and "Tequila Sunrise."

By this time, the band was itching to rock harder and go beyond the country-rock idiom. "We got put into that category and we filled that slot," said Henley. "I knew, no matter how much our music would change, we would never escape that category."[3] In an effort to give their sound a harder edge, the group added guitarist Don Felder. After sessions in London with Johns yielded little that the band were happy with, they returned to Los Angeles and finished their third album, *On the Border* (1974), with producer Bill Szymczyk. The third time proved to be the charm for the Eagles, as "Best of My Love" earned the group their first No. 1 single and helped *On the Border* become the band's first album to crack the Top 20.

With *One of These Nights* in 1975, the Eagles finally hit pay dirt. The title track and the album both reached No. 1, while "Lyin' Eyes" and "Take It to the Limit" also hit the Top 5. As the band began working on their next album,

Asylum released a *Greatest Hits* collection that went platinum out of the box. Meanwhile, Leadon left the group and was replaced by Joe Walsh, who had already made a name for himself with the James Gang and as a solo artist.

Hotel California in 1976 proved to be the band's definitive moment and most successful album. It debuted at No. 1 and included two chart-topping singles: the title song and "New Kid in Town." By this time the Eagles were also selling out stadiums and arenas on their concert tours. At their height as the most successful band in America, Meisner quit and was replaced by Timothy B. Schmit, who had also followed Meisner in Poco.

It took the Eagles three years of arduous sessions to follow *Hotel California* with the aptly named *The Long Run* in 1979. It was also a No. 1 album and featured a chart-topping hit with "Heartache Tonight" and two Top 10s with the title song and "I Can't Tell You Why." But it was clear from the varied quality of the album's content that the Eagles were losing creative steam. After a 1980 live album, the group called it quits.

Only Henley went on to have a solo career that rivaled that of the Eagles in artistic achievement and appreciable sales and chart success. But when the group reunited in 1994, they were immediately able to headline stadiums and arenas like they'd never been away. And with sales of their *Greatest Hits* album surpassing 25 million, the Eagles are arguably the most successful American rock band ever.

Linda Ronstadt

Country-rock singer Linda Ronstadt served as a locus for both the California sound and the country-rock genre and helped take both to the top of the pop and country charts. Her most popular albums, produced by Peter Asher—an Englishman who had enjoyed hit-single success during the British invasion of the early to mid-1960s in the duo Peter & Gordon—showcased choice song selections from the best contemporary songwriters as well as past artists. The Eagles first coalesced as her backing band, which at other times featured some of the best players from the California scene. As critic John Rockwell noted, "Of the principal Los Angeles rock stars

Linda Ronstadt, 1978. Courtesy of Photofest.

of the '70s, it has been Linda Ronstadt who best combined artistic integrity and mass commercial success."[4]

Arizona native Ronstadt arrived in Los Angeles in the late 1960s as the singer for the folk-rock group the Stone Poneys, who landed the song "Different Drum" (written by Monkee Michael Nesmith) in the Top 20 in 1968. Going solo the following year, she mixed material from contemporary folk writers and songs from the country canon on her first two solo albums, which both had a strongly country flavor. By her self-titled third release in 1971, Ronstadt's sound began to lean as much on rock as country, and she started pulling material from the songbooks of her peers on the Los Angeles scene like Jackson Browne and Neil Young. The song credits on *Don't Cry Now* in 1973 almost read like a who's who of Los Angeles singer-songwriters, yet the album also hit No. 5 on the country charts.

Ronstadt's pop and rock breakthrough began in 1974 on *Heart Like a Wheel*, her first outing with Asher, which landed singles in the Top 5 with songs from the past like "You're No Good" and "When Will I Be Loved?" The pop sheen with rock kick, country flavors, and soul inflections that Asher brought to Ronstadt's work carried five more albums into the pop and country Top 5 through the end of the decade, and she became a consistent presence on pop, country, AOR, and adult contemporary radio. On 1978's *Living in the USA* and '80's *Mad Love*, Ronstadt incorporated new-wave sounds and songs into her reliable formula.

In the 1980s, as her presence as a pop-rock star waned, Ronstadt varied her musical approach, recording three successful albums of pop classics from the years before rock (with string arrangements by frequent Frank Sinatra collaborator Nelson Riddle), an album of Mexican American songs, and a best-selling country project with Dolly Parton and Emmylou Harris titled *Trio* (1987). Her knack for straddling genres, charts, and audiences marks Ronstadt as one of the leading female singers of the late 1970s.

Jackson Browne

One of the most acclaimed singer-songwriters to emerge in the early 1970s, Browne was the boyish bard of the southern California scene. His work was marked by sensitivity, literacy, and the conflicts and conundrums one encounters as adulthood overtakes youth.

His 1972 self-titled debut album on the Asylum label—also home to the Eagles and Ronstadt—was preceded by his reputation as a writer, thanks to his songs being covered by Tom Rush, the Nitty Gritty Dirt Band, and others. *Rolling Stone* praised the "awesome excellence" of his first release, which featured David Crosby on harmony vocals. "It's not often that a single album is sufficient to place a new performer among the first rank of recording artists. Jackson Browne's long-awaited debut album chimes in its author with the resounding authority of an *Astral Weeks*, a *Gasoline Alley*, or an *After the Gold Rush*."[5] The album also contained the biggest chart single of his career, "Doctor My Eyes," which reached No. 8.

By his second release the following year, *For Everyman*, Browne had joined forces with his musical foil, multi-instrumentalist David Lindley, whose lap-steel playing became a trademark of Browne's sound. *Late for the Sky* in 1974 solidified his reputation as a chronicler of the emotional life behind the southern California dream, which Browne finally articulated best on *The Pretender* in 1976, which thanks to regular airplay on album radio reached No. 5 on the charts and went platinum. *Running on Empty* in 1978, which reflected on life on the rock 'n' road, was partly recorded live in concert as well as on his tour bus. Though Browne's consistent excellence as a writer was starting to show cracks, the album rose to No. 3 on the charts. He closed out the decade with *Hold Out*, which finally took Browne to No. 1 even as his writing seemed to lose its impact and relevance. In the 1980s, Browne turned his attention to social and political matters and faded from prominence. Yet his first four albums are near-perfect articulations of the California sound and some of the most poetic and emotive rock songwriting of the decade.

Fleetwood Mac

One of the supreme ironies of the mid- to late 1970s southern California sound is that one of its most successful acts was composed of three natives of

Fleetwood Mac (left to right) Mick Fleetwood, Stevie Nicks, John McVie, Christine McVie, and Lindsey Buckingham, 1978. Courtesy of Photofest.

THE ORIGINAL FLEETWOOD MAC

In a story that is a litany of ironies, the group's name comes from its rhythmic backbone of drummer Mick Fleetwood and bassist John McVie rather than any of the many star players and singers at the band's forefront. The two had worked together in John Mayall's Bluesbreakers before starting the band in 1967 with another Mayall alumnus, guitarist Peter Green. They became an out-of-the-box sensation in the United Kingdom, but despite frequent tours of the United States in the early 1970s, they failed to connect in America until 1975. But when they did, it would be in such a big way as to make the group superstars.

Prior to that, Fleetwood Mac would suffer one of the most checkered histories of any band in rock and roll. Although Peter Green was the band's musical focus, he left the group in 1970, suffering from the ravages of drug abuse and psychological problems. Guitarist Jeremy Spencer then became the musical pivot, but in 1971, in California on a U.S. tour, he mysteriously disappeared to later be discovered among a religious cult. In 1974, the band's manager booked an ersatz "Fleetwood Mac" on an American tour while the actual band members took a break from the road. And between 1967 and '74, a total of five guitarists would join and leave the band.

England and two other musicians who migrated to Los Angeles from northern California. Yet Fleetwood Mac were nearly as definitive a southern California band as the Eagles, racking up a string of classic hit songs, selling millions of albums, and packing arenas and stadiums with a sound that was miles away from the group's origins as a British blues band. Thanks to a style that mixed crafty pop-rock with soft romanticism and mystical ethereality—depending on the singer and writer of the song—Fleetwood Mac ruled the soft-rock movement of the late 1970s.

The origins of the Fleetwood Mac that rose to stardom came in 1970 when the group replaced guitarist Peter Green with pianist and vocalist Christine Perfect, who married John McVie the following year and took his surname. By 1974, the group's core of Mick Fleetwood and the McVies had moved to Los Angeles and, in the wake of legal battles with their manager, attempted once more to find new members and continue on.

The English threesome was joined in 1975 by guitarist, singer, and songwriter Lindsey Buckingham and singer and songwriter Stevie Nicks. The duo, who were also a couple at the time, had migrated to Los Angeles from northern California and released one largely overlooked album as Buckingham-Nicks.

The album the quintet recorded that year, titled simply *Fleetwood Mac*—also the title of the original group's '68 debut—signaled a radical change from the band's previous blues-based style. "From listening to *Fleetwood Mac*, you'd think this once-definitive British blues band was a Southern California pop group—and you'd be right," noted *Circus* magazine. The review observed how the band, "which not long ago seemed to be unraveling, has new life and plenty of newfound charm" and praised the release as "an easy-going, immensely playable record."[6] Just how playable it was would soon be evident, thanks to three voices and writers: Christine McVie, who supplied charming soft rock; Nicks with her haunting wail of a voice and sometimes supernatural song tales;

and Buckingham, who would increasingly prove himself a skillful pop-rock craftsman.

The album took some time to find an audience. But by the following year, it started yielding hit singles like the No. 20 McVie song "Over My Head" and her "Say You Love Me" and Nicks' "Rhiannon (Will You Ever Win)," which hit No. 11. The singles propelled the album to No. 1 and eventual quintuple platinum sales status in the United States.

Even as Fleetwood Mac finally broke through commercially, the internal disarray that had plagued the group since the beginning continued to threaten the band's survival. The relationships of the McVies and Buckingham and Nicks broke up, and for a spell Nicks and Fleetwood became a couple, prompting the media to characterize the group as a rock 'n' roll soap opera. The band responded by titling its next album in 1977 *Rumours*, which was indeed marked by romantic tensions in the songs within. It nonetheless yielded four Top 10 singles: the No. 1 hit "Dreams" as well as "Go Your Own Way," "Don't Stop," and "You Make Loving Fun." The album won the Album of the Year Grammy Award and spent thirty-one weeks at No. 1 on the charts, finally unseated by Michael Jackson's *Thriller*, one of the few albums to ever outsell the more than 25 million copies that *Rumours* moved worldwide.[7]

Buckingham's increasing mastery of recording techniques and pop experimentalism dominated the double release *Tusk* in 1979, another Top 5 album from which the group scored two more Top 10 singles with the title track and "Sara." Another double album *Live* followed in 1980. Christine McVie, Nicks, and Buckingham all then embarked on solo careers. But in 1982, the band again hit No. 1 with *Mirage*, which featured the No. 4 pop single "Hold Me."

Since then, Fleetwood Mac intermittently carried on, replacing the absent Buckingham and Nicks during the early 1990s with other musicians. In 1993, Christine McVie retired from the band, but since the late 1990s, Buckingham, Nicks, Fleetwood, and John McVie have continued to record and tour as Fleetwood Mac. The band remains the superstar group of soft rock, setting musical, chart, and sales standards that have yet to be equaled within the genre. Though almost as celebrated for their tempestuous internal relationships as their music, Fleetwood Mac nonetheless created an enduring body of work from 1974 to the end of the decade that continues to enchant listeners.

The Steve Miller Band

Dallas, Texas, native Miller was a blues fanatic who landed in San Francisco in the late 1960s to become part of the psychedelic music scene. Over his first five albums, the singer, guitarist, and songwriter used his blues base to create some of the most intelligent and progressive music to emerge from the Bay Area music community but never rose above being a second-tier act within that particular rock music scene.

That all changed when Miller's song "The Joker" from the album of the same name hit No. 1 in 1974. Thanks to subsequent songs like "Fly Like an Eagle," "Rock'n Me," "Take the Money and Run," and "Jet Airliner" that were pop hits and standards on AOR playlists, Miller became one of rock music's most consistent hit makers of the mid- to late '70s. The strength of his catchy, economical songs and light rock sound is proven by the fact that his 1978 album *Greatest Hits 1974–1978* has sold over 13 million copies. The cultural impact of Miller's music may not have been significant, but his songs were a major part of 1970s rock music.

The Doobie Brothers

Few, if any, bands epitomized rock and roll's shift from being a serious cultural and political force in the late 1960s to becoming good-time party music than the Bay Area–bred Doobie Brothers. After all, this is a group who took the name for their brotherhood from a slang word for a marijuana joint.

In their first incarnation from 1971 to 1976, the group combined rocking boogie, a touch of funk, country-rock, and a knack for pop hooks to score pop and FM rock radio hits like "Listen to the Music," "China Grove," "Long Train Runnin'," "Black Water" (the group's first No. 1 single), and "Take Me in Your Arms (Rock Me)." Their albums consistently went gold, and the group was a reliable presence on the U.S. concert circuit.

When singer, guitarist, and writer Tom Johnston bowed out of the band in 1975 due to health problems, he was replaced by singer, songwriter, and keyboard player Michael McDonald, who had previously played with Steely Dan. With McDonald's songs and deep soul shout of a voice up front, the group's sound shifted to a rock-inflected classic R&B style. The hits on AM and FM radio kept coming through the end of the decade with "Takin' It to the Streets," "It Keeps You Runnin'," "Minute by Minute," and "What a Fool Believes" (which earned the group their second No. 1 single and a Grammy for Record of the Year in 1979). The new sound also lifted the group to million-seller status. The band's consistent flow of popular songs made the Doobie Brothers an essential part of the rock sound of the 1970s.

Little Feat

Little Feat never achieved a commercial success to match their press raves, devoted cult following, and the esteem they enjoyed among fellow artists and musicians. Yet Little Feat were "a great American band, a band as quintessentially SoCal as the Beach Boys, as rootsy as the Band, as funky as the Meters, as cerebral as Steely Dan," wrote music critic Bud Scoppa in his liner notes to a 2000 Little Feat compilation.[8]

The band's musical significance stems from what was a dynamic if also uneasy match of a visionary leader—singer, songwriter, and guitarist Lowell George—with a set of musicians gifted enough to articulate his eclectic notion of American rock music. And what a notion it was, drawing from the Southern R&B groove, the blues and country traditions, the arty innovations of Captain Beefheart and Frank Zappa's Mothers of Invention, and the harmonic beauty of the California sound—to name some but hardly all of the ingredients found in the Little Feat style. Inject all that with strains of psychedelia and surrealism, and you have at least an approximation of the eclecticism that was both Little Feat's greatest quality as well as their commercial downfall.

The band began in 1969 with the lineup of George and bassist Roy Estrada—both of whom had played with Zappa's Mothers—and keyboardist/singer Bill Payne and drummer Richie Hayward. The band's 1971 self-titled debut and follow-up *Sailin' Shoes* the following year both failed to dent the charts despite critical acclaim, and the group parted ways for a number of months. Regrouping with Kenny Gradney replacing Estrada on bass and second guitarist Paul Barrere and percussionist Sam Clayton joining the fold, they released *Dixie Chicken* in 1973. Constant touring began to win the group a coterie of worshipful fans, thanks to one of the most dynamic live shows in rock at the time. The group members also became busy session players on many albums by acts within the southern California scene and elsewhere, and George's trucker anthem "Willin' "—which appeared on both the first and second album by the group—became a modern standard as it was covered by numerous other artists, most notably Linda Ronstadt.

After 1974's *Feats Don't Fail Me Now*, with which the band finally managed to crack the Top 40 of the album charts, Payne and Barrere started to challenge George's somewhat autocratic leadership. As a result, the group's sound grew more improvisational and jazz-inflected on the studio albums *The Last Record Album* in 1975, *Time Loves a Hero* in 1977, and *Down on the Farm* in 1979, as well as the double album live set *Waiting for Columbus* in 1978. In '79, George broke up the band and recorded a solo album, *Thanks I'll Eat It Here*. While on tour to promote it, George died of a heart attack in Washington, D.C. on June 29, 1979.[9]

The rest of the group reunited in 1988 with, initially, Pure Prairie League singer Craig Fuller taking George's place. The band would enjoy some of the commercial success that originally eluded them and would eventually dub themselves "The Jamband's Jamband."[10] But Little Feat, the second edition, never approximated the musical glories they created with George at the helm. And long after his death, Lowell George remains a venerated rock talent for his crafty and ingenious songwriting, soulful vocals, and a distinctive slide-guitar style—praised in *Rolling Stone* by Scoppa for the way it would "howl and roar like a tractor trailer in the midst of a steep, mountainous descent"[11]—that was as innovative as the work of the also-deceased Duane Allman.

COUNTRY-ROCK

The American country-rock sound in large part grew out of the music of the Byrds and Buffalo Springfield. The pivotal event that started the country-rock trend was when the Byrds added Georgia-bred Gram Parsons for the 1968 album of straight-ahead country music, *Sweetheart of the Rodeo*, recorded in Nashville, which was almost antirock heresy at the time. Parsons and bassist Chris Hillman left the band soon after to form the Flying Burrito Brothers, whose cosmic country-rock set the standard for the style, while Byrds leader Roger McGuinn continued the Byrds in a rocking country style. Meanwhile, after the breakup of Buffalo Springfield in 1968, guitarist and singer Richie Furay and guitarist Jim Messina started Poco, a breezy and bouncy country-rock band that enjoyed FM radio and concert popularity but never found mass success.

Nonetheless, these groups inspired a slew of country-flavored rock bands in the early 1970s and can rightly be called the founding fathers of the Americana movement of the 1990s. By the era this volume covers, 1974 to 1980, country-rock had either gone big-time, as with Californians like the Eagles and Linda Ronstadt, or faded as a widespread trend. Yet its influence remained especially pervasive in soft rock, and a number of significant country-rock acts continued to make music during this period.

America

A threesome formed in England by the sons of American servicemen that became a duo early in their recording career, this group distilled the California country-rock sound into lightweight but immensely popular pop fodder in the early to mid-1970s. America hit No. 1 on the American charts in March 1972 with their first single, "Horse with No Name," which sounded uncannily like a Neil Young outtake and actually unseated Young's "Heart of Gold" from the top slot.[12] However, *Rolling Stone* reviewer John Mendelsohn took the song to task for the "mawkish sentiments and banal, pimply hyperboles [that] abound therein."[13]

Which is to say that America did not get much respect from the critical cognoscente, as they were seen as offering a sweet and sometimes cloying form of country-rock with little, if any, of the content found in the best stuff. But the band did score with programmers and listeners of pop and adult contemporary radio with such Top 10 pop hits as "Ventura Highway," "I Need You," "Tin Man," "Lonely People," and "Sister Golden Hair" (which was their second

No. 1) between 1972 and 1975. By the late 1970s, America faded from the top of the charts, although the group did land another song in the Top 10, "You Can Do Magic," in 1982.

The Marshall Tucker Band

This South Carolina band was the country-rock wing of the Southern rock movement and brought to the sound both jazzy saxophone and flute inflections as well as extended instrumental jams that presaged the jam-band sound that became popular in the 1990s. Debuting in 1973, the group had a number of its 1970s albums certified gold and cracked the Top 20 in 1977 with "Heard It in a Love Song," which propelled their album *Carolina Dreams* to sales of over a million. In contrast to the Southern boogie of their Dixie peers, the Marshall Tucker Band showed that the '70s sounds of the South could be smooth, mellow, and countrified without sacrificing appeal.

The Charlie Daniels Band

The North Carolina–bred guitarist and fiddler Daniels made a living as a Nashville session player and even had a song recorded by Elvis Presley before forming the Charlie Daniels Band in the early 1970s. Coming from a country background but inspired by the Southern rock of the Allman Brothers, his country-rock succeeded in winning him hits and fans in both the rock and country camps. A 1973 novelty single inspired by the clash between rednecks and longhairs, "Uneasy Rider," was a Top 10 hit for Daniels. He hit the Top 30 two years later with "The South's Gonna Do It" but truly struck pay dirt in 1979 with his fiddle song "The Devil Went Down to Georgia," which went to No. 3 on the pop charts and was certified a gold single. In the late '70s and early '80s, his annual multiartist Volunteer Jam concerts in Nashville helped cement ties between Southern rock and country artists. As the 1980s dawned, Daniels began injecting his conservative political views into his music with the hits "In America" and "Still in Saigon."

BRITISH ROCK GOES POP AGAIN

With the British invasion, artists from the United Kingdom brought rock and roll back into the U.S. pop charts. By the 1970s, England was still having its effects on the American rock and roll scene, but as much for the hard rock of acts like Led Zeppelin as anything else. But the rise of soft rock allowed the British knack for pop-rock to reassert itself, and a number of British superstars arrived—or in the case of Paul McCartney, continued—to be an integral part of the pop music of the 1970s.

Wings (left to right) Jimmy McCulloch, Joe English, Linda McCartney, Paul McCartney, and Denny Laine, c. 1975. Courtesy of Photofest.

Paul McCartney and Wings

"Ballads and babies—that's what happened to me," quipped McCartney of his post-Beatles career.[14] Hyperbole perhaps, but as the softer and more melodic and musically traditional of the creative team of Lennon/McCartney, he was well poised to become a soft-rock superstar in the 1970s. After debuting as a solo act with his *McCartney* album in 1970, the man who would later be knighted as Sir Paul decided to get back to being in a band. So he formed Wings, which also featured the musical contributions of his wife Linda.

The group got off to a slow start in 1971 with *Wild Life*, which received a sound drubbing by music critics. Wings finally earned a No. 1 single in 1973 with the ballad "My Love" off the album *Red Rose Speedway*, which also hit No. 1. *Band on the Run* in 1973 found McCartney approaching the artistic glories of his Beatles days on another No. 1 album that even England's usually hard-nosed *New Musical Express* succinctly hailed as "a great album."[15] It yielded the band another No. 1 single with the title track as well as Top 10 hits with "Helen Wheels" and "Jet."

From that point on into the early years of the 1980s, McCartney and Wings settled into a pattern, continuing to hit No. 1 on the U.S. pop charts with "Listen to What the Man Said," "Silly Love Songs," "With a Little Luck," "Coming Up," and McCartney's 1982 duet with Stevie Wonder, "Ebony and Ivory." The band also topped the album charts with *Venus and Mars* (1975), *Wings at the Speed of Sound* (1976), *Wings over America* (1976), and McCartney's solo effort *Tug of War* (1982), though critics consistently upbraided McCartney for producing pop fluff that hardly befitted a former Beatle. By the mid-1980s, the ripple effect of having been a Beatle no longer carried McCartney to the top of the charts. But throughout the 1970s, McCartney remained an almost constant presence on the rock-music scene, proving to himself and fans, if maybe not the critics, that there was life after the Fab Four.

Elton John

If any artist in the 1970s achieved a career trajectory similar to what the Beatles did in the 1960s, it was Elton John. With his writing partner Bernie Taupin,

John was part of a creative duo as prolific and gifted as the Lennon/McCartney team. But the varied and exceptionally catchy and high-quality songs the two composed was only part of what made Elton John the most successful and sensational pop superstar of the 1970s.

As *All Music Guide* observes,

> Initially marketed as a singer-songwriter, John soon revealed he could craft Beatlesque pop and pound out rockers with equal aplomb. He could dip into soul, disco, and country, as well as classic pop balladry and even progressive rock. His versatility, combined with his effortless melodic skills, dynamic charisma, and flamboyant stage shows made him the most popular recording artist of the '70s.[16]

Born Reginald Dwight, John had made his way as a backing musician and songwriter for hire in England before finally starting to release singles and then his first album, which failed to attract attention, in the late 1960s. But once his second album *Elton John* was released in America in 1970, he soon racked up an impressive string of chart successes.

With the exception of his 1971 live album *11-17-70*, which reached No. 11, every one of the twelve albums that John released between 1971 and '76 hit the Top 10, and seven of them topped the charts. During the same time period, John landed sixteen singles in the Top 10, seven of them No. 1 hits. He also, of course, sold millions of records. And the impressive numbers do not even begin to quantify the enduring appeal of tunes like "Your Song," "Rocket Man," "Tiny Dancer," "Crocodile Rock," "Daniel," "Goodbye Yellow Brick Road," "Don't Let the Sun Go Down on Me," "Someone Saved My Life Tonight," and many others.

John also became one of the hottest tickets on the U.S. concert circuit—selling out stadiums and the nation's largest arenas—as well as becoming one of the decade's most visible and outspoken musical celebrities. Eventually awarded a British knighthood, Sir Elton John helped define

Elton John, c. 1976. Courtesy of Photofest.

the notion of rock superstar in the era when that term became part of the lex-icon. His chart action started to wane toward the latter part of the decade, and eventually his pop stardom would be eclipsed by Michael Jackson. Yet John's place in the highest reaches of the rock and roll pantheon is secure. In fact, given the emotional impact of his music and the consistent quality of his best work, John probably deserves the "King of Pop" title more than Jackson (who actually gave himself that sobriquet). The 1970s was the decade of Elton John, and much of the music he made continues to sound as fresh and timeless today.

Eric Clapton

Even before he became a rock superstar with Cream and Blind Faith in the late 1960s, his English fans were declaring, "Clapton is God." Yes, he was and remains one of the greatest guitarists in rock and roll. But Clapton was also known as a modest and even shy man, and it is not idle speculation to wonder if the pressure of such stardom and admiration was a factor in his becoming addicted to heroin in the early 1970s.

So when Clapton returned to action in 1974 with *461 Ocean Boulevard* after overcoming his drug problem, it is no surprise that it was just as much an album of songs and singing as it was a guitar player's record. And it was his concentra-tion on developing those other aspects of his artistry that made the hard-rock pioneer and guitar god also become a soft-rock star in the mid-1970s.

He celebrated his sobriety with a gold No. 1 single off *461 Ocean Boulevard*—his cover of Bob Marley's "I Shot the Sheriff." In 1978, he enjoyed another gold single with the Top 5 hit "Lay Down Sally" and hit No. 16 with the ballad "Wonderful Tonight," both off his 1977 *Slowhand* album. The fol-lowing year he hit the Top 10 again with "Promises" off the *Backless* album. Be-coming known as a singer and songwriter enabled Clapton to flesh out his superstardom beyond hot guitar licks, and he continued to show his knack for affecting mainstream soft-rock balladry years later in 1992 when he hit No. 2 on the Hot 100 with "Tears in Heaven," written after the tragic death of his son Conor.

Rod Stewart

As the singer for the Jeff Beck Group and then Faces, Rod Stewart and his raspy voice were the epitome of raw rocking. Drawing from blues, soul, coun-try, folk, and '50s rock and roll in those bands as well as with his own solo releases starting in 1969, the swaggering singer, songwriter, and master of well-chosen covers was one of the most critically admired figures in rock and roll. He had also captured the ear of U.S. pop audiences in 1971 with the No. 1 hit "Maggie May" from his third solo album, *Every Picture Tells a Story*. But from the point when he left Faces in 1975 and moved to America, Stewart was plagued by accusations that he had abandoned his rock and roll roots to "go Hollywood." Yet Stewart's career certainly did not suffer from the change even if his rock credibility was forever tarnished.

The indication that his sound was shifting came on 1975's aptly titled *Atlantic Crossing*, his sixth solo release. "Coming as it does amidst sweeping changes in Stewart's career and personal life, the unsettling nature of *Atlantic Crossing* isn't that much of a surprise," opined critic John Morthland in *Creem* magazine. "It's simply Rod Stewart trying to get a firm footing on some new ground, succeeding stupendously a couple times but more often falling a little short. . . . and if two great songs and eight near-misses don't add up to a failure, neither can it be considered very satisfying."[17]

But the fears of critics soon proved well founded. Yet at the same time, Stewart's career leapt to a new and higher level of pop success. *A Night on the Town* in 1976 became his first million-selling album and reached No. 2 on the charts, propelled by the No. 1 gold single "Tonight's the Night (Gonna Be Alright)." *Foot Loose & Fancy Free* the following year hit No. 2 thanks to the gold No. 4 single "You're in My Heart (The Final Acclaim)." But the track "Hot Legs," as popular as it was on FM rock radio, struck some fans of his older work as almost a parody of the style Stewart developed with Faces. With "Do Ya Think I'm Sexy" in '79, Stewart jumped into the heart of the disco movement and racked up another No. 1 single that sold over a million copies. But the artist who had started the decade as one of rock's great hopes had become a pop star by the dawn of the 1980s, albeit one who some say had sold out but also sold millions of records.

The Bee Gees

The initial aversion of rock audiences to disco brought some scorn to the Bee Gees after the group's participation on the 1977 *Saturday Night Fever* soundtrack album—the best-selling soundtrack of all time.[18] But the English-born Gibb brothers, who had launched their career in Australia in the 1960s, had always been more a pop act than a rock band. And they started applying their amazing sibling vocal harmonies to danceable R&B on 1974's *Mr. Natural*.

The Bee Gees topped the pop charts with gold singles well before *Saturday Night Fever* with "Jive Talkin'" from 1975's *Main Course* and "You Should Be Dancing" off *Children of the World* in 1976. Of course those successes hardly compared to the phenomenal success that *Saturday Night Fever* brought the group, which enjoyed three No. 1 singles from the album: "Stayin' Alive," "How Deep Is Your Love," and "Night Fever." Similarly, 1979's *Spirits Having Flown* also yielded three more chart-topping singles with "Tragedy," "Too Much Heaven," and "Love You Inside Out."

Lightning did not strike again with the group's participation in the film version of *Sgt. Pepper's Lonely Hearts Club Band* in 1978: though the album reached No. 5 on the charts, the film bombed. And by the beginning of the 1980s, the Bee Gees' hot streak started to cool. But during their 1970s heyday, the Bee Gees were one of the best-selling acts in the world and certified superstars, enjoying unprecedented play for a white act on black-music radio. And ultimately the funky R&B work that made the Bee Gees the kings of disco music transcended the trend thanks to rock-solid songcraft, sophisticated arrangements, and the trademark Bee Gees harmonies.

Dire Straits

Arriving in England amidst the punk and new wave craze, Dire Straits were certainly an anomaly. The band's laid-back, highly American style was informed by country and blues, and leader Mark Knopfler's wiry guitar riffs signaled the arrival of a new 6-string star. But given the context, many had no idea what to make of the band at first blush.

"Not an obvious little band, this," observed a *New Musical Express* reviewer of a 1977 London pub show by the group.

> On the face of it, Dire Straits tread a hack course through easy rocking American vapidity, minus the Californian harmonies and surface gloss that distinguishes most L.A. product from everything else, and hence is mundane in the sweaty environs of London town. Or so I thought when I encountered them some months ago. . . . What sets Dire Straits apart is the slide from the commonplace to the sublime. . . . [A] casual listen could miss the inherent strength, and it may take some tuning in to pick up on the considerable subtleties Dire Straits possess, but the effort is well worth the reward.[19]

American listeners did not seem to miss the subtleties. Thanks to the No. 4 hit "Sultans of Swing," the group's self-titled debut album in 1978 reached No. 2 and went platinum. *Communiqué* the following year reached No. 11 and went gold, and *Making Movies* in 1980 was a Top 20 gold album. The band did not hit No. 1 in the United States until 1985 with Knopfler's acerbic observation on MTV and the pop-music game, "Money for Nothing," from the album *Brothers in Arms*, which spent nine weeks in the top spot. Dire Straits became an American AOR staple from their first release and in the 1980s were one of the best-selling bands in the world. But more important, the band demonstrated that the soft-rock audience was open to musical sophistication and intelligent, if not downright intellectual, songs—a quality that speaks well for soft rock's contribution to American popular music.

NOTES

1. DeCurtis et al. 1992, 539–540.

2. Shapiro 1995, 44.

3. Ibid., 55.

4. DeCurtis et al. 1992, 542.

5. Bud Scoppa, review of *Jackson Browne*, *Rolling Stone*, March 2, 1972.

6. Bud Scoppa, review of *Fleetwood Mac*, *Circus*, November 1975.

7. See http://www.roughguides.com.

8. *Hotcakes & Outtakes: 30 Years of Little Feat*, liner notes by Bud Scoppa, Rhino, 2000.

9. See http://www.roughguides.com.

10. See http://www.littlefeat.net.

11. Bud Scoppa, review of *Sailin' Shoes*, *Rolling Stone*, March 30, 1972.

12. See http://www.allmusic.com.

13. John Mendelssohn, *Rolling Stone*, April 27, 1972.

14. See http://www.roughguides.com.

15. Charles Shaar Murray, review of *Band On The Run*, *New Musical Express*, January 19, 1974.

16. See http://www.allmusic.com.

17. John Morthland, review of *Atlantic Crossing*, *Creem*, December 1975.

18. See http://www.riaa.com.

19. Paul Rambali, "Dire Straits: Hope & Anchor, Islington, Live Review," *New Musical Express*, October 8, 1977.

SINGER-SONGWRITERS: ROCK GROWS UP

John Borgmeyer

The generation born in the post–World War II "baby boom" grew up with rock music. The books in this series have covered the adolescent jubilation expressed in early rock and roll, as well as the teenage rebellion that fueled the protest and psychedelic songs of the late 1960s. In 1970, the baby boomers became adults—and, in some ways, so did rock music.

That year saw important harbingers of change in rock culture. Paul McCartney officially announced that the Beatles had broken up in April. More gravely, autumn brought the deaths by drug overdose of both Jimi Hendrix and Janis Joplin. At a time when John Lennon, Bob Dylan, and Paul Simon were approaching the age of thirty, the events of 1970 prompted members of the counterculture generation to reflect on their mortality and their future.

Before she died, Joplin declared that the freedom her generation sought came only when there was nothing left to lose. Indeed, it is one thing to tear one system down, but without a new system to replace the old one, freedom can seem more like . . . drifting. For the baby boomers, the pleasures of "free love" faded as the divorce rate skyrocketed; the drugs that had once offered freedom now seemed like prisons of abuse and addiction; disillusionment with political utopianism sent people searching inward for moral clarity. As the rock 'n' roll generation shook off their parents' traditional attitudes and beliefs, by 1970 they faced the much more difficult challenge of crafting workable alternatives.

The baby-boom generation was by now accustomed to having its preoccupations sold back to them as rock culture. As adults, their soul-searching was expressed by a new breed of introspective singer-songwriters. Theirs was a style Bruce Pollock called "the Middle of the Dirt Road . . . a certain woodsy crossroads of folk and blues, country and middle of the road pop . . . a sound which the baby boom middle class would eventually salvage as their own, effectively making it the most popular sound of the period, if not the entire decade."[1] In an American rock context that included the bombastic forms of progressive rock and heavy metal, as well as aggressive funk from black artists like Sly Stone and George Clinton's Funkadelic, the singer-songwriters couched their pensive lyrics in rustic sounds and images of flannel shirts and dusty jeans. In an age of diet soda, space travel, plastic, and sprawling suburbs, the middle of the dirt road led toward a fantasy of a more earth-friendly, "natural" way of living and spoke to the rock generation's deep longing for psychological roots and "authenticity."

Singer-songwriters in the 1970s were strongly influenced by Bob Dylan's folk roots and the literary craft of his songwriting. Perhaps the most literary of all was Leonard Cohen, who set his abstract, poetic lyrics to lush accompaniment on his 1974 album *New Skin for the Old Ceremony*. In 1975 one of Cohen's backup singers, Janis Ian, released her most famous song, "At Seventeen," which captured the nostalgia and focus on "personal issues" that characterized the spirit of the times.

Also traveling the "middle of the dirt road" was Laura Nyro, whose jazz-tinged *Smile* in 1976 exemplified the way singer-songwriters attempted to mythologize their personal experience. Jackson Browne built his career in the mid-'70s with romantic confessions, with his 1974 album *Late for the Sky* reflecting a doomed view of personal relationships at a time when the divorce rate had begun to skyrocket.

Instead of focusing on their own personal lives, songwriters like Gordon Lightfoot and Carole King spoke through historical narrative and created characters. Lightfoot's ballad "The Wreck of the Edmund Fitzgerald," for example, hit No. 2 and earned the songwriter a Grammy nomination in 1977. King, meanwhile, sang of young streetwalkers and drug addiction on her 1973 album *Fantasy*.

Fortunately, it was not all gloom and doom. Tom Waits channeled Jack Kerouac in his 1978 album *Blue Valentine*, which was by turns gritty and comic. Randy Newman and Loudon Wainwright III offered wicked satire, on albums like Newman's *Good Old Boys* in 1974 and Wainwright's hit song "Dead Skunk" in 1973.

For a while in the early 1970s, it looked as if all of rock was headed toward the dirt road, but by 1976 it was clear that most of

Carole King, c. 1976. Courtesy of Photofest.

the singer-songwriters did not have the vision to sustain the movement. Aside from their own limitations, the singer-songwriters were doomed by punk and disco—two styles as far from the dirt road as can be—and by the debut of MTV in 1981. Still, artists like Suzanne Vega and Tracy Chapman had hits as singer-songwriters in the decades to follow, and MTV eventually created a series called *Unplugged*, on which popular artists (from rapper L. L. Cool J. to rockers like Nirvana) strapped on acoustic guitars and gave their hits a spin on the dirt road. The remainder of this chapter deals with singer-songwriters who managed to survive the rock audience's ever-shifting taste.

JOHN LENNON AND GEORGE HARRISON

Since the Beatles had led the rock generation from "I Wanna Hold Your Hand" to "Strawberry Fields Forever," it is fitting perhaps that two former Beatles—John Lennon and George Harrison—also made the music that kicked off the "Me" decade.

John Lennon made one of rock's most introspective, personal statements with his 1970 album *John Lennon/Plastic Ono Band*. Lennon and his artist wife, Yoko Ono, wrote the songs after "primal scream" therapy sessions; Lennon explores his relationship to his parents and his place in the world on songs like "Mother," "I Found Out," and "Look at Me."

Subsequent releases included uneven material as Lennon spent the 1970s battling the U.S. government's attempts to deport him, beginning in 1971. In November 1980 he released *Double Fantasy* with Ono, and its success seemed to revitalize Lennon as a public artist. It was a short-lived reprise. Only three weeks later, Mark David Chapman shot Lennon to death in New York City.

Similar to Lennon's scream therapy was George Harrison's consulting of Eastern mysticism for answers to the confusion of the age, and he offered the fruits of somber spiritual meditations on his 1970 double album *All Things Must Pass*. Reflecting the

George Harrison performs during the mid-1970s. Courtesy of Photofest.

era's quest for spiritual meaning, many of the tunes, like "My Sweet Lord," are straightforward prayers. Harrison set the precedent for all-star charity concerts with his two benefit shows for Bangladesh in 1971. On *Living in the Material World* in 1973, Harrison showed that there is a fine line between spiritual questioning and sanctimonious preaching. After the forgettable 1974 album *Dark Horse* and an unsuccessful tour, and a 1975 collection of leftovers called *Extra Texture (Read All About It)*, Harrison released the more upbeat *Thirty-Three & 1/3* in 1976. *George Harrison* in 1979 was also lighter, but by 1980 his audience had left him.

BOB DYLAN

In the 1960s, Bob Dylan established himself as one of the giants of American music and a voice for the counterculture. His albums during that period redefined folk with protest songs like 1963's "Blowing in the Wind," while his 1965 album *Bringing It All Back Home* invented folk rock and introduced a new poetic depth to rock lyrics. After *Blonde on Blonde* in 1966, Dylan suffered a motorcycle accident, the exact nature of which is unclear. By many accounts the wreck was not very serious, but it gave him a chance to retreat from his intense fame for several years.

After a trio of lackluster albums in 1969, 1970, and 1973, critics suggested Dylan had lost his artistic focus. As a flesh-and-blood man, however, the early '70s were some of his best years. He had married Sara Lowndes in 1965, and he settled down to domestic life with their children (the couple would eventually have five) in Woodstock, New York; he dabbled in film and painting, made music for fun, and read widely.

In 1974 he released the album *Planet Waves*, his first official release recorded with his longtime touring group, known simply as the Band. Songs like "Wedding Song," "Forever Young," "You Angel You," and "Something There Is About You" show Dylan in love—a distinct contrast to his earlier political and psychedelic material. *Planet Waves* became his first No. 1 album on the strength of a tour where Dylan and the Band played forty of the biggest theaters and sports stadiums in America—the first major stadium tour of the rock era. With all 658,000 tickets eventually sold for an average of $8 (pricey by the day's standards), the tour was a huge financial windfall, grossing approximately $5 million.

Led by guitarist Robbie Robertson, the Band delivered raw, hard-rocking versions of classic Dylan songs that recalled their heyday. In 1966, however, Dylan's devoted folk music fans booed and howled abuse; in 1974 it was the same aggressive sound, but the audience greeted Dylan as if he were a counterculture hero returning home. "Everybody cheered and acted like, *Oh I loved it all along*," said Robertson. "There was something kind of hypocritical in it."[2]

The shows from the 1974 tour opened with an explosive rock set by Dylan and the Band. Dylan left the stage after a few songs so Robertson and the Band could perform their solo hits like "The Weight" and "Cripple Creek." After intermission, Dylan performed solo with a harmonica and acoustic guitar. On the tour's opening night—January 3, 1974, in Chicago—Dylan's performance of "It's Alright Ma (I'm Only Bleeding)" resonated especially strongly among an audience engrossed in the unfolding Watergate drama. When Dylan sang his famous line that even the president must stand naked, the crowd roared and held aloft cigarette lighters and matches in a spontaneous show of unity. A photograph of the flickering flames appeared on the cover of *Before the Flood*, a 1974 live album recorded on tour, and the practice of waving lighters became an American concert tradition.

Dylan occupied the highest echelon of rock stardom, and although he was not usually an extravagant spender, in the mid-'70s he spared no expense on a strange, lavish mansion north of Los Angeles, California. Bob and Sara changed their minds regarding design frequently as construction progressed, and eventually fifty-six artisans took up residence on the couple's front lawn. They would stay for two years until the $2.5 million, twenty-room home was finally complete. Ironically, though, cracks developed in Dylan's marriage during their home's construction, as Bob and Sara started bickering about various aspects of the project. After living quietly as a husband and father, Dylan readopted the rock 'n' roll lifestyle during Tour '74, putting more strain on his relationship with Sara. He spent most of 1974 living in Minnesota, away from his wife. During this time of obvious turmoil in his marriage, he wrote the songs for *Blood on the Tracks*, released in 1975.

Widely regarded as a masterpiece, the album shows the artist ruminating on the nature of mature human relationships. Before releasing the album, Dylan rerecorded some songs that he deemed too forthrightly autobiographical— particularly the angry "Idiot Wind." By blurring the songs' lyrical edges, Dylan made them more cryptic and, perhaps, more universal. Penned, it seemed, for a specific person, the album produced several hits that in some ways reflected the mood of an aging rock audience. People reminiscing on failed early loves no doubt identified with "Tangled Up in Blue," while "Shelter from the Storm" spoke for protesters weary of political confrontation. The album was released to universal acclaim in January and went to No. 1. *Rolling Stone* considered *Blood on the Tracks* so significant that the editors devoted the magazine's entire review section to the record.

In the summer of 1975, Dylan returned to the neighborhood where he started his career, New York City's Greenwich Village. There he met theater director and lyricist Jacques Levy, and the two embarked on what would be the first sustained period of co-writing in Dylan's career. Their first song together was "Isis," an allegorical epic about a man who leaves his woman for an ill-fated graverobbing adventure. Levy's theatrical sense influenced their next important collaboration, "Hurricane," a dramatic song about middleweight boxer Rubin

"Hurricane" Carter, who was serving a life sentence in New Jersey for a triple murder he claimed he did not commit. Carter's 1974 memoir, *The Sixteenth Round*, made the boxer's case for innocence a cause célèbe.

Both "Isis" and "Hurricane" appeared on Dylan's most commercially successful release, the 1976 album *Desire*. Every song on the album, except for "One More Cup of Coffee" and "Sara," a final plea to his estranged wife, were written with Levy. Yet it sounds like a Dylan album, perhaps because it was recorded under Dylan's preferred conditions—hectic, chaotic, nearly out of control. The core of his band included Rob Stoner on bass, Howie Wyeth on drums, Emmylou Harris singing backing vocals, and Scarlet Rivera, who joined the band after Dylan saw her walking down the street with her violin in New York City.

These musicians formed the backbone band for Dylan's next tour, which would become known as the Rolling Thunder Revue. The concept for the tour was of a traveling carnival, a barnstorming group of musicians playing small towns in a vaudeville style—an idea of which Dylan was always fond. Friends and fellow artists, like poet Allen Ginsberg, songwriters Ramblin' Jack Elliott and Joan Baez, and playwright Sam Shepard crammed onto tour buses for a cocaine-fueled cross-country rolling circus documented in the 1978 film *Renaldo and Clara*.

The Rolling Thunder Revue culminated in a star-studded benefit concert for Rubin "Hurricane" Carter at Madison Square Garden in December 1975, featuring boxing icon Muhammad Ali speaking to Carter via telephone from the stage. Dylan played another, less successful, benefit for Carter in 1976. At a retrial that year, Carter was returned to prison, where he would stay until a federal judge overturned the previous convictions and finally set Carter free in the late 1980s. Meanwhile, the 1976 leg of the Rolling Thunder Revue was, as one Dylan biographer put it, "like watching a house burn down."[3] Sara showed up for some of the gigs as her marriage to Bob was clearly collapsing. Dylan's personal turmoil infused the performances with palpable intensity and rage. When the tour finally wound down, he returned to his fantasy home—and the hard realities of his personal life—in California.

It was a dark time for Dylan. Sara filed for divorce in March 1977, and the case devolved into a bitter custody battle. This year Dylan recorded more songs telling veiled stories of his relationship with Sara, but the lyrics were so dark and angry they were never recorded. In 1978 the four-hour film *Renaldo and Clara* debuted to almost unanimous criticism; he had spent $1.25 million of his own money on the project, and its failure smashed his hopes of directing more films. "I've got a few debts to pay off," he told a newspaper. "I had a couple of bad years. I put a lot of money into the movie, built a big house . . . and there's the divorce. It costs a lot to get divorced in California."[4]

To pay the bills, Dylan launched a 1978 world tour of Japan, the Far East, Europe, and the United States during which he played 140 shows for almost 2 million people. Although it grossed more than $20 million, it was a strange show where Dylan's greatest hits were reworked with incongruous new arrangements—"Don't Think Twice, It's All Right" was performed as a reggae song, with "It's Alright Ma (I'm Only Bleeding)" as hard rock. Dylan retained the touring band's orchestral sound for his next album, *Street Legal*, recorded after the first leg of the tour and released in 1978. Although *Street Legal* hit No. 11, critics considered it a weak album. Combined with the flop of *Renaldo and Clara* and the messiness of his public divorce, as Oliver Trager wrote, it was "as if critics were waiting in the alley, knives sharpened," eager to debunk the myth of Bob Dylan.[5]

On tour Dylan was surrounded by Christian women, particularly Carolyn Dennis, Mary Alice Artes, and Helena Springs, all backup singers in his band. Dylan's public conversion to Christianity coincided with a spiritual revival sweeping the music business and much of counterculture America that was by now weary of the drug abuse, alcoholism, and decadent living inspired by the selfishness of the era. There is a famous legend of Dylan's encounter with saving grace in a Phoenix hotel room, and in 1979, he started attending Bible studies with Artes at the Vineyard Fellowship—a small evangelical church near Los Angeles founded by singing pastor Kenn Gulliksen with a membership that included several well-known musicians. With his baptism, Dylan joined the swelling ranks of Americans that called themselves "born-again Christians."

Religious imagery had always appeared in Dylan's lyrics—not surprising, perhaps, because he had been raised Jewish. As a Jew, though, his conversion fascinated the press while offending many of his friends and family—not to mention many fans, who had long found inspiration in Dylan's condemnation of dogmatic institutions. His next album, 1979's *Slow Train Coming*, was his most overtly religious album to date.

It was the story of the artist at a crossroads, recorded with Dire Straits guitarist Mark Knopfler as bandleader. Songs like "Gotta Serve Somebody" (for which he received his first Grammy Award in 1980) presented life as a choice one must make between being saved or being lost, an ultimatum longtime fans never expected Dylan would present. His concerts were marked by the confusion a pot-smoking audience felt when Dylan inundated them with a crop of religious songs they did not know, interspersed fire-and-brimstone that revealed Dylan's preoccupation with the end of the world (a popular trope in the born-again movement). The heckling he endured surpassed even that of his first electric shows in 1965–1966, when he was booed almost every night. "I went out on tour and played no song that I had ever played before live," Dylan said. "I thought that was a pretty amazing thing to do. I don't know any other artist who has done that."[6]

His hellfire bent continued with the release of *Saved* in 1980. Critical reception to the album and gospel shows indicated Dylan fans liked the artist better when he was telling them to think for themselves, instead of appearing onstage as some kind of savior. "When practically every tune on an album is thanking God for something, it gets a wee bit redundant to hear it again . . . and again," wrote Trager.[7] After 1981 Dylan stopped performing all-gospel shows; since then his conversion has become a topic of argument for the legions of fans who carefully scrutinize Dylan's work and speculate on his motives.

His 1981 album *Shot of Love* fared even worse than *Saved*, reaching only No. 33, even though it bears fewer overt religious overtones, and it is considered his last good album before a low period in the '80s. For Dylan, the decade began with the death of John Lennon, terrible reviews and upset friends in the wake of his conversion, lawsuits with former manager Albert Grossman, and fear caused by threats from a stalker named Carmel Hubbel. The death of his close friend Howard Alk cemented Dylan's feelings that his career was going off track.

Through the 1980s, Dylan remained as inscrutable as ever. The album *Infidels* in 1983 seemed to suggest a new interest in orthodox Judaism, while the glitzy remix on 1985's *Empire Burlesque* obscures the strength of the songs. Yet with *Oh Mercy* in 1989, Dylan proved he could still write meaningful, fully conceived songs on politics, love, society, and spirituality. Today Dylan the artist is still strong, while Dylan the man remains as mysterious as ever.

NEIL YOUNG

With a voice that could howl with rage or plead like a wounded child, Neil Young articulated the hopes and frustrations of an aging counterculture. After playing with Buffalo Springfield in the late 1960s, Young began a solo career during which he defined the intimate singer-songwriter genre and anticipated punk with his rock band Crazy Horse. He released his solo debut, *Neil Young*, in 1969 at the age of twenty-three. That year he played with two completely different bands. Crosby, Stills & Nash added Young to lend a gritty tone to the 1969 album *Déjà vu*, of which Young's "Helpless" is a highlight; also that year, Young released *Everybody Knows This Is Nowhere*, backed by the loud, ragged Crazy Horse. On his own, Young helped define the emerging singer-songwriter genre in 1970 with *After the Gold Rush*, a collection of bare acoustic songs.

For the next three decades, Young would continue to cross between rock and folk boundaries, willfully hopping genres to the point that in the early 1980s Geffen Records sued Young for allegedly violating his contract by recording "unrepresentative" songs. Record executives forever hoped Young would re-create the sentimental touch of 1972's *Harvest*, featuring the dewy romanticism of "Heart of Gold."

As the middle of the dirt road got crowded with artists like James Taylor and Carly Simon, Young found that "traveling there soon became a bore, so I headed for the ditch."[8] By releasing unpolished live material on *Time Fades Away* in 1973, it seemed as if Young was trying to shake himself away from the music industry's tendency to classify artists into marketable genres.

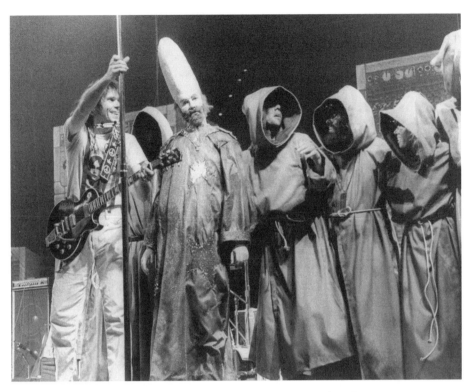

Neil Young during the Rust Never Sleeps Tour, 1979. Courtesy of Photofest.

He recorded an acoustic follow-up to *Harvest* called *Homegrown* but shelved it and reunited with Crazy Horse, a garage-rock band closer to punk than the singer-songwriters. The band's guitarist, Danny Whitten, and roadie Bruce Berry had died drug-related deaths when Young reunited with them to record *Tonight's the Night*. Released in 1975, it documented the allure and the danger of the rock 'n' roll lifestyle.

Young's 1975 album *Zuma* reflected his tug-of-war between rock and folk, featuring both Crazy Horse and Crosby, Stills & Nash. After making the retrospective album *Decade* in 1977, Young released two great albums—*Comes a Time* in 1978 and *Rust Never Sleeps* in 1979, which Don McLees calls "arguably Young's richest musical achievement."[9] On *Comes a Time* Young returned to the dirt road. His old fans were thankful, even though *Comes a Time* avoided the excessive sentimentality of *Harvest*. *Rust Never Sleeps* is commonly characterized as Young's response to punk, with the song "Out of the Blue" aimed at Sex Pistols singer Johnny Rotten. The album's portrayal of the human element in rock—and its reprisal of risk-averse corporate blandness—comes from an artist who had so far managed to successfully navigate the rock industry and still make the music he wanted to.

Young continued his musical duality with the acoustic *Hawks and Doves* in 1980 and the abrasive *Re-ac-tor* in 1981. Then he left Reprise Records for

Geffen; the company was not pleased with the 1982 album *Trans*, where he responded to the computer age by distorting his voice with synthesizers. Nor did Geffen appreciate Young's rockabilly effort *Everybody's Rockin'* in 1983—the company sued Young, accusing him of intentionally making "uncharacteristic" albums. Young finished out his Geffen contract with *Landing on Water* in 1986 and *Life* in 1987, before returning to Reprise for the rest of his career. His tour supporting 1990's *Ragged Glory* featured the post-punk noise rock of Sonic Youth and Social Distortion, and Young's profile rose when popular bands like Pearl Jam cited the influence of Young's music and anticorporate posture. Uncompromising to the end, when Young was elected to the Rock and Roll Hall of Fame as a member of Buffalo Springfield in 1997, he replied with a letter decrying corporate control of the event and declined to attend the ceremony.

JOHN DENVER

If the middle of the dirt road had a dead center, John Denver was there. He carefully cultivated an image so nonthreatening that it inspired the ironic urban legend that he had actually been a sniper in Vietnam. Untrue, of course, but a popular story because Denver was perhaps the most purposefully pleasant of all the singer-songwriters.

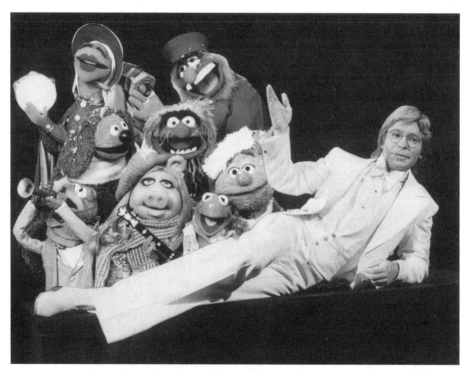

John Denver and the Muppets on *A Christmas Together*, 1979. Courtesy of Photofest.

Henry John Deutschendorf Jr. took his stage moniker from the name of his favorite city. With 1969's *Rhymes & Reasons*, featuring "Leaving, on a Jet Plane," Denver projected himself as the sensitive mountain man with songs like "Take Me Home Country Roads" and "Sunshine on My Shoulders." Articulating each word with utmost precision, he sang in a soaring twang full of warm sentiment and devoid of any sharp emotion.

In 1974—the year Colorado's governor declared him the state's poet laureate—Denver released *Back Home Again*, featuring his song "Thank God I'm a Country Boy," which would become one of his biggest hits. Music, however, was not Denver's only claim to fame. In 1976 he started the Windstar Foundation, an environmental education organization, and he appeared on the big screen starring opposite George Burns in the 1977 movie *Oh, God!* After a successful appearance on *The Muppets* television show, Denver made two television specials and two records with the puppets.

In the 1980s, Denver invested his fame in promoting humanitarian and environmental causes. By the 1990s, Denver's squeaky-clean image and prolific media presence made him the subject of jokes. He has been glorified, however, since his death in 1997, at age fifty-three, when he crashed an experimental fiberglass aircraft in California.

PAUL SIMON

In 1970 Simon made his last studio album with Art Garfunkel, *Bridge over Troubled Water*. It has sold more than 10 million copies on the strength of Simon's articulate lyrics and incorporation of black gospel styles. Spinning tales of life, death, and love in middle-class America over folk songs tinged with African sounds and rhythms, Simon made music that probed the psyche while embracing the world.

Where *Bridge* was grand, his 1972 solo debut *Paul Simon* was modest. On the album cover Simon peers out from beneath the fuzzy hood of a thick winter coat, as if retreating from the exposure of fame. Simon reflects on time and age with "Mother and Child Reunion," and on "Me and Julio Down by the School Yard" he weaves a playful tale atop a Latin shuffle. Simon explored gospel more fully with the No. 2 hit "Love Me Like a Rock" on his 1973 follow-up,

Paul Simon, c. 1978. Courtesy of Photofest.

There Goes Rhymin' Simon. It was the work of a pop veteran reflecting on youth in songs like "Kodachrome" and expressing a hard-won, deeply felt love on "Something So Right."

The 1975 album *Still Crazy After All These Years* sounded both mature and melancholy. With this collection of personal confessions, secular spirituals, and urban folktales Simon evoked the gently depressed mood of the mid-1970s; behind the childlike rhymes of "50 Ways to Leave Your Lover" was the tale of a disillusioned romantic trapped with a woman he cannot bear to leave.

Simon's songs are cinematic in their deft use of specific detail, and in 1980 he turned to film to express his vision. He wrote, directed, and starred in *One Trick Pony*, a glum tale of a wandering musician with a failing marriage and a fading career. The movie got mixed reviews and bombed financially. The accompanying soundtrack laments the loss of personal connection in an age of pop culture and mass media; but it is hard for listeners to fully believe the superstar Simon singing as a lonely nobody.

After the film, Simon's career seemed to lack focus, as evidenced by his 1981 reunion with Garfunkel for a free concert for 400,000 people in New York City's Central Park. A short-lived but successful reunion tour followed, but Simon's next solo album, 1983's *Hearts and Bones*, sold only 400,000 copies (*Still Crazy* sold 2 million), even though it contained Simon's typically strong writing. In 1986 Simon enjoyed a resurgent popularity with *Graceland*, a record influenced by his extensive study of South African music and his collaboration with a ten-member a cappella church group called Ladysmith Black Mambazo. The jubilation and freedom in their music elevated Simon's whimsical, scatting vocals to transcendent heights, and the record was a huge commercial success. It sold 4 million copies and spawned a world tour that included many of the album's African musicians. The 1990 follow-up, *Rhythm of the Saints*, was a softer, dreamier return to African rhythms and less commercially successful. His tour, however, was punctuated by a triumphant return to Central Park, where Simon and his band played a free concert to 750,000 people. Fitting, perhaps, that a songwriter who had described growing old with such poetic accuracy would age so gracefully himself.

TIM BUCKLEY

By 1973, the ubiquity of singer-songwriters made them easy for critics to stereotype as spaced-out hippies or underground figures, offering half-baked solutions to the world's problems or the details of their latest breakup. The eccentric work of Tim Buckley, however, defied easy categorization.

The music Buckley made over his short career—he died of a drug overdose at twenty-eight—was like the shifting moods of a dream. He incorporated folk, rock, funk, and jazz styles beneath poetic lyrics that were more psychological than didactic or confessional. His signature, however, was his voice. With a range of five-and-a-half octaves, Buckley's voice swooped dramatically from high to low, from whispers to howls, conveying an emotional intensity unique in rock music.

Buckley began his career as a singer-songwriter after hooking up with Herb Cohen, who managed both comedian Lenny Bruce and Frank Zappa's group, the Mothers of Invention. The nineteen-year-old Buckley signed with Elektra records and released his debut, *Tim Buckley*, in 1966. He composed seven of the twelve original tunes with high-school friend and poet Larry Beckett, with whom Buckley would collaborate throughout his career.

Elektra greeted the delicate 1967 follow-up, *Happy/Sad*, with great enthusiasm, and the company's promotional money made Buckley a star. Thematically, *Happy/Sad* fit in with the San Francisco hippie scene, but in a 1974 interview Buckley distanced himself from the political pretensions of the counterculture: "I'm not a reporter," he said.

> I go on energy and spirit and not anything metaphysical or religious or anything like that. I feel in fact that sometimes that's dangerous, because it gets in the way of the one-to-one thing with people. You start seeing and feeling that you see an all-knowing force in the universe, when you should be dealing with getting it on with your old lady or neighbor or something . . . mowing the lawn and drinking on the weekend. You get away from the simple things. Trying to solve the problems of the universe is a bunch of nonsense a lot of the time.[10]

After releasing *Happy/Sad* and *Blue Afternoon* in 1969, Buckley embarked on more musically adventurous territory. *Lorca*, released in 1970, contains only five tracks, although no track is shorter than five minutes. Delving into the free-form jazz-rock style that Miles Davis had popularized around that time, Buckley shrugged off the conventions of singer-songwriter folk. Fans startled by this new direction would be more shocked by the even more abstract *Starsailor*, also released in 1970. Fans outright rejected the difficult album, which left Buckley furious at first, then depressed. The record sold poorly, and his live performances of this era often lacked enthusiasm; nearly broke, Buckley turned to alcohol and drugs.

In an attempt to regain his following, Buckley released three rock albums, starting with *Greetings from L.A.* in 1972. The songs were simple, rhythmic, and played by a straightforward rock lineup. *Sefronia* followed in 1973, refining the rock style of *Greetings*, and Buckley's live performances displayed a renewed vigor, as he had apparently learned to moderate his drug use. *Look at the Fool*, in 1974, veered toward funky soul, with critics suggesting it as the most derivative album in Buckley's catalogue. Although Buckley had curbed his heroin addiction, his lower tolerance left him susceptible to an overdose. On June 28, 1975, he consumed a fatal combination of drugs and alcohol.

Beauty and tragedy also trailed Buckley's son Jeff, whose voice soared to the same heights as his father's. His 1994 debut album *Grace* put the younger Buckley on the cusp of superstardom before he died, at the age of thirty, trying to swim in the Mississippi River near Memphis.

CAT STEVENS

Cat Stevens, wrote Bud Scoppa, "is much like his songs: straightforward and completely guileless. He has the beautifully open kind of face you'd wish for in a friend. Upon seeing Cat Stevens, it's nearly impossible to maintain a cynical attitude, regardless of one's attitude toward his music."[11] Critical opinion of Stevens' music ranged from affection to outright hostility; regardless, he was one of the most commercially successful singer-songwriters of the 1970s.

The British-born Stephen Demetre Georgiou published his first song, "I Love My Dog," as Cat Stevens in 1966. He established himself in the folk-singer scene with the 1967 albums *Matthew and Son* and *New Masters*. That year, he was hospitalized with a near-fatal case of tuberculosis. During his recovery, he began experimenting with various world religions, a preoccupation reflected in his 1970 comeback album, *Mona Bone Jakon*. It featured more ambitious folk-pop arrangements and a blossoming spirituality that would eventually draw him away from music altogether.

Stevens entered his most commercially successful period with 1970's *Tea for the Tillerman*, which went to No. 8 in the United States. The 1971 follow-up, *Teaser and the Firecat*, went to No. 2 on the strength of overtly religious songs like "Morning Has Broken," "Moonshadow," and "Peace Train," which have become Stevens' most popular works. The album remains popular—it reached triple platinum status in 2001.

Commercial success continued with *Catch Bull at Four*, in 1972, which went to No. 1. Artistically, however, Stevens was flailing as he dabbled in the bloated styles of progressive rock. The dark *Foreigner*, released in 1973, featured the eighteen-minute "Foreigner Suite" and was decried by critics as thin and vapid. Stevens worked best playing happy songs as sort of a nondenominational, nature-loving guru, as indicated by the success of 1974's *Buddha and the Chocolate Box*, which marked a return to the folk-pop that made him a star.

The quasi-spiritual—some critics would say pretentious—airs of prog-rock seemed to appeal to Stevens, as he released a 1975 concept album called *Numbers*. It presumed to tell the tale of a race of space aliens called the Polygons and featured more of Stevens' vague spirituality. Again, however, he returned to folk-pop with 1977's *Izitso*, his ninth straight gold album—and his last.

By the time Stevens released his last album, *Back to Earth*, in 1978, record labels were ditching singer-songwriters as disco, punk, and new wave leapt to the foreground of American rock. That year, Stevens finally quit dipping his toe in various religious waters and plunged into Islam. He changed his name to Yusuf Islam and renounced popular music. Islam later moderated his views on music, although he sparked outrage in America in 1989 when he seemed to endorse a religious edict that put a price on the head of Salman Rushdie, author of *The Satanic Verses*, a book some Islamic fundamentalists found offensive. Fans of the former Cat Stevens could hardly imagine that the writer of "Peace Train" would support revenge killing, and indeed Islam toned down his rhetoric after the uproar.

JAMES TAYLOR

Understated, personal, and tranquilizing, James Taylor's records offered a soothing antidote to heads ringing with the electrified political anthems of the late 1960s. Singing in a calm, unaffected voice over a simple acoustic guitar, Taylor's music captured a generation's transition from the frustrating tumult of radical politics to a preoccupation with the self. Perhaps Taylor could articulate inner turmoil so clearly because he had done his share of soul-searching before breaking through into pop music.

After dropping out of a New England prep academy at sixteen to start a band with his brother Alex, Taylor checked himself into a psychiatric hospital in Massachusetts. By 1968, the twenty-one-year-old Taylor's addiction to heroin prompted another hospital stint. After a motorcycle crash further sidelined his fledgling music career, he finally released his breakthrough album, *Sweet Baby*

James Taylor performs at New York's Bottom Line club in May 1978. © Neal Preston/Corbis.

James, in 1970. With songs inspired by his stay in a mental institution, especially the hit "Fire and Rain," Taylor spoke to adult baby boomers interested in reflecting on the experiences of youth. Both "Fire and Rain" and *Sweet Baby James* broke into the Top 5 in October 1970, prompting interest in Taylor's previously ignored debut, *James Taylor*, originally released in 1969 on the Beatles' Apple Records label.

In the spring of 1971, Taylor appeared on the cover of a *Time* magazine article that declared him a founder of the "singer-songwriter" trend, marking what the magazine called "the cooling of America."[12] As he toured the United States that year, his 1971 album *Mud Slide Slim and the Blue Horizon* spent the summer in the Top 10 on the strength of "You've Got a Friend," his duet with Carole King. The song won Taylor the 1971 Grammy Award for Best Male Pop Vocal Performance.

After disappearing from the limelight for more than a year, Taylor in fall 1972 married Carly Simon, already a popular singer-songwriter in her own right, and together the two reigned as the hip scene's power couple. Despite the buzz, sales figures fell off for Taylor's next two albums—*One Man Dog* in 1972 and *Walking Man* in 1974—even though they both went gold.

Gorilla in 1975 marked a comeback of sorts for Taylor when he covered Marvin Gaye's 1964 hit "How Sweet It Is (to Be Loved by You)." The song reached the Top 5; the album, infused with soft rock and R&B and themes of sex rather than Taylor's usual despair, broke into the Top 10. *In the Pocket*, released in 1976, was his seventh album, and that year Warner Brothers marked the end of their contract with Taylor by releasing *Greatest Hits*. It has remained a big seller, eventually topping 10 million copies.

Taylor then signed with Columbia Records to release *JT* in 1977. Again, Taylor went into the Top 5 by covering an older song—this time it was the 1959 hit "Handy Man" by Jimmy James. The album sold more than 2 million copies, and the song earned Taylor another Grammy for Best Male Pop Vocal Performance. After *JT*, Taylor took a two-year break from making records to write songs for the Broadway musical *Working*. It was not successful, but two of the songs—"Millworker" and "Brother Trucker"—appeared on Taylor's next album, *Flag*, in 1979. It went double platinum on the strength of yet another cover, the 1963 hit "Up on the Roof" by the Drifters. In the fall Taylor performed at the "No Nukes" concert in Madison Square Garden with Jackson Browne, the Doobie Brothers, and Bruce Springsteen; that performance eventually yielded a triple album and a live concert movie.

In 1980 Taylor toured the United States, beginning a period of heavy traveling, often overseas, that helped him sustain his popularity as tastes shifted and most other singer-songwriters fell from view. He released *Dad Loves His Work* in 1981, his last album for four years, spawning "Her Town Too," a collaboration with J. D. Souther and Waddy Wachtel that hit the Top 10—it was Taylor's most successful original song since "Fire and Rain." In 1983, he and Simon divorced. He continued to make music steeped in the vein of the sensitive singer-songwriter music he had pioneered in the '70s. While critics often applied adjectives like "sensitive" and "sweet" to Taylor in a spirit of derision, his legions of fans considered them compliments.

CARLY SIMON

Like James Taylor, Carly Simon was another popular singer-songwriter in the early 1970s who emerged from an upper-class background and, like Taylor, started her musical career in a family band. Her father, Richard Simon, co-founded the Simon and Schuster publishing company, so Carly and her sister Lucy had little to lose when they embarked on a musical career in the Greenwich Village scene in the mid-1960s.

On her 1971 solo debut *Carly Simon*, she ruminates on relationships and reflects the conflicted feelings of her generation. On "That's the Way I've Always Heard It Should Be," the narrator yearns for the ideal "happily ever after" marriage while fearing the passionless life she believes has trapped her parents. On songs like "Alone" and "Another Door," Simon speaks to the soaring expectations that her generation placed on romantic relationships. Men and women had come to believe the goal of life was a perpetual state of individual happiness, and they expected their romantic partners to provide material, psychological, emotional, and sexual satisfaction. When their relationships inevitably

James Taylor and Carly Simon perform during the filming of Daniel Goldberg's 1980 film, *No Nukes*. © Muse/The Kobol Collection.

failed to meet such high standards, they found themselves, as Simon suggested, closing one door and optimistically opening another.

"That's the Way I've Always Heard It Should Be," co-written with Jacob Brackman, reached the Top 10 and helped propel Simon's follow-up album, 1971's *Anticipation*, to gold status and earned her the 1971 Grammy Award for Best New Artist. Her third album, *No Secrets*, in 1972 adopted a rock sound and included the No. 1 hit "You're So Vain," produced by Richard Perry. It would become her signature song. Mocking the self-absorption of a rich and famous lover, the song's mystique was enhanced by her high-profile marriage that year to fellow singer-songwriter James Taylor.

Her 1974 album *Hotcakes* featured a pregnant Simon on the cover, indicating that the record would chronicle a happier chapter in her life. It became her third consecutive gold album on the strength of her duet with Taylor on "Mockingbird," a remake of a hit by Inez and Charlie Foxx. By this time, new trends in music like disco, punk, and the soft rock of bands like Fleetwood Mac were pushing singer-songwriters off the charts; Simon did her best to adapt.

Simon shed the "mommy" image for the cover of 1975's *Playing Possum*, which showed Simon crouching in black knee-high leather boots and a skimpy outfit, perhaps an attempt to fit with the flamboyant eroticism of the ascendant disco scene. It was another Top 10 album, but the 1976 follow-up *Another Passenger* was a commercial disappointment. Her career was buoyed, however, by "Nobody Does It Better," the theme song for the 1977 James Bond film *The Spy Who Loved Me*. Her 1978 album *Boys in the Trees* went gold with a Top 40 duet with Taylor on "Devoted to You." Confessional pop ballads could hardly be more out of fashion at this time, however, evidenced by the lackluster sales of *Spy* in 1979 and *Come Upstairs* in 1980.

That year, Simon collapsed onstage during a performance, and she would limit her live appearances for the rest of the decade. *Torch* in 1981 consisted of nonrock covers, a prelude to the "easy listening" trend. With her songwriting waning and her marriage to Taylor dissolved, Simon stayed out of the spotlight for most of the 1980s, briefly reviving her career by making songs for movies, including "Coming Around Again" from *Heartburn* and "Let the River Run" from *Working Girl*, a song that would win her another Grammy Award.

JONI MITCHELL

With a clear, ringing voice and ambitiously poetic lyrics, Joni Mitchell epitomized the 1970s singer-songwriter trend. Her first four albums, beginning with *Joni Mitchell* in 1968, *Clouds* in 1969, *Ladies of the Canyon* in 1970, and *Blue* in 1971, were couched in the folk style popular in the mid-1960s. As her career progressed, however, she embraced rock and jazz, creating a sophisticated music that would outlast many of her more bland contemporaries.

Her 1972 album *For the Roses*, with its complex chord structures constructed with piano and woodwind sounds, hinted at her growing affinity for jazz—this at a time when Miles Davis and the Mahavishnu Orchestra were popularizing a new jazz-rock hybrid. She hit her commercial high-point with the follow-up *Court and Spark* in 1974, featuring orchestral arrangements and a full-band, jazz-oriented sound. That album produced her biggest hit, "Help Me," which peaked at No. 7.

She would continue her experiments in the jazz-pop vein for the rest of the 1970s, and her risk-taking produced various re-sults. Her 1974 live album *Miles of Aisles* featured her earlier songs reworked into jazzier tunes by her backing band, the L.A. Express. She experimented with African influences on 1975's *The Hissing of Summer Lawns*, which sounded like a deliberately anticommercial challenge from an artist al-ways suspicious of the rock industry. While it drew some critical scorn at the time, it prefigured the "world music" embrace of

Joni Mitchell. Courtesy of Photofest.

artists like Sting and Paul Simon more than a decade later.

Her 1976 album *Hejira* was a more subdued plunge into confessionalism. On songs like "Coyote" and "Song for Sharon," Mitchell reflected on age, mar-riage, fame, and death over stripped-down tracks often consisting of just guitar, drums, and the bass playing of jazz-rocker Jaco Pastorius. She continued on an experimental path with 1977's *Don Juan's Reckless Daughter*, on which she ex-perimented with Latin rhythms, but by then her lyrics seemed to lack the in-spiration of her earlier poetic efforts, and even die-hard fans started to question her artistic direction. Her collaboration with jazz great Charles Mingus for the 1979 album *Mingus* testified to the aimlessness of much late '70s jazz-fusion, as does Pat Metheny's noodling solos on 1980's *Shadows and Light*.

In the 1980s, Mitchell remained an artistic voice, with her 1985 album *Dog Eat Dog* attacking right-wing politics. Her 1988 album *Chalk Mark in a Rain-storm* criticized the greed of an era where it seemed that Mitchell's generation had either given up their search for "meaning" or perhaps tried to find it in an unabashedly material culture.

Billy Joel, 1978. Courtesy of Photofest.

BILLY JOEL

Billy Joel, one of the most commercially successful singer-songwriters of the 1970s and 1980s, incongruously began his career playing in a heavy-metal duo called Atilla. He released his solo debut *Cold Spring Harbor* in 1971, but he did not become a star until he released *Piano Man* on Columbia Records in 1973. The title track reflected Joel's experience playing piano-bar gigs in Los Angeles, and it established Joel as a singer-songwriter with a gift for spinning sentimental stories of big-city characters.

Cultivating the image of a scruffy balladeer, Joel released *Streetlife Serenade* in 1974, and he sold out concerts at Carnegie Hall and Lincoln Center in New York City on the strength of the album's single "The Entertainer," which celebrated the life of an itinerant musician and lamented the comodification of his art. Joel moved back to New York City in 1975, at a time when Bruce Springsteen was also making it big with his poetic celebrations of blue-collar life.

Sticking with his urban themes, that year Joel recorded *Turnstiles*, featuring the hit "New York State of Mind," and released the album in 1976. His 1977 follow-up, *The Stranger*, would be the biggest commercial success of his career, hitting No. 2 and eventually selling more than 10 million copies. It produced three singles that made the Hot 100 chart—"Only the Good Die Young," "Movin' Out (Anthony's Song)," and "Just the Way You Are." The 1978 follow-up, *52nd Street*, would become Joel's first No. 1 album. Between 1978 and 1981, Joel would earn five Grammy Awards, including a Best Rock Vocal Performance, Male for his 1980 album *Glass Houses*—his second straight No. 1 album. It also spawned his first No. 1 single, "It's Still Rock and Roll to Me."

Joel's knack for literary hit-making continued in the 1980s. *The Nylon Curtain* in 1982 chronicled the strife of blue-collar workers in Allentown, Pennsylvania, and Vietnam veterans. "Uptown Girl," from his 1983 album *An Innocent Man*, chronicled what he thought was his unlikely marriage to supermodel Christie Brinkley. In recent years, Joel has dabbled in classical compositions and film scores, but the enduring popularity of his storytelling pop is evidenced by the fact that in 1999 his total worldwide record sales topped 100 million, and he was inducted into the Rock and Roll Hall of Fame.

JOAN BAEZ

Joan Baez is usually remembered as the godmother of interpretive folk music. Although she never abandoned socially conscious music or activist causes, she started to write her own songs and express more commercial ambition in the late '60s and early '70s.

Baez turned toward pop in earnest when she switched from Vanguard Records to A&R Records to release *Come from the Shadows* in 1972. *Where Are You Now, My Son?* in 1973 included the original song "A Young Gypsy," which some have called one of her best; side two consists of Baez's musical travelogue of her trip to Hanoi in 1972, including the sounds of American bombs exploding in the city.

She hit her commercial zenith with *Diamonds & Rust* in 1975. "If I'd done another political album at this point, I'd have been bankrupt. I had no money left," Baez told *Let It Rock* in 1975. "So I went into the record company and said, 'Okay fellas—how do you make one of those albums that sells? If it feels comfortable to me, I'll do it.' . . . Well it wasn't QUITE as crass as that."[13] Baez did a series of promotional radio and television interviews to support the record, and they paid off as the album went gold. Critics, however, accused Baez of abandoning political activism.

It was a charge she could understand, since she famously blamed Bob Dylan for abandoning her when he stopped writing political anthems in the late 1960s. While she spent the mid-'70s writing books on her experiences in Hanoi and with Amnesty International, even Baez followed the general trend of retreating from politics toward more personal matters—in this case, her son. "Believe me, I want to go march with all my heart," said Baez. "But, sadly, the world will still be in this state when I'm ninety years old and right now my priority is to spend time with Gabriel."[14]

The songs on *Gulf Winds* in 1976 were self-written—reportedly during her stint on Dylan's Rolling Thunder Revue tour—although critics suggest the album is overwritten. It was her last album with A&R, and it marked a period of decline for Baez as rock fashion passed her by. She released *Blowin' Away* in 1977 on CBS' Portrait Records, but left the label after *Honest Lullaby* in 1979. Her 1980 live album *European Tour* was not even released in the United States. It would be another seven years before she released another record in America, although in 1993 she enjoyed a resurgence when Vanguard released a triple album retrospective, titled *Rare, Live & Classic*.

VAN MORRISON

In the mid-'70s, many a singer-songwriter made "spiritual" songs, full of words like "truth" and "soul." The majority of these tunes could more accurately be described as songs *about* spirituality. The best songs by Van Morrison, by contrast, exude a mystical quality of which it has been said: "He is not singing it, it is singing him."[15]

Morrison had been summarily forgotten by the rock masses after his first Top 10 hit, 1967's "Brown Eyed Girl," fell off the charts. With a voice that channeled Ray Charles, a gift for writing emotional music, and a pudgy, un-rockstar appearance, it was perhaps inevitable that Morrison would become a favorite among rock critics. It happened after he released the brooding *Astral Weeks* in 1968, and he achieved moderate fame with the follow-up *Moondance* in 1970.

The early '70s was a time of great creative outpouring from Morrison. He was married, living in California, and writing joyful songs of domestic bliss covered on 1970's *His Band and the Street Choir*—which yielded his biggest hit, "Domino," which went to No. 9. He went on to release *Tupelo Honey* in 1971, *Saint Dominic's Preview* in 1972, *Hard Nose the Highway* in 1973, and a live album, 1974's *It's Too Late to Stop Now*, which showcased his transcendent performances with the Caledonia Soul Orchestra.

The good times did not last for Morrison, however, as 1973 saw the breakup of both his group and his marriage. He left California and returned to his native Belfast, Northern Ireland, to chronicle his emotional tumult in 1974's *Veedon Fleece*. It would be Morrison's last record for three years before another creative burst that began with the appropriately named *A Period of Transition* in 1977. The next year he released *Wavelength* and went on his first tour in five years. But Morrison, who had apparently always been plagued by stage fright, turned in uneven performances and even left the stage in the middle of a set in 1979. Beginning with *Into the Music* in 1979, Morrison produced a string of records into the '80s on which the notoriously erratic artist meditated on themes of rebirth and healing. In 1990, Mercury released *The Best of Van Morrison*; it would be his best-selling album, earning him a new generation of fans and cementing his place as one of rock and roll's great artists.

BRUCE SPRINGSTEEN

In a 1973 article titled "Was Bob Dylan the Previous Bruce Springsteen?" Steve Turner wrote that "the surest way of killing a man these days is to liken him to the late Bob."[16] Although reports of Dylan's "death" proved to be premature (1975's *Blood on the Tracks* is a masterpiece), critics and record executives at the time were on the lookout for a figure who would express the hopes and fears of the '70s the way Dylan had done in the 1960s. The "next Dylan" label had been applied to artists like Kris Kristofferson, John Prine, and Loudon Wainwright III, but none fulfilled the promise. So when *Rolling Stone* editor Jon Landau wrote in 1974 that "I saw rock and roll's future and its name is Bruce Springsteen,"[17] the stage was set for either a revolution or a dramatic flameout.

The comparisons were obvious. Springsteen had the same hungry, rugged image, the same tendency to cram songs with long strings of metaphorical lyrics. Like Dylan, Springsteen transformed hard-luck stories from the social underbelly into epic allegories. In 1973, the twenty-three-year-old Springsteen was signed to Columbia Records by John Hammond, who had also signed a young Dylan a decade before.

On his first two albums that year, *Greetings from Asbury Park, N.J.* and *The Wild, the Innocent & the E Street Shuffle*, Springsteen set his tales in the dead-end working-class environs of his hometown. He built a cult following touring the East Coast with his E Street Band, and amidst a feverish buzz he released *Born to Run* in 1975. It was his first great album and the first suggestion that he might actually live up to all the Dylan comparisons. Songs like "Backstreets" and "Thunder Road" were full of poetic lyrics capturing the wild restlessness and spiritual yearning of backstreet characters, who were all far removed from the glitz and glam that dominated mid-'70s rock.

Springsteen had already been nicknamed "The Boss," and his performances with the E Street Band—Clarence Clemons on saxophone, Steve Van Zandt on guitar, Roy Bittan on piano, Danny Federici on organ, Garry Tallent on bass, and Max Weinberg on drums—were already extending to three hours and becoming legendary for their intensity. "What a band," wrote Bud Scoppa after seeing them perform at the Roxy in Los Angeles in 1975. "Even without the boss they'd be one of the best in the business. With him they're practically un-rivalled. You don't think of words like 'resonance' or 'majesty' when they happen in front of you—you think, 'Man, this is fun, and I'm really happy, and I don't ever want it to end.'"[18]

Even though Springsteen appeared on the covers of both *Time* and *Newsweek* in October 1975, his ascendancy to superstardom would not be smooth, as the hype prompted an expected backlash. Furthermore, Springsteen got mired in a legal dispute. He had become friends with Landau, who quit his job at *Rolling Stone* to help produce *Born to Run*, and Springsteen wanted him to produce his next album. Springsteen's manager, Mike Appel, refused, and the two sued each other. In 1976, a judge's ruling prohibited Springsteen from working with Landau.

After a 1977 settlement, Springsteen and Landau were finally free to collaborate on the 1978 album *Darkness on the Edge of Town*. The record expressed "the walled-up sensation that pounds at your gut, the daytime monotony that leads to nighttime explosion,"[19] but, as some critics noted, the legal tension and long studio sessions might have suppressed the sense of humor that graced *Born to Run*. Springsteen seemed to be getting more serious. Songs like "Factory" showed a new affinity with the working men that had been typecast as villains by the adolescent counterculture. In 1979 Springsteen took a tentative step further into the political fray when he headlined two shows to benefit Musicians United for Safe Energy (MUSE), which raised money for antinuclear groups following the Three Mile Island accident. The concerts included Jackson Browne, James Taylor, Carly Simon, and the Doobie Brothers, but Springsteen was the only performer who refused to make public statements against nuclear power, and he joined the bill only on the condition that no money would go to political candidates.

The River in 1980 was Springsteen's first No. 1 album, on which he continued to deepen his political content while reveling in the joyful simplicity of good-time rockers like "Crush on You" and "I'm a Rocker." With this record he truly attained national stardom, but he would ascend even higher. With the introspective *Nebraska* in 1982 and the 1984 epic *Born in the U.S.A.*, Springsteen attained the iconic Dylanesque status that had always seemed to be his destiny.

NOTES

1. Pollock 1993, 146.
2. Sounes 2001, 275.
3. Ibid., 303.
4. Ibid., 314.
5. Trager 2004, 589.
6. Sounes 2001, 331.
7. Trager 2004, 541.
8. DeCurtis et al. 1992, 327.
9. Ibid., 328.
10. Childs, *ZigZag*, October 1974.
11. Bud Scoppa, *Crawdaddy!*, June 1971.
12. DeCurtis et al. 1992, 480.
13. Valentine, *Let It Rock*, December 1975.
14. Ibid.
15. DeCurtis et al. 1992, 446.
16. Steve Turner, *NME*, October 1973.
17. DeCurtis et al. 1992, 620.
18. Bud Scoppa, *Phonograph Record*, November 1975.
19. Cohen, *Creem*, September 1978.

PUNK ROCK: THE ART OF NOISE

Rob Patterson

By its very name, punk rock suggests both musical simplicity and an attitude to go with it. An emphasis on rock and roll basics was at the core of the punk movement that emerged in the mid-1970s, stressing short, concise, three- or four-chord songs played with speed and aggressiveness. Equally integral was a stance and manner that reflected two of the meanings of the word "punk": a rebelliousness and snottily delinquent attitude—witnessed in the *noms de guerre* of Sex Pistols Johnny Rotten and Sid Vicious—as well as a musical naiveté that manifested itself in punk rock's anyone-can-do-it ethos. As such, the movement was a fierce rejection of the musical proficiency and complexity and the stylistic breadth found in the prevailing trends, as well as the trappings associated with mainstream rock and roll at the time.

At its purest, punk music is defined by a popular slogan of the time: "loud, fast rules." The forcefully played and sung songs of the Ramones, the Sex Pistols, and the early Clash, with their speedy tempos and rapid-fire chording, epitomize the early punk musical ethos. Punk lyrics frequently expressed anger, frustration, alienation, political outrage, nihilism, and ennui. Punk music and its surrounding subculture also spawned an accompanying antifashion movement that included everything from ripped T-shirts, jeans, and short-cropped hair to more outrageous looks that included bondage gear, safety pin piercings, and sometimes outrageous hairdos.

Punk was rock music boiled back down to its basics and played with a confrontational attitude that asserted that this is what true rock and roll should be. But the punk movement also included groups with broader musical and lyrical approaches, and some of those who helped define the style—like the Clash—evolved into more sophisticated and musically diverse acts.

Punk and new wave music (see Chapter 7, "A New Wave of Rock") arose almost concurrently even though new wave is sometimes referred to as "post-punk." Some acts that were seminal artists in the punk movement, especially such Americans as Television and Patti Smith, had new-wave elements in their music from the beginning. Yet their primacy in the development and rise of the punk movement predicates that they be discussed in this chapter. Other bands that were also part of the early punk-rock scene, such as New Yorkers like Talking Heads and Blondie or English acts like the Pretenders and the Police, are for the purposes of this history identified as new wave due to such factors as the pop elements, ethnic styles, and art-music influences found in their sounds.

The delineations between punk and new wave and categorizations that are made here may seem almost arbitrary or appear to be a matter of splitting rather thin hairs. At the time both genres emerged it was all considered "new music," and the terms "punk" and "new wave" were often used interchangeably. But punk provided the initial rallying cry as well as the first powerful kicks at the door of the popular music scene—punk was the spark that fired a paradigm shift in popular music that continued through the college rock of the 1980s into the alternative and modern rock at the end of the twentieth century.

Punk and new wave were both reactions to the myriad musical, performance, image, and even lifestyle excesses of the prevailing rock styles of the time, at least in the viewpoint of the artists making this new music as well as the initial fans it attracted. The movement eschewed a wide range of popular musical styles and approaches that had become popular as the 1960s flowed into the next decade: the trippy extended jams and good-time hippie vibes of the Grateful Dead; the self-reflection and romanticism of the early singer-songwriters and soft-rock acts; the musical ambitiousness and intricacy of progressive rock; and the bombast, macho posturing, and musical grandstanding of hard rock, as punk rockers viewed it all. Punk also rejected the long, stylish hair and fancy and flashy garb of many of the big-time rockers of the early to mid-'70s, as well as such accoutrements as groupies and chauffeured limousines. Punk and early new wave were also a reaction to the growth of live rock concerts into arenas and stadiums, taking rock and roll back into clubs and small theaters. The rise of disco music in the early 1970s as a soundtrack for a nightlife focused on pleasure and fashion was a final musical development that helped breed punk rock as an angry retort to the state of contemporary music.

Ultimately, punk rockers felt that rock and roll had moved away from its core musical styles and values and that its performers had been seduced by its growth as an industry and subsequent success into making music that no longer reflected the basic lives and concerns of teenagers and young adults. The original rock and roll of the 1950s was teenaged music (even if made by adults such as Bill Haley) that expressed the feelings and concerns of youth. And as such, much of it was suffused in its lyrics with the confusion, alienation, discomfort, and downright rebellion—all emotional elements of adolescence and early youth. These traits could still be heard in the rock and roll revival that followed the British invasion of the early to mid-1960s, and the American garage rock of that era also harkened back to such musical and lyrical themes.

But by the early 1970s—from the perspective that would spawn the new music of the mid-decade—the music and lyrics as well as artist images and lifestyles within rock and roll had grown bloated, indulgent, pretentious, hedonistic, and ultimately divorced from the basics of the music. Rock and roll, which in its early days had been a form of terse economy and musical minimalism, had become grander and more complex. And in content and context—from the simmering sexuality of an act like Led Zeppelin to the fantastical tales spun by Yes to the musical sweetness of Crosby, Stills & Nash—much of rock music had forsaken the concerns of common youths as well as largely abandoned the impact of simple, concise songs fashioned from a few basic chords and played with fervor and drive to deliver basic (if sometimes also still eloquent and ingenious) messages.

OLD SOUNDS BEGET NEW MUSIC

A major irony of the mid-1970s new music movement was that it was so tied to and influenced by older antecedents. "One of the punk things was going to the past to pick the right influences out," explains John Holmstrom, a founder of New York's influential *Punk* magazine.[1]

The punk-rock rebel stance and attitude can be traced as far back as country upstart Hank Williams. The music and the look of such 1950s rock and roll pioneers as Elvis Presley (prior to joining the army) and rockabilly legends Eddie Cochran and Gene Vincent were iconic predecessors of punk rock. (To wit, the cover of the Clash's *London Calling* album in 1979 copied the graphic design of an early Presley record sleeve.) The basic and economical three-or-so-chord songs with driving rhythms of 1950s rock and roll formed the model for the basic punk-rock style, as did its common themes of teenage angst and rebellion.

A number of the British invasion bands that followed in the wake of the Beatles also influenced and inspired the artists who created punk rock with both their music and attitude: the early Rolling Stones and Who, the Animals, the Kinks, and the Yardbirds. At about the same time, American rockers like the Bobby Fuller Four (whose 1966 hit "I Fought the Law" became a signature song for the Clash), ? and the Mysterians, the Seeds, the Standells, and a slew of Stateside garage-rock bands and one-hit wonders also created a style that would later be described as punk rock. Again, basic and driving guitar-based rock and roll and outsider lyrical perspectives helped provide the model for punk rock.

Later 1960s influences on punk include the dark and coarse sound and decadent subject matter of the Velvet Underground as well as the raw and raucous sounds of MC5 and the Stooges. The brash British glam rock of David Bowie, T-Rex, and Mott the Hoople and the arty decadence of Roxy Music were historically closer touchstones for many of the musicians that created punk rock, especially in England, along with the noisy and dissonant creations of avant-garde deconstructionists like Can. The most immediate predecessors of punk were the New York Dolls, whose shambling music and androgynous image in the early 1970s could be considered the first rumblings of punk, and, at the same time, the simple, droll, and almost naïflike songs of Boston's Jonathan Richman and his band the Modern Lovers.

The term "punk rock" first entered the rock lexicon in an article written by critic Dave Marsh in the April 1971 issue of *Creem* magazine, where he coined it to describe the music of ? & the Mysterians. The following year, Elektra Records released *Nuggets*, a twenty-seven-act compilation of songs by early psychedelic and garage-rock bands. The set was compiled by music journalist Lenny Kaye—later guitarist with the Patti Smith Group, one of the New York punk scene's founding acts—who applied the punk-rock tag to the music within the collection in his liner notes. Kaye's description of that music also fits the punk rock that followed: "Most of these groups . . . were young [and] decidedly unprofessional. . . . [T]hey exemplified the berserk pleasure that comes with being on-stage outrageous, the relentless middle-finger drive and determination offered only by rock and roll at its finest."[2]

THE SOCIAL AND CULTURAL CONTEXTS OF PUNK

An undercurrent of dissatisfaction with the current state of rock and roll music in the early 1970s was not the sole factor that led to the rise of punk rock. As indicated by the prevalence of social and political observations, commentary, and sloganeering in the music, punk also had its cultural origins.

The idealism and social movements of the 1960s had already played out into such results as the end of American involvement in Vietnam in 1973 and the spread of 1960s countercultural notions and fashions into the mainstream of American life, especially among the nation's youth. At the same time, President Richard Nixon had instituted détente with the Soviet Union and opened relations with communist China, mitigating the dangers of the Cold War. But as international conflicts and dangers faded, the struggles of the youth movement with the U.S. government, followed by the Watergate scandal, had given rise to a new atmosphere of cynicism regarding traditional American values and assumptions. By the early 1970s, economic stagnation had set in with sustained inflation and rising unemployment, exacerbated by the Arab oil embargo that followed the 1973 Yom Kippur War in the Middle East.[3]

The long Vietnam War had ended, but the hopeful dreams of the 1960s had dissipated. For some Americans, escapism was a response to this malaise, something for which mainstream rock and roll provided an ideal soundtrack. But an undercurrent of dissatisfaction also simmered within this atmosphere, and punk rock caught its flame from this climate of pessimism and a lack of new social ideals and hopes like those that had characterized the previous decade. In a parallel progression, while rock and roll in the 1950s and 1960s had been a major force at the forefront of social and political change, by the early 1970s it had become much like just another consumer product.

In England, the economy had been on the decline through the 1960s and was crippled even further by frequent nationwide trade strikes in the early '70s. The country's economy was suffering its worst downturn since the years following World War II, and unemployment reached record-high levels by the mid-1970s.[4] This bleak outlook was succinctly expressed by the Sex Pistols when the group declared that there was "no future" in their antimonarchist rant "God Save the Queen." While conditions in America were certainly better, both nations seemed in a state of listlessness, if not decline.

It is no surprise that within this atmosphere the punk-rock movement first came into being in New York City and London, both of which were their nation's major urban cultural centers. In both cities, punk rock was the latest wrinkle in a long line of bohemianism and as such quickly attracted like-minded writers, visual artists, and filmmakers. It was a music that arose from the urban underground and was created to some degree by rebels, outsiders, and malcontents, as well as musicians and fans-turned-musicians frustrated by or alienated from the rock and roll mainstream that had become big business. A major philosophy within the punk ethos was that anyone could be a musician and start a band. High unemployment and relatively cheap housing in the depressed areas of New York and London facilitated the free time needed to start bands and play early gigs for little or no money. Similarly, the pessimism bred by bleak economic conditions found expression in punk music.

As punk music began to take hold in those cities and elsewhere, a subculture arose around it. Sometimes crude and cheaply published "fanzines" like *Punk* in New York and *Sniffin' Glue* in London started up to document and tout this new music, paralleling the "do it yourself" (DIY) ethos of the bands. The music also attracted the attention of New York's alternative newsweeklies, the *Village Voice* and *Soho Weekly News*, as well as the voracious editorial maws of England's four national weekly music papers, *Melody Maker*, *New Musical Express*, *Sounds*, and *Record Mirror*. New nightclubs and venues for these budding acts to play began to proliferate. As this underground movement began getting attention, it quickly spread to other major cities such as, notably, Los Angeles and San Francisco in America and Manchester and Liverpool in the United Kingdom.

Since major record labels were initially reluctant about signing this new music, artists began releasing their own seven-inch vinyl singles, and entrepreneurs started independent labels like Stiff Records in London and Slash and SST in Los Angeles to record and promote the burgeoning movement. In America, the open formats of college radio stations helped expose punk to young listeners. And along with punk grew a community of associated artists and designers to create record sleeves and posters and photographers and film-makers to visually document the scene. The rock press, which had grown out of the underground in the early 1970s and proliferated, provided a major forum for punk music to gain a good deal of its initial exposure.

The result was a punk subculture with its own look, nightclubs, publications, and everything from slang to dance styles to social mores. It also spawned a punk style that was largely a rummage sale of antifashion garb from the most basic and cheapest to outrageous and shocking, all of it announcing a "don't give a damn" posture. Hairstyles ran the gamut from cropped and chopped to wildly colored and cut, exemplified by the tall "Mohawk" Indian brush cut with shaved sides. Early punk shows were often confrontational and anarchic, with audiences spitting on the performers—an expression of antistardom sentiment especially prevalent in England, where it was called "gobbing"—and fans bouncing and jumping in place to the music in a dance of sorts known as the "pogo," named for the pogo stick. By the early 1980s, punk also spawned slam dancing (in which audience members slammed against one another) and stage diving (where fans climbed onto the stage and dove back into the crowd). Conversely, many performers confronted their audiences with everything from exhortations to insults to sulking indifference. Punk was a primal set of attitudes and rituals that were driven by negativity, outrage, and defiance.

The archetypal punk attitude was to be rebels with or without a cause. It was a throwback to earlier eras of rock as rebellion, and punk also rebelled against how rock had become an integral part of the larger culture. One definition of the word "punk" is delinquent, and punk music largely embraced that stance in a fashion similar to how early rock and roll was seen by outsiders and derided as a cause of juvenile delinquency. To be a punk was to emphatically not give a damn, even if that seems like a contradiction in terms, especially since punk rock was passionately oppositional. It was rock 'n' roll and its surrounding culture at its most contrary and sometimes antisocial. Given the attitude, it is no surprise that punk culture had a drug subculture that embraced heavy drinking and hard drugs, especially heroin (which a large number of punk musicians were or became addicted to and some died from), which ran counter to the prevalence of cocaine in both the mainstream rock and disco circles. Where the underground rock of the 1960s had been the light side of liberation and rebellion, punk was the darker flipside.

A REVOLUTION FROM A RETURN TO SIMPLICITY

The punk musical ethos in its primal state eschewed, if not rejected, the notions of musicianship and instrumental proficiency that were valued in mainstream rock by the early 1970s. The core of the punk sound was a basic 4/4 rhythm that was, in its most distilled form, as removed from rock and roll's blues and country antecedents as rock could be. Punk vocals were often shouting and sneering or sometimes droll and dispassionate—and in many cases far less harmonic than rock and roll singing had been in the past. The truest punk bands were small and simple combos that played only the fundamental chords and rhythms and little more, and soloing was kept to terse minimums. Speed and fast-paced tempos were the primary approach, and most of the songs were short and structurally simple. It was rock 'n' roll stripped down to its very basic components—guitars, bass, drums, sometimes keyboards, and singers—and such essential elements as a few chords, verses, and a chorus, delivered with high energy and fervent commitment. And from this simplicity and zeal came music of incredible raw power, to borrow a phrase from an album title by punk touchstones the Stooges.

The lyrics of punk songs matched the music with frequently terse expressions of angry and negative feelings and observations. American punk acts tended more to write songs with personal and social lyrical themes, while political expressions were more common with the British acts. And the mode of expression was often declamations, declarations, accusations, and rants. Song titles like "Pretty Vacant" and "Anarchy in the U.K." by the Sex Pistols, "I'm So Bored with the U.S.A." and "Hate and War" by the Clash, and "Blitzkrieg Bop" and "Now I Wanna Sniff Some Glue" by the Ramones on their debut albums convey a sense of the subject matter of the first punk bands. Punk songs were broadsides that were intended to arouse, shock, and outrage listeners.

In just about every way, punk was a countercurrent to most everything that mainstream rock and roll represented in the early years of the 1970s. It was also a pendular swing back to musical basics similar to the one that occurred some ten years earlier with the British invasion, which had come about a decade or so after the birth of rock and roll. Although a number of the major bands that punk scorned were initially derided by these snotty new acts, the movement's impact was such that, by later in the decade, superstar acts like the Rolling Stones and the Who would acknowledge punk in their music. Most of the more enduring bands that created this new (if also in some ways very retrogressive) music eventually broadened their styles, made music that was more accomplished and complex, added ethnic styles and greater rhythmic diversity, and became more sophisticated in their lyrical approaches and melodies. Like early rock and roll and some of the rock music movements that came later, it was an initially underground and antiestablishment phenomenon from which eventually emerged artists that sold millions of records and became part of the mainstream. Ultimately, punk music succeeded in its implicit goal of changing the state of music, though not quite in the ways the movement intended or expected.

NEW YORK PUNK

Punk rock first became a local scene and then a musical force in New York City. And it was a ripe locale for such a movement to take birth, as epitomized by the *New York Daily News* headline of October 30, 1975: "Ford to City: Drop Dead."[5] New York was in a fiscal crisis and in danger of going bankrupt, and President Gerald Ford had rejected the city's appeal for federal help. The grim economic outlook combined with the city's long tradition as a bohemian haven to foster an outsider underground rock scene in Lower Manhattan.

At the time punk began brewing, New York had a dearth of music clubs. Max's Kansas City, where the Velvet Underground and New York Dolls had played, closed in 1974 and reopened under new management the following year. The Mercer Arts Center, which was home base for the Dolls, also closed the following year. But the opening of CBGB on the Bowery in late 1973 eventually led to the club being ground zero for the punk movement, even though the club's name stood for the styles of music owner Hilly Kristal initially booked: country, blues, and bluegrass.

Although New York was the birthplace of punk, the scene that developed there was far more musically variegated than the English punk movement that arose soon after. As *Punk* magazine founder John Holmstrom notes, in 1976: "there were only two authentic punk rock bands in New York at the time (The Ramones and The Dictators) and most of the 'kids' who hung out at CBGBs were just an assortment of college kids, hippies, ex-glam rockers and weirdos. Not a single 'punk' among them."[6] Yet the new music created in New York sparked the rise of both punk and new wave and established the city as a new rock center for decades to follow.

Television

The music made by Television is more often typed as new wave than punk, although their jagged chord structures, angular rhythms, and the sinuous and sometimes modal guitar lines of Tom Verlaine and Richard Lloyd placed the band in a class all its own. But they played a number of fundamental roles in the development of punk, and by the time the group broke up in 1978, the new wave movement was only beginning to rival punk in widespread public attention.

The group originated in New York City in the early 1970s as the Neon Boys, a short-lived trio composed of guitarist and singer Verlaine, bassist Richard Hell, and drummer Billy Ficca that released two independent singles but never performed live. At the end of 1973, they morphed into Television with Lloyd joining on guitar. After debuting in early March of '74 at the Townhouse Theatre, Verlaine persuaded Hilly Kristal, the owner of CBGB, to let them play there on a Sunday night, March 31.[7] The booking opened the door for the Ramones and then the Patti Smith Group to also play the club and led to CBGB becoming the live performance epicenter for punk rock in New York.

Hell left the band in April of 1975 to join the Heartbreakers and later lead the Voidoids and was replaced by Fred Smith. Later that year, the group released a 45 on tiny Ork Records, "Little Johnny Jewel (Parts One and Two)," one of the first and most influential singles from the New York scene. Although the group had recorded a demo for Island Records produced by Brian Eno (ex-Roxy Music) when Hell was still in the band, they did not release an album until *Marquee Moon* in February 1977. It was greeted with such rapturous acclaim as "[t]he most powerful and passionate rock to come out of anywhere in a dog's age" in New York's *Village Voice* and "[a]n obvious, unashamed classic" by *Sounds* in the United Kingdom, which also later named it 1977's album of the year.[8] In April 1978, Television released the album *Adventure* and broke up later that year.

Although Television never achieved significant chart or sales success, their musical impact was considerable. The foursome were hailed for making "some of the most astounding music of our time" by *Melody Maker* in the United Kingdom,[9] where their influence, especially after a sold-out May 1977 tour, echoed through the sound of many guitar-based post-punk bands that followed.

Among the original acts to break out from the early CBGB scene, Television were widely admired by both their peers and fans as the scene's most musically visionary and dynamic act. Although garage-band rock may have been the band's musical launching pad, Television suggested and presaged what the back-to-basics revolution of punk could grow into in their brief, five-year run.

Patti Smith

Poet, singer, songwriter, and provocateur Patti Smith was both a seminal and iconic figure in the punk-rock movement. She was the first artist from the New York punk scene to release an independent single and major-label album and tied punk to New York's literary and artistic undergrounds as well as the bohemian tradition. She also all but pioneered a new imagery for female rockers that embraced androgyny and eschewed glamour. Smith helped punk gain credibility when she earned nods of approval from Bob Dylan and Bruce Springsteen. And she was instrumental in helping punk music break into the mainstream when she scored a Top 20 hit with "Because

Patti Smith performs at the Roxy in Hollywood, 1976. Courtesy of Photofest.

the Night," co-written with Bruce Springsteen. The music she created demonstrated the breadth punk could achieve, ranging from raucous and almost amateurish garage rock to avant-garde experimentalism, all of it laced with her poetic lyrics.

Born on December 31, 1946, in Chicago, Smith came of age in a working-class environment in southern New Jersey, a social outcast whose dreams of a bohemian life were fed by French symbolist poets, Bob Dylan, and the Rolling Stones. She dropped out of community college and then worked a factory job before moving to New York City in 1967. She befriended photographer Robert Mapplethorpe, playwright Sam Shepard—with whom she co-wrote the play *Cowboy Mouth*—and, later, music critic Lenny Kaye, compiler of the *Nuggets* collection.

On February 10, 1971, Kaye accompanied Smith to a poetry reading at St. Mark's Church in downtown Manhattan. In the years that followed she published her first book of poetry, wrote for rock magazines, read her poetry as an opener for the New York Dolls at the Mercer Arts Center in Greenwich Village, and continued to perform with Kaye on occasion. Keyboard player Richard "DNV" Sohl joined them in the spring of 1974, and the group began performing at venues like CBGB and Max's Kansas City. They also recorded a single (with Television's Tom Verlaine on guitar) released on Smith's own Mer Records label—a cover of the rock classic "Hey Joe" backed with her own rock poetry composition "Piss Factory," inspired by her time on the factory assembly line.

After guitarist Ivan Kral joined the group in 1975, they played a seven-week residency at CBGB that resulted in Smith being signed by Arista Records. With drummer Jay Dee Daugherty on board, she recorded *Horses* with producer John Cale from the Velvet Underground. With a sexually ambiguous cover portrait of Smith by Mapplethorpe, it was released in November of that year and went on to crack the Top 50 of the *Billboard* album charts, signaling that the burgeoning punk-music movement in the downtown New York clubs had commercial potential. On it, Smith reworked Van Morrison's hit with Them, "Gloria,"

 PUNK CREATES NEW MUSICAL ROLES FOR WOMEN

Although punk rock's aggression and occasional violence reflect a strong testosterone content in the music, the punk movement also helped liberate women musicians from certain accepted limitations prior to its emergence in the 1970s. Before then, women in rock were generally—with a few exceptions like the hard-rock band Heart—lead singers or singer-songwriters whose image, styles, and messages were highly feminine and traditional.

Patti Smith's androgyny and rock-star posture suggested that women could play the rock game on the same terms as men. The Los Angeles all-woman band the Runaways, even though they were created by male rock svengali Kim Fowley, proved that women could also play guitars, bass, and drums and rock with the same sort of approach that men had been taking for years. On leaving the Runaways, guitarist, singer, and songwriter Joan Jett achieved long-term success with a style that rocked as hard as any male band. The guitar playing of Ivy Rorschach of the Cramps demonstrated how a woman could play wild roots-rock riffs with as much imagination and abandon as men, while into a punk-rock rave-up; experimented with reggae rhythms on "Redondo Beach"; mixed extemporaneous poetry and rock and roll improvisation on "Birdland"; and fused her tale of homosexual rape, "Horses," with the soul dance classic "Land of a Thousand Dances." All told, the record presented rock and roll as a redemptive force with a subtext declaring that anyone can pick up an instrument and be a rocker.

Smith stayed true to her basic rock and roll roots while displaying growing mastery of record making on *Radio Ethiopia* in 1976 and two years later with *Easter*, which reached No. 20 on the album charts after its single "Because the Night" hit No. 13 on the radio charts. After releasing *Wave* in 1979, which also cracked the Top 20, she married Fred "Sonic" Smith from MC5 (not to be confused with Television bassist Fred Smith), one of her rock and roll heroes, and retreated from recording and touring to give birth to and raise their two children. During that time she released an album made with Smith, *Dream of Life*, in 1988. After her husband's death in 1994, she returned to an active recording and touring career, continuing to create rock and roll that mixed rebellion and redemption and was imbued with personal and artistic maturity.

 PUNK CREATES NEW MUSICAL ROLES FOR WOMEN *(continued)*

Tina Weymouth of Talking Heads showed that a girl could hold down the bass guitar bottom end as handily as any man.

In England, Siouxsie Sioux (née Susan Dallion) was one of the original group of Sex Pistols fans known as the Bromley Contingent who was inspired by the anyone-can-do-it ethos of punk to form the Banshees (whose original drummer was Sid Vicious). With her wild makeup and hairstyles and sharp vocal attack, Sioux turned traditional female rock imagery inside out. Similarly, punk fans Marion Elliot and Susan Whitby became Poly Styrene and Lora Logic and started X-ray Spex. Though short-lived, the group's classic single "Oh Bondage, Up Yours" announced that sexually outrageous themes were no longer just the province of male rockers. The UK punk scene also fostered all-female bands like the Slits and the Raincoats that were the direct antecedents of the 1990s riot grrl movement.

Punk took women beyond the domain of girl groups, sensitive folk-rock troubadours, or singing for all-male bands. It signaled that females could play, sing, and write anything in rock that men could and could bring to it all a liberated female approach and perspective that began to change rock from being primarily a boys' club.

The Ramones

The Ramones were the epitome of punk rock with their stripped-down sound, terse songs, tight and high-tempo delivery, and teenage toughie garb of T-shirts, tight jeans, sneakers, and black leather jackets, all topped with bowl haircuts. "Eliminate the unnecessary and focus on the substance" is how original drummer Tommy Ramone characterized the group's approach. By doing so, they became the first truly punk band of the new music movement, helped spark the British scene when they played the United Kingdom in 1976, and left a legacy of twenty-one studio and live albums before retiring in 1996.

The Ramones (left to right) Johnny Ramone, Tommy Ramone, Joey Ramone, and Dee Dee Ramone. Courtesy of Photofest.

In early 1974, singer Jeffrey Hyman (Joey Ramone), guitarist John Cummings (Johnny Ramone), bassist Douglas Colvin (Dee Dee Ramone), and drummer Thomas Erdelyi (Tommy Ramone)—all friends from the upper-middle-class Forest Hills neighborhood in the New York borough of Queens—first played together. They took the brotherly surname from a pseudonym that Paul McCartney used on occasion.

The third of the new groups to play CBGB, the Ramones won a deal with Sire Records in 1976. Their eponymous debut album cost $6,400[10] and was recorded in less than a week and released on March 23 of that year. As the second major-label album from the downtown New York scene, it reinforced the notion that it was a movement to be reckoned with. With its musical concision and verve, Joey's adenoidal vocals, and a cover that made the group look like a teenaged gang, *Ramones* all but shouted the notion of punk music. The group followed it with two more albums—*Leave Home* in January 1977 and *Rocket to Russia* the following November—that in eighteen months all but codified the punk-rock style. "Pure, white rock and roll with no blues influence" is how Johnny described it. On their first four albums were songs that became Ramones standards as well as prime examples of the punk musical and lyrical style: "Gimme Shock Treatment," "I Wanna Be Sedated," "Rockaway Beach," and "Sheena Is a Punk Rocker."

The Ramones were also the first of the New York bands to play London. Ironically, it was at the Roundhouse Theater on July 4, 1976—the American bicentennial. The show and the band's first album a few months earlier helped inspire and fuel the burgeoning English punk scene.

In 1978 Tommy left the band and Marc Bell (Marky Ramone), formerly with Richard Hell and the Voidoids, joined on drums. In 1979, the group gained significant mainstream exposure by appearing in and writing the title song for the Roger Corman film *Rock'n'Roll High School*. The foursome finished out the decade by recording *End of the Century* with legendary producer Phil Spector. The "Do You Remember Rock'n'Roll Radio?" from that 1980 album celebrated the glories of the three-minute-or-less pop song that was at the heart of the Ramones' style.

The original threesome that started the band remained intact until Dee Dee left the group in 1988. The Ramones finally retired in 1996, followed not long after by the successive deaths of Joey (2001), Dee Dee (2002), and Johnny (2004). The group was celebrated in the 2003 documentary film *End of the Century: The Story of the Ramones*, and the popularity of T-shirts bearing the Ramones logo (adapted from the U.S. national seal) long after the band's heyday and demise attests to their iconic stature as standard bearers of the punk-rock ethos. With their shouted "one-two-three-four" song countdowns and chant of "hey, ho, let's go," the Ramones were the personification of punk-rock team spirit.

Richard Hell/The Heartbreakers/The Voidoids

Richard Hell was, if anyone, the original punk rocker. "He was this wonderful, bored, drained, scarred, dirty guy with a torn t-shirt," recalled Malcolm McLaren of seeing Hell with Television.[11] The Englishman then exported Hell's style and ideas back to London and infused them into the Sex Pistols. But Hell, despite his seminal role, did not get his songs fully heard in either Television or the band he joined after leaving that group, the Heartbreakers (with ex-New York Dolls Johnny Thunders and Jerry Nolan), with whom he played for only a few months. He formed the Voidoids in 1976 and released an EP independently later that year before putting out *Blank Generation* on Sire in 1977. The title track became a definitive punk anthem (the Sex Pistols drew from it to write their song "Pretty Vacant"), but thanks to the adventurous guitar work of Robert Quine, the Voidoids were punk with an arty edge. Hell released one other album with the Voidoids in the early '80s and has since established himself as a published writer of poetry and prose as well as an actor.

The Dead Boys

The Dead Boys pushed the envelope of punk raucousness, outrageousness, and anarchism with a live show that mixed wild and driving music with onstage mayhem. Though the group only recorded two studio albums and lasted for a mere four years, from 1975 to 1979, the Dead Boys nonetheless had a lasting significance and impact. When the band arrived in New York from Ohio in 1976, it was a clear signal that the punk-music phenomenon was rippling into the heartland. Their song "Sonic Reducer" remains a punk classic, later performed by Pearl Jam in their live shows in the 1990s. Guns N' Roses recorded the band's "Ain't It Fun" on *The Spaghetti Incident?*, their 1993 album of punk-music covers, signifying how the band's music echoed well beyond their rather brief run.

The band's roots go back to a Cleveland group of the early 1970s, Rocket from the Tombs, which included Dead Boys guitarist Cheetah Chrome (née Gene O'Connor) and drummer Johnny Blitz (John Madansky) as well as David Thomas and Peter Laughner, who went on to form Pere Ubu. After the band broke up in 1975, Chrome and Blitz started a group called Frankenstein with guitarist Jimmy Zero (William Wilden), bassist Jeff Magnum (Jeff Halmagy), and singer Stiv Bators (Steve Bator). Playing music in the spirit of the Stooges, they found the Cleveland club scene hard to crack. The band's members had befriended the Ramones and the Heartbreakers as those acts came through Cleveland on tour and, sensing a more welcoming atmosphere in New York, moved to the Big Apple. The band changed their name to the Dead Boys and, with the help of Joey Ramone, started playing CBGB. The club's owner Hilly Kristal became their manager, and the group soon signed a deal with Sire Records.

The Dead Boys released the aptly titled debut album, *Young Loud and Snotty*, in 1977 and toured England with the Damned that year. A second release the following year, *We Have Come for Your Children*, suffered from inappropriate production by Felix Pappalardi, who had produced Cream and played bass in the hard-rock band Mountain. Not long after its release, Blitz suffered serious injuries when he was mugged on the street in New York, and the group broke up soon after. A live album recorded at CBGB under duress for Sire, *Night of the Living Dead Boys*, was released on the independent Bomp! label in 1981, but only after Bators rerecorded the vocals he had originally made a mess of to stymie Sire's plans. Bators went on to appear in the 1981 John Waters movie *Polyester* and play with Brian James of the Damned in the Lords of the New Church from 1982 to 1989. He died on June 4, 1990, in Paris after being hit by a car.[12]

The Dictators

Started in 1974 and hailing primarily from the Bronx, the Dictators were the most direct descendants of MC5, the Stooges, and the New York Dolls within the New York scene. Classified as "proto-punk" by some, the Dictators actually embodied the traditional definition of "punk" as snotty delinquents through the celebration of lowbrow culture and loud and hard-driving power-chord rock. The group's three albums from 1975 to 1978 never caught on beyond New York City with much more than a cult following, but their roaring, guitar-based sound and cheeky love for the tackiness in modern pop culture was as essentially punk in nature as the music made by any of the bands of that era.

The Cramps

Combining a rockabilly base with psychedelia and horror-movie culture, the Cramps all but invented the "psychobilly" sound that many groups would later follow. Started in 1977 by guitarist and singer Lux Interior and guitarist and singer Ivy Rorschach, the Cramps melded hillbilly wildness and B-movie and late-night TV culture with an urban intelligence and theatricality. Starting out by releasing their own 45s, the band collected their early songs on the 1979 EP *Gravest Hits* before releasing their debut album, *Songs the Lord Taught Us*, in 1980. The band have continued into the twenty-first century to create wild and wooly post-1950s rock with a ghoulish slant.

LONDON CALLING

Punk started its rise in New York City, but it was in England where the notion reached its apotheosis. The Sex Pistols took punk rock's musical and conceptual ideas to their snottiest and most shocking apogee in their rather brief blaze of twisted rebellious glory, sealing the band's mythos by ending with a crash and burn. The Clash first delineated a true-believer credo for punk rock and then expanded it and built upon it to create a powerful and multifaceted legacy that includes U.S. charts hits and albums that sold in the millions. And such a swarm of other bands arose under the punk banner that England, by the latter part of the decade, usurped the center of the punk-rock movement from New York and became the music's most fecund breeding ground if not spiritual homeland.

England was ripe for such a phenomenon to take hold. Postwar English youth had also embraced musically defined subcultures with specified ethos and modes of dress with far more commitment and zeal than American youth, as with the smart up-to-date Mods and rock traditionalist Teddy Boys that clashed in the mid-1960s. National radio, TV, and daily newspapers as well as four weekly national music papers—whose tone was more in the British tabloid tradition than the more studious American rock-music press—spread new music and trends quickly across the small island nation.

The traditional English cultural propriety also helped breed an even stronger oppositional character in the nation's punk bands and movement. This also meant that punk music's outrages were far bigger news. And the lyrical messages of English punk rock were far more political in nature, in this era of British national discontent, than those of the American bands.

In New York, punk took hold and grew when it found a live performance venue, CBGB, which opened its doors to the music and its fans and became a home base where the scene grew and flourished. In London, the catalytic force was a person: Malcolm McLaren. Influenced by the confrontational Situationist art movement and an admirer of the British rock management moguls of the late 1950s and 1960s, he ran a number of boutiques selling hip and sometimes outrageous rock fashions on London's Kings Road and for a while managed the New York Dolls at the tail end of their career. The shop he ran with designer Vivienne Westwood, SEX, became a gathering place for the early members of London's punk scene, and his canny instinct for media manipulation helped bring punk, via the Sex Pistols, to national attention in England.

But McLaren only exploited a musical underground that was already burgeoning by the mid-1970s in London, finding its way into the London music clubs and eventually—via music on new independent labels like Stiff Records and the major labels—capturing public attention beyond the initially small London scene. Thanks to the United Kingdom's national music press, daily newspapers, radio, and television, punk disseminated rapidly throughout the island nation. Although punk may have started in New York, it was so eagerly embraced by British youth—and many of its acts enjoyed chart single and album hits—that England became the spiritual homeland of punk music.

The Sex Pistols

It is fitting that the group that became the Sex Pistols began in early 1974 on equipment stolen from Roxy Music, David Bowie, Rod Stewart, and the studios of the British Broadcasting System—the first two musical touchstones for these budding punks, the latter pair targets of punk rage and resentment. Guitarist Steve Jones was a working-class lad with a larcenous bent and a love of rock 'n' roll who left home at fifteen to soon end up living with the family of his schoolmate, drummer Paul Cook. Fans of the first two aforementioned acts as well as the Faces (whom Stewart would abandon for glitzy stardom) and the New York Dolls, they started a band called the Strand in a rehearsal studio on the King's Road.[13]

As author Jon Savage notes in *England's Dreaming*, his comprehensive account of the birth of London punk rock, "Jones and his satellites had accepted the pop fantasy of transformation hook, line, and sinker, but they were ordinary youths with their noses pressed against the window, and no way in." Jones, a habitué of SEX, hectored McLaren, who he knew had managed the Dolls, for a number of months to see his band.

"The accepted view of the Sex Pistols is that McLaren, Svengali-like, hoisted a group of no hopers to international stardom, that he is the group's alpha and omega," writes Savage. "In fact, it was Steve Jones that had the idea of putting the group . . . together with McLaren."[14] McLaren did put Jones and Cook together with Glen Matlock, a proficient musician who worked at SEX part-time and had some musical proficiency. It was also McLaren who dubbed the band the Sex Pistols, a name that also promoted his shop. And he suggested

The Sex Pistols during a concert in 1977 (left to right) Sid Vicious, Paul Cook, Johnny Rotten, and Steve Jones. Courtesy of Photofest.

that they audition John Lydon, a sneering ne'er-do-well who hung around the King's Road and SEX, as the band's singer. McLaren's situationist tactics played a significant role in the agitprop within the band's look, message, and the publicity tactics and stunts that gained them attention. But the Sex Pistols were born and bred by the youthful discontent of Jones, Cook, and Lydon, while Matlock brought the musical refinement that the three lacked that would later get him fired from the group.

The budding band played its first show on November 6, 1975.[15] Lydon had by then acquired the name Johnny Rotten for the poor state of his teeth as well as his attitude. He lived up to the name with his onstage demeanor and confrontational attitude with audiences, and Sex Pistols shows were almost always marked by riotous and sometimes violent behavior by Rotten and, in time, their growing legions of fans.

McLaren managed to book the band at colleges in London, where they left most of their few listeners unimpressed. But they did start winning some fans and followers and inspired others to start similar bands. On February 12, 1976, the band played its first London club gig at the Marquee, opening for the pub-rock band Eddie and the Hotrods.[16] The show—where, among other stunts, Rotten smashed the headliners' equipment—earned the Pistols their first review in *New Musical Express*. The band continued to play London's clubs and shows in the rest of the country, usually leaving both outrage and converts in their wake. Following the punk festival at the 100 Club in late September, the group was signed by EMI Records on October 8.[17] The group's first single, the snarling "Anarchy in the U.K.," was released in late November.

On December 1, the Sex Pistols appeared on the local London evening show *Today* (replacing Queen, who canceled). Spurred on by host Bill Grundy, Jones called Grundy a "dirty bastard . . . dirty fucker . . . fucking rotter." The incident made front-page headlines in the next day's tabloids—"The Filth and the Fury," announced the *Daily Mirror*—and immediately thrust the band into the British national spotlight.[18]

As a result of the controversy, the group's "Anarchy" tour of England later that month suffered from a string of cancellations, and EMI eventually dropped the band. A&M Records then signed and also dropped the group almost immediately when the drunken band members trashed the company's offices after the celebration of their signing. During this time, Matlock was fired and replaced by Lydon's friend Sid Vicious (née John Ritchie), a regular on the punk scene with little musical talent but considerable punk attitude.

By May 1977, the group's reputation had made it nearly impossible to secure gigs, but Virgin Records did step in to offer the group yet another contract. The release of their antimonarchist single "God Save the Queen" at the end of the month was timed to coincide with the upcoming Jubilee Week celebration of Queen Elizabeth's twenty-fifth year on the throne. Record plants refused to press the disc and major stores declined to stock it, yet it was still one of England's best-selling singles the week it came out. Further controversy came with a concert played on a boat on the River Thames the next week, after which McLaren and some of the band's fans were arrested.

By the fall of 1977, the band's debut album, *Never Mind the Bollocks, Here's the Sex Pistols*, was finally released in the United Kingdom on Virgin and by Warner Bros. Records in America. Many British record stores again refused to stock the band's music, yet the album still sold enough to top the UK charts.

In January 1978, the Sex Pistols embarked on a chaotic twelve-day tour of America. Following McLaren's confrontational approach, the group toured through the South and Southwest, even playing country music venues in Texas. The tour ended on January 14 with a show at San Francisco's Winterland concert hall, after which Lydon quit the band. He went on to form the punk/noise band Public Image, Ltd. Vicious, addicted to heroin, landed in New York City with his girlfriend Nancy Spungen. Early on the morning of October 12, Spungen was stabbed to death in the couple's room at the Chelsea Hotel, and Vicious was charged with the crime.[19] After a court hearing on February 1, Vicious overdosed on heroin and was found dead the following morning.[20]

The Sex Pistols only released one genuine album. But as English writer Jon Savage noted in *Sounds*, *Never Mind the Bollocks* was "powerful" and "authentic" and "a very good rock & roll album."[21] With its blasting guitar work and Rotten's snarling voice carrying its message of anger, defiance, and anarchy, it is an essential punk-rock document that sounds as dangerous as the band's reputation. Although the Sex Pistols created far more controversy than they did actual music, the group's one album conveys the threat they posed to the established musical, social, and political order with a chilling potency.

The Clash

If the Sex Pistols were the promise of punk shattered soon after leaving the starting gate, the Clash were punk rock's potential fulfilled both musically and commercially. From basic punk-rock beginnings, the group matured into an expansive musical act whose rock sound encompassed rockabilly, reggae, and rap music, to name a few flavors the Clash brought to their music. Their early punk polemics grew into a radical and global left-wing political viewpoint. And the band eventually scored American chart hits and sold millions of records, becoming one of the top bands of the early 1980s as well as one of the acknowledged great rock bands of all time.

The Clash (left to right) Nicky Headon, Mick Jones, Joe Strummer, and Paul Simonon, 1978. Courtesy of Photofest.

The Clash started in early 1976 when guitarist, singer, and songwriter Joe Strummer (née John Mellor) left his pub-rock band the 101ers after seeing the Sex Pistols play. He was introduced to guitarist Mick Jones and bassist Paul Simonon of the ever-changing group London SS by the band's manager, Bernie Rhodes, a former associate of Malcolm McLaren, and London SS morphed into the Clash. The group played their first show on July 4, 1976, opening for the Sex Pistols.[22] After playing the few shows that were not canceled on the Sex Pistols' "Anarchy" tour in December of that year, the Clash were signed by CBS Records early in 1977.

The group's eponymous debut album released later that year was a full-throttle rock tour de force on which songs like "White Riot," "Career Opportunities," and "I'm So Bored With the U.S.A." captured the rebellious anger of British punk in full flower. CBS Records in America resisted releasing it until 1979 (with a different set of tracks from the UK version), following the 1978

U.S. release of the band's second album, *Give 'Em Enough Rope*. By this time, the Clash had already had chart success in England and had become one of the top UK punk bands.

Two U.S. tours in 1979 won the band a growing U.S. following, and the band brought classic American musical styles into their sound on the two-record set *London Calling*, which cracked the U.S. Top 30 in 1980, thanks to Jones' atypically poppy song "Train in Vain," which reached No. 23 on the pop singles charts. With the sprawling three-disc set *Sandinista!* in 1981, the Clash musically mixed roots styles with ethnic sounds from Latin music and Jamaican dub while sharpening both their global political messages and social observations in their lyrics. By now a popular U.S. concert attraction, the band released the single disc *Combat Rock* in 1982. The album reached No. 7 on the charts, and the single "Rock the Casbah," bolstered by MTV playing its video, reached No. 8. The following year, Strummer and Simonon booted Jones from the band and later recorded the best forgotten *Cut the Crap* with two new guitarists before the group finally disbanded in 1986.

Strummer went on to act in films, record soundtracks, play with the Pogues, and enjoy a solo career before dying from a heart condition on December 22, 2002. After leaving the Clash, Jones enjoyed success with his band Big Audio Dynamite. In 2003, the Clash were inducted into the Rock and Roll Hall of Fame, a fitting tribute for an act that brought insight and articulation to punk's political and social concerns while weaving strains from rock both old and new, along with world music, into the punk-rock sound.

The Stranglers

Forming in 1974 in southern England, this foursome were the earliest UK band to display a punk sensibility, though their keyboard-driven sound was tied to an earlier brand of rebel rock that resembled the Doors, with whom they also shared a dark worldview. Older than most of the other musicians in the punk scene, the Stranglers also wrote songs from a more sardonic viewpoint. Hence songs like "Peaches" (i.e., women's breasts) and "Bring on the Nubiles" caused the Stranglers to be seen as misogynists rather than a band who were willing to take ideas right to the edge, as they also did on "I Feel Like a Wog," using the derogatory British term for dark-skinned foreigners. This confrontational sensibility extended to a contentious relationship with the press and even their audiences. In 1977, the group released two albums— *Rattus Norvegicus* and *No More Heroes*—that won them some attention in America. The Stranglers have continued to release albums and perform into the twenty-first century, and even though the band never enjoyed substantial record success in the United States, the group's early work holds up well with time, thanks to the undercurrent of almost absurdist humor that spiced their punk sensibility.

The Damned (left to right) Rat Scabies, Dave Vanian, Captain Sensible, and Brian James, 1978. Courtesy of Photofest.

The Damned

The Sex Pistols and the Clash were the English punk acts that ultimately commanded widespread attention. But the Damned were the first of the original London bands to release a single ("New Rose" in 1976) and an album (*Damned, Damned, Damned* the following year), both on the Stiff Records label. They were definitive punk-rock documents, but the group's anarchic stage show was matched by a constantly shifting membership and breakups and reformations in the late '70s and mid-'80s. Surprisingly, the Damned nonetheless continued to record and tour in a variety of configurations led by singer Dave Vanian and guitarist Captain Sensible into the twenty-first century. Even though the Damned never reached a large American audience, they influenced later successful acts like the Offspring (who recorded the Damned song "Smash It Up" for the 1995 *Batman Forever* soundtrack).

Generation X

This band's most lasting legacy is their name, which was later used to describe the grunge rock generation, and the fact that it launched singer Billy Idol to solo stardom in the 1980s. In fact, Idol's breakthrough solo song, "Dancing

Generation X take a break during a recording session. (Left to right) Tony James, Mark Laff, Bob Andrews, and Billy Idol, 1979. Courtesy of Photofest.

with Myself" (written about masturbation), first appeared on the band's third and last album, 1981's *Kiss Me Deadly*. Lasting from 1976 to 1981, Generation X created a musical legacy that stretched from pure punk to near bubblegum. Bassist Tony James went on to form Sigue Sigue Sputnik in the 1980s, marking Generation X as more important for their influence than for their music.

The Buzzcocks

Started in 1976 by guitarists Pete Shelley and Howard Devoto after seeing an early Sex Pistols show, the Buzzcocks were the first band to emerge from Manchester, sparking a scene that would make the city England's most musically influential locale in the 1980s. They were one of the groups on the Sex Pistols' "Anarchy" tour, but unlike many of their punk brethren, the Buzzcocks combined punk energy with fluent musicianship and a knack for creating concise and catchy pop-punk songs like "Orgasm Addict" (their debut single) and "What Do I Get?" The group broke up in 1981 but reunited by the end of the decade and remain among the more influential and respected punk acts by many groups that followed in their wake.

The Boomtown Rats

Formed in Ireland in 1975, this quintet were punk in attitude and lyrical themes, but musically their sound reflected old-school rock influences and became more broad and sophisticated over their career. A year after forming, the band relocated to London, secured a record deal, and started landing singles in the UK charts. In America, the Rats were only one of many British punk acts with the release of their first two albums in 1977 and 1978. The following year, the group released a single, "I Don't Like Mondays," inspired by a California teenager who explained her murderous shooting spree with that line. The song only reached No. 73 (it hit No. 1 in Britain) but focused U.S. media attention on the band. As the group's career waned in the mid-1980s, singer Bob Geldof organized Band Aid in 1984 to record the single "Do They Know It's Christmas?" and raise funds for African famine relief. He followed that in 1985 with Live Aid, which mounted simultaneous benefit shows in London and Philadelphia that featured some of rock music's biggest stars. The group broke up in 1986, and Geldof was later awarded a British knighthood for his charity efforts, marking him as the one punk-rock musician who actually succeeded in effecting significant social change.

Joy Division

This Manchester outfit reached legendary status when singer Ian Curtis committed suicide in 1980 on the eve of the band's first U.S. tour. But their true legacy is creating a post-punk sound that was less assaulting and more moody and ambient than the original punk bands, a sound that echoed later in groups like fellow Brits the Smiths. Founded in 1977, Joy Division began to open the punk sound to synthesizers over the one EP and two albums recorded before Curtis died. The remaining members formed New Order in 1981 and became a top modern-rock band in the 1980s.

AMERICAN WEST COAST PUNK

The "California sound" of Crosby, Stills & Nash, the Eagles, Jackson Browne, Linda Ronstadt, and others were, with their melodic music and post-hippie sensibilities, the epitome of everything punk was opposed to. Yet on their home ground, a punk scene followed those in London and New York to in fact solidify punk music within American rock and create some of the most muscular and political punk music made in the United States.

X

This Los Angeles band took their name from the last letter of the airline code for the city's airport, but it made a fitting punk monitor for the one

California act of this movement whose musical legacy was world class. Never a great commercial success beyond being a mid-level record-selling and concert-circuit act, X were nonetheless the most important and influential West Coast punk band.

Although their 1980 debut *Los Angeles* was a platter of searing and driving politicized punk rock, X brought to punk a background that allowed the group to expand their style in the '80s with everything from country to hard rock. The band started in 1977 after bassist and singer John Doe and singer Exene Cervenka met at a poetry reading. It was their intellectualism that gave the group its sharp lyrical edge and their shared vocals that gave the band a distinctly different sound. Guitarist Billy Zoom, the son of a jazz musician, had already garnered a rep as a hot 6-string gun playing surf music and rockabilly and drummer D. J. Bonebrake had played in jazz bands and was fond of the art and noise rock of Captain Beefheart.

These influences and their musical abilities brought X quickly to the forefront of the budding L.A. scene. As an entertainment industry town and the home of the sweet and mellow California sound, the city was ripe for an underground counterpart to the prevailing zeitgeist. "It was just an open city," Doe later recalled of L.A. punk's birth, so the attitude was, "Let's just make music happen."[23]

Los Angeles and its 1981 follow-up *Wild Gift* were produced by Ray Manzarek of the Doors and contained such signature songs as "We're Desperate" and "White Girl," as well as a pummeling cover of the Doors song "Soul Kitchen" that signaled X as the heir apparent for the L.A. rebel-rock crown. Both albums were critical hits in the United States and United Kingdom, and the band followed them with four more high-quality releases marked by continuing growth and musical expansion until breaking up in 1987. Doe went on to a solo musical career and film acting, while Cervenka became a respected poet and spoken-word artist. The band reconvened in 1993 and has continued to do so on occasion since.

Black Flag

This Los Angeles hardcore punk group formed in 1977 but became one of America's major punk acts in the 1980s with singer Henry Rollins as their frontman. Founding member Greg Ginn started SST Records to release the band's music, and the label later became an influential force in punk, thanks to albums by the Minutemen, Meat Puppets, Hüsker Dü, Soundgarden, and others. By the time Rollins joined in 1981, Black Flag had begun mixing metal into their sound, presaging the rise of grunge music a decade later. After Black Flag broke up, Rollins continued to be a punk media personality as the leader of his own band, spoken-word artist, book publisher, and occasional actor. Black Flag were pivotal in carrying American punk into the 1980s and spawning a continuing southern California punk scene.

The Dead Kennedys

The most influential and enduring band from the San Francisco punk scene were the Dead Kennedys. As the name implies, the group was America's most provocative as well as political punk band, along the lines of the British punk acts. Led by singer Jello Biafra, the group formed in 1978 and debuted with the indie single "California Über Alles." A second single, "Holiday in Cambodia," was followed by Biafra's campaign for San Francisco mayor (in which he garnered a surprising number of votes). In 1980, the DKs, as fans called them, released their first album, *Fresh Fruit for Rotting Vegetables*, on the IRS Records label. Biafra then started his own label, Alternative Tentacles, to release music by his band and others (which would years later result in a lawsuit by his fellow band members for what they claimed were unpaid royalties). Into the 1980s, the Dead Kennedys emerged as one of America's leading punk bands. The inclusion of a graphic poster by artist H. R. Giger in their 1985 album *Frankenchrist* led to the band being tried for obscenity in California, though charges were dropped after a trial that ended in a hung jury, and Biafra's political profile as a free speech activist was raised further by the incident. The Dead Kennedys were one of the main progenitors of American hardcore punk.

PUNK ROCK LIVES ON

Although pure punk receded for the most part back into the underground, and the punk sound split into styles like hardcore, ska punk, Goth rock, riot grrl, and other variations, punk continued to yield star acts and exert a major influence on rock music well past 1980. U2 bowed at the dawn of the decade as an Irish punk band to become one of rock's major international acts into the next century. Nirvana and the other grunge bands of the 1990s were direct descendants of punk rock. And in the 1990s, the California punk band Green Day would become a million-selling act. Though punk rock may not have appreciably changed politics or society, it did draw rock music back to its primal power, and the punk movement that began in the mid-1970s continues to reverberate throughout modern rock.

NOTES

1. Savage 1993, 133.
2. Liner notes, *Nuggets*, 1972/1998.
3. See http://usinfo.state.gov/products/pubs/history/ch12.htm.
4. Savage 1993, 108.
5. See http://www.brainyhistory.com.
6. See http://www.punkmagazine.com.
7. See http://www.marquee.demon.co.uk.
8. Ibid.

9. Ibid.

10. McNeil and McCain 1997, 229.

11. Ibid., 198.

12. See http://www.stivbators.com.

13. Savage 1993, 72–77.

14. Ibid., 71.

15. Matlock 1991, 65.

16. Savage 1993, 151.

17. Ibid., 255.

18. Ibid., 257–259.

19. Ibid., 509–510.

20. Ibid., 527–528.

21. Jon Savage, review of *Never Mind The Bollocks, Here's The Sex Pistols, Sounds,* November 5, 1977.

22. Gray 1995, 171.

23. *X: The Unheard Music,* 1986.

A NEW WAVE OF ROCK

Rob Patterson

New-wave music was neither a style nor a sound, and even as a musical movement it was far more amorphous and indefinable than punk rock, with which it emerged more or less contemporaneously. Defining what new-wave music was is similar to the adage about the five blind men and the elephant: Depending on which groups under the very broad new-wave rubric you happen to examine, the music varied widely in its sound.

Nonetheless, the term "new wave" is instructive. As discussed in the previous chapter, what became known as punk and new wave was initially described simply as new music. And like punk music, though there was newness and even modernity within the new-wave approach and some of the sounds, much of it drew, as rock music has always done, from older styles. And it was indeed a wave, in that new-wave music by the end of the decade had become both a commercial force and an influence on the sound and state of contemporary rock and roll.

Like punk, new wave was also both a response to and a reaction against the prevailing styles of rock that dominated the sales charts, radio playlists, and concert circuit in the early to mid-1970s. And similar to punk, much of it was marked by musical simplicity and economy, even when sometimes the ideas behind the music were cerebral. It was also yet another emergence of an underground music into the mainstream. But unlike punk, there was no core ethos to new-wave music, and some punk purists scoffed at much of what was known as new wave and even accused new-wave groups of co-opting punk for commercial ends.

The origin of the term "new wave" does offer an analogous idea of what new-wave music was and how much of it sounded. It was originally used to describe the new breed of French cinema directors (*nouvelle vague*) that emerged from and around the magazine *Cahiers du cinéma* at the end of the 1950s. It was a cinematic trend that was linked to the post–World War II generation youth movement as well as the literary works of the French existentialists and as such often dealt in such themes as alienation and absurdity. New-wave cinema also challenged the traditional narrative structure and visual lexicon of film and began as an independent film movement, making films on low budgets outside the studio system.

New-wave music was similar to the French film movement in many ways. It was a reassertion of youth into a mainstream rock-music scene that had matured and in its first emergence was heavily touted by the music press. It was also, to a large degree, a movement that embraced modernism in musical, topical, and stylistic terms, even though a number of schools of music within new wave were revivalist. In fact, it could be said that new wave was the beginning of postmodernism in rock music. And as with punk, many new-wave acts got their start on independent labels.

It is unclear just when the term "new wave" was applied to the new music of the mid-1970s that did not fit within the parameters of punk. New wave had already become a popular description for modern developments with other forms of art as well. But credit for making the term stick probably goes to Sire Records, who marketed the new acts they had signed in the mid-1970s, like the Ramones, Talking Heads, and Richard Hell and the Voidoids with an ad campaign and sampler album that declared, "Don't Call It Punk," and suggested new wave as an alternative description. The intent was obviously to overcome resistance with both radio programmers and mainstream rock fans to the radicalism of punk, and as such the campaign implied what later turned out to be true—that new-wave music did have considerable commercial appeal.

In some quarters, new wave continued to be called new music, and it was also sometimes known as "skinny tie music" due to the popularity of thin neckties worn by some of the bands and fans. But ultimately "new wave" stuck as an apt description for a new generation of artists with a decidedly different set of sounds and themes that by the end of the 1980s became an integral part of the overall American rock scene.

ONE WAVE, MANY SOUNDS

The antecedents of new-wave music are much the same as those of punk rock, delineated in the previous chapter. Like punk rock, new-wave artists embraced many previous styles and artistic influences that were all but forsaken by most popular mainstream rock bands by the early 1970s.

The music of David Bowie and Roxy Music—with their use of costumes, high fashion, decadent subject matter, and modernistic sounds—certainly presaged new wave as its most direct antecedents. Technological advances of the

1970s like compact, portable keyboard synthesizers and more sophisticated and advanced effects processors for guitars also offered new and modern sounds for new-wave artists to experiment with. As recording technology also advanced in the 1970s, multitrack recordings and a greater range of effects processing and more powerful noise reduction filters allowed rock records to be mixed with a cleaner overall sound and greater separation of instruments. Progressive noise-rock bands—such as Can, Gong, and Henry Cow—that deconstructed traditional song and musical structures also helped provide new blueprints for modern music.

New-wave music was also postmodern in the way many of its acts grabbed bits and pieces from a wide variety of sounds and recombined them into pastiches that included everything from garage rock to bubblegum to noise rock to glam to dance music, sometimes in the same song. The music also had a highly modernist slant in a good deal of its lyrical content, which was frequently laced with such expressions of modern anomie as irony, detachment, antiromanticism, fatalism, and alienation. New wave also brought art-music elements like unconventional harmonics and unusual song structures into the mainstream rock sound. Similarly, it introduced arresting visual elements with the myriad fashions and hairstyles that were radically different, and also more contemporary and even futuristic, than the post-hippie garb of mainstream rock acts in the early and mid-1970s. New wave infused modernity and technology into rock and expanded the music's vocabulary beyond its blues, country, R&B, and folk roots.

Since new wave encompasses such a diversity of styles, it is divided here into a number of major schools. One of the most successful areas of new-wave music was new rock and pop, in which the bands took the rock sound and created a different and more modern approach. Other new-wave bands drew from underground art music and modern visual art approaches and philosophies to create new forms that were more cerebral than what had come before. On the other hand, new wave music was also a launching pad for a number of acts that emerged from or were influenced by the back-to-basics sound of the English underground pub-rock movement of the early 1970s. Finally, a number of English artists drew from the rhythms of Caribbean music like ska and reggae to create a rock version of those sounds that bore the energetic influence of punk rock. New-wave music drew from styles and strains that were both older and modern, but in contrast to the prevailing rock styles popular in the mid-1970s, it all sounded quite new and different.

A NEW UNDERGROUND AND MAINSTREAM

Punk helped strip away some of the pretensions and excesses, both musical and otherwise, that had arisen in the early 1970s as rock-music acts became superstars. What had once been both an art and business of pop songs and

45 RPM singles had evolved into albums and full-length musical packages and concepts rather than a collection of songs, abetted by the growth of FM album radio. Punk in its truest spirit stripped the music back to the three-minute or less song with three or four chords, and its movement was kick-started by crucial singles, a number of them on independent labels. New wave took that distilled essence and created a pop music for the modern age.

By the end of the decade, as punk-rock acts either broke up or entered the mainstream, and the hardcore punk movement receded underground, new-wave music had become part of the popular music landscape. It was being played on commercial pop and rock radio stations and was a college radio staple and had been embraced by the major labels while also still being released by a burgeoning community of independent record companies. A national circuit of new-wave clubs had emerged, and mainstream live music venues were featuring new-wave acts. At the same time, the influence of the waning disco scene had intermingled with new wave to spark the opening of "rock disco" dance clubs that featured new-wave music. When MTV ("Music Television") began broadcasting its initial offering of music-video clips twenty-four hours a day in the summer of 1981, new-wave music was one of the main styles it featured, ensuring that the new sounds that were created in the 1970s became a major element in rock music throughout the 1980s.

Music journalist Ken Tucker observes in *The Rolling Stone Illustrated History of Rock & Roll*, "At its most adventurous, American alternative rock contradicts the myth that the only worthwhile popular music is made by subliterate teens with nothing more on their minds than girls and inebriants."[1] Although that statement may be hyperbolic—and ignores the fact that girls and inebriants were also subject matters and pastimes for punk rockers and new-wave musicians—it does symbolically represent the sea change that new-wave music brought about in rock music.

Punk initially blasted at the barricades of accepted rock conventions in the mid-1970s. New-wave music then poured into the breech and tore down the walls separating underground sounds from the mainstream. It may also have created its own set of clichés and conventions, but new-wave music did change the nature of rock music—and to some degree the audiences and industry around it—in a permanent manner. It brought rock music to the end of the century and into the next millennium as something very different from what it was at the dawn of the 1970s.

NEW ROCK AND POP

Rock music came out of the 1960s into the '70s with longer and more expansive songs as well as album-length concepts and even rock operas. New wave narrowed the focus back to the more economical pop-song structure, drawing from pop styles of the past that the underground rock of the late 1960s and mainstream rock of the early 1970s had eschewed for more complex approaches. New-wave acts pilfered the grab bag of pop from bubblegum to the early Beatles and buffed it up for a new era and reconnected rock with pop-music styles and forms.

The B-52's

Masters of party rock, kitsch, and musical mirth, the B-52's "came together for the purest of rock & roll reasons: to amuse themselves at parties," notes *The Rolling Stone Illustrated History of Rock & Roll*.[2] The group—the first of many to emerge from the college town of Athens, Georgia—was formed in October 1976 by a gang of friends after drinks at a Chinese restaurant, and played their first show at a party the following Valentine's Day. Their 1978 independent single "Rock Lobster" caught the attention of national music critics and won the band gigs at punk and new-wave clubs in New York City, where they later relocated.

Warner Bros. Records signed the B-52's and released their self-titled first album in 1979. The rereleased "Rock Lobster" and "Planet Claire" became underground and dance club hits, with the latter finally reaching No. 56 on the pop singles chart the following year. "Private Idaho," from the band's second album in 1980, *Wild Planet*, also became a popular dance single and hit the lower reaches of the pop charts.

The group became standard-bearers of new-wave pop and MTV regulars in the early 1980s alongside acts like Blondie and the Cars. After guitarist Ricky Wilson died of AIDS in October 1985, the band took an extended hiatus. When they returned to action in 1989 with *Cosmic Thing*, the B-52's finally achieved a major commercial breakthrough with two successive singles that both hit No. 3 on the pop charts: "Love Shack" and "Roam."

With their retro, rummage-sale fashion and the beehive hairdos of singers Kate Pierson and Cindy Wilson, the B-52's were champions of camp. Their sound mixed surf music, go-go dance rhythms, and bubblegum, topped with wacky lyrics, in a fashion that helped make post-disco dance music popular with rock fans. Calling themselves "the World's Greatest Party Band," the B-52's deserve the title, thanks to their infectious sense of fun both on record and in concert.

Blondie

"They like to think of themselves as 'pop punks,'" said *Trouser Press* of this New York band in 1977[3]—an apt summary of what Blondie was about. One of the first bands to play CBGB, New York's punk central, the group went on to chart No. 1 singles with "Heart of Glass" in 1979, "Call Me" in 1980, and "Rapture" and "The Tide Is High" in 1981. That success made this group one of the premier new-wave acts.

Blondie, 1978. Courtesy of Photofest.

The band was started in 1974 by guitarist Chris Stein and singer Debbie Harry, who had worked as a bunny at the New York Playboy Club. Named for the platinum-haired Harry, the group asserted that "Blondie is a band" in promo campaigns even if she was the media focal point whose breathy vocals distinguished the group's sound. After a self-titled debut in 1976 on the independent Private Stock label, Blondie jumped to Chrysalis Records. With *Plastic Letters* the following year, the group began to score chart hits in the United Kingdom, where they became a consistent radio presence and star act. With the 1978 album *Parallel Lines*, Blondie began to hit in the United States. The group continued to release albums and tour through 1982, when internal tensions and Stein's illness from the autoimmune disease pemphigus caused the group to split up. In 1998, a recovered Stein and Harry regrouped the act with two other members and began releasing albums and touring again.

Though Blondie started out with a pop-punk style, the group came to epitomize the eclecticism of new wave. Their sound incorporated garage rock, bubblegum, punk, '60s girl group pop, and art-rock and later added reggae and disco, which Blondie was instrumental in getting rock audiences to accept.

The Cars

The Cars were the first band from the new wave to achieve rapid and sustained commercial success. They did so with a canny mix of the ironic detachment pioneered by David Bowie and Roxy Music, a chilly and glossy modernist musical sound, meticulously crisp production by superstar producer Roy Thomas Baker (who had worked with Queen), a deftly Warholian grasp of pop symbolism in the band's look and packaging, and a sound that had touches of both highly adult decadence and catchy bubblegum-flavored riffs and hooks. "The Cars have achieved success the way Henry Ford built autos—by creating interchangeable, streamlined riffs that are assembled to mass-produce pop hits," observed rock scribe Roy Trakin in *New York Rocker*. "[T]he Cars have reduced pop passion to a chilly science of precision."[4]

The group came together in Boston in 1976, led by singer, guitarist, and primary songwriter Ric Ocasek. After they made a splash on the local club scene, Elektra Records signed the group and released their self-titled debut in May 1978. Singles like "Just What I Needed," "My Best Friend's Girl," and "Good Times Roll" edged into the pop Top 40 and lifted the album to No. 18 on the Top 100 and propelled it to sales of 1 million by the end of the year. Successive albums like *Candy-O* (1979), *Panorama* (1980), *Shake It Up* (1981), and *Heartbeat City* (1984) all hit the Top 10 of the pop album charts and sold over a million copies on the strength of songs like "Drive," "Magic," "Shake It Up," and "You Might Think," among others, that received heavy pop and album-rock radio play. Once MTV started broadcasting in 1981, videos by the Cars were regularly aired on the channel. By the mid-1980s, the group's popularity started to wane, and in 1988 the band finally called it a day.

Still popular as an oldies act on rock radio, the Cars created a definitive commercial new-wave rock sound by their use of wiry guitar tones and synthesized keyboard riffs matched with the affected vocal styles of Ocasek and bassist Benjamin Orr. Although the Cars never achieved the critical favor earned by some of their peers, the group was one of the prime forces in bringing new wave into the rock mainstream. The continuing popularity of the Cars with rock fans is evidenced by a number of their original albums and greatest-hits collections earning multiplatinum status well into the 1990s and after.

The Jam

This decidedly English trio was the new-wave band most firmly linked to the rock and pop of the mid-1960s, drawing its sound from the Who as well as the Beatles, Small Faces, the Kinks, and American soul. Combined with their frequent stage garb of stylish '60s suits, the Jam revived the British Mod look and sound for a new generation. Although they became a top act in Great Britain, the Jam never managed a substantial American breakthrough.

Led by singer, guitarist, and songwriter Paul Weller with Bruce Foxton on bass and Rick Buckler on drums, the origins of the Jam precede new wave. Starting out in the suburban community of Woking near London in the early 1970s, the group, unlike so many other rock bands of the time, enjoyed the support of Weller's parents. Their earliest rehearsals were in Weller's bedroom, and his father John was the band's manager.

John Weller hustled early gigs for the fledgling band at Woking pubs and other venues and by 1974 started getting the group booked into London music clubs. The rising punk and new-wave movement had its influence on the Jam, further heightening the trio's concise and energetic sound, which combined Weller originals with rocked-up versions of soul classics.

Signed to Polydor in early 1977, the Jam hit No. 40 on the British single charts with their first single, "In the City." Their debut album of the same name reached No. 20 in the United Kingdom and was compared by many critics to *The Who Sings My Generation*. A second album released later in 1977, *This Is the Modern World*, carried on in the same vein. Then 1978's *All Mod Cons* found Weller's songwriting moving into a more mature and sophisticated vein and landed in the UK Top 10. The band's difficulty finding an American audience was compounded by a mismatched U.S. tour billing in '78 opening for Blue Öyster Cult.

By 1979, the Jam began scoring a string of Top 5 UK singles that continued until the group broke up in 1982. On *The Gift* that same year, the group had expanded its sound with accents like horns and a deeper soul groove that Weller continued to explore in his later band the Style Council.

Still teenagers when they won their record deal in 1977, the Jam expressed a sense of youthful excitement mixed with touches of alienation that paralleled punk on songs like "In the City," "The Modern World," "Strange Town," and "When You're Young." The Jam's reassertion of mid-1960s British rock styles and values would be echoed in the 1990s by such English superstar acts as Oasis and Blur.

The Knack

Few groups were more critically reviled in this era than the Los Angeles band the Knack. "The Knack's presumption of what-they-want-to-hear was a betrayal of the energy and integrity that have made the new wave and alternative rock in America so provocative," notes writer Ken Tucker in *The Rolling Stone History of Rock & Roll*.

The Knack burst out of a budding Los Angeles power-pop scene in 1979 to hit No. 1 with their debut single "My Sharona" and also topped the album charts with their first album, *Get the Knack*,[5] which went gold and then platinum quickly after its release. Although genuine new-wave acts like the Cars and Blondie had already enjoyed singles success, the Knack's rapid ascension from being virtual unknowns to chart-topping stardom led to charges that the band was ripping off new-wave music for commercial gain.

The way their label, Capitol Records, marketed the band did not help matters. After all, this was the label that launched the Beatles in the United States now asserting that history was repeating itself by packaging and titling the Knack's debut in the same fashion as *Meet the Beatles!* The group's logo copied that of the early Beatles, the band wore thin-lapel suits and ties like the young Fab Four, and their tight and hooky melodies were clearly modeled on the original Beatles style. Damning the Knack even further with critics was the highly salacious if not downright sleazy lyrics of the songs penned by Knack guitarist and singer Doug Fieger. It all added up to make the Knack seem calculating—if not crass—even if the group enjoyed a brief but powerful reign as the flavor of the moment in teenybopper pop. But the backlash was so strong that one clever entrepreneur started marketing items bearing the slogan "Knuke the Knack."

Another single from *Get the Knack*, "Good Girls Don't," hit No. 11 on the charts. But the band's fall was almost as rapid as their rise. A second album in 1980 attempted to defy the band's many critics with its title, *But the Little Girls Understand*. But the critics were ready with their pencils sharpened to a razor point. Writer Charles Shaar Murray in England's *New Musical Express* declared the album "distressingly formulaic" and "strictly flyweight," remarking how on one track "they rock hard enough to make the Bay City Rollers sound remarkably like the Clash by comparison. . . . The Knack bear roughly the same relation to rock and roll as radiation poisoning does to nuclear power."[6] The album hit No. 15 on the *Billboard* Hot 100 and sold enough to be certified gold, but the Knack were rapidly on the wane. Their next album, 1981's *Round Trip*, barely cracked the Top 100 even if it did show signs of some genuine musical creativity. The group split up soon after its release, and reunions in 1991 and 1998 were largely met with indifference.

The Knack remain little more than a footnote in new-wave music even though their success did demonstrate that power pop—a style that had been bubbling under the mainstream throughout the 1970s—could have large-scale commercial appeal. But the main significance of the Knack is how the band's rejection by the initial new-wave audience proved that the music's core listeners valued a degree of musical integrity in the acts even as those artists started to become part of the star system.

The Pretenders

"I'll never be a man in a man's world," declared Pretenders singer, songwriter, and guitarist Chrissie Hynde in 1980.[7] By the time she made that statement, Hynde had proven herself a woman who had triumphed in the man's world of rock and roll. With their debut album that year, the Pretenders hit the Top 10 of the American album charts, helping to prove that new wave had commercial muscle with an album that went gold and later sold over a million.

Rock stardom had been a longtime goal for the determined Hynde, who migrated from her native Ohio to England in 1973. She penned music journalism for *New Musical Express*, worked at Malcolm McLaren's SEX shop, and had played and sung in a number of musical ventures, including a short stint in London SS with Mick Jones and Tony James, later of, respectively, the Clash and the Damned.

Hynde was an integral part of London's original punk scene. But when she began putting together the Pretenders in 1978, the first single she released was a cover of "Stop Your Sobbing" by Ray Davies of the Kinks (who Hynde would later marry), with her own song "The Wait" on the flip side. Thanks to the A-side's meld of classic rock and punk attitude, it reached the UK Top 40 in 1979. Two more singles—Hynde's songs "Kid" and "Brass in Pocket"—preceded the band's 1980 eponymous first album, which topped the UK charts. By that time the band's lineup had coalesced into Hynde with guitarist James Honeyman-Scott, bassist Pete Farndon, and drummer Martin Chambers.

With Hynde's piquant mix of tough and sweet in front of the lean and muscular band, the Pretenders continued to enjoy U.S. chart and radio success with 1981's *Pretenders II*. Farndon was fired from the band the next year due to his heroin addiction, and not long after Honeyman-Scott died in a drug-related incident. Farndon overdosed the following year, but Hynde added new members to the band and has carried on with the Pretenders into the twenty-first century, proving that a woman can be a guitar-playing rocker on her own terms right beside the boys.

Split Enz

The first band from New Zealand to achieve global success, Split Enz blended Beatlesque songs with contemporary musical accents to create indelible modern pop that earned them a measure of American popularity in the 1980s. Though the band started as an arty and theatrical combo in New Zealand in the early 1970s, and by the middle of the decade had won homeland and Australian success, they finally hit a groove in the late '70s when the ever-shifting lineup coalesced around singers, songwriters, and guitarists Tim Finn (one of the group's founders) and his younger brother Neil.

Though they had been taken under the wing of Roxy Music's Phil Manzanera in the mid-1970s and migrated to England, Split Enz did not achieve a commercial breakthrough until 1980's *True Colours*. The single "I Got You" hit No. 53 on the U.S. charts while also going Top 20 in the United Kingdom and topping the Australian charts for ten weeks. The group became a regular U.S. concert attraction and enjoyed regular play on MTV into the mid-1980s. After Split Enz broke up in 1985, Neil Finn formed Crowded House, a band that also included his brother Tim for an album. The group became a pop-rock powerhouse in America, thanks to the Top 10 hit songs "Don't Dream It's Over" and "Something So Strong," eventually selling more than a million copies of their 1986 self-titled debut.

Squeeze

The most decidedly traditional pop band of the new-wave movement, Squeeze was started in 1974 by the songwriting team of guitarists and singers

Glenn Tilbrook and Chris Difford. With Difford providing quintessentially English lyrics set to melodies by Tilbrook, the duo were frequently hailed as the Lennon/McCartney of new wave.

Starting out in the pubs of South London, the group also included keyboard player Jools Holland, who brought his boogie-woogie keyboard skills and wacky personality to the mix. A 1977 debut EP, *Packet of Three*, was produced by John Cale and released on the Deptford Fun City label by their original manager, Miles Copeland, who also managed the Police. It won the group a deal with A&M Records, which in 1978 released the band's Cale-produced, eponymously titled debut (which was titled *U.K. Squeeze* in the United States to avoid confusion with an American band of the same name). The spunky set was not fully representative of their sound, which was better defined on 1979's *Cool for Cats* and 1980's *Argybargy*. Though the group had pop hits in the United Kingdom, they earned an American audience through frequent U.S. touring.

Holland left the band after *Argybargy*, eventually becoming a UK TV star as the host of a number of popular music programs. He was replaced by keyboard player and singer Paul Carrack from the pub-rock band Ace. *East Side Story* in 1981 was produced by Elvis Costello and managed to launch a single into the Top 50 of the U.S. pop charts with "Tempted," which was sung by Carrack (whose voice was also heard on Ace's 1975 No. 3 U.S. pop hit "How Long"). The group had won such a fervent New York City-area following through shows and album radio play that they were able to headline Madison Square Garden on June 18, 1982. The group broke up the next year, and Difford and Tilbrook became a duo act until they re-formed Squeeze in 1985 and carried on until breaking up again in the late 1990s. Although Squeeze never achieved high-level stateside success, they built a devoted U.S. fan base that persisted over two decades and showed that the mid-1960s British pop-rock style had its place within new wave.

XTC

One of the supreme ironies of new-wave music is that XTC is the one major group from the movement that never broke up and continues to create music at the time this volume was written. XTC never enjoyed major chart success in the United States and United Kingdom and stopped touring in 1982, but the highly intelligent and hook-laden pop-rock created by main members Andy Partridge (guitar and vocals) and Colin Moulding (bass and vocals) has won XTC a devoted cult following that has enabled them to continue releasing critically acclaimed albums.

Started in 1976 in the quiet bedroom city of Swindon, west of London, XTC were signed to Virgin Records in early 1977. Their first album releases— *White Music* and *Go 2*—featured progressive and sometimes fractured pop-rock that would easily type the band as art-rockers as much as new pop-rock, in part due to the influence of keyboard player Barry Andrews, who left the band in early 1979 (and later played with Robert Fripp and Shriekback).

Drums and Wires, released in 1979, found XTC moving into a more modernist pop-rock sound, with guitarist and keyboard player Dave Gregory replacing Andrews. *Black Sea* in 1980 and *English Settlement* in 1982 continued to refine the XTC sound of sophisticated rock with pop twists. In '82, Partridge's ongoing stage fright led him to bolt from the stage at a show in Paris on the first song, cancel an entire British tour, and then play only one show of an American tour before flying back to England and canceling the rest of that tour.

XTC carried on as a studio outfit, creating what many acknowledge as the band's masterpiece in 1986 with the Todd Rundgren–produced *Skylarking*. Having taken the British pop-rock sophistication of such icons as the Beatles and the Kinks in the mid- to late 1960s to new realms and sometimes even greater heights, XTC are arguably, as writer Stephen Thomas Erlewine asserts in *All Music Guide*, "the great lost pop band."[8]

ART MUSIC

Rock's maturation beyond teenage music and pop ditties opened its doors to many outside influences by the end of the 1960s. The concurrent rise of modern art and conceptualism began exerting a strong influence on the music with new wave. The movement also opened rock to more intellectual approaches. A number of new-wave bands were started by art students, who applied artistic concepts to the music they created. Hence this segment of the movement is the most modern in sound and approach and brought new and progressive forms and themes to further enhance what began as a fairly simple musical form.

Devo, wearing their famous "dome hats," 1980. Courtesy of Photofest.

Devo

Hailing from the industrial city of Akron, Ohio, Devo took the notion of new wave to its fullest conceptual expression and musical modernism. The band—led by art students Mark Mothersbaugh and Jerry Casale—based an entire Devo conceptual universe on the notion that mankind was devolving within a modern and highly technological society, hence the name Devo. This was expressed musically with a sound that was primarily created with synthesizers and electronic drums and featured mechanistic rhythms. The lyrics reflected on the state of man within a technologically advanced world. Matching uniforms gave the group's members the look of drones, and a complete visual and philosophical imagery expressed their devolutionary concept.

Starting out in 1972, the band released singles on its own Booji Boy label and England's Stiff Records before signing with Warner Bros. Records and releasing their first album, produced by musical modernist Brian Eno, in 1978. The group won a cult following and later rose into the mainstream with the No. 14 pop single "Whip It" from their 1980 album *Freedom of Choice*. When MTV went on the air, Devo's strong visual imagery was perfectly suited to the notion of video music, and the clip for "Whip It" received heavy play on the channel. By the end of the 1980s, Mothersbaugh and Casale put the group on the back burner to concentrate on soundtrack and video work. Even though Devo never became a star act, their influence echoed through covers of their songs by Nirvana, Soundgarden, and others. No other act in new wave took the notion of modern life and music to such full fruition.

Pere Ubu

This highly influential Cleveland-based band never enjoyed commercial success beyond an underground following, but Pere Ubu has continued to create unique and provocative music since the group was first formed in 1975. Emerging from the local group Rocket from the Tombs, which also yielded members of the Dead Boys, Pere Ubu was founded by singer David Thomas (a.k.a. Crocus Behemoth) and guitarist Peter Laughner (who left Pere Ubu in 1976 and died early in 1977). Their debut self-released single, "30 Seconds Over Tokyo," in 1975 was one of the earliest U.S. punk/new-wave singles.

The group's first album, 1978's *The Modern Dance*, introduced a style that was dissonant and fractured, drawing from art-rock antecedents to create a sound that reflected contemporary industrial decay. Atop it was the keening wail of Thomas vocals. Pere Ubu put out five more albums through 1980 and continued its prolific output, in various configurations fronted by Thomas, into the next century. Echoes of the Pere Ubu sound can be heard in such varied later acts as the Pixies and Nine Inch Nails, demonstrating how Pere Ubu set the tone for a genuinely modernist art-rock with an apocalyptic edge.

Talking Heads

"Talking Heads epitomize the American new wave, out of New York, via art school, Harvard and the Village lofts. . . . Theirs has been called the music of intellectualism," noted *Melody Maker* writer Penny Valentine in 1978.[9] The music of Talking Heads on their 1970s albums was arty and cerebral, with angular song structures and rhythms, and themes of alienation, detachment, and absurdity—not unlike the French new-wave film directors. Topped with the

Talking Heads (left to right) Jerry Harrison, David Byrne, Chris Frantz, and Tina Weymouth play a concert in Central Park, 1980. Adrian Belew joins the original Talking Heads for the concert. © Corbis.

keening, nervous, and almost strangled vocals of singer, guitarist, and primary songwriter David Byrne, Talking Heads, as the name implies, were quintessentially modernist in their initial approach.

The group originated at the Rhode Island School of Design, where Byrne and drummer Chris Frantz played in a band called the Artistics. Frantz also shared an art studio with Tina Weymouth, an avid fan of the group who would become his wife. By 1974, all three of them had moved to New York City, where they lived together in a lower Manhattan loft and started the band. In June 1975, they first played CBGB as the Talking Heads, opening for the Ramones. By November of the next year the group were signed to Sire Records. Also in the fall of 1977, Harvard-educated Jerry Harrison, who had been a member of Jonathan Richman's band Modern Lovers, started playing selected shows with the group and joined as a full-time keyboard and guitar player early in 1977.

In September of that year, the group released *Talking Heads: 77*, which contained the signature song "Psycho Killer." Sung from a psychopath's point of view, the song was a pastiche of elements: snippets of French in the lyrics, a "fa fa fa" chorus borrowed from an Otis Redding song, a martial beat, and touches of bubblegum rock. Its postmodernist cut-and-paste structure exemplified the new and highly original sound that Talking Heads developed.

On 1978's *More Songs about Buildings and Food*, the group began working with producer Brian Eno. The group cracked the Top 30 of the album and pop charts thanks to their cover of Al Green's "Take Me to the River." Over two more albums with Eno—*Fear of Music* in 1979 and *Remain in Light* in 1980—the Talking Heads sound became fuller and more expansive and began to incorporate such elements as funk and African polyrhythms.

During the 1980s, Talking Heads were one of the most esteemed and critically acclaimed modern music bands, scoring a Top 10 pop single with "Burning Down the House" in 1983. The group's 1984 Jonathan Demme–directed concert film *Stop Making Sense* is regarded as one of the best films ever made of a rock performance. In 1980, Frantz and Weymouth started a side project, Tom Tom Club, that enjoyed dance-club hits with "Genius of Love" and "Wordy Rappinghood." By the time Talking Heads officially broke up in 1991, they had become one of the preeminent and most influential modern rock bands.

POST-PUB ROCK

In the early 1970s, a back-to-basics movement arose in England that featured bands playing older, simpler, roots-oriented music in pubs. Its top groups like Brinsley Schwarz, Dr. Feelgood, Ducks Deluxe, and Bees Make Honey never became pop stars in the United Kingdom and failed to make any significant dent on the American scene. But with the rise of new wave, this new traditionalism became a part of the movement as pub rock's seasoned musicians and the songwriters influenced by its reverence for '50s rock, soul, and country found greater outlets and audiences for such sounds. Many of these acts stand apart from what new wave morphed into during the 1980s, but they also created some of its most accomplished music within new wave as well as the traditional rock and roll form.

Elvis Costello

When Elvis Costello emerged in 1977, the venomous undertone in his voice and lyrics combined with the full-barrel pace of most of his songs found him typed as the

Undated photo of Elvis Costello in concert. Courtesy of Photofest.

"angry young man" of new wave as well as the most musically and lyrically literate of punks. "I never was an angry young man," Costello later said. "I was always an angry old man."[10]

Although that statement bears some of Costello's own mythmaking, it does reflect his mature command of older musical styles, which he fashioned into what is probably the most dynamic and intelligent of new-wave music. With his facile wordplay, rich melodic sense, almost encyclopedic knowledge of popular music, and unerring eye for human and political issues and conflict, he has often been described as the most important rock songwriter since Bob Dylan. The fact that he remains a vital and creative musical force and the subject of consistently high critical acclaim well into the first decade of the twenty-first century backs that contention.

Born Declan Patrick McManus in 1954 and raised in Liverpool by a musician and bandleader father and mother who ran a record store, Costello was steeped in popular and classical music from an early age. By the early 1970s he was playing London clubs and pubs with the group Flip City and as D. P. Costello (the maiden surname of one of his great-grandmothers).

When Stiff Records set up shop in London in late 1976 and advertised for artists in the English music press, a demo by Costello was one of the first to arrive. He was promptly signed and recorded his debut album, *My Aim Is True*, in a twenty-four-hour session with members of the expatriate California band Clover as his backup band and Nick Lowe producing. In an act of true punk-rock hubris, he took the first name of the king of rock 'n' roll. By the time the album was released in the United Kingdom in July 1977, Costello had formed his band the Attractions: Steve Nieve on keyboards, Bruce Thomas on bass, and Pete Thomas (no relation) on drums.

With song titles like "No Dancing," "Blame It on Cain," "Less Than Zero," and the ironic "I'm Not Angry," as well as a tough and terse musical feel, *My Aim Is True* slotted neatly into the burgeoning punk consciousness, though the album's most enduring song is the ballad "Alison." The disc won immediate attention from the English music press and soon reached the Top 20 in the UK album charts. Another single, the reggae-inflected "Watching the Detectives," also became a No. 15 British pop hit.

That July, CBS Records was holding its annual international convention in London. Costello and the Attractions set up at noontime across the street from the hotel and began playing as the company's executives left for lunch. The group was quickly arrested, but Columbia A&R man Gregg Geller was suitably impressed enough to buy the album and sign Costello to Columbia Records.

My Aim Is True was released later that year in America and was hailed in the U.S. music press. The album eventually peaked at No. 32 on the *Billboard* album charts the following year.[11] Costello also sparked controversy when he appeared on NBC's *Saturday Night* and early into his performance of "Less Than Zero" stopped the band and launched into his as-yet-unrecorded anticorporate radio diatribe, "Radio Radio." He was subsequently banned from the show and did not appear on *Saturday Night* again for another two decades.

Costello's stunning songcraft and the fierce and dynamic virtuosity of the Attractions helped land his subsequent albums into the upper reaches of the U.S. album charts through the end of the decade: 1978's *This Year's Model* (which hit No. 30), 1979's *Armed Forces* (No. 10), and 1980's *Get Happy!!* (No. 11). Regular U.S. touring and consistent critical acclaim helped secure Costello's presence in the American rock scene.

Ian Dury

Though little more than a commercial footnote in U.S. new wave, Ian Dury & the Blockheads created some of the early movement's most charming and memorable songs: "Sex & Drugs & Rock & Roll," "Hit Me with Your Rhythm Stick," and "Reasons to Be Cheerful (Part 3)"—all of which were Top 10 UK hits in the late 1970s. Crippled by polio since childhood, Dury—with his eccentric charm—first found favor in the early 1970s as the singer for pub-rockers Kilburn and the High Roads. Signed to the London indie label Stiff Records, Dury teamed with keyboard and guitar player Chaz Jankel to create a sound that melded English dance hall, soul, jazz, and dance music with a pop flair. Dury's 1977 album *New Boots and Panties!!* became a worldwide million seller thanks to a style that, for all his distinctiveness from the rest of new wave, certainly exemplified the notion of that term by being decidedly different, original, entertaining, sometimes slyly provocative, and utterly danceable. Dury later enjoyed further success as an actor before dying of cancer in 2000.

Joe Jackson

On his first album, *Look Sharp!*, Joe Jackson was grouped with Elvis Costello and Graham Parker as one of new-wave music's angry young songwriting Englishmen—a perception that did not truly fit any of them, least of all Jackson. One of the most accomplished musicians of the new-wave scene, he had studied at the London Academy of Music and played with England's National Youth Orchestra while working in rock, pop, and cabaret acts in London in the early to mid-1970s.

Inspired by punk and new wave, he recorded demos of pared-down, attitudinal songs in the late '70s that won him a deal with A&M Records and led to the release of *Look Sharp!* in 1979. As critic Charles Shaar Murray noted in *New Musical Express*, the album "resembles a parallel-universe alternate take on the first Elvis Costello album. The ringing, contoured pop melodies, the jaundiced, skeptical lyrics and the crisp vocals recall the Big El, with the important proviso that Joe Jackson seems to be resisting hostility and alienation."[12]

It may have been that thematic difference that helped Jackson land the song "Is She Really Going Out With Him?" at No. 21 in the *Billboard* Hot 100. *Look*

Sharp! reached No. 20 on the charts and was awarded a gold album later that year. Jackson followed his debut later in 1979 with *I'm the Man*, an album in a similar vein that reached No. 22 on the charts.

He soon began expanding his musical output with the Caribbean-inflected *Beat Crazy* in 1980 and the jump blues of *Joe Jackson's Jumpin' Jive* the next year. In 1982, Jackson released *Night and Day*, an album of sophisticated pop marked by Latin music flavors and a strong Cole Porter influence (as acknowledged in the Porter homage of its title, the name of one of Porter's best-known songs). The set yielded the hit pop singles "Steppin' Out" (which reached No. 6) and "Breaking Us in Two" (No. 18) and climbed to No. 4 on the album charts, earning Jackson a second gold record. Jackson continued from there to explore a wide variety of musical modes, including classical, winning a Grammy Award in 2000 for his *Symphony No. 1*.

Jackson was viewed by some as an interloper in the new-wave music scene. Yet "Is She Really Going Out with Him?" was pivotal in breaking pop radio open to the new-wave school of songwriting, and he demonstrated how new wave provided a very big tent, within which a variety of talents could utilize the movement as a springboard to successful musical careers.

Graham Parker

The most firmly traditionalist singer-songwriter of the new-wave movement, Graham Parker recalled Bob Dylan and Van Morrison in his songs and singing and had a hard-edged, roots-oriented rock sound. He fit into the punk and new-wave scene and was seen as one of its "angry young men" due to an approach that critic Ken Tucker called "tempestuously articulate."[13] But throughout his career on a number of major and independent labels, Parker has consistently remained his own man musically and professionally. Annotator Jimmy Guterman sums up Parker in his liner notes for the best-of collection *Passion Is No Ordinary Word* as "vivid, barbed rock & roll, with enough nods in the direction of reggae, folk and classic pop to sketch the range of his ever-widening ambitions."[14] Add soul as another major influence to that description to summarize the old-school rock renewal Parker achieved within new wave.

Londoner Parker played in pubs with R&B-oriented bands in the early to mid-1970s and pumped gas by day before one of his demos was heard by Dave Robinson, who had managed Brinsley Schwarz and ran a recording studio at the Hope & Anchor and would soon co-found Stiff Records.

Robinson became Parker's manager and surrounded him with a band—dubbed the Rumour—composed of some of the pub rock scene's best musicians, and soon after Parker won a deal with Mercury Records. His first album in 1976, *Howlin' Wind*, leaned heavily on Parker's Dylan and Morrison influences and immediately caught the ears of music critics. *Heat Treatment* later that year delved into a tougher rock and soul sound and garnered Parker even further critical raves, though his music failed to connect commercially in

America even though he scored chart action with singles and albums in the United Kingdom. Over the musically spotty *Stick to Me* (1977) and live two-disc set *The Parkerilla* (1978), he grew increasingly frustrated with what he saw as his label's inability to effectively market his music.

The screed "Mercury Poisoning" was the B-side of a single that announced his switch to Arista Records, where Parker cut what many feel was his best work, 1979's *Squeezing Out Sparks*, followed by *The Up Escalator* in 1980—both of which hit No. 40 on the album charts. Parker then split with the Rumour, sundering what had been, at least in live performance, a musical match of singer and songwriter with a band on the order of Bob Dylan and the Band and Bruce Springsteen and the E Street Band.

Through the 1980s and into the early 1990s, Parker moved from Arista to Elektra, Atlantic (where he never released an album), RCA, and Capitol Records, yet never cracked the mainstream. He has continued to make interesting if sometimes inconsistent music on independent labels. His 1970s releases still signal a major talent who, sadly, was not able to commercially capitalize on his considerable potential. Yet Parker's best work remains some of the most powerful songwriter rock of that or any era.

Rockpile/Dave Edmunds/Nick Lowe

The band Rockpile—which served as a recording and touring vehicle for the solo careers of guitarist, singer, and songwriter Dave Edmunds and bassist, singer, and songwriter Nick Lowe and released only one album as a group—was the most unlikely and stylistically atypical group within new-wave music. The band's peppy, stripped-down style was a throwback to the rock of the 1950s and early to mid-1960s, recalling Chuck Berry, Buddy Holly, and the Everly Brothers as well as the variations on the styles of those artists by such later British acts as the Beatles, the Rolling Stones, and the Kinks. Yet the band's relationship to new wave and punk goes beyond such obvious connections as Lowe's production of early albums—by the Damned, Graham Parker, and Elvis Costello—and the fact that he released the first single on the influential London new-wave label Stiff Records on August 14, 1976.[15]

Edmunds had been the guitarist for the late 1960s English band Love Sculpture—best known for his 6-string workout on Khachaturian's "Sabre Dance"—before embarking on a production career and shifting his musical orientation to old-school rock 'n' roll. He befriended Lowe after producing an album for Lowe's band Brinsley Schwarz. The two formed Rockpile with guitarist, singer, and songwriter Billy Bremner and drummer Terry Williams in the mid-'70s, and the group served as the band for albums by Edmunds like *Get It* (1977), *Tracks on Wax 4* (1978), and *Repeat When Necessary* (1979) and Lowe's *Pure Pop for Now People* (1978) and *Labour of Lust* (1979). The group finally released an album as Rockpile with 1980's *Seconds of Pleasure* and also backed Carlene Carter (daughter of country-music legend June Carter and, at the time, Lowe's wife) on her 1980 album *Musical Shapes*. Rockpile split up not longer after the band's sole release, and both Lowe and Edmunds returned to solo careers and production work.

Rockpile were the primary roots-rock force within new wave music, part of the return to simplicity, but in their case also with substantial musical proficiency. Known for their barreling and rollicking live shows (during which the band never played a slow number), Rockpile helped spark a revival of rock 'n' roll basics that echoed through the American roots-rock bands of the 1980s and the Americana movement that emerged in the 1990s.

REGGAE AND SKA MEET ROCK

This particular strain of new wave started, quite naturally, in England. Jamaica was once part of the British Empire and remains in the Commonwealth, and England has a substantial Jamaican and Caribbean population. Music from the islands had been a presence in the English music scene and on the UK pop charts since the 1960s. What new-wave musicians did with it is inject a new energy and rock attitude and give it contemporary twists to create some of the most interesting and charming music within the movement.

2 Tone Bands: The Specials, the Selecter, Madness, the English Beat

The Coventry, England–based 2 Tone label was the epicenter of a community of groups influenced by the pre-reggae Jamaican sounds of ska and rock steady, marked by speedy, offbeat shuffles. More up-tempo than reggae, these styles leant themselves to a punk-influenced rock approach that became a late '70s rage in the United Kingdom and found an audience in America. Jerry Dammers, leader of this movement's founding band, the Specials, started 2 Tone to release music by his band and, later, recordings by the Selecter and other acts. The other two major bands within this trend, Madness and the English Beat, also recorded early singles that were released on 2 Tone.

The 2 Tone name refers to the multiracial makeup of many of the new rocking ska bands and the checkerboard pattern that was the label's graphic flag. The music's makers and fans adopted the look of mid-1960s Jamaican "rude boys" (roughly translated as street toughs): porkpie hats, thin lapel suits, knit shirts, and loafers. The music served as an ameliorative to the high racial tension in the United Kingdom at the time and introduced U.S. rock audiences to ska and rock steady, an influence that echoed later in the music of such bands as late 1990s stars No Doubt. Though the music never gained a wide audience in America, it was an integral part of the dance-club scene of the late 1970s into the '80s.

The Specials formed in 1977 with keyboard player and songwriter Jerry Dammers as their de facto leader and key conceptualist. Their debut single,

"Gangsters," was a UK hit, and the band's Elvis Costello–produced debut album caught the ears of American critics and new-wave fans. The group's most memorable song, "Ghost Town," was an evocative expression of England's economic tribulations in the 1970s. Singer Terry Hall, guitarist and singer Lynval Golding, and percussionist and singer Neville Staples split from the group to form Fun Boy Three and enjoy even greater stateside attention in the 1980s. The Specials made strong political and social statements in their lyrics and were fervently antiracist in their song topics, membership, and musical approach.

The Selecter started as an ad hoc instrumental combo that consisted of members of the Specials and some friends. It spun off into a full-fledged act with feisty singer Pauline Black, releasing one truly classic album, *Too Much Pressure*, in 1980. The group's peppy, infectiously danceable sound was matched by strong political and social commentary but also displayed a pop flair as heard in their popular song "On My Radio."

The members of London-based Madness were known as "the nutty boys" for their antic music and stage show. Originating in 1976 as a ska group called the Invaders, by 1978 the band had mutated into Madness, taking their name from a song by Jamaican ska artist Prince Buster. Their 2 Tone single and tribute to Buster, "The Prince," became a UK hit, followed onto the British charts by the Buster song "One Step Beyond." Madness became one of Great Britain's most successful singles bands in the early 1980s and charted a No. 7 pop single in the States in 1983 with "Our House," thanks to heavy MTV play of its video.

Madness, 1979. Courtesy of Photofest.

Originally named the Beat but later called the English Beat to avoid confusion with an American band of the same name, this Birmingham group were distinguished by the alternating white/black lead vocals of Dave Wakeling and Ranking Roger (née Roger Charley). They won respect with ska purists by bringing former Prince Buster saxophonist Saxa into the act but also expanded on the ska sound to create a hybrid Caribbean-inflected, pop-soul sound. They were introduced on 2 Tone by their zippy remake of Smokey Robinson's "Tears of a Clown." The English Beat style found fruition on their 1982 album *Special Beat Service*, from which the videos for the songs "Save It for Later" and "I Confess" enjoyed considerable MTV play. The group then split apart, with Wakeling and Roger starting General Public and guitarist Andy Cox and bassist Dave Steele joining forces with singer Roland Gift to form the popular 1980s pop band Fine Young Cannibals.

The Police

This trio, which was formed in London in 1977, was the one new-wave act to achieve international superstardom. Though inspired by punk and its energy, their success came thanks to a style that fused a progressive pop-rock sound with reggae. It took the Police from playing shows on their first U.S. tour in 1978—where, at some venues, there were only a few more people in the audience than onstage—to selling out New York's Shea Stadium in August 1983.

The Police (left to right) Sting, Stewart Copeland, and Andy Summers. © Corbis.

All three members were experienced and accomplished musicians. Singer, bassist, and main songwriter Sting (née Gordon Sumner) had played in jazz bands. Drummer Stewart Copeland, an expatriate American, had been in the progressive-rock band Curved Air. And guitarist Andy Summers had played with a later version of 1960s hitmakers the Animals as well as with other British rock bands. The stripped-down and highly focused style of the Police made the most of their musical abilities. And with Sting's knack for penning offbeat songs with strong pop appeal, the Police managed to springboard from early shows on the UK punk circuit to become one of rock music's all-time classic bands.

Sting compositions like "Roxanne" (which cracked the Top 40 of the U.S. singles charts) and "Message in a Bottle" helped propel the band's first two albums, *Outlandos d'Amour* (1978) and *Regatta de Blanc* (1979), to, respectively, No. 23 and 25 on the album charts. A tour playing Third World countries following their second album helped the group eventually win a global audience.

Zenyatta Mondatta in 1980 elevated the band to star status in the United States on the strength of the singles "Don't Stand So Close to Me" and "De Do Do Do, De Da Da Da" both of which hit No. 10. *Ghost in the Machine* the following year secured the Police as one of rock and roll's reigning acts and brought the band their first Top 5 single with "Every Little Thing She Does Is Magic." With *Synchronicity* in 1983, the Police created their masterwork and achieved chart and sales success that would ensure their place in the rock-music pantheon. The album and single "Every Breath You Take" both topped the charts for months and *Synchronicity* eventually sold 8 million copies in America.

The album also proved to be the group's swan song. Internal tensions throughout their career and Sting's increasing dominance of the band and its material led the Police to go on what they first called a sabbatical, albeit one that has never ended aside from reuniting for benefit shows and brief recording sessions together in 1986. Sting went on to a solo career that has continued his international stardom.

New wave reached its highest musical achievements via the Police, whose highly modern rock sound and ethnic rhythms made them a global presence. The continuing appeal of Sting's songs is underlined by the 5 million U.S. sales of a 1986 greatest hits package. Though the group released only five original albums, their best music balanced musical sophistication and progressivism with the simplicity of just three musicians playing together to create some of the finest modern rock of the 1980s.

NEW MUSIC FOR THE 1980s AND BEYOND

Ironically, the new music revolution for which the Sex Pistols led the charge ultimately resulted in the popular 1980s English band Duran Duran, who were the antithesis of all that punk represented with their pretty-boy looks, smooth and danceable modern music, and videos peppered with scantily clad models. Like every significant musical revolution, punk and new wave became absorbed into the mainstream. What the new-wave underground of the 1970s started became the pop-rock of the 1980s.

New wave spawned a plethora of modernist pop bands whose sound often featured synthesizers and effects-laden guitars and whose lyrics and imagery carried whiffs of postmodern decadence: A Flock of Seagulls, Berlin, Culture Club, Depeche Mode, the Eurythmics, INXS, Pet Shop Boys, Simple Minds, and Tears for Fears, to name some of the most successful. Its more decadent strains prompted the rise of Goth rock, while new-wave dissonance was an antecedent of industrial rock.

The movement became more focused on acts like these in the 1980s, yet it still had its varied stylistic strains. Adam and the Ants started with punk and added tribal beats to the sound. The Stray Cats took rock revivalism to its deepest origins by playing 1950s rockabilly. The Go-Go's melded California pop with the '60s girl-group vibe. Australia's Men at Work distilled the reggae influence of the Police into bouncy pop confections. And R.E.M. emerged from Athens, Georgia to give mid- to late 1960s jangling guitar pop a musical, intellectual, and philosophical depth, eventually inheriting the Police's mantle as a modern-rock band that commanded musical respect while also selling millions of records.

When MTV began broadcasting on August 1, 1981, the first video it played was a decidedly new wave song in style and theme: *Video Killed the Radio Star* by the Buggles. New wave's vivid fashion and style sense and high conceptual content made it ideal for MTV's visual music programming, and the channel took what had been breaking through on radio at the end of the '70s and beamed it into the living rooms of America. As a result, new wave became permanently integrated into rock music's mainstream.

At the same time, the proliferation of college radio in the 1970s as an alternative to commercial radio combined with new wave to foster the college rock of the 1980s. Hence new wave both went mainstream and helped create an enduring underground by the dawn of the decade. Though new-wave music was initially scoffed at by many of the mainstream guitar rockers of the 1970s as well as their fans, it brought about a sea change that usurped guitar rock's prominence and relegated that music to what became known as "classic rock." New wave sparked the blaze of musical modernism that followed in the 1980s and '90s, bringing rock and roll, for sometimes better and other times worse, firmly into the future.

NOTES

1. DeCurtis et al. 1992, 573.
2. Ibid., 576.

3. Ira Robbins, "Blondie around the World," *Trouser Press*, November 1977.

4. Roy Trakin, review of *Shake It Up*, *New York Rocker*, 1982.

5. See http://www.allmusic.com.

6. Charles Shaar Murray, review of . . . *But The Little Girls Understand*, *New Musical Express*, March 15, 1980.

7. Vivian Goldman, "The Pretenders: Hynde Sight," *Melody Maker*, January 28, 1980.

8. Stephen Thomas Erlewine, http://www.allmusic.com.

9. Penny Valentine, "Talking Heads," *Melody Maker*, January 28, 1978.

10. Schinder 1996, 296.

11. See http://www.allmusic.com.

12. Charles Shaar Murray, review of *Look Sharp!*, *New Musical Express*, 1979.

13. DeCurtis et al. 1992, 580.

14. Guterman 1993.

15. McCann 1992.

ROCK ON THE BIG SCREEN

Chris Smith

Ever since Bill Haley's classic "Rock around the Clock" was played over the opening credits of the 1955 teen rebellion film *Blackboard Jungle*—causing young moviegoers to slash theater seats and teachers to lock their doors at night—film and rock music have had a special relationship. It was not rock then, of course; it was the nascent rock 'n' roll, music written for the feet and executed through the pelvis. Bill Haley, Little Richard, Elvis Presley, Chuck Berry, and Fats Domino were the earliest instigators, and after the success of *Blackboard Jungle* their music could be heard streaming from every movie house in town as Hollywood tried to capitalize on this gateway to underage audiences.

There were plenty of films through the 1950s and 1960s that either had rock music but were not truly rock films, or vice versa. It could be said (and, in fact, has been) that the earliest rock films practically predated rock and roll itself, with James Dean's existential angst in 1955's *Rebel Without a Cause* and Marlon Brando's proto-hippie outsider ("What're you rebelling against?" "Whatta ya got?") in 1953's *The Wild One*. Though lacking rock music, the films are important markers of rebellious rock attitudes that would permanently shape the relationship between rock and film. On the flip side of the coin was the plethora of films with rock soundtracks that followed *Blackboard Jungle* but had little to do with the relationship between the music and the nature of the characters. The most memorable of this set was the long string of Elvis films that were simply vehicles for ticket sales. With few exceptions—notably 1957's *Jailhouse Rock* and 1958's *High School Confidential*—these movies and their countless imitators often limited the relationship between rock and film rather than enhanced it.

The years between 1964 and 1973 were utterly magical for rock music, as well as its relationship to the movies. The Beatles' surprisingly intelligent 1964 film *A Hard Day's Night* left all formulas behind and opened the door for imaginative cross-pollination between rock and the big screen. Rock soundtracks became intimately tied to the film's subject matter in movies like 1967's *The Graduate*, 1968's *Yellow Submarine*, 1969's *Easy Rider*, 1973's *American Graffiti*, and 1973's *Mean Streets*. Documentaries about the rock life ("rockumentaries") found popularity through D. A. Pennebaker's 1967 Bob Dylan portrait *Dont Look Back* and the Beatles' 1970 *Let It Be*, while straight-up concert performance films like 1965's *The T.A.M.I. Show*, 1968's *Monterey Pop*, and the 1970 gem *Woodstock* found new—and very profitable—ways to portray live concerts on the big screen.

Woodstock was not only a benchmark in concert footage technique but a marker for the end of hippie idealism. Though filmed at the peak of the peace and love movement, the movie was released soon after the tragic Altamont Festival and only months before the shootings at Kent State, the breakup of the Beatles, and the deaths of hippie icons Jimi Hendrix and Janis Joplin. The warm, community-centered flower-power movement of the 1960s quickly gave way to a more self-centered and narcissistic 1970s, and the relationship between rock and film followed suit.

ROBERT STIGWOOD AND THE ROCK MUSICAL

Perhaps the largest impact rock music made on the moviegoing public in the 1970s was through that tried and true marriage wherein the music and the film's story gain equal billing: the musical. The musical has maintained a presence in the *Billboard* charts since the charts debuted in 1955. Of the thirty-one film soundtracks that reached No. 1 in the chart's first twenty-five years (1955–1980), fifteen of them were musicals. In both the 1950s and 1960s, four of each decade's ten top charting albums were musicals.

Musicals and their soundtracks were a staple of entertainment through 1965, a year when five of the nine top-charting albums were soundtracks, and four of those were musicals—*Roustabout*, *Help!*, *Mary Poppins*, and *The Sound of Music*. However, with the British invasion, the advent of folk rock and psychedelia, the FM radio explosion, and the birth of the music festival came new movie genres that would make musicals passé: the rockumentary and the concert film. Though the musical maintained a sacred place as a form of Broadway theater, it was not until the mid-1970s that the film musical rebounded from a decade-long slump with a string of successful interpretations of Broadway hits (*Jesus Christ Superstar* and *Grease*) and film-musical versions of landmark rock albums (*Sgt. Pepper's Lonely Hearts Club Band* and *Tommy*). The man behind these films was one of Britain's most successful music industry professionals, Robert Stigwood.

The Australian-born Stigwood migrated to the United Kingdom at a young age, working in the early 1960s with some of the first independent artists and engineers who attempted to operate outside the strict record-label system. By 1965 he was one of the busiest men in the industry, operating as agent, manager, promoter, publisher, and producer for his artists. Soon he had a hand in dealings with some of the top British acts of the day, including the Graham Bond Organization, John Mayall's Bluesbreakers, the Who, and Cream, and nearly took over for George Martin as manager of the Beatles (a move that was stopped by the band, who reportedly disliked Stigwood).

After launching Australian act the Bee Gees in the United Kingdom and becoming one of Britain's top music executives by the late 1960s, Stigwood expanded into theater production, putting together a highly successful version of *Hair* for the London stage. *Hair* had become a major hit in the United States as the first rock musical, and after its success in London, Stigwood became an even larger player with productions such as *Oh Calcutta!*, *Pippin*, and *Sweeney Todd*. Stigwood's theater success led him to take a shot at the American film industry, debuting in 1973 with a screen version of the popular rock musical *Jesus Christ Superstar*. Nominated for an Oscar for best music, the film would lead Stigwood to a host of further collaborations between music and film. Over the course of the 1970s, Stigwood would make a lasting mark in American cinema by producing the musicals *Tommy*, *Grease*, and *Sgt. Pepper's Lonely Hearts Club Band* and almost single-handedly launching the short-lived disco craze with *Saturday Night Fever*.

Tommy, 1975

Based on the classic 1969 Who album of the same name, *Tommy* tells the story of Tommy Walker, a boy struck deaf, dumb, and blind when he witnesses his father's murder. Tommy shuts out the world but becomes addicted to a pinball game, soon achieving fame and fortune as a master player and eventually becoming a messiah figure to a band of followers.

The film has become something of a cult classic, featuring performances by actors Jack Nicholson and Ann-Margret (who famously rolls around a room full of baked beans in one scene), as well as some of rock's hottest musicians of the time, including Eric Clapton, Elton John, Tina Turner, and the members of the Who. Pete Townshend, who composed the original album, received an Oscar nomination for best music.

The original album is considered the first "rock opera," creating an entirely new subgenre of storytelling rock albums soon copied by other artists such as Jethro Tull and on the theater stage by *Jesus Christ Superstar*, *Godspell*, and *Joseph and the Amazing Technicolor Dreamcoat*. Three versions of the *Tommy* album found their way into the *Billboard* Top 5: the original reaching No. 4 in 1970; an orchestral version by the London Symphony Orchestra (featuring singing by the Who, Steve Winwood, Rod Stewart, and Ringo

The Who star in Ken Russell's 1975 film, *Tommy*. © RBT Stigwood Prods/Hemdale/The Kobol Collection.

Starr) climbing to No. 5 in 1973; and the film soundtrack topping out at No. 2 in 1975.

Grease, 1978

The longest-running Broadway musical until toppled by *A Chorus Line* in the 1980s, *Grease* was an enormous success when Stigwood brought it to the big screen.[1] What the stage version had in longevity, the film version matched in sales, for a short period one of the highest-grossing films of all time. The movie established actor John Travolta—who had broken out the previous year in the Stigwood-produced disco drama *Saturday Night Fever*—as a major star and included British/Australian pop singer Olivia Newton-John in her first major film.

A campy snapshot of 1950s teenage mores, *Grease* features Travolta as Danny Zuko, a leather-jacket-clad Chicago high schooler trying to woo the prim and proper Sandy Olsson (Olivia Newton-John) without appearing un-cool to his friends. Four of the film's songs reached the Top 5 as singles: "Hope-lessly Devoted to You"; "Grease," a slightly out-of-place disco piece written by Stigwood client Barry Gibb; and two Travolta/Newton-John duets, "You're the

One That I Want" and "Summer Nights." The album topped the charts for twelve weeks, and the film remains one of the highest-grossing musicals in American cinema.

Sgt. Pepper's Lonely Hearts Club Band, 1978

Like *Tommy*, the film *Sgt. Pepper's Lonely Hearts Club Band* was based on a landmark 1960s album (in this case the Beatles' eponymous 1967 release, believed by many critics to be the greatest rock album ever). Unlike *Tommy*, the film version of *Sgt. Pepper's* was distant from the original album's story line, and the Beatles (who had broken up years before) played no role in the making of the film beyond the use of their songs, which were performed in the movie by an A-list of musicians and actors, including Peter Frampton, George Burns, Donald Pleasence, Steve Martin, Alice Cooper, Aerosmith, Billy Preston, and Earth, Wind and Fire.

With the members of Stigwood's act the Bee Gees—one of the hottest bands in the world at the time—performing alongside Frampton in the lead roles, and more than two dozen classic Beatles songs reinterpreted in glitzy Hollywood splendor, the film could not help but be a hit. Unfortu-

The cast of Randal Kleiser's 1978 film *Grease*. Shown from left (standing) Olivia Newton-John, John Travolta, Jeff Conaway, Stockard Channing; (kneeling) Dinah Manoff, Kelly Ward, Didi Conn, Michael Tucci; (lying down) Barry Pearl. Courtesy of Photofest.

nately, it did not even come close. Although Stigwood was coming off major successes with *Grease* and *Saturday Night Fever* in the previous two years, *Sgt. Pepper's* turned out to be a major flop, called by *Rolling Stone* "one of the worst movies ever made" and a "fiasco so unique it should win some kind of award for ineptness beyond the normal call of duty."[2]

Part of the blame rested on the decision to not allow any of the actors to speak except for George Burns, who narrates a story line that essentially strings one Beatles song after another together in haphazard fashion. The soundtrack fared much better, peaking at No. 5 on the charts, but a far cry from the success of the original album, which topped the charts for fifteen weeks. Ironically, George Martin (the man behind the original 1967 release) also produced the film soundtrack, which *Rolling Stone* quipped "proves conclusively that you can't go home again in 1978. Or, if you do, you better be aware of who's taken over the neighborhood."[3]

Other Musicals

Notwithstanding the poor quality and reception of *Sgt. Pepper's*, the musical continued its bounce in the late 1970s with a string of film adaptations of popular plays. In 1978, the Broadway musical *The Wiz*—a soul version of the 1939 film *The Wizard of Oz*—was brought to the big screen with Michael Jackson as the scarecrow, Lena Horne as the good witch, Richard Pryor as the Wiz, and a poorly cast Diana Ross as Dorothy, who many critics felt was much too old for the part. Though the stage version won a Tony for best musical, the reworked story translated poorly on the screen, and the flashy effects were unable to camouflage the tired fairy tale behind the curtain.

The following year brought three very different musicals into movie theaters: a screen version of the original rock musical *Hair*, an autobiography of choreographer Bob Fosse in *All That Jazz*, and a puppet road show in *The Muppet Movie*. Though *All That Jazz* and *The Muppet Movie* had little to do with rock, their critical and commercial success helped continue the musical trend, while *Hair* helped prolong theater's interest in rock movies with counterculture themes.

Despite the fact that *Hair* the film followed ten years after *Hair* the musical—with the hippie movement it portrays long since dead—the movie is fairly faithful to the original's plot, capturing the sexuality, spirituality, drug use, class wars, and conflicts of conscience that comprised the late 1960s. The film was directed by Milos Forman, who had won critical acclaim (and a Best Director Oscar) several years earlier with *One Flew Over the Cuckoo's Nest*, written by one of hippie counterculture's most vibrant luminaries, Ken Kesey. The success of film musicals in the 1970s carried the genre into the next decade, for better—the brilliant paean to Chicago blues *The Blues Brothers* and the modern–dance-centered Alan Parker film *Fame*, both released in 1980—and for worse, with the numerous subpar imitations of *Grease* and *Saturday Night Fever*, among them 1980's *Xanadu*, 1982's *Grease 2*, and 1983's *Staying Alive*.

CONCERT FILMS

The two most important musical events of the 1960s—the 1967 Monterey Pop Festival in Monterey, California, and the 1969 Woodstock Music and Art Fair in upstate New York—are universally recognized as seminal launching points for a host of important bands that would shape rock music for decades. However, this justifiable position often overshadows these events' contribution to film as well.

Though there were concert films before Monterey and Woodstock, the performance documentaries of these two shows—each released a year after the event—set new standards for capturing concerts on celluloid and became benchmarks in concert film. More than a crucial record of the music scene in 1967 San Francisco (which it was), *Monterey Pop*—through its director D. A. Pennebaker—made a special effort to focus on the audience as well as the performers, capturing not just live music but the effect it had on the audiences, an essential ingredient for the performer/audience interaction that heavily flavored the nascent rock-festival scene.

Woodstock was an entirely different type of concert film. Going even further to convey the audience experience and the behind-the-scenes moments, the film went far beyond capturing the musical performances to relate a larger story—a full narrative that begins long before the first guitar is plugged in and reaches far beyond the edge of the stage. Director Mike Wadleigh brilliantly montages two and three camera angles on the screen at once, providing the viewer with almost too much to take in, a cinematic trip that won the film an Academy Award for Best Documentary. *Woodstock* and *Monterey* demonstrated what could be done with concert footage beyond mere re-presentation, leading to a number of performance films through the 1970s that were as often derivative as innovative but continued rock's presence in the theater.

By the mid-1970s a number of concert films were released (or recorded and released much later) showcasing the performance talents of rock's top acts: Pink Floyd giving a surreal performance in a volcano crater in 1972's *Live at Pompeii*; the Rolling Stones touring North America in 1969 for the tragic *Gimme Shelter* and in 1972 for the serious-fans-only *Ladies and Gentlemen, the Rolling Stones*; seminal San Francisco bands closing down the Fillmore for good in 1972's *Fillmore*; the Grateful Dead showcasing their live chops at San Francisco's Winterland in 1974 for *The Grateful Dead Movie*.

Like these, most concert films throughout the 1970s focused on a single act or even a single performance. While some hint at a larger rock picture, many of them are enjoyable only to fans of the specific group: the extended, winding strains of prog-rock band Yes in 1975's *Yessongs*; the fantasy-laden skits accompanying Led Zeppelin's Madison Square Garden performance in 1976's *The Song Remains the Same*; the sheer pleasure of watching Neil Young caress his guitar in 1979's *Rust Never Sleeps*; and the nostalgic waxing for Beatles tunes by Paul McCartney's group Wings in 1980's *Rockshow*. A few concert films of the period, however, bring a bit more to the table and serve as important documents of the era.

Good to See You Again, Alice Cooper, 1974
Alice Cooper: Welcome to My Nightmare, 1975

Some rock stars live for the camera. And as one of the originators of "shock rock"—a form of rock that relies on sensational and occasionally over-the-line stage antics designed to offend the audience—Alice Cooper was bound to make some videos. Though many of these efforts were destined for television audiences or straight to VHS cassette, his 1974 concert film *Good to See You Again, Alice Cooper* and 1975 follow-up *Alice Cooper: Welcome to My Nightmare* found their way to the big screen in limited release.

The former captures Cooper at his absolute peak, with his band still intact and riding the wave of their 1973 hit album *Billion Dollar Babies* (the band was named "Alice Cooper" but centered around the antics of frontman Vincent Furnier, who adopted the name for himself and kept it when he went solo in 1975). Despite some questionable editing decisions, including footage from black-and-white movies inserted between songs, the film is a valuable archive of one of heavy metal's iconic groups in their heyday.

The second release, *Welcome to My Nightmare*, sought to buoy Cooper's solo image after his original band dissolved. The film was an even more dramatic vision of Cooper's theatrics, practically a musical play that highlights Cooper's macabre horror-film influences while never taking itself too seriously. Though filmed while Cooper was still at the peak of his popularity with the eponymous album reaching the Top 5, the film and album mark the beginning of Cooper's quick slide into musical mediocrity as he became a parody of the genre he helped create.

The Blank Generation, 1976

Aesthetically, *The Blank Generation* is one of the worst documentaries in rock. The video is grainy and jumpy and was shot without sound, so the music added later (from the bands' demo tapes and other performances) does not match the music being performed on the stage. Its technical drawbacks make the film nearly unwatchable, and its lack of content information makes it a uniquely uninformative documentary. One has the sense of being trapped in their neighbor's living room watching a home movie of their teenager's new band.

Its saving grace, however, is that it manages to capture what has rarely been captured in any kind of music—the beginnings of a new genre. *The Blank Generation* was shot during the very stirrings of New York's punk scene in 1975, when bands would venture forth from the garage to gather at CBGB in New York's Greenwich Village and let loose their anticorporate angst. Viewers witness the earliest stages of punk/new-wave gods like Patti Smith, David Byrne, Richard Hell, the Ramones, and Blondie. Some critics have commented that the film's amateurish and haphazard direction is the perfect medium to convey the germination of an amateurish and haphazard genre such as punk rock. Nevertheless, it can hardly be denied that a music documentary suffers if you cannot hear the music. Had the filmmakers thought to pack a microphone, *The Blank Generation* would be one of the key jewels in the rock-doc crown; as it stands, it is at least a minor treasure.

The Last Waltz, 1978

On the opposite end of the spectrum from *The Blank Generation* stands one of rock's most celebrated concert films, *The Last Waltz*. Both the subject matter and the aesthetic representation are anti-punk, with some of the most commercially successful acts in the country captured for the viewer in smooth, sweeping dolly shots framed by plush curtains, elaborate candelabras, and massive chandeliers. Directed by Martin Scorsese, *The Last Waltz* celebrates the 1976 final performance of the Band, featuring an all-star lineup that included Bob Dylan, Ronnie Hawkins, Dr. John, Neil Young, Neil Diamond, Joni Mitchell, Paul Butterfield, Ringo Starr, Van Morrison, Eric Clapton, Emmylou Harris, and Muddy Waters.

Though Scorsese is known as a top film director, his involvement in rock music—working as a cameraman and editor for documentaries such as *Gimme Shelter* and *Woodstock* and later incorporating rock into films such as *Mean Streets*—is sometimes overlooked. With *The Last Waltz*, Scorsese established a template for rock music documentaries: a series of powerful, well-shot performances interspersed with revealing personal interviews and just enough backstage drama to make the audience feel like they are a part of the performance. Though the performers make the show, it is Scorsese—with a 150-page script, some of Hollywood's finest technicians, detailed camera and lighting cues, and a $1.5 million shooting budget—that makes the movie.

A number of performers on stage during Martin Scorsese's 1978 film, *The Last Waltz*. © United Artists/The Kobol Collection.

ROCKUMENTARIES

The line between concert film and rockumentary is a thin one. Every rockumentary includes at least some performance footage, and a well-crafted film such as *The Last Waltz*—incorporating both coverage and commentary—could easily fit into either category. For these pages, however, the films are organized by the subjective criterion of purpose, whether a film was primarily meant to entertain the audience with a good show (a concert film) or inform the audience with a "backstage" peak at the artist's life (a rockumentary).

Ever since D. A. Pennebaker's revealing 1967 documentary *Dont Look Back*, in which he uses unobtrusive camerawork to capture Bob Dylan during his most important artistic phase, filmmakers have sought to gain a behind-the-scenes understanding of artists and play those private moments on the big screen. By designing inconspicuous cameras and microphones, Pennebaker and his collaborators changed the authorship of the documentary from the filmmaker to the subject. "Their epiphany was to use sound—essentially dialogue—as the organizing principle for documentaries. This way they could dispense with intrusive narrations and let the interaction of the subjects tell the story."[4] After *Dont Look Back*, audiences felt they had a right to know what was going on behind the curtain, and filmmakers delivered. Often consisting of a blend of concert footage, interviews, and postured semicandid moments to convey a sense of intimacy, rockumentaries through the 1970s continued to dish out the lives of rock stars in healthy doses to the moviegoing public.

Jimi Hendrix, 1973

Janis, 1974

Journey Through the Past, 1974

Renaldo and Clara, 1977

The passing of Jimi Hendrix and Janis Joplin in 1970 was a crippling blow to the raw, blues-based rock of the 1960s and marked a rise in popularity of the polished, self-centered rock of the 1970s. The retrospectives of their work, *Jimi Hendrix* and *Janis*, were released several years after the artists had died and America's musical climate had changed considerably. With Dylan releasing subpar albums, the Beatles long gone, Led Zeppelin past their best records, the Rolling Stones beginning a long, slow slide into mediocrity, and punk still years away, 1973–1974 was the perfect time to remind rock fans what the premier artists could get out of an audience, and these two films do it with dramatic excellence. With powerful footage from late 1960s concerts—Monterey Pop and Woodstock among them—and candid interviews with the artists' friends and colleagues, *Janis* and *Jimi Hendrix* are how rockumentaries should be made for the average viewer, providing informative and highly entertaining tributes to rock's brightest stars.

Conversely, the Neil Young showcase *Journey Through the Past* and Dylan's self-directed, four-hour epic *Renaldo and Clara* are not for the average viewer. Obsessed devotees of Young and Dylan often hail the films as visionary master-pieces, but average rock fans are irritated by long, wordless interludes, bizarre scenes that seem completely out of context, and stream-of-consciousness edit-ing that seems to favor the artists' "vision" over a coherent story line. Though worth watching just to see the excellent performances of Dylan and Young in their prime, viewers should be aware of the films' eccentricities, particularly *Renaldo and Clara*—made from 400 hours of footage from Dylan's Rolling Thunder tour—which constantly battles with itself to determine its identity as either an uninformative documentary or a barely entertaining feature film.

The Kids Are Alright, 1979

Consisting mainly of concert footage from various Who performances and television appearances over the band's first fifteen years, *The Kids Are Alright* is a treasure trove of long-forgotten clips, demonstrating the Who's over-the-top stage persona that made them one of the most exciting rock groups in the world. The interviews that occasionally surface between songs reveal the per-sonalities of the individual band members—Pete Townshend's philosophical introspection, Roger Daltrey's mouthy sarcasm, John Entwistle's affected bore-dom, and Keith Moon's camera-mugging unpredictability—and add important material to any Who fan's collection.

The Punk Rock Movie, 1978
Punk in London, 1978
The Great Rock 'n' Roll Swindle, 1980
Punk and Its Aftershocks, 1980

The essence of mid-1970s British punk and the films that sought to chroni-cle the phenomenon can be summed up in Malcolm McLaren's exhortation from the 1980 Sex Pistols documentary *The Great Rock 'n' Roll Swindle*: "Forget about music and concentrate on creating generation gaps."

Such marketing genius is worthy of McLaren's talent for exploitation and the lack of talent that he exploited in late 1970's UK punk. These releases from Britain and West Germany chronicle London's burgeoning punk scene and the new-wave movement that would follow in its footsteps. The films run the gamut of the British scene, from pre-MTV Billy Idol and Siouxsie and the Banshees in *The Punk Rock Movie*, to the Clash at their absolute peak in *Punk in London*, to the unabashed commercialism of McLaren and the Sex Pistols in *The Great Rock 'n' Roll Swindle*, to mod and ska rockers in *Punk and Its After-shocks*.

Though varying in video and audio quality and documentary style, these films feature a punk/new wave who's who of performances and interviews, including the Sex Pistols, Madness, the Jam, the Pretenders, the Specials, the Kinks, the Boomtown Rats, the Police, the Clash, X-ray Spex, Billy Idol, and Siouxsie Sioux.

D.O.A., 1980

While Britain produced a slew of documentaries on the Sex Pistols and the rise of the London punk movement, American audiences saw their own film about punk's rise and fall with *D.O.A.* Centered around the Sex Pistols' 1978 tour of the United States, the movie features performances by such early punk bands as Generation X (with Billy Idol), Sham 69, the Rich Kids, and X-ray Spex, as well as plenty of Sex Pistols footage and commentary from concertgoing fans. Its most notable feature, however, is a famous in-bed interview with Sid Vicious and Nancy Spungen not too long before their tragic end.

ROCK-THEMED MOVIES

As rock music progressed from soundtrack fodder to theme material, the film industry began to produce movies wherein rock constituted the picture rather than the frame. The early 1970s saw a number of films, such as *American Graffiti* and *Mean Streets*, that used rock music to great effect in their story lines. As rock music continued to fragment, build new audiences, and gain wide commercial viability through the decade, the late 1970s saw a run of films built around rock rather than just using rock for background noise.

Beyond the aforementioned musicals and rockumentaries, Hollywood began producing feature films with rock themes—usually either biopics of famous rock figures or fictional stories inspired by rock's historic events and personalities. According to legendary critic Greil Marcus, by the end of the 1970s "more than two decades of rock and roll had expanded the music's audience enormously . . . events in rock history could now be taken, by filmmakers and by a broad, mass audience, as historical events pure and simple. No special audience or genre premise was needed to justify rock as subject matter."[5]

Saturday Night Fever, 1977

Though Robert Stigwood famously brought musicals such as 1975's *Tommy*, 1978's *Grease*, and 1978's *Sgt. Pepper's Lonely Hearts Club Band* to the big screen, his biggest success was with a feature film that, though not a musical, had a major impact on the American music scene by providing a massive boost to the disco craze of the mid-1970s. Of all American musical forms, disco has perhaps made the largest impact over the shortest period of time. Though rarely considered a form of rock (thus not widely covered in this text), its impact on American culture was significant, and though it had been around since the early 1970s, the catalyst for its success on a wide scale was Stigwood's group the Bee Gees and their involvement with a little film called *Saturday Night Fever*.

Based on a *New York* magazine article that detailed the Saturday night adventures of a pack of Brooklyn youth, *Saturday Night Fever* is the story of Tony Manero, a big fish in the little pond of Brooklyn disco. Manero is played by John Travolta, the teenage heartthrob who would enjoy even bigger success the following year with the lead in Stigwood's film version of *Grease*.

The combination of Stigwood, Travolta, and the Bee Gees' soundtrack resulted in a massive hit. *Saturday Night Fever* was the perfect crossover of film and soundtrack success. Paramount greatly underestimated box-

Karen Lynn Gorney and John Travolta star in John Badham's 1977 film, *Saturday Night Fever*. Courtesy of Photofest.

office proceeds at about $20 million and had no interest at all in sponsoring the soundtrack.[6] When all was said and done, the film grossed more than $300 million at the box office and another $75 million in rentals. The soundtrack, meanwhile, won a Grammy for Album of the Year and spent an amazing twenty-four weeks at No. 1—longer than all of the Rolling Stones and Who albums of the decade combined—ultimately breaking a slew of chart and sales records in both the album and singles categories.

Eventually both the film and the soundtrack would be listed among the most successful releases of all time, providing a sudden explosion of interest in what was still a somewhat underground disco scene—thousands of discos, roller discos, disco cruises, and all-disco radio stations sprung up overnight. The Bee Gees were already a thriving group, but the soundtrack made them instant superstars, leading to two more subsequent No. 1 albums for the band. Unfortunately, other film producers smelled the green and pounced on the disco trend, releasing subpar *Saturday Night Fever* imitations designed primarily as marketing gimmicks to use films and soundtracks to help sell each other, like 1978's *Thank God It's Friday*, 1979's *The Music Machine*, 1980's *Can't Stop the Music*, and the unfortunate 1983 *Saturday Night Fever* sequel, the Sylvester Stallone–directed *Staying Alive*.

American Hot Wax, 1978
The Buddy Holly Story, 1978

One of the more respectable and enduring forms of the movie/music collaboration was in the form of biopic, films that attempted to tell the true (though often overdramatized) story of a rock star or personality who had made a lasting impact on the music world. Since the 1970s, numerous excellent films have been made about great rock figures, including 1987's *La Bamba* (Ritchie Valens), 1991's *The Doors* (Jim Morrison), and 2005's *Ray* (Ray Charles). But among the earliest were the loving 1978 treatments of two rock pioneers, Alan Freed and Buddy Holly.

As Paramount Pictures' follow-up to *Saturday Night Fever* and *Grease*, the film *American Hot Wax* had a lot to live up to. The story of Alan Freed, the DJ who brought early blues-based rock to mainstream audiences, *American Hot Wax* covers a one-week period in 1959 when rock and roll was creating its first real buzz. Though the film was accused of oversentimentalizing Freed, *American Hot Wax* was credited with digging deep into rock's childhood and bringing to the big screen the excitement of its first words, living up to its tagline, "You shoulda been there." According to critic Greil Marcus, "It caught what early rock felt like; it made you understand why and how it changed so many lives."[7]

The same could be said about Buddy Holly, the subject of the classic *The Buddy Holly Story*. Starring a memorable Gary Busey in an Oscar-nominated performance, the film recounts the short life of one of rock's greatest heroes, who was tragically killed in a plane crash at twenty-two years old (according to songwriter Don McLean, the day that music died). Like *American Hot Wax*, the film had limited critical and commercial appeal but simultaneously created an appreciation for the nostalgia-inducing new genre. As *New York Times* music critic Janet Maslin later said of the genre, "Films like these . . . are better admired for their innocence and simplicity than faulted for their lack of sophistication."[8]

The Rose, 1979

The big-screen debut of legendary actress/singer Bette Midler, *The Rose* was one of the few rock-themed films beyond *Saturday Night Fever* that succeeded at the box office, largely on the strength of Midler's performance for which she was nominated for a Best Actress Oscar. Midler had originally turned down the script but reconsidered when some changes were made to reflect her own struggle as a musician.

The film's producers insisted that the fictional Rose—a popular but insecure rock star exhausted by constant commitments—is a loose composite of the careers of Jimi Hendrix, Jim Morrison, and Janis Joplin, but the film was originally called *Pearl* (Joplin's nickname), and at times Midler's deep-blues warbling, affected southern drawl, and bawdy language are dead-on Janis. The film's soundtrack was as successful as the movie, reaching No. 12 on the charts with its title track peaking at No. 3.

I Wanna Hold Your Hand, 1978

Simply by virtue of being a comedy, the Steven Spielberg–produced *I Wanna Hold Your Hand* stands out from the host of other 1970s rock films. A witty tale of adventurous teenage girls in the grip of Beatlemania, the film follows the group as they try to crash the *Ed Sullivan Show* during the Beatles' first U.S. tour in 1964. Though the movie did poorly at the box office, it was well liked by critics and launched the career of its director, Robert Zemeckis, who would go on to direct memorable classics such as *Back to the Future*, *Who Framed Roger Rabbit*, and *Forrest Gump*.

FM, 1978
Rock 'n' Roll High School, 1979

With the success of rock films came the inevitable low-budget schlock that hoped to capitalize on the enormously successful film/soundtrack formula generated by *Saturday Night Fever*. Although an entire chapter could be devoted to films that abused rock and roll rather than honored it, we will just cite two here as examples: the 1978 radio station send-up *FM* and the 1979 vehicle for the Ramones, *Rock 'n' Roll High School*.

Neither of them films as much as marketing tools, these two gems were seemingly created for the sole purpose of promoting a product. In *FM*, the product is the soundtrack, a strong collection of the 1970s' best rock hits played by the radio station in the film (this was long before rock compilations became a dime a dozen). For *FM*—described by one critic as "an advertisement for its own soundtrack"[9]—the formula worked, with the poorly received movie nonetheless pushing the soundtrack to No. 5 on the charts. *Rock 'n' Roll High School* was not so lucky. Created by B-movie legend Roger Corman, the cheesy teen exploitation film is an undisguised commercial for the Ramones, the seminal punk band that star in the film and appear prominently on the soundtrack. Shot for only $300,000, *Rock 'n' Roll High School* and its soundtrack bombed at both the box office and the record stores.

CHARTING THE SOUNDS

Film soundtracks have had a home in the pages of *Billboard* since the charts premiered in 1955 and have maintained a continuous presence through the period covered in this volume. In fact, out of the ten highest-charting albums during this twenty-five-year period, five of them were music soundtracks: 1955's *Love Me or Leave Me*, 1958's *South Pacific*, 1961's *Blue Hawaii*, 1961's *West Side Story*, and 1977's *Saturday Night Fever*. Listed below are all of the rock soundtracks that premiered on the charts between 1974 and 1980 (soundtracks that largely represent other genres—such as country, soul, and symphonic—are excluded), plus the highest chart position they reached and the notable artists who appear on the album.

Lisztomania (1975)

Peak position: 145

Notable artists: Roger Daltrey and Rick Wakeman (both add lyrics to compositions of Franz Liszt). Daltrey plays the lead role of Liszt; Ringo Starr plays the Pope.

Tommy (1975)

Peak position: 2

Notable artists: Elton John, the Who, Eric Clapton, and Tina Turner. The original 1969 Who album *Tommy*, upon which the film is based, only reached the No. 4 position but lasted longer on the charts than the band's next three best-charters combined.

All This and World War II (1976)

Peak position: 48

Notable artists: Tina Turner, Rod Stewart, Leo Sayer, Elton John, Bryan Ferry, Peter Gabriel, Keith Moon, Roy Wood, and Jeff Lynne (all performing John Lennon and Paul McCartney songs). Elton John's cover of "Lucy in the Sky with Diamonds" rose to No. 1 on the singles chart.

The Song Remains the Same (1976)

Peak position: 2

Notable artists: Led Zeppelin (from a live performance at New York's Madison Square Garden).

Saturday Night Fever (1977)

Peak position: 1 (for twenty-four weeks)

Notable artists: KC and the Sunshine Band, the Bee Gees, the Trammps, and Kool and the Gang. The soundtrack won a Grammy for Album of the Year and became one of the best-selling albums of all time.

American Hot Wax (1978)

Peak position: 31

CHARTING THE SOUNDS (continued)

Notable artists: Jerry Lee Lewis, Screamin' Jay Hawkins, Buddy Holly, Chuck Berry, Bobby Darin, Little Richard, and the Drifters.

Animal House (1978)

Peak position: 71

Notable artists: Sam Cooke, Stephen Bishop, Lloyd Williams, and Paul and Paula.

The Buddy Holly Story (1978)

Peak position: 86

Notable artists: Gary Busey (performs all of Buddy Holly's songs on the album).

FM (1978)

Peak position: 5

Notable artists: Tom Petty, Foreigner, Steely Dan, Steve Miller, the Doobie Brothers, Billy Joel, Boz Scaggs, the Eagles, Joe Walsh, Jimmy Buffet, Boston, Bob Seger, Linda Ronstadt, Dan Fogelberg, Queen, James Taylor, and Randy Meisner.

Grease (1978)

Peak position: 1 (for twelve weeks)

Notable artists: Frankie Avalon, Sha Na Na, Frankie Valli, Olivia Newton-John, and John Travolta. Two Travolta/Newton-John duets reached the Top 5 as singles—"You're the One That I Want" and "Summer Nights"—and both reached No. 1 in the United Kingdom.

The Last Waltz (1978)

Peak position: 16

Notable artists: Bob Dylan, the Band, Ronnie Hawkins, Dr. John, Neil Young, Neil Diamond, Joni Mitchell, Paul Butterfield, Ringo Starr, Van Morrison, Eric Clapton, Emmylou Harris, and Muddy Waters.

Sgt. Pepper's Lonely Hearts Club Band (1978)

Peak position: 5

Notable artists: Aerosmith, Billy Preston, Peter Frampton, the Bee Gees, and Earth, Wind and Fire (all performing Beatles songs).

Hair (1979)

Peak position: 65

Notable artists: Music from the original Broadway score, performed by the film's cast.

The Kids Are Alright (1979)

Peak position: 8

CHARTING THE SOUNDS *(continued)*

Notable artists: The Who (the soundtrack to a documentary film featuring various interviews and hits from the band's first fifteen years).

More American Graffiti (1979)
Peak position: 84

Notable artists: Bob Dylan, Country Joe and the Fish, Chuck Berry, Bill Haley, Del Shannon, and the Beach Boys.

Quadrophenia (1979)
Peak position: 46

Notable artists: The Who, James Brown, the Kingsmen, and Booker T. and the MG's (the soundtrack is from a film based on the Who's original *Quadrophenia* album released in 1973).

Rock 'n' Roll High School (1979)
Peak position: 118

Notable artists: Devo, the Ramones, Todd Rundgren, Brian Eno, Alice Cooper, Chuck Berry, and Nick Lowe.

The Rose (1979)
Peak position: 12

Notable artists: Bette Midler (also starred in the film). The title track claimed the No. 3 spot on the singles charts.

The Blues Brothers (1980)
Peak position: 13

Notable artists: The Blues Brothers (John Belushi and Dan Aykroyd as Jake and Elwood Blues), Aretha Franklin, John Lee Hooker, James Brown, and Ray Charles. The film, as well as the Blues Brothers band, were based on a *Saturday Night Live* skit.

Caddyshack (1980)
Peak position: 78

Notable artists: Journey and Kenny Loggins.

Flash Gordon (1980)
Peak position: 23

Notable artists: Queen (composed the entire soundtrack).

McVicar (1980)
Peak position: 22

Notable artists: Roger Daltrey, Kenney Jones, John Entwistle, and Pete Townshend.

CHARTING THE SOUNDS *(continued)*

One Trick Pony (1980)

Peak position: 12

Notable artists: Paul Simon (also starred in the film).

Roadie (1980)

Peak position: 125

Notable artists: Teddy Pendergrass, Styx, Eddie Rabbitt, Cheap Trick, Jerry Lee Lewis, Joe Ely, Alice Cooper, Blondie, Roy Orbison, Emmylou Harris, Pat Benatar, and Stephen Bishop.

Times Square (1980)

Peak position: 37

Notable artists: The Cure, the Ramones, Talking Heads, Patti Smith Group, Joe Jackson, Suzi Quatro, Roxy Music, XTC, the Pretenders, and Lou Reed.

Urban Cowboy (1980)

Peak position: 3

Notable artists: Joe Walsh, the Charlie Daniels Band, Bonnie Raitt, Linda Ronstadt, the Eagles, Jimmy Buffet, Boz Scaggs, and Bob Seger.

NOTES

1. Green 1987, 234.

2. *Rolling Stone*, October 5, 1978.

3. Ibid.

4. David Dallon, "D. A. Pennebaker: I Film while Leaping from My Chair," *Gadfly*, April 1999.

5. Miller 1980, 398.

6. Denisoff and Romanowski 1991, 222.

7. Miller 1980, 40.

8. Denisoff and Romanowski 1991, 734.

9. Ibid., 319.

A-TO-Z OF ROCK, 1974–1980

Bold-faced words refer to other entries in the A-to-Z chapter.

AC/DC. One of the few Australian bands to have a significant impact on American rock music, the heavy-metal act AC/DC enjoyed a run from 1973 through the end of the decade as the top rock act down under with albums such as *T.N.T.*, *High Voltage*, *Let There Be Rock*, and *Powerage*. Finally in 1980 the group broke through in the States with their massive seller *Highway to Hell*, followed by the even more successful 1981 release *Back in Black*. Though lead singer Bon Scott died (and was replaced by Brian Johnson) between the two albums—both Johnson and Scott gave AC/DC a unique sound with their full-throated screams, accented by the crunchy guitars of Scottish brothers Angus and Malcolm Young—the band continued their meteoric rise in America to become one of the world's top metal acts. (See Chapter 3, "Corporate and Mainstream Sounds: Rock Is Dead, Long Live Rock!")

Aerosmith. Considered by some to be a later, American version of the **Rolling Stones**, the Boston blues-rock outfit Aerosmith debuted with *Aerosmith* in 1973 but did not make a splash on the charts until their third album, 1975's *Toys in the Attic*, a must-have classic that included their memorable tunes "Sweet Emotion" and "Walk This Way." After *Toys in the Attic* found its way to No. 11 on the charts, the band's follow-up *Rocks* the next year made it as far as No. 4 and turned the bar band into a stadium headliner. Largely defined by the emotive antics of singer Steven Tyler and powerful blues riffs of guitarist Joe Perry (a duo eerily similar to the Stones' Mick Jagger and Keith Richards), the band reached their peak in the mid- to late 1970s before drug abuse and internal friction took their toll, leading to a brief breakup before reuniting to become a major draw again—as well as an MTV favorite—in the late 1980s and beyond. (See Chapter 3, "Corporate and Mainstream Sounds: Rock Is Dead, Long Live Rock!")

Ambient Music. Largely the creation of early electronica pioneer **Brian Eno**, ambient music was meant to provide soothing, subtle sounds that could be heard and ignored at the same time. Eno's first ambient album, 1975's *Discreet Music*, involved a pair of synthesizer melodies processed through a system of tape-delay loops and a recast Pachelbel's *Canon* with a shifted tempo. The album was so calming that hospitals played it in maternity wards. Eno's later albums, 1978's *Ambient 1/Music for Airports* and 1982's *Ambient 4/On Land*, helped inspire the "New Age" music of the 1980s and later influenced the "ambient techno" dance music in the 1990s. (See Chapter 2, "Progressive Rock in the 1970s: But Is It Art?")

America. The sons of air force personnel stationed in London, guitarists Dan Peek, Gerry Beckley, and Dewey Bunnell formed this **soft rock** trio in 1970 after graduating high school. Following a successful debut in the United Kingdom, the band moved to the United States, where their self-titled American debut spent five weeks at No. 1 in 1972, aided by their No. 1 single "Horse with No Name." Four of their next five albums found their way into the Top 10, introducing **MOR** staples such as "Ventura Highway," "Sister Golden Hair," and "Lonely People" into the soft-rock canon. With their easy-on-the-ear vocals and **Neil Young**–flavored melodies, the group enjoyed moderate success through the 1970s before falling out of favor with audiences. (See Chapter 4, "The Softer Side of Rock.")

AOR. An acronym for "album-oriented rock," AOR took root in the 1960s when adventurous DJs tired of playing the same singles over and over, as was the standard on AM radio. FM DJs began playing any track they wished from rock albums rather than just the most popular hits, leading to the phenomenon of albums reaching large sales with no hit singles (though this was a two-way street, as artists at the time had begun thinking in terms of cohesive albums rather than singles). As FM radio increased in popularity, eventually overtaking AM radio, AOR came to be seen as its own genre, with bands marketed for their entire works rather than their most popular songs. In the 1970s, AOR bands such as **Led Zeppelin**, **Pink Floyd**, and **Yes**—whose albums were considered more than just the sum of their parts—gained massive audiences and helped further the idea of an album being a cohesive unit rather than just a collection of individual songs.

***Autobahn* (1974).** **Kraftwerk** is one of the strangest groups ever to break into the pop mainstream. In a mid-1970s atmosphere of glitter and glamour, the four musicians that made up Kraftwerk prided themselves on their "anti-image," as if their personalities had been fully consumed by the electronics they used to construct this album of masterful soundscapes. The twenty-two-minute title track re-creates a drive along Germany's most famous highway, complete with the whooshes and buzz of passing traffic over a hypnotic beat. At a time when many artists were either glorifying or demonizing technology, Kraftwerk simply embraced it, and this groundbreaking album prefigures a whole new genre of electronic music that would follow in the decades to come.

The Average White Band. An early 1970s all-white **funk** band from Scotland, the Average White Band—or AWB—was a rarity in the black-dominated soul world. When their sophomore album, *AWB*, rose to No. 1 on the American charts in 1974, the group were well placed for a successful career in funk and **disco**. Later that year, however, drummer Robbie McIntosh died of an accidental drug overdose, casting a pallor over the band's future work. The group had moderate success through the remainder of the 1970s, particularly with their 1975 No. 1 single "Pick Up the Pieces." (See Chapter 1, "Funk, Jazz-Rock, and Fusion: The Rhythm Revolution.")

Bachman-Turner Overdrive. Consisting of Fred Turner and the Bach-man brothers—Robbie, Randy, and Tim—this Canadian party-rock band hit it big in 1974 when their sophomore album *Bachman-Turner Overdrive II* reached No. 4, aided by their hit single "Takin' Care of Business." After their next album *Not Fragile*, released the same year, reached No. 1 and yielded the hit "You Ain't Seen Nothing Yet," the band began a slow slide into mediocrity, steadily losing members and fans through the 1970s.

Bad Company. Having the good fortune to sign with **Led Zeppelin**'s new Swan Song label at the height of Zep's fame in 1974, British rockers Bad Company maintained a steady presence on the charts through the end of the decade, with their 1974 debut *Bad Company* reaching No. 1 and their four subsequent 1970s albums all breaching the Top 20. The group of respected rock veterans—drummer Simon Kirke (Free), vocalist Paul Rodgers (Free), bassist Boz Burrell (King Crimson), and guitarist Mick Ralphs (Mott the Hoople)—would release later classic-rock station staples such as "Bad Company," "Ready for Love," "Feel Like Making Love," "Shooting Star," "Rock 'N' Roll Fantasy." Though never topping the success of these first few albums, the band would continue with regular releases (and occasional roster changes) into the next century. (See Chapter 3, "Corporate and Mainstream Sounds: Rock Is Dead, Long Live Rock!")

The Band. Along with the Flying Burrito Brothers and the Byrds, the Band are considered among the fathers of country-rock, particularly appreciated for their role as **Bob Dylan**'s regular backing band in the late 1960s and on Dylan's *Planet Waves* album in 1974. A major concert draw (particularly with Dylan in 1974), the Band released the live *Before the Flood* in 1974 and *The Basement Tapes* in 1975, the latter a must-have for folk-rock fans, consisting of material recorded with Dylan in 1967. In 1976 the group decided to call it quits at an all-star jam captured on film by Martin Scorsese for the seminal **rockumentary** *The Last Waltz*.

The Bee Gees. Though remembered as the kings of **disco**, particularly for their association with the enormously popular soundtrack for *Saturday Night Fever*, the Bee Gees began as a soulful rock act, with most of their critical success coming in the late 1960s and early 1970s. Their early albums, however, did not hold a candle in terms of commercial success to their late-1970s disco hits on 1977's *Saturday Night Fever*, 1979's *Spirits Having Flown*, and 1979's *Greatest Hits*, which spent a combined thirty-one weeks at No. 1 and produced several No. 1 hits, including "How Deep Is Your Love," "You Should Be Dancing," "Tragedy," "Too Much Heaven," "Night Fever," and what is perhaps disco's signature song, "Stayin' Alive." (See Chapter 4, "The Softer Side of Rock.")

The B-52's. A **new-wave** band whose members considered themselves the masters of party rock, the B-52's were known for their campy, retro appearance—beehive hairdos and garage-sale attire—as much as their fun sing-a-long tunes. After forming in Athens, Georgia, in 1976, the group moved to New York after catching the attention of record companies and scored underground hits with their singles "Rock Lobster" and "Planet Claire." One of the original bands to make Athens a musical hotspot, the B-52's mixed surf music and go-go with amusing lyrics to let the rock world know it was all right to boogie without taking yourself too seriously. (See Chapter 7, "A New Wave of Rock.")

Black Flag. A hardcore, anarchist **punk-rock** group formed in southern California in 1977, Black Flag is seen as one of the original West Coast punk bands that followed in the footsteps of East Coast punkers the **Ramones.** Their dabbling with heavy metal and instrumentals made the band more eclectic than many punk outfits, and even though the group saw only minor success until the 1980s (after which some felt they betrayed the punk aesthetic), the group were highly respected for their commitment to the anticorporate, do-it-yourself work ethic, releasing their albums under founder/guitarist Greg Ginn's SST Records. (See Chapter 6, "Punk Rock: The Art of Noise.")

***The Blank Generation* (1976).** Despite its poor video quality and almost unbearable audio problems, *The Blank Generation* is one of rock's most important video documents. Filmed in 1975 at New York's **CBGB** (though, sadly, without accompanying audio), the film captures the **punk-rock** and **new-wave** movements in their very infancy, with some of the earliest performances by **Patti Smith**, David Byrne, **Richard Hell**, the **Ramones**, and **Blondie.** (See Chapter 8, "Rock on the Big Screen.")

Blondie. Named after the hair tint of their distinctively breathy lead singer Deborah Harry—occasionally referred to as if Blondie were her actual name—this late 1970s rock band exemplified the eclectic mix of sounds **new-wave** acts were bringing into pop. With No. 1 hits through the late 1970s and early 1980s like "Heart of Glass," "Call Me," "The Tide Is High," and "Rapture," the group demonstrated facility blending sounds as diverse as **punk**, reggae, and **disco** and brought a certain credibility to pop by being one of the earliest bands to play

CBGB, New York's legendary launching pad for some of the most important punk and new-wave acts. (See Chapter 7, "A New Wave of Rock.")

***Blood on the Tracks* (1975).** At a time when confessional albums were all the rage, this is as close as the enigmatic **Bob Dylan** ever came to baring his soul. Recorded during the breakdown of his marriage, *Blood on the Tracks* is by turns melancholy ("Tangled Up in Blue"), angry ("Idiot Wind"), and peaceful ("Shelter from the Storm"). Also represented is one of Dylan's classic narratives, "Lily, Rosemary and the Jack Of Hearts." The tracks were first recorded in New York, but during the Christmas holidays with his family in Minnesota, Dylan assembled a pickup band he had never met before and rerecorded peppier versions of the songs. A few of the original recordings can be found on 1985's *Biograph* and *The Bootleg Series, Volumes 1–3*, released in 1991.

Blue Öyster Cult. One of the few heavy-metal bands to earn both critical and commercial appeal in the 1970s—thanks in part to the producing and songwriting talents of Sandy Pearlman and Richard Meltzer, both rock critics, as well as occasional contributions from lauded **punk** rocker **Patti Smith**—Blue Öyster Cult found respect early on with their first three albums between 1972 and 1974: *Blue Öyster Cult, Tyranny and Mutation*, and *Secret Treaties*. Though known for their energetic, lasers-and-smoke live performances, the band was also appreciated for their intelligent lyrics and melodies, penning several memorable hits near the turn of the 1980s, including "Godzilla," "Burnin' for You," and "Don't Fear the Reaper." (See Chapter 3, "Corporate and Mainstream Sounds: Rock Is Dead, Long Live Rock!")

***Born to Run* (1975).** After two mediocre albums in 1973—*Greetings from Asbury Park, N.J.* and *The Wild, the Innocent & the E Street Shuffle*—the twenty-four-year-old **Bruce Springsteen** needed a hit record if he hoped to live up to "the next **Bob Dylan**" mantle that record executives and journalists were laying on him. It was recorded with a massive budget, and it sounds huge: layers of guitar, vocal echoes, massive drums, and songs that have been described as either epic or overblown. Regardless, *Born to Run* was meant to be Springsteen's kick-down-the-door album, and it was, providing him with a crop of songs well suited to his legendary marathon concerts.

Boston. An out-of-nowhere smash success with their 1976 self-titled debut (with 17 million copies sold and still counting, one of the most successful debuts in rock history), Boston helped define the so-called "**corporate rock**" sound of the late 1970s, which included soaring, emotive guitar solos and high-register harmonies. Although *Boston* was largely recorded in techno-genius Tom Scholz's basement before even having a band assembled or a record deal signed, the full, multilayered sound gives the album and its sequels a feeling like highly polished arena rock captured on vinyl. Though Scholz's notorious perfectionism has led to long periods—as much as eight years—between albums, the group was influential in making "power-pop" such a driving force in

1980s rock. (See Chapter 3, "Corporate and Mainstream Sounds: Rock Is Dead, Long Live Rock!")

Boston (1976). Although it peaked at No. 3, **Boston's** self-titled debut quickly became the best-selling debut album in history upon its release in 1976—a title finally snatched by Whitney Houston a decade later. To date, the record—featuring the hit singles "More Than a Feeling" (No. 5), "Long Time" (No. 22), and "Peace of Mind" (No. 38)—has sold 17 million copies in the United States alone. Although generally pegged as the quintessential "**corporate rock**" album by (non)merit of its huge, radio-friendly hooks and painstakingly perfect production (its massed harmonies and anthemic, soaring guitars seemingly constructed specifically for maximum arena/stadium impact), most of the album was in fact recorded in group mastermind Tom Scholz's basement on a 12-track recorder before he even had a record contract (or, for that matter, a band).

Bowie, David (b. 1947). One of rock's most chameleonlike figures, David Bowie found fame in the early 1970s as glam rock's most prominent figure, performing glitzy, androgynous theater-rock as the characters Ziggy Stardust and Aladdin Sane. In 1974 he immersed himself in the **Philadelphia sound**, releasing Philly-inspired hits such as "Young Americans" and the No. 1 hit "Fame" (co-written with **John Lennon**) and donning the character of the Thin White Duke, a persona aided by Bowie's growing drug habit. By mid-decade, Bowie changed his tune again, moving toward a more **krautrock**-inspired simplicity, incorporating electronica into his albums and working with **ambient music** pioneer **Brian Eno**, as well as helping **punk** godfather Iggy Pop relaunch his career by producing his 1977 albums *The Idiot* and *Lust for Life*. By the late 1970s Bowie was a major figure in rock, releasing a steady stream of albums and appearing in the occasional odd film into the next century.

Brown, James (b. 1928). Raised on gospel music, James Brown spent his life singing in church before becoming one of the central soul/**funk** figures in American music. Known as "hardest working man in show business," Brown was a prolific performer and recording artist, notoriously rehearsing his band to perfection. After putting six singles in the Top 10 between 1965 and his zenith in 1968, Brown entered the 1970s at the top of his profession, but sank through the decade as personal problems affected his career and competing funk acts crowded him out of the limelight. Though his 1974 double album **The Payback** was his last truly great release, Brown was enormously influential in the popularization of funk, soul, and **disco** in the 1970s, influencing acts such as **George Clinton** and **Kool and the Gang**.

Browne, Jackson (b. 1948). The archetypical "sensitive" **singer-songwriter**, Jackson Browne's laid-back songs of personal pain spoke to a generation of baby boomers coming to terms with adulthood. A native of West Germany, Browne grew up in California and built his reputation as a songwriter on the folk-music scenes in Los Angeles and New York City in the 1960s. His songs were recorded by the Byrds, the **Eagles**, and **Linda Ronstadt**, and after four solo albums Browne broke through with his platinum album *The Pretender* in 1976. His career hit a commercial high point with *Running on Empty* in 1977, and Browne put his fame toward political activism, most famously protesting nuclear power. Browne continued to pen hits on both love and politics throughout the '80s, with songs like "Lawyers in Love" and "Tender Is the Night," and after disappearing for years, he staged something of a comeback with a 1993 gold record, *I'm Alive*. (See Chapter 4, "The Softer Side of Rock.")

Buckley, Tim (1947–1975). One of the more difficult to appreciate among the **singer-songwriter** set, Tim Buckley zigzagged between simple, commercially viable work and awkward, abstract creations, all marked by his passionate delivery and remarkable five-and-a-half-octave vocal range. After suffering setbacks in the early 1970s due to poor reception of his more inaccessible albums, Buckley started to produce more straightforward material, though to little success. Buckley died of a drug overdose in 1975 after a tour on which he controlled his habit, thus lowering his tolerance. Later rock fans rediscovered Buckley—who had never been a commercial success—and the 1990s saw a critical appreciation for his more avant-garde work that eluded him while he was alive. (See Chapter 5, "Singer-Songwriters: Rock Grows Up.")

The California Sound. See Soft rock

The Cars. One of the most enduring bands to bring **new wave** into the 1980s, the Cars found a niche somewhere between *Happy Days* classic and **Talking Heads** ironic that brought them a litany of catchy pop hits such as "My Best Friend's Girl," "Just What I Needed," "You're All I've Got Tonight," "Good Times Roll," "Shake It Up," and "You Might Think," eschewing new wave's trademark eclecticism for a narrow range that found favor with radio stations and the charts. Fronted by singer Ric Ocasek's studied ironic detachment, the band's bouncy guitar jangles and uncomplicated synthesizers were a recipe for head-on, teenie-bopper pop-rock that made for an entire catalogue of safe fodder for later classic-rock stations. (See Chapter 7, "A New Wave of Rock.")

CBGB. If not the birthplace of **punk rock** and **new wave** in the United States, the New York music venue CBGB at least deserves the title of nursery. Opened in December 1973 by Hilly Kristal to show country, blues, and bluegrass acts (hence the club's name), Kristal soon began allowing bands like **Television** and the **Ramones** to perform on Sundays when the venue was not usually open. The following summer **Patti Smith** played a seven-week residency at CBGB, and the club's Rock Festival Showcase Auditions brought acts such as Smith, **Talking Heads**, **Richard Hell**, the Ramones, and **Blondie** to the stage, captured on the 1976 film ***The Blank Generation***, which chronicles the very stirrings of rock and new wave in New York. (See Chapter 6, "Punk Rock: The Art of Noise.")

The Clash. Although the **Sex Pistols** were London's first well-known **punk** band, the Clash soon overshadowed them as the best punk London had to offer. Incorporating roots and reggae sounds into their material, the Clash fused the raw power of punk with folk rock's idealism and **new wave**'s eclecticism. Starting out as an opening act for the Sex Pistols in 1976, the Clash became one of the United Kingdom's top punk bands before their material was released in the United States in 1978, replacing the Pistols' unfocused nihilism with left-wing politics. With two U.S. releases and American tours, the band earned a respectable enough following to bring their 1979 release *London Calling* into the Top 40, a rare feat for punk bands. The double album (which the band insisted be priced as a single) is often mentioned among rock's most important releases, incorporating reggae, ska, and rockabilly into its songs and bringing a more world-aware punk into the new decade. (See Chapter 6, "Punk Rock: The Art of Noise.")

Clinton, George (b. 1940). The master of 1970s **funk**, George Clinton—along with his bands **Parliament and Funkadelic** (sometimes combined as P-Funk)—married **James Brown**'s rhythm with Jimi Hendrix's psychedelia and **Frank Zappa**'s bizarre craftsmanship to create a sound and an image that has since been copied by a generation of desperately hip artists. His heavily layered acid-soul was an exciting **fusion** that made his audiences jump and groove to Clinton's summary exhortation: "Let your booty do its duty." Albums from his two bands, such as 1974's *Up for the Down Stroke*, 1975's *Chocolate City*, and 1976's *Mothership Connection*, became funk lodestones, influencing later genres such as hip-hop to maintain a connection to their soul and R&B roots. (See Chapter 1, "Funk, Jazz-Rock, and Fusion: The Rhythm Revolution.")

Corea, Chick (b. 1941). One of America's premier jazz pianists, Armando Anthony "Chick" Corea found fame in the late 1960s playing on **Miles Davis**'s landmark albums *In a Silent Way* and *Bitches Brew*. In the early 1970s, through collaborations with other artists and with his own band Return to Forever, Corea helped establish jazz **fusion** as a unique blend of jazz and rock. (See Chapter 1, "Funk, Jazz-Rock, and Fusion: The Rhythm Revolution.")

Corporate Rock. A catchall—and unfairly ambiguous—term for a certain combination of sound and success in the late 1970s and early 1980s, corporate rock is less a genre of music as much as a waste bin for critics to toss in bands that were tremendously successful but lacked the personality that would make them easier to classify. Usually used in the derogatory sense to dismiss arena and stadium bands like **Boston**, **Styx**, **Supertramp**, **Foreigner**, and **Journey**, corporate-rock bands often featured the powerful guitar work of heavy metal (though with much less distortion) and the tender themes of **soft rock** (though at a much higher volume, sung at a much higher pitch). Though often written off by critics for their pop sensibilities and commercial melodic hooks, corporate-rock bands featured some of the most talented musicians of the period, including the distinctive, piercing register of singer Steve Perry (Journey), the unerring melodic instincts of Mick Jones and Lou Gramm (Foreigner), and the sophisticated production techniques of Tom Scholz (Boston). (See Chapter 3, "Corporate and Mainstream Sounds: Rock Is Dead, Long Live Rock!")

Costello, Elvis (b. 1954). A self-proclaimed "angry" musician, Liverpoolian Elvis Costello was among the more political and outspoken of **new wave**'s standard-bearers. His independence, gifted songwriting, and nasal tone have earned him comparison to **Bob Dylan**, a slot he filled nicely during Dylan's lack of appreciable output during the new-wave heyday of the late 1970s and early 1980s. As a solo artist, Costello (born Declan McManus) has endured for decades beyond many new-wave acts, gathering airplay for releases into the twenty-first century even as his older hits, such as "Alison," "Oliver's Army," and "Radio Radio," seem timely—and often timeless—by comparison. (See Chapter 7, "A New Wave of Rock.")

Davis, Miles (1926–1991). One of jazz music's most legendary figures, Miles Davis is also one of the most important contributors to rock music who was not a rock musician himself. As creator of groundbreaking jazz and **fusion** albums such as 1959's *Kind of Blue*, 1969's *In a Silent Way*, and 1970's *Bitches Brew*, the trumpet player and composer stretched the boundaries of jazz to include rock elements and helped launch the careers of many great fusion artists such as **Chick Corea**, **Herbie Hancock**, and **John McLaughlin**. (See Chapter 1, "Funk, Jazz-Rock, and Fusion: The Rhythm Revolution.")

Denver, John (1943–1997). Perhaps the most deliberately pleasant of all the mid-1970s **singer-songwriters**, John Denver (born Henry John Deutschendorf Jr.) cultivated a nonthreatening, down-home image. Songs like "Take Me Home Country Roads," "Sunshine on My Shoulders," "Leaving, on a Jet Plane," and "Thank God I'm a Country Boy" have become American classics, campfire sing-alongs utterly devoid of any unpleasant emotion. Denver was also a movie star, appearing in the 1977 film *Oh, God!* with George Burns, and he collaborated frequently with the Muppets. He died at age fifty-three, when he crashed an experimental fiberglass aircraft in California. (See Chapter 5, "Singer-Songwriters: Rock Grows Up.")

Devo. A clever combination of **progressive**'s artsy anomie, **new wave**'s ironic detachment, and a **Zappa**-meets-**B-52's** sense of humor, Devo centered their image on the trope of musicians in a technology-controlled, posthuman universe. With its art-student leaders Mark Mothersbaugh and Jerry Casale rarely reaching beyond synthesized instruments, the band incorporated mechanical beats to make it sound as if humans were barely needed to create the music at all—even their name, Devo, is meant to encapsulate the concept of the inevitable devolution of humans into the machines they create. With few memorable tunes beyond their 1980 single "Whip It," the band never saw major commercial success but are remembered for their detachment from music's pomp that was the ultimate end for new wave. (See Chapter 7, "A New Wave of Rock.")

Dire Straits. A British rock act centered around the subtly stinging guitar work of Mark Knopfler, Dire Straits was a band out of pace with the rest of the rock world that nonetheless managed to hit the big time with intelligent lyrics and mellow melodies. As **disco** and **new wave** were battling for supremacy on the radio, Dire Straits emerged at the tail of the decade with their No. 4 hit "Sultans of Swing" from 1978's *Dire Straits*, followed by 1979's *Communiqué* and 1980's *Making Movies*, all of which reached the Top 20 in the United States. Although their biggest hit would not come until 1985 when the MTV-friendly hit "Money for Nothing" propelled the album *Brothers in Arms* into the top spot for nine weeks, the band's first three albums seemed to be the last gasp of the complex yet understated musical sophistication that began disappearing from rock in the early 1970s. (See Chapter 4, "The Softer Side of Rock.")

Disco. A short-lived but immensely popular genre in the late 1970s, disco was either something you loved or hated—there often seemed to be no middle ground. Rooted in the grooves of early 1970's **funk** and the mid-1970s **Philadelphia sound**, disco replaced the unreachable rock superstar with an elaborate dance floor, allowing the audience to be the performers rather than passive worshippers. Originally a somewhat underground scene, disco was launched to national prominence with the 1977 blockbuster film and album *Saturday Night Fever*, making gods of the **Bee Gees** (though most disco artists were faceless, a few, like Donna Summer and the Bee Gees, became icons of the 120 beat-per-minute sound). (See Chapter 1, "Funk, Jazz-Rock, and Fusion: The Rhythm Revolution.")

Discreet Music (1975). After leaving the groundbreaking group **Roxy Music** in the early 1970s, and before he would go on to produce hit records for **Talking Heads** and U2, **Brian Eno** stepped away from pop structures to create some of the first electronic **ambient music**. Designed to help relieve the stress of modern urban life, Eno used a system of two reel-to-reel tape records to layer sounds—the songs never really "go anywhere," but they evolve and decay with time. Eno created other parts of the album by editing and altering the pace of a classical music score. The result is delicate, beautiful music that unfolds and closes like a flower.

D.O.A. (1980). Centered around the **Sex Pistols**' 1978 tour of the United States, the documentary film *D.O.A.* features performances by such early **punk** bands as Generation X (with Billy Idol), Sham 69, the Rich Kids, and X-ray Spex, as well as plenty of Sex Pistols footage and commentary from concert-going fans. Known mainly for its famous in-bed interview with Sid Vicious and Nancy Spungen not too long before their tragic end, the film also includes valuable news and concert records that might otherwise have been lost to the ages. (See Chapter 8, "Rock on the Big Screen.")

The Doobie Brothers. Something of a vigorous, funked-up version of **Steely Dan**, the Doobie Brothers brought a hip-swaying energy to early 1970s radio with soulful **jazz-rock** hits like "Listen to the Music," "Jesus Is Just Alright," "China Grove," and "Black Water," their first No. 1 in 1974. With the addition of Steely Dan veterans Michael McDonald and Jeff Baxter in 1975 (joining the guitarists behind the Doobies' sound, Pat Simmons and Tom Johnston), the Doobie Brothers continued to sell out large venues and score platinum success with songs like "What a Fool Believes" and "Minute by Minute," rounding out the decade with four Grammy Awards in 1980. (See Chapter 1, "Funk, Jazz-Rock, and Fusion: The Rhythm Revolution.")

Double Fantasy (1980). Taken by itself, **John Lennon**'s final album can be faulted for its too-slick production and for Lennon's decision to include songs from his wife, Yoko Ono, who was not much of a tunesmith. Yet these criticisms are beside the point. *Double Fantasy* is Lennon's most mature and sentimental work, as he sings to his wife ("Dear Yoko") and his son ("Beautiful Boy [Darling Boy]"). This album shows Lennon at forty, five years after he gave up music, and on the eve of his assassination. He is on the verge of growing old gracefully and, it seems, happily—which makes the songs all the more poignant, and one can only wonder what further gems Lennon might have crafted had his comeback lasted more than one album.

Dylan, Bob (b. 1941). It would be impossible to overestimate Bob Dylan's impact on popular music and American culture. A comic and insightful figure many have compared to Charlie Chaplin or Huckleberry Finn, he broke new ground for pop music several times, and his best albums are American classics. His worst albums, however, are forgettable, and the early 1970s were not friendly to him. But in 1974 Dylan staged a major arena tour and a year later released another masterpiece, ***Blood on the Tracks***—fueled by the painful breakup with his wife—that is still hailed as perhaps his greatest work. The remainder of Dylan's 1970s was dominated by a long, carnival-like tour known as the Rolling Thunder Revue, from which Dylan got several albums, a TV special, and the poorly received documentary film *Renaldo and Clara*. Dylan topped off the odd decade with a conversion to Christianity, leading to a lackluster 1980s and the belief that Dylan's best years were long behind him. (See Chapter 5, "Singer-Songwriters: Rock Grows Up.")

The Eagles. Beginning as a backing band for popular country rocker **Linda Ronstadt** in 1971, the Eagles went on to become poster boys for the soft **California sound** of the 1970s and eventually one of the most successful rock acts of all time. The group was founded by Glenn Frey, Don Henley, Bernie Leadon, and Randy Meisner, though the latter two left in the mid-1970s, and three more faces—Don Felder, Joe Walsh, and Timothy Schmit—came on board at various points during the decade. At a time when the **singer-songwriter** movement was receiving massive airplay, the Eagles took the singer-songwriter aesthetic and applied it to a group format, creating tender ballads and personal stories with a full rock backing. At the peak of their success between 1975 and 1979, the group sent four albums to the top of the charts for a combined twenty-seven weeks at No. 1. Among them were **Hotel California** and *Their Greatest Hits 1971–1975*, both of which became among the best-selling albums in rock history. (See Chapter 4, "The Softer Side of Rock.")

Earth, Wind and Fire. One of the most popular—and most talented—**funk** bands of the decade, Earth, Wind and Fire traded hits with funkmeister **George Clinton** throughout the 1970s with their blend of funk, soul, jazz, gospel, Latin, and African folk rhythms. Their colorful outfits and elaborate stage productions augmented their catchy grooves to make them a popular tour band as well. Averaging more than an album a year into the 1980s, the group hit the Top 10 with every release between 1975 and 1981, many of them spawning Top 40 singles as well. (See Chapter 1, "Funk, Jazz-Rock, and Fusion: The Rhythm Revolution.")

Electric Light Orchestra. One of the rare **progressive** bands to bring classical musicians into their fold (rather than using a mellotron or electronic technology to synthesize orchestral sounds), the Electric Light Orchestra was also one of the few prog-rock groups to flourish as progressive music began declining in the late 1970s. Though the group was formed in 1969—with Roy Wood, Jeff Lynne on guitar, and Bev Bevan on drums, later joined by string and horn players—ELO did not break out until their 1974 album *Eldorado* found its way into the Top 20, aided by the Top 10 single "Can't Get It Out of My Head." Though earlier minor hits marked the band as distinctly progressive, their 1975 release *Face the Music* demonstrated their capacity for change as the band moved toward a **disco** sound with hits like "Evil Woman" and "Strange Magic." With even larger hit albums through the late 1970s and early 1980s, and ambitious, science-fiction–themed tours, the band became an FM-radio staple before eventually breaking up in 1983. (See Chapter 2, "Progressive Rock in the 1970s: But Is It Art?")

Emerson, Lake & Palmer. The trio of Keith Emerson, Greg Lake, and Carl Palmer comprised one of **progressive rock**'s supergroups, riding the wave of classical-influenced rock to produce influential studio albums such as 1973's *Brain Salad Surgery* and live releases such as their 1974 triple album *Welcome Back My Friends to the Show That Never Ends*, making them one of the most successful groups of the period. As one of the most elaborate stage bands in rock, ELP spent the mid-1970s touring with thirty-six tons of equipment and occasionally an entire symphony backing them. Such excess would eventually doom progressive music to be edged out of the charts by the simplicity and populism of **punk rock**. (See Chapter 2, "Progressive Rock in the 1970s: But Is It Art?")

Eno, Brian (b. 1948). Standing alongside Jimi Hendrix as one of the most creative studio innovators in rock, Brian Eno was largely responsible for the popularization of electronica and **ambient music** in the 1970s and 1980s. Eno built his reputation as an inventive keyboard player in the British group **Roxy Music** before going his own way in 1973, first working with Deep Purple's brilliant Robert Fripp on tape looping techniques and then with many other musicians on accidental and ambient music. By using the studio as an instrument on albums such as 1975's *Discreet Music* and 1978's *Ambient 1/Music for Airports*, Eno pioneered recording techniques that would influence **progressive**, **new wave**, New Age, dance, and pop music for decades. (See Chapter 2, "Progressive Rock in the 1970s: But Is It Art?")

Fleetwood Mac. After releasing a dozen albums in the late 1960s and early 1970s to very limited success, the **soft-rock** group Fleetwood Mac picked up guitarist Lindsey Buckingham and singer Stevie Nicks for their self-titled 1975 album, which slowly crawled to the top of the charts in 1976. Their next studio album, 1977's *Rumours*, was an unexpected hit, spending thirty-one weeks at the top of the charts—the highest-charting rock album ever until Michael Jackson's *Thriller* occupied the No. 1 spot for thirty-seven weeks in 1983. Though originally a British blues band, Fleetwood Mac came to symbolize the California sound almost as much as the **Eagles**, with *Rumours* spawning some of West Coast rock's most memorable hits, including "Dreams," "Don't Stop," "You Make Loving Fun," and "Go Your Own Way." (See Chapter 4, "The Softer Side of Rock.")

Foreigner. One year after **Boston** came out of nowhere to release a smash debut and sell out arenas, the power-pop outfit Foreigner performed the same feat with their No. 4 self-titled debut in 1977, featuring the three Top 20 hits "Feels Like the First Time," "Long, Long Way from Home," and "Cold as Ice," an auspicious start to a career as one of the top rock outfits of the late 1970s and early 1980s. Foreigner's next three albums—1978's *Double Vision*, 1979's *Head Games*, and 1981's *4*—all made the Top 5 as well, introducing some of **corporate rock**'s biggest anthems, including "Waiting for a Girl Like You," "Juke Box Hero," "Hot Blooded," and "Urgent." Powered by the dominating vocals of Lou Gramm (who later went on to moderate solo success) and catchy melodic and lyrical hooks of Gramm and guitarist/songwriter Mick Jones, the band personified as well as any act the blend of rock guitar and pop hooks that marked corporate rock. (See Chapter 3, "Corporate and Mainstream Sounds: Rock Is Dead, Long Live Rock!")

Frampton, Peter (b. 1950). See *Frampton Comes Alive!* (1976)

Frampton Comes Alive! **(1976).** If the 1970s taught us anything, it is that the quickest route toward collecting one's allotted fifteen minutes of fame is to release a double-live album. Guitarist/singer Peter Frampton had already had enough minor brushes with fame to be considered something of a has-been (rather than a nobody) when *Frampton Comes Alive!* gave him not only the biggest hit of his career but one of the biggest live albums in rock (it eventually sold more than 6 million in the United States and 18 million worldwide). Though more an artifact of its time than essential listening today, Frampton's nice-guy-guitar-hero charm still shines through on the sing-along favorites "Show Me the Way" and "Do You Feel Like We Do," while the album's third Top 10 single, "Baby, I Love Your Way," remains inescapable on every easy-listening radio station in the modern world. Frampton himself is harder to come by, as he never came close to repeating *Comes Alive!*'s success. (See Chapter 3, "Corporate and Mainstream Sounds: Rock Is Dead, Long Live Rock!")

Funk. A popular 1970s genre featuring syncopated rhythms, strong base-lines, danceable grooves, and shouted lyrics, funk was an energetic and upbeat style largely influenced by predominantly black American musical forms such as soul and gospel. Popularized in the late 1960s by artists such as **James Brown**, the Meters, and Sly and the Family Stone, funk's infectious rhythms made stars of '70s acts like **Earth, Wind and Fire**, **Kool and the Gang**, and the inappropriately named **Average White Band** (white but far from average). (See Chapter 1, "Funk, Jazz-Rock, and Fusion: The Rhythm Revolution.")

Funkadelic. See **Parliament/Funkadelic**

Fusion. One of the few genres almost entirely attributable to one person, fusion grew out of jazz master **Miles Davis**'s jazz-rock experiments at the turn of the decade, particularly on his 1970 album *Bitches Brew*. Although bands such as Chicago, Electric Flag, and Blood, Sweat & Tears incorporated horns and jazz techniques into their late 1960s albums, their efforts were limited when compared to Davis' true melding of jazz and rock (hence, the work of Davis and his imitators is called "fusion," while mainstream rock that borrows from jazz is termed "jazz-rock"). Jazz-rock continued its popularity in the 1970s with acts like **Joni Mitchell**, the **Doobie Brothers**, and **Steely Dan**, while fusion saw further development through Miles Davis' former bandmates **Chick Corea**, **John McLaughlin**, and **Herbie Hancock**, as well as world musicians such as Ry Cooder and Carlos Santana. (See Chapter 1, "Funk, Jazz-Rock, and Fusion: The Rhythm Revolution.")

Genesis. Although largely remembered in the United States as a Phil Collins–led, 1980s pop band, Genesis was fairly successful in the early and mid-1970s as a **progressive** act led by the flamboyant Peter Gabriel. Thickly layered recordings and theatric stage performances earned them the typical progressive reputation as overblown and dramatic, but the band endured from their beginnings in 1967 to become a popular British attraction. With the release of their powerful 1974 *The Lamb Lies Down on Broadway*, the band was introduced to American audiences. Subsequent albums such as 1976's *A Trick of the Tail* and 1978's *. . . And Then There Were Three* slowly crept up the American charts, helping the group earn a large following in the United States by the early 1980s. (See Chapter 2, "Progressive Rock in the 1970s: But Is It Art?")

Grease (1978). Originally a very successful theater production (the longest-running Broadway play until the 1980s), *Grease* was adapted for the big screen by **Bee Gees** manager **Robert Stigwood**, who had a smash hit the previous year with *Saturday Night Fever*. Securing John Travolta's place as a major teen heartthrob and introducing singer Olivia Newton-John to the big screen, *Grease* became one of the highest-grossing films of all time. The soundtrack perched at the top of the charts for twelve weeks, with four of the film's songs reaching the Top 5 as singles: "Hopelessly Devoted to You"; "Grease"; and two Travolta/Newton-John duets, "You're the One That I Want" and "Summer Nights." (See Chapter 8, "Rock on the Big Screen.")

Hancock, Herbie (b. 1940). Through his association with **Miles Davis** in the mid-1960s, Herbie Hancock was on the forefront of the jazz and rock blend that would become **fusion**. After he formed the Headhunters and released the hit record *Head Hunters* in 1973, fusion found popular appeal and pushed jazz-rock further into the mainstream. Hancock continued his experiments with jazz, rock, and electronica through the 1970s, becoming a well-known innovator in these genres as well as soul, **funk**, world, and hip-hop. (See Chapter 1, "Funk, Jazz-Rock, and Fusion: The Rhythm Revolution.")

Heart. Led by the Wilson sisters—Ann on vocals and Nancy on guitar—the Seattle/Vancouver band Heart was an original and forceful hard-rock act that broke out in the States with their 1976 powerhouse debut *Dreamboat Annie*, which was recorded for an independent Canadian label but climbed to No. 7 in the United States. Striking a balance between delicate guitar fretwork and hard-driving rhythms, the group became a steady presence on the charts, with 1977's *Little Queen*, 1978's *Magazine*, 1978's *Dog & Butterfly*, and 1980's *Bebe Le Strange* and *Greatest Hits/Live* all finding homes in the Top 20. Though the band suffered a slump in the early 1980s, they came back with a vengeance with several hit singles in 1986 and 1987, their new work in regular play on MTV while their harder, earlier material became staples of classic rock radio. (See Chapter 3, "Corporate and Mainstream Sounds: Rock Is Dead, Long Live Rock!")

Hell, Richard (b. 1949). Believed by many to have been the original source of **punk** fashion, Richard Hell (born Richard Meyers) played guitar and sang for the early punk group **Television** before leading the short-lived New York punk bands the Heartbreakers and the Voidoids. Hell's spiked hair and torn clothes were reportedly an homage to the French poet Arthur Rimbaud and became the default fashion for punk bands and fans, particularly after **Sex Pistols** manager **Malcolm McLaren** dolled up his band to (literally) look like Hell. With the Heartbreakers, Hell formed what may have been punk's first supergroup, combining his talents with former New York Dolls Jerry Nolan and Johnny Thunders. Hell soon left to form the Voidoids, whose nihilistic song "Blank Generation" became an anthem for the burgeoning **new-wave** movement. (See Chapter 6, "Punk Rock: The Art of Noise.")

***Horses* (1975).** One of **punk rock**'s seminal foundation albums, **Patti Smith**'s *Horses* was perhaps the first punk album to receive both critical and popular acclaim, making a respectable showing at No. 47 on the charts when the few punk albums around at the time could not be found in the record stores. Produced by the Velvet Underground's John Cale with a cover photo of Smith by famed avant-garde photographer Robert Mapplethorpe, *Horses* demonstrates the power of punk interpretations with commanding covers of the **Van Morrison** classic "Gloria" and Cannibal and the Headhunters' tune "Land of a Thousand Dances" (renamed "Land"). Smith's deliberately primitive and loose style on *Horses* presaged both the punk and **new-wave** sounds of mid-1970s New York City.

***Hotel California* (1976).** Considered by many to be the **Eagles**' finest hour, the release of *Hotel California* established the band as the definitive authors of the **California sound**, the album being the third of four consecutive Eagles records to top the charts for a combined twenty-seven weeks. With the group's classic lineup of Joe Walsh, Don Felder, Glenn Frey, Randy Meisner, and Don Henley, *Hotel California* captured the band at their tightest, using lush, intricate vocals and guitar work to interpret personal and heavily metaphorical lyrics that seemed sweet to the ear but bordered on a subtle nihilism. Generating the **soft-rock** classics "Hotel Calfornia," "New Kid in Town," "Life in the Fast Lane," "Wasted Time," and "Victim of Love," the album went platinum many times over and eventually became one of the best-selling albums in rock.

Ian, Janis (b. 1951). Janis Ian was a precocious **singer-songwriter** who scored her first hit song, "Society's Child," in 1966, when she was only fifteen. Ian has since released nineteen albums following her self-titled debut in 1967. The zenith of her commercial success came with her 1975 album *Between the Lines*, which included her most famous song, "At Seventeen." The singer's reflection on teenage alienation, from the point of view of a mature adult, epitomizes the nostalgia and emphasis on personal psychic issues that characterized the baby-boom generation in the mid-1970s. (See Chapter 5, "Singer-Songwriters: Rock Grows Up.")

Jackson, Joe (b. 1954). Regarded by critics as a softer, cuddlier version of **Elvis Costello**, fellow-Englishman Joe Jackson just caught the tail of the **new-wave** movement as it was scurrying into the 1980s. His 1979 debut *Look Sharp!* found its way to No. 22 on the charts, aided by his most memorable hit, "Is She Really Going Out with Him?"—a catchy ditty more **Cars**-like than anything Costello ever wrote. As many new-wave artists did before and since, Jackson used his pop-rock beginnings to explore more diverse world flavors such as Latin and Caribbean sounds in his 1980s releases. (See Chapter 7, "A New Wave of Rock.")

Jazz-rock. See **Fusion**

Joel, Billy (b. 1949). Billy Joel was one of the most commercially successful **singer-songwriters** of the 1970s and 1980s. He released his solo debut, *Cold Spring Harbor*, in 1971, but he did not become a star until he released *Piano Man* on Columbia Records in 1973. The title track reflected Joel's experience playing piano-bar gigs in Los Angeles, and it established Joel as a singer-songwriter with a gift for spinning sentimental stories of big-city characters. His 1977 album *The Stranger* would be the biggest commercial success of his career, hitting No. 2 and eventually selling more than 10 million copies. It produced three singles that made the Hot 100 chart—"Only the Good Die Young," "Movin' Out (Anthony's Song)," and "Just the Way You Are." The 1978 follow-up, *52nd Street*, would become Joel's first No. 1 album. His knack for literary hitmaking continued in the 1980s with hits like "Uptown Girl." The enduring popularity of his storytelling pop is evidenced by the fact that in 1999 his total worldwide record sales topped 100 million, and he was inducted into the Rock and Roll Hall of Fame. (See Chapter 5, "Singer-Songwriters: Rock Grows Up.")

John, Elton (b. 1947). One of the most successful international acts of the 1970s, Elton John (born Reginald Dwight) combined the showmanship of glam rock with the energy and catchiness of pop and an eclectic array of influences—including **disco**, soul, country, hard rock, and glam—to create a versatile and charismatic appeal. Between 1972 and 1975, John's seven original albums (including a Greatest Hits package) spent a remarkable thirty-nine weeks at the top of the charts. At the height of his fame, his 1975 release *Captain Fantastic and the Brown Dirt Cowboy* became the first album in chart history to debut at No. 1, a feat that has rarely been repeated since. John was also one of the most successful touring acts in the world, selling out the largest arenas wherever he went and leaving behind a string of memorable hit tunes— "Your Song," "Rocket Man," "Tiny Dancer," "Crocodile Rock," "Daniel," "Goodbye Yellow Brick Road," "Don't Let the Sun Go Down on Me," "Someone Saved My Life Tonight," just to name a few—that have endured for decades. (See Chapter 4, "The Softer Side of Rock.")

Journey. Although Journey's most commercial success would not come until the early 1980s, this **corporate-rock** outfit—complete with power ballads, high-range vocals, and impressive guitar solos—was active long before corporate rock had a name. Founded by guitar virtuoso Neal Schon and keyboardist Gregg Rolie in 1973, both of whom had previously played in Santana, the group saw limited success until singer Steve Perry joined the band in 1978 for their fourth album, *Infinity*, which began the band's march up the ranks of the Top 40. Perry's distinctive and powerful high-pitched vocals coupled with Schon's bouncy guitar grooves moved the group to the forefront of the corporate-rock set with five consecutive Top 10 albums in the early 1980s. (See Chapter 3, "Corporate and Mainstream Sounds: Rock Is Dead, Long Live Rock!")

Judas Priest. Helping to usher in the 1980s with a faster, more intense heavy metal was the grinding English act Judas Priest. Formed by guitarist Kenneth Downing, bassist Ian Hill, singer Rob Halford, and guitarist Glenn Tipton, the band's black-leather and spikes wardrobe spawned a fashion code that would soon make speed-metal fans discernible from mere hard rockers. Though they formed in 1969, it took two independent releases and eight years of touring the United Kingdom and Europe before they could find an audience in the States. After three moderately successful American releases that helped popularize a new wave of U.S.-bound British metal, the band broke out in 1979 with their live *Unleashed in the East*, spawning a series of hit records that would make them one of the most popular heavy-metal acts of the 1980s. (See Chapter 3, "Corporate and Mainstream Sounds: Rock Is Dead, Long Live Rock!")

Kansas. One of the bands that straddled the **progressive** and **corporate-rock** genres with thickly layered guitars and keyboards and Steve Walsh's soaring vocals, Kansas was an **AOR** staple in the mid-1970s. After their first three albums failed to make much of an impression, the group broke through in 1976 with *Leftoverture*, featuring their first Top 40 hit "Carry On Wayward Son." The follow-up, 1977's *Point of Know Return*, featured the group's most famous hit "Dust in the Wind," which exhausted the band's fifteen minutes of fame. Though they released a steady stream of albums into the late 1980s, only a few songs stood the test of time to find homes on later classic rock stations.

King, Carole (b. 1942). With her husband Gerry Goffin, Carole King co-wrote songs like "On Broadway," "Up on the Roof," and "Locomotion" that defined the rock sensibility in the 1960s. After eight years off the charts—and following her divorce from Goffin—King staged an impressive comeback when her 1971 solo album *Tapestry* sold more than 13 million copies to date and made King a pop sensation. With *Music* in 1971 and *Rhymes and Reasons* in 1972, King veered into an overly sentimental tone that plagued many **singer-songwriter** albums in the mid-'70s, yet both albums went gold. *Fantasy*, in 1973, was an edgier album where King transcended the inherent limitations of her own experience by speaking through characters like Hollywood streetwalkers and bored suburban housewives. Her 1974 album *Wrap Around Joy* went gold (and produced the No. 1 hit "Jazzman"), as did *Thoroughbred* in 1976. After that she left Ode Records and moved to Capitol, a transition that marked a decline in her commercial success. (See Chapter 5, "Singer-Songwriters: Rock Grows Up.")

The Kinks. One of the first rock bands to approximate a heavy-metal sound (with the seminal singles "You Really Got Me" and "All Day and All of the Night" in the mid-1960s), the Kinks seemed destined for a roller-coaster career, losing their American audience in the late 1960s after being banned from the United States for a few years for rowdy behavior, then regaining a following with their surprise hit "Lola" in 1970, then losing their fans again with a less accessible sound in the early 1970s, and finally winning popular support again with a return to straightforward rock (and a sudden reappreciation of their earlier material) in the late 1970s. With a string of Top 40 albums between 1977 and 1983, as well as the popular hit "Come Dancing" in 1983, the Kinks stood toe-to-toe with many of the **punk** and **new-wave** acts for whom they had laid the groundwork more than a decade earlier. (See Chapter 3, "Corporate and Mainstream Sounds: Rock Is Dead, Long Live Rock!")

KISS. Few bands in rock have been as successful as KISS at becoming massive stars as parodies of their own genre, or left as big a legacy. With the fashion sense of the New York Dolls and the cheesy music of **Rod Stewart**'s lesser material, KISS was not so much hard-rock music as wuss-metal theater. Sporting bondage attire, face paint, and seven-inch platform boots, and employing all manner of pyrotechnics and other stage craft available, the band created a cult of heavy metal that was actually headbanging fun rather than darkly serious and depressing. More than just a flashy rock act, KISS were a brand, pimping out KISS-themed comics, lunch boxes, action figures, baseball cards, and an array of other items that made them the band of choice for the thirteen to eighteen set. The quartet of Paul Stanley, Gene Simmons, Ace Frehley, and Peter Criss sold mediocre albums through the early 1970s but became known for their wild stage act, earning them massive sales for their 1975 live album *Alive!*, followed by a quick string of hit albums including *Destroyer*, *Rock and Roll Over*, and *Love Gun*, making them the first band in history to have four albums on the charts simultaneously. Their fun, headbanging hits like "Rock and Roll All Nite" and "Detroit Rock City" are icons of the pop/metal mix that became a major commercial enterprise in the 1980s. (See Chapter 3, "Corporate and Mainstream Sounds: Rock Is Dead, Long Live Rock!")

The Knack. Critically derided for taking **new wave** from alternative to mainstream (though they were not the first new-wave artists to score chart success), the Knack leaped out of the closet with their memorable 1979 debut *Get the Knack* (modeled after the Beatles' debut *Meet the Beatles!*) and its chart-busting single "My Sharona." The band's rapid popular ascension doomed it immediately in the eyes of the new-wave critics, who, in the late 1970s, liked to approve music before people were allowed to enjoy it. Although another single from the same album, "Good Girls Don't," also found popular success, the band's star fell as quickly as it had risen, demonstrating that although new-wave sounds could enjoy heavy chart success, it takes a certain amount of street credibility to endure as a new-wave band. (See Chapter 7, "A New Wave of Rock.")

Kool and the Gang. Described by **funk** originator **James Brown** as "the second-baddest out there,"[1] Kool and the Gang epitomized the spirit of boogie with their dance-inducing instrumentals and hooting vocals, making party music respectable. With hits throughout the decade such as 1974's "Jungle Boogie," 1979's "Ladies Night," and 1980's "Celebration," the band left a trail of R&B and **disco** memories in its wake, continuing to place songs in the Top 10 until the late 1980s. (See Chapter 1, "Funk, Jazz-Rock, and Fusion: The Rhythm Revolution.")

Kraftwerk. The brainchild of German avant-garde composers Ralf Hütter and Florian Schneider, Kraftwerk helped bring about the electronica movement in the United States in the mid-1970s with their surprise No. 5 hit *Autobahn*. Hütter and Schneider used synthesizers and programmed drum machines to create pulsating electronic rhythms and synthesized swooshes, simulating a drive along the famous German highway. Though *Autobahn* was the duo's only American hit, Kraftwerk introduced **krautrock** to U.S. audiences and helped pave the way for the electronica movement. (See Chapter 2, "Progressive Rock in the 1970s: But Is It Art?")

Krautrock. Several decades after World War II, Germany sought to move forward with cultural productions that represented the most avant-garde comments on modernity. In their music, the rock form known as "kosmiche" (cosmic) relied heavily on technology (in the form of synthesizers and studio effects) to produce progressive compositions that ironically commented on the dehumanizing effects of technology. In Britain and the United States this music was dubbed "krautrock," led by bands such as **Kraftwerk**, Neu!, Can, Faust, and **Tangerine Dream**. (See Chapter 2, "Progressive Rock in the 1970s: But Is It Art?")

***The Last Waltz* (1978).** One of rock's most celebrated concert films, the Martin Scorsese–directed *The Last Waltz* is a highly polished record of the **Band**'s final performance on Thanksgiving Day in 1976. With an elaborate set, sophisticated camera work, and a $1.5 million shooting budget, it might be rock's most elaborate concert documentary. Along with the Band, the all-star lineup includes **Bob Dylan**, Ronnie Hawkins, Dr. John, **Neil Young**, Neil Diamond, **Joni Mitchell**, Paul Butterfield, Ringo Starr, **Van Morrison**, Eric Clapton, Emmylou Harris, and Muddy Waters. (See Chapter 8, "Rock on the Big Screen.")

Led Zeppelin. Few critics have written about Led Zeppelin without employing at least a few superlatives: loudest, wildest, most talented, and others. Rivaling **Elton John** and the **Eagles** for the title of most successful act of the 1970s, Zeppelin was certainly the most influential on later music, as learning the intro to "Stairway to Heaven" or "Black Dog" became a rite of passage for hopeful teenage guitarists ever since. With all nine of their albums reaching the Top 10 between 1969 and 1980 (when the band broke up after the death of drummer John Bonham), and six of them spending a combined twenty-eight weeks at No. 1, Zeppelin were the iconic 1970s supergroup, flying from gig to gig in Lear jets and trashing $1,000-a-night hotel rooms as they toured. As Jaan

Uhelzki wrote in *Creem* in 1975, "They have become the longest-lasting model for those culturally bankrupt 'trendies' to follow. Underage masses walk, talk, dress, and dope like Zep. They have become a necessary trapping for the terminally hip, as well as providing the audial backdrop for any social gathering."[2] Such fame was not undeserved—Robert Plant's screeching vocals, John Paul Jones' thick basslines, John Bonham's thunderous drumming, and Jimmy Page's versatile and brilliant guitar work, coupled with the band's adventurous forays into other styles such as folk, reggae, Celtic, and raga, made them one of rock's all-time seminal bands. (See Chapter 3, "Corporate and Mainstream Sounds: Rock Is Dead, Long Live Rock!")

Lennon, John (1940–1980). After the Beatles broke up in 1970, Lennon embarked on a solo career that was carefully scrutinized by fans around the world. That year, he collaborated with his future wife, the artist Yoko Ono, on *Plastic Ono Band*, a sharply introspective album that ushered in the "Me Generation" and confessional songwriting. *Imagine* followed in 1971, and the title track has become a pop standard. Through the early 1970s Lennon battled the Nixon administration's unsuccessful attempts to have him deported on a 1968 drug conviction, but otherwise he spent the decade on a retreat from music to raise a family with Ono. His eagerly anticipated comeback album **Double Fantasy** in 1980 earned him critical kudos and a Grammy for Album of the Year, a triumphant return cut tragically short when Lennon was assassinated outside the Dakota apartment building in New York City that December. (See Chapter 5, "Singer-Songwriters: Rock Grows Up.")

Lightfoot, Gordon (b. 1938). This Canadian **singer-songwriter** was heavily influenced by **Bob Dylan** in the 1960s. Lightfoot first broke into pop when Peter, Paul and Mary's recording of his song "For Lovin' Me" hit the U.S. Top 40 in 1965. Lightfoot released fourteen original albums over the next twenty-eight years, mining personal experience for his first hit performance, "If You Could Read My Mind," which hit No. 5 in 1971, while the album of the same name went gold. Reflecting the literary bent of some singer-songwriters, Lightfoot also spun historical yarns in his music. In 1975, a ship named the *Edmund Fitzgerald* sank in Lake Superior, and Lightfoot spent three days writing "The Wreck of the Edmund Fitzgerald." A year later the song hit No. 2, and it earned Lightfoot a Grammy nomination in 1977. Although his records and tours enjoyed modest success in America in the mid-1970s, Canada treated Lightfoot like a poet laureate. In 1980 he was named Canada's male singer of the previous decade, and in 1997 he received the Governor General's award—the highest official Canadian honor. (See Chapter 5, "Singer-Songwriters: Rock Grows Up.")

***London Calling* (1979).** Regarded as one of **punk**'s most sophisticated releases, the **Clash** double-album *London Calling* (priced, at the band's insistence, as a single album) was an eclectic mix of punk, ska, reggae, jazz, and rockabilly that stunned critics and fans and established the Clash as punk rock's reigning instigators. By tying punk to other music genres the Clash moved punk beyond a simple reactionary fad and into the realm of respected rock subgenre. Where many punk acts were somewhat nihilistic, especially Clash forerunners the **Sex Pistols**, the Clash wore their politics on their sleeves, particularly in tracks like "London Calling," "Spanish Bombs," and "The Guns of Brixton." The cover art—a concert photo of bassist Paul Simonon smashing his guitar surrounded by text imitating Elvis Presley's 1956 debut album—is often mentioned among the best album covers in rock.

Lynyrd Skynyrd. The short and tragic story of Lynyrd Skynyrd is one of the great legends of rock music. Second in the southern rock scene only to the Allman Brothers, who served as their inspiration in the early 1970s, Lynyrd Skynyrd were the alternative to metal-based hard rock in the 1970s, bringing audiences a taste of southern boogie in heavy doses with their legendary live performances. The band's 1974 hit "Sweet Home Alabama" became the anthem for southern pride, and songs like "Free Bird," "You Got That Right," "What's Your Name," "Gimme Three Steps," and "Saturday Night Special" endured to become classic-rock staples. Releasing six albums since their debut in 1973, the band met a tragic end in 1977 when their plane crashed during a U.S. tour, killing several members of the group. (See Volume 3, Chapter 4, "The South Rises Again.")

The Mahavishnu Orchestra. See McLaughlin, John

***Marquee Moon* (1977).** The long-awaited first release from **Television**, the group that began the New York **punk** and **new-wave** movements, *Marquee Moon* is hailed as a punk classic. Though the album was not released until punk had spread around the United States and England—three years after Television first appeared at **CBGB**—its power and passion earned it critical praise and an enduring legacy as one of the finest examples of punk in its peak year. The album never earned much sales or airplay, but Television's cultish fans felt it so crystalized the punk sound that it was hailed as "post-punk" while punk itself was still in diapers.

McCartney, Paul (b. 1942). The most successful Beatle after the band's breakup in 1970, Paul McCartney remained in the spotlight through the decade with his popular **soft rock** act Wings. Under various permutations of the name "Paul McCartney and Wings," the band scored eight consecutive Top 10 albums between 1971 and 1979 (plus a Greatest Hits package), with five of them topping the charts. Leaving behind a trail of bouncy radio favorites such as "Let 'Em In," "My Love," "Band on the Run," "Helen Wheels," "Silly Love Songs," and "With a Little Luck," Wings were a staple of **MOR** programming in the 1970s. (See Chapter 4, "The Softer Side of Rock.")

McLaren, Malcolm (b. 1946). One of the most important figures in the birth of London **punk**, Malcolm McLaren ran an anti-fashion store called

SEX, at which he formed the band the **Sex Pistols** in 1975 as something of a marketing gimmick. McLaren had previously managed the seminal proto-punk group the New York Dolls during the downward slope of their career and borrowed the look of New York punk **Richard Hell** to adorn the Sex Pistols in ripped clothing and spiked hair, a look soon imitated by punk fans. McLaren promoted the barely talented Sex Pistols with intentionally confrontational publicity gimmicks that often got the group banned from playing and releasing records but nonetheless earned them a large cult following in London's underground music scene. (See Chapter 6, "Punk Rock: The Art of Noise.")

McLaughlin, John (b. 1942). One of the most revered **fusion** and world-music artists, guitar virtuoso John McLaughlin has been making waves in rock since his association with **Miles Davis** in the late 1960s, when he brought his formidable skills to Davis' landmark album *Bitches Brew*. Known for his ability to play in odd meters with startling speed and clarity, McLaughlin brought critical attention to fusion, jazz, and world music (particularly Indian) with his 1970s groups Shakti and the Mahavishnu Orchestra, as well as through his collaborations over the decades with some of the world's finest musicians, including Miles Davis, jazz pianist **Chick Corea**, flamenco guitarist Paco de Lucia, Latin-rock guitarist Carlos Santana, fusion guitarist Al DiMeola, and many of India's most talented instrumentalists. (See Chapter 1, "Funk, Jazz-Rock, and Fusion: The Rhythm Revolution.")

MFSB. Largely credited for creating the **Philadelphia sound**, MFSB (Mothers, Fathers, Sisters, Brothers) was the house band for Philadelphia International, the record label formed in 1971 that became a powerhouse for soul musicians as Motown was on the decline. The band's 1974 largely instrumental hit "TSOP (The Sound of Philadelphia)" went to No. 1 and, with its lush strings and driving beat, created a blueprint for the **disco** that would soon follow. (See Chapter 1, "Funk, Jazz-Rock, and Fusion: The Rhythm Revolution.")

Miller, Steve (b. 1943). One of the major San Francisco acts during the psychedelic heyday of the late 1960s, Steve Miller elevated his group the Steve Miller Band to the national stage in 1973 when he traded in psychedelic blues for catchy pop on *The Joker*, taking the album to No. 2 on the charts and scoring a No. 1 single with the title track. The band peaked with their 1976 follow-up *Fly Like an Eagle* and 1977 *Book of Dreams*, which featured an army of **AOR** favorites such as "Fly Like an Eagle," "Jet Airliner," "Jungle Love," "Swingtown," "Rock'n Me," and "Take the Money and Run," making the Steve Miller Band one of the top touring acts by the end of the decade. (See Chapter 3, "Corporate and Mainstream Sounds: Rock Is Dead, Long Live Rock!")

Mitchell, Joni (b. 1943). A folkie troubadour who helped launch the **singer-songwriter** movement with her albums *Joni Mitchell* in 1968, *Clouds* in 1969, *Ladies of the Canyon* in 1970, and *Blue* in 1971, Mitchell took a decidedly different direction after her popular 1974 album *Court and Spark*, which demonstrated a distinct leaning toward jazz. Mitchell continued a marked departure from rock with increasingly experimental jazz and world-beat albums through the 1970s, including 1974's live *Miles of Aisles*, 1975's African-influenced *The Hissing of Summer Lawns*, 1978's Latin-infused *Don Juan's Reckless Daughter*, and her 1979 collaboration with jazz great Charles Mingus on *Mingus*. (See Chapter 5, "Singer-Songwriters: Rock Grows Up.")

The Moody Blues. By 1974, the Moody Blues had enjoyed major tour popularity and Top 5 chart success with seminal albums like 1967's *Days of Future Passed*, 1970's *A Question of Balance*, 1971's *Every Good Boy Deserves Favour*, and 1972's *Seventh Sojourn*. But in 1973 the pioneering **progressive** act had dissolved, leaving a trail of greatest hits, live albums, and solo projects in their wake through the 1970s, reuniting in 1978 to find moderate success through the 1980s but largely living off their reputation as one of the first bands to bring large-scale progressive music to the United States. (See Chapter 2, "Progressive Rock in the 1970s: But Is It Art?")

MOR. As radio programming research improved in the late 1960s, certain types of programming techniques brought about categories such as AOR (album-oriented rock or adult-oriented rock), AC (adult contemporary), and MOR (middle-of-the-road). MOR programming was a means of gaining adult listeners who wanted less abrasive rock, a format that helped launch a number of **soft-rock** and **singer-songwriter** acts to stardom. MOR programming is generally marked by melodic rock that was contemporary but not radically advanced.

***More Songs about Buildings and Food* (1978).** An important transition from art-punk to **new wave**, **Talking Heads**' sophomore album *More Songs about Buildings and Food* brought the band increased attention as progenitors of a new style of intelligent modern rock, particularly through the memorable interpretation of the Al Green classic "Take Me to the River," one of the group's few popular singles. With the band's groovy beats and melodic synthesizer work and David Byrne's affected, slightly off vocals, the album foreshadows the modern-rock movement that would take over college radio stations over the following decade. Particularly important is the introduction of experimental producer **Brian Eno**—the father of **ambient music** and godfather of electronica—a long-lived collaboration between Eno and the band that would make Talking Heads one of new wave's most significant acts.

Morrison, Van (b. 1945). Van Morrison grew up in Belfast, Northern Ireland, and started his career singing soul hits to American soldiers stationed in Europe. He developed his singing and songwriting style as a leader of Them in the early 1960s, then scored hits writing now-classic rock songs like "Gloria" and "Brown Eyed Girl." Morrison was mostly unknown in America, however, until his 1968 album *Astral Weeks* made him a critical darling. In the 1970s he achieved moderate fame with hits like "Domino" and "Wild Nights," and his legendary live performance is captured on the 1974 album *It's Too Late to Stop*

Now. His fame seems to have only increased over the years as his soulful arrangements and passionate voice continue to draw new fans. (See Chapter 5, "Singer-Songwriters: Rock Grows Up.")

Mothership Connection (1976). One of the great all-time **funk** albums by perhaps the greatest funk band ever, *Mothership Connection* launched **George Clinton**'s group **Parliament** into superstardom and figured prominently in the development of hip-hop music in the '80s and '90s. For this album, Clinton added former **James Brown** hornplayers Fred Wesley and Maceo Parker into the sprawling Parliament family, and their presence made *Mothership Connection* an important evolution from the more conventional R&B style of Parliament's earlier records. On songs like "Mothership Connection (Star Child)" and "Give Up the Funk (Tear the Roof Off the Sucker)," Clinton established a quasi-spiritual doctrine devoted to the Funk, and the dense rhythms continue to reverberate in countless rap songs.

Never Mind the Bollocks, Here's the Sex Pistols (1977). Considered by many to be **punk rock**'s most important record, *Never Mind the Bollocks, Here's the Sex Pistols* was the **Sex Pistols**' only official album. After being picked up and dropped by both EMI and A&M record labels, the group found a home with Virgin Records long enough to release the album. Banned in many record stores and on radio stations for its use of the word "Bollocks" (considered a curse word by some Londoners), as well as for its anti-monarchy rants in the songs "God Save the Queen" and "Anarchy in the U.K." (which had been released as singles much earlier), the album nonetheless reached No. 1 on the UK charts and No. 106 on the U.S. charts, both amazing feats considering the album's troubles in the United Kingdom and that the band had never toured the United States. Though the Sex Pistols would not last beyond their first album, *Never Mind the Bollocks* came to be seen as the ultimate example of punk music's nihilism, and the phrase "no future"—from "God Save the Queen"—would become an enduring punk motto.

New Wave. Originally coined to categorize experimental French filmmakers of the late 1950s, the term "new wave" carries with it notions of absurdity and alienation. As an American and British musical genre of the mid- to late 1970s, the style was a separation of rock from the overly produced **progressive** bombast of the late 1960s and early 1970s, yet still carrying on progressive's more cerebral aspects, if in something of an alienated manner. Many of the minimalist, postmodern new-wave acts of the late 1970s—such as **Talking Heads**, **Elvis Costello**, the **B-52's**, and the **Cars**—saw careers that lasted much longer than those of most **punk-rock** bands (you can only be angry for so long, but you can be ironic forever), thus having a heavy impact on the sound of the 1980s. (See Chapter 7, "A New Wave of Rock.")

A Night at the Opera (1975). Excessively over-the-top, eclectic, ambitious, and shamelessly absurd even by **Queen** standards, *A Night at the Opera* put an end to critics' casual dismissal of the group as a second-rate **Zeppelin** clone. Not that those same critics *liked* the record, but they did have to think up new and original ways to express their hatred for Freddie Mercury and company, who proved here that they sounded like *nobody* else on earth except Queen. Never again would heavy metal, prog-rock, baroque, pop, British music hall, and yes, opera come together so boldly on one album—or, for that matter, one song, as on the album's hit number "Bohemian Rhapsody." Mama mia, indeed.

Night Moves (1976). Released hot on the heels of his breakthrough double live album, 1975's *Live Bullet*, **Bob Seger** and the Silver Bullet Band's terrific *Night Moves* officially completed the veteran Detroit rocker's transition from the Midwest's best-kept secret to multiplatinum superstar, second only to **Bruce Springsteen** in the "blue-collar rock" field. Spawning the classic rock hits "Mainstreet," "Rock and Roll Never Forgets," and the No. 4 title track, *Night Moves* was a popular (No. 8 on the charts and 5 million sold to date) *and* critical success: It is hard rock with a street poet's heart, shot through with bittersweet nostalgia but ultimately uplifting, as Seger assures his own aging generation that it is *still* okay to tear loose and rock out on the far side of thirty.

Nugent, Ted (b. 1948). Known as the Motor City Madman, the Detroit-bred Ted Nugent was one of hard rock's more exciting acts of the late 1970s. Originally finding limited fame with the Amboy Dukes in the late 1960s, Nugent went solo (with a backing band) in 1975, releasing a string of popular, if somewhat unsophisticated, Top 40 albums, whose better-selling singles included the primal tracks "Cat Scratch Fever," "Yank Me, Crank Me," and "Wango Tango." Onstage, however, Nugent was an all-out entertainer, dressing as a caveman and swinging onto stage on a rope, making him something of a primeval icon for hard rockers. (See Chapter 3, "Corporate and Mainstream Sounds: Rock Is Dead, Long Live Rock!")

Nyro, Laura (1947–1997). Nyro falls into what can be called the "romantic visionary" school of **singer-songwriters** who mythologized their own personal experience with lyrics reflecting the sensibilities of Beat writers like Jack Kerouac and Allen Ginsberg. She released her debut album in 1966, when she was just nineteen; two years later, she released *Eli and the Thirteenth Confession*, a collection of vignettes influenced by Broadway, folk, gospel, and pop that showed young musicians that singer-songwriters could work from a broader musical palette than just an acoustic guitar. At the age of twenty-four, Nyro announced her retirement from the music business, but she returned with the jazz-tinged *Smile* in 1976. Though she released only four more albums over the next twenty years, Nyro is remembered as one of the more imaginative of the young 1960s folkies and an early figure in the singer-songwriter movement. (See Chapter 5, "Singer-Songwriters: Rock Grows Up.")

The Ohio Players. An early 1970s R&B group, the Ohio Players broadened their horizons after their 1973 hit "Funky Worm" broke the Top 20.

Though the band dabbled in stomping blues, tender ballads, explosive **funk-rock**, and dance anthems, they were just as known for their risque album covers, featuring seductively posed women shot by *Playboy* photographer Richard Fegley. "Funky Worm" was later resurrected in the Los Angeles hip-hop of the 1990s. (See Chapter 1, "Funk, Jazz-Rock, and Fusion: The Rhythm Revolution.")

***One Nation Under a Groove* (1978).** This **Funkadelic** album is a pinnacle for **George Clinton** in many ways. Here his groundbreaking combination of Jimi Hendrix–style guitar pyrotechnics and dance-floor rhythms finds its most successful expression. This is also Clinton's most positive articulation of his "unity through groove" philosophy that stood against the racial, sexual, and social segregations of "straight" society. *One Nation Under a Groove* is perhaps the best of a genre known as "black rock," with the cut "Who Says a Funk Band Can't Play Rock?!" answering its own question. It is also Funkadelic's most popular album, going platinum on the strength of the title cut, which stands as one of the great dance anthems of all time.

Parliament/Funkadelic. Commonly known as P-Funk, Parliament/Funkadelic was a combination of two bands led by **funk**-master **George Clinton** in the 1970s. While Parliament (originally a doo-wop group known as the Parliaments) was mainly a **James Brown**–style soul group, Funkadelic was more of a psychedelic funk band, incorporating the styles of their influences that ranged from Jimi Hendrix to Sly Stone to the Beatles. Both bands had hits in the 1970s, and dozens of musicians traveled in and out of both bands. "P-Funk" also refers to the elaborate style of funk largely brought about by Clinton and bandmate (and former James Brown colleague) Bootsy Collins, a heavily layered groove that was carried on by many of the bands' members through their solo projects and eventually heavily sampled by later hip-hop acts. (See Chapter 1, "Funk, Jazz-Rock, and Fusion: The Rhythm Revolution.")

***The Payback* (1974).** This two-album release appeared just as **James Brown**'s groundbreaking career was about to flag—not that you would know it from the seventy-three minutes of scorching **funk** on these eight songs. His band in 1974 included Fred Wesley, Maceo Parker, St. Clair Pinckney, Jimmy Nolen, and Jabo Starks, and the notoriously demanding Brown had them so well rehearsed that the extended rhythmic jams never seemed to wander or lose a degree of intensity. Indeed, Brown's band was one of the most awesome forces in rock music, and they are at their energetic best on cuts like "Shoot Your Shot" and "Mind Power." It would be Brown's last unquestionably great album—but an explosive sendoff, indeed. (See Chapter 1, "Funk, Jazz-Rock, and Fusion: The Rhythm Revolution.")

Pere Ubu. Formed in 1975 by singer David Thomas (a.k.a. Crocus Behemoth) and guitarist Peter Laughner, Pere Ubu was one of the earliest **punk/new-wave** bands to throw their hat into the arena with their 1975 self-released single "30 Seconds over Tokyo." The Cleveland-based outfit waited until 1978 to release their first full album, *The Modern Dance*, featuring an introduction to their startling sound that was simultaneously modern and heavy, like a garage band formed by Edgard Varèse. Though the proto-punk outfit never benefited from wide commercial acceptance, Pere Ubu enjoyed a devoted underground following through the years and are claimed by some to be one of the most important American bands in the history of rock. (See Chapter 7, "A New Wave of Rock.")

Philadelphia International. See **The Philadelphia Sound**

The Philadelphia Sound. In 1971, the successful songwriting team of Kenny Gamble, Leon Huff, and Thom Bell founded the Philadelphia International record label, hiring the group **MFSB** as the house band. With Gamble and Huff running the label and Bell operating as an independent producer, the three of them created what became known as the Philadelphia sound, using MFSB to back up a number of popular R&B artists—including Harold Melvin and the Blue Notes, Teddy Pendergrass, the O'Jays, and the Stylistics—with lush strings, heavy bass, and propulsive rhythms. The distinctive sound and the popularity of its artists made Philadelphia International the last great hit factory, creating the sound that would soon be the template for **disco**. (See Chapter 1, "Funk, Jazz-Rock, and Fusion: The Rhythm Revolution.")

***Physical Graffiti* (1975).** Led **Zeppelin**'s untitled fourth album, from 1971, is the one everybody buys first (it has that "Stairway" song on it). But *Physical Graffiti*—released at the absolute pinnacle of Zeppelin's reign as the gods of '70s metal—is the band's desert island disc. Across its four-sided sprawl, Zeppelin's chart-topping sixth album explores every angle, nook, and cranny of the band's sound: from the Middle Eastern mystery of "Kashmir" to the Middle Earth-y, acoustic beauty of the instrumental "Bron-Yr-Aur"; from the terrifying metallic blues of "In My Time of Dying" to the funky stomp and crunch of "Trampled Under Foot"—everything that made Zeppelin *Zeppelin* is right here.

Pink Floyd. Rising from the avant-garde club scene in late 1960s London, Pink Floyd built a following as an influential art-rock band to become one of the major rock acts of the 1970s. Their transition from cult darlings to bonafide rock gods came in an instant with their phenomenally successful 1973 release *Dark Side of the Moon*, which spent fourteen years on the American charts—the most successful charting in history. The band built on their reputation of producing "space rock" to create three more monumental albums by the end of the decade—1975's **Wish You Were Here**, 1977's *Animals*, and 1979's *The Wall*, another major success that spent fifteen weeks at No. 1 and went on to become one of the top-selling rock albums of all time. (See Chapter 2, "Progressive Rock in the 1970s: But Is It Art?")

The Police. Though initially playing UK **punk** clubs shortly after they formed in 1977, the Police's minimal production and reggae-tinged grooves—two hallmarks of late 1970s **new wave**—gave them a distinct sound that earned them relatively rapid chart success and eventually a worldwide following. Charting such memorable songs as "Roxanne," "Message in a Bottle," "Don't Stand So Close to Me," and "De Do Do Do, De Da Da Da" in their first few years, the band's songs became part of the soundtrack for the 1980s as they grew to be one of new wave's most successful acts. Defined largely by the sparse, muted guitarwork of Andy Summers and the baby-soft vocals of singer Gordon Sumner (a.k.a. Sting), the group disbanded shortly after reaching their peak with the highly successful *Synchronicity* in 1983. (See Chapter 7, "A New Wave of Rock.")

The Pretenders. One of the more successful **punk/new-wave** hybrid acts to emerge from the UK scene in the late 1970s, the Pretenders are thought by many to be an American band, due to their talented and highly credible lead singer Chrissie Hynde. Though originally from Cleveland, Ohio, Hynde moved to London, where she worked at **Malcolm McLaren**'s SEX store (origin of punk icons the **Sex Pistols**), wrote for respected Brit music journal *New Musical Express*, and played with later punk luminaries Mick Jones (the **Clash**) and Tony James (the Damned), before finding a place on the UK charts with her new band, the Pretenders. Though they would not release their critically acclaimed and commercially successful debut, *Pretenders*, until 1980, the hard-driving yet technically sophisticated band is often lumped together with 1970s new-wave acts, with whom they share many characteristics. (See Chapter 7, "A New Wave of Rock.")

Progressive Rock. Growing out of the largely British, classically influenced rock of the late 1960s, progressive rock persevered through the 1970s in the form of symphonic rock (**Electric Light Orchestra, Yes,** the **Moody Blues**), krautrock (**Kraftwerk, Tangerine Dream**), art-rock (**Pink Floyd**), and avant-garde (**Frank Zappa, Brian Eno**). Often marked by stage theater, elaborate production, and excessive showmanship (or in the case of krautrock and **ambient music**, excessive minimalism), progressive music eventually collapsed under its own weight, giving way in the late 1970s to the much more populist and accessible **punk-rock** movement. (See Chapter 2, "Progressive Rock in the 1970s: But Is It Art?")

Punk Rock. Largely a reaction to the pomposity of **progressive rock**, the shallow showiness of **disco**, and the untouchable celebrity of the biggest rock stars, amateur rockers came out of their garages and onto small club stages in the mid-1970s to return rock music to the basic energy of its three-chord structures and call it punk rock. The genre was foreshadowed from the mid-1960s to the early 1970s by such protopunkers as the **Kinks**, the Stooges, and the New York Dolls. Soon after the venue **CBGB** opened in 1973 in New York, acts such as the **Ramones, Television,** and the **Patti Smith** Group began a series of shows there that kickstarted the punk-rock and **new-wave** movements in America. Soon after, London would follow suit with groups like the Damned, the **Sex Pistols,** and the **Clash,** beginning a sudden punk movement in England, subsequently influencing punk on America's West Coast. (See Chapter 6, "Punk Rock: The Art of Noise.")

Queen. One of the few full-on rock bands to rival **Led Zeppelin**'s international domination (and sheer talent) in the 1970s, Queen was a uniquely gifted combination of Brian May's blinding guitarwork and Freddie Mercury's operatic vocals. Running the gamut from deadly serious to fun and bouncy, and incorporating glam, heavy metal, opera, ragtime, Caribbean, rockabilly, and blues into their work, the band would achieve rock immortality with a string of hits that included "Another One Bites the Dust," "We Will Rock You," "We Are the Champions," "Killer Queen," "Under Pressure," "Somebody to Love," "Crazy Little Thing Called Love," and their "Stairway to Heaven"–esque classic "Bohemian Rhapsody." Unlike many rock groups, the members of Queen considered themselves equal members of the band (despite press attention usually focused on Mercury), and each contributed hits to the group. Though Queen never saw quite the level of success in the United States that their rivals Led Zeppelin did, they were considered the Beatles of the 1970s in Great Britain, ultimately placing just behind the fab four for England's most popular act of all time. (See Chapter 3, "Corporate and Mainstream Sounds: Rock Is Dead, Long Live Rock!")

The Ramones. Formed in Queens, New York, in 1974 by a group of childhood friends who all adopted the surname "Ramone" for the band, the Ramones are considered by many to be New York's first full-on **punk** act. Sharing New York's **CBGB** stage with other early punk acts **Television** and **Patti Smith,** the Ramones' songs were simple, loud, and short—a tune rarely went over three minutes, and for longer sets they would just play everything twice. With very little blues influence, the Ramones seemed to sidestep rock's classic traditions and leap right for the jugular with high-energy, three-chord simplicity. As the first American punk band to tour England in 1976, the group ignited the nascent London punk scene, influencing the **Sex Pistols,** the Damned, and the **Clash,** all of whom would become seminal punk acts themselves. Although the band never scored a Top 40 album or single, they released a surprising amount of material for a punk band and endured longer than any of their contemporaries, eventually retiring from the stage in 1996. (See Chapter 6, "Punk Rock: The Art of Noise.")

Rockumentary. Shorthand for "rock documentary," the rockumentary is generally a combination of a biography and a concert film, featuring performances by and interviews with the featured artist and often others. D. A. Pennebaker's 1967 **Bob Dylan** film *Dont Look Back* was a model for "rock docs" to come, featuring performances, interviews, and unobtrusive behind-the-scenes footage that allowed the subjects to tell their own story. In the 1970s, rockumentaries and concert films ranged from the collection of existing **Who** footage that became 1979's *The Kids Are Alright* to the semifictional 1978 Bob Dylan project *Renaldo and Clara* to the big-budget filming of the **Band**'s final concert in 1978's ***The Last Waltz***. (See Chapter 8, "Rock on the Big Screen.")

The Rolling Stones. Although by many critics' standards the Rolling Stones released their finest albums between 1968 and 1973, their material through the 1970s was still worthy of their name, and the band remained as commercially successful as ever, with every studio album through the end of the decade reaching No. 1 and spawning at least one Top 20 single. As the 1980s loomed, the band returned to top form with 1978's *Some Girls* and 1980's *Emotional Rescue*, spawning the hits "Miss You," "Emotional Rescue," "Shattered," "She's So Cold," and "Beast of Burden." With these albums the band borrowed **disco** beats to give themselves a more contemporary sound, a formula that served the band well as they remained among the world's top touring acts into the next century. (See Chapter 3, "Corporate and Mainstream Sounds: Rock Is Dead, Long Live Rock!")

Ronstadt, Linda (b. 1946). One of rock's largest female stars of the 1970s, Linda Ronstadt struggled with minor fame for several years with her band the Stone Poneys and on solo projects before jumping to the top of the charts in 1974 with *Heart Like a Wheel*. A move away from her country-rock origins, the album launched Ronstadt in a pop direction and opened the door for experimentation with later albums using Latin, country, big band, **new wave**, and even lullabies. Ronstadt's eclectic interests made her a chart-straddling phenomenon, often placing songs on several charts at once and covering tunes by an array of contemporary **singer-songwriters** as well as classic rockers from the 1950s and 1960s. For her self-titled 1972 album and tour Ronstadt assembled a quartet that would go on to become the **Eagles**, with whom she would later share massive fame as two of soft rock's biggest acts of the decade. (See Chapter 4, "The Softer Side of Rock.")

Roxy Music. One of the more iconoclastic of the early 1970s **progressive** bands, Roxy Music built a loyal following in Britain with their driving rhythms and the affected mannerisms of its singer Bryan Ferry. Also helping to gain an audience were the unusual experimentations of keyboard player **Brian Eno**, who left the group after their second album in 1973. Though the band never gained popular appeal or chart success in the United States, they developed a loyal cult following and were hailed by critics as purveyors of sleek, compelling rock and roll. (See Chapter 2, "Progressive Rock in the 1970s: But Is It Art?")

***Rust Never Sleeps* (1979).** **Neil Young**'s incisive ode to the music industry, *Rust Never Sleeps* came as his strongest collection in years, the album paralleling the acoustic/electric structure of **Bob Dylan**'s 1965 record *Bringing It All*

Back Home. Young begins with "My My Hey Hey (Out of the Blue)," a message to **Sex Pistols**' singer Johnny Rotten that concludes the album as an electric version with different lyrics, "Hey Hey My My (Into the Black)." Young managed to shake off creative rust by constantly exploring pensive acoustic music along with explosive rock, and on *Rust Never Sleeps* he executes both extremes in the service of great songs.

Saturday Night Fever (1977). Possibly the best combination of film and soundtrack success in movie history, the **disco** drama *Saturday Night Fever* won big at both the box office and the record store, grossing more than $300 million in ticket sales and sitting at the top of the *Billboard* charts for twenty-four weeks.[3] The film was based on a *New York* magazine article about disco-crazed Brooklyn kids out on a Saturday night and featured a young John Travolta in the film that made him a star. Providing a massive boost to the fledgling disco phenomenon, the film's success spawned a major increase in disco-themed venues and radio stations, not to mention generated a series of poor imitations in the theaters. (See Chapter 8, "Rock on the Big Screen.")

Seger, Bob (b. 1945). With a trio of Top 10 albums—1976's **Night Moves**, 1978's *Stranger in Town*, and 1980's chart-topping *Against the Wind*—Bob Seger found himself second only to **Bruce Springsteen** as America's working-class poet-hero at the turn of the 1980s. Before adopting the Silver Bullet Band to back him in 1975 for a well-received live double-album, Seger had been churning out bar-band rock to limited success for more than a decade, giving his late 1970s releases a maturity and blue-collar appeal that fans could relate to in hits such as "Rock and Roll Never Forgets," "Against the Wind," "Feel Like a Number," "We've Got Tonight," "You'll Accomp'ny Me," "Night Moves," and "Old Time Rock & Roll." Such nostalgia-inducing fare made him a favorite among the over-thirty crowd, a formula that served him with a continuous stream of Top 10 albums through the 1980s—always carefully crafted and paced a few years apart—making him the rare reliable rock star. (See Chapter 3, "Corporate and Mainstream Sounds: Rock Is Dead, Long Live Rock!")

The Sex Pistols. The baddest boys London could muster in the bad-boy genre of **punk rock**, the Sex Pistols were not the first punk rockers or—by far—the best, but they manufactured the punk image and attitude that is so closely identified with the music. Founded in 1975 by guitarist Steve Jones and manager **Malcolm McLaren**—who ran the store SEX that gave the band its name—the Sex Pistols were mostly made up of local delinquents who hung out around the seedy King's Cross area of London. McLaren had formerly managed the protopunk New York Dolls and borrowed the idea of spiked hair and torn clothes from New York musician **Richard Hell** to give the Sex Pistols an anti-authority style. Long on attitude but short on talent, the band received notoriety for publicity stunts manufactured by McLaren, including having the band play their antimonarchy song "God Save the Queen" from a boat on the River

Thames, coinciding with Queen Elizabeth's twenty-five-year anniversary on the throne. Fronted by singer Johnny Rotten (John Lydon) and bassist Sid Vicious (John Ritchie), who was added to the group in 1977, the group managed only one album, **Never Mind the Bollocks, Here's the Sex Pistols**, and a two-week tour of the United States before calling it quits but nonetheless managed to become one of the most influential punk rock bands of their time. (See Chapter 6, "Punk Rock: The Art of Noise.")

***Sgt. Pepper's Lonely Hearts Club Band* (1978).** Though based on the landmark 1967 Beatles album—claimed by many rock cognoscenti to be the greatest rock album ever—the film version of *Sgt. Pepper's* existed at the opposite end of the spectrum, called by *Rolling Stone* "one of the worst movies ever made."[4] Despite enlisting the acting and musical support of **Peter Frampton**, George Burns, Donald Pleasence, Steve Martin, Alice Cooper, **Aerosmith**, Billy Preston, the **Bee Gees**, and **Earth, Wind and Fire**, the film flopped in the theaters, with the soundtrack reaching a respectable No. 5 on the charts. (See Chapter 8, "Rock on the Big Screen.")

Shakti. See **McLaughlin, John**

Simon, Carly (b. 1945). With a recording career that resembles one big musical diary, Carly Simon's albums reflected the mid-'70s fixation on the ups and downs of romance at a time when the American divorce rate had begun to soar. On songs like "That's the Way I've Always Heard It Should Be," from her 1971 debut, Simon reflects the conflicted feelings of a generation that both fears and craves intimate relationships. Simon's own marriage to **James Taylor** fueled her music and her fame and lent mystique to her 1972 No. 1 hit "You're So Vain." (See Chapter 5, "Singer-Songwriters: Rock Grows Up.")

Simon, Paul (b. 1941). As the songwriting force behind the 1960s folk duo Simon and Garfunkel, and later as a solo artist, Simon has established himself as one of rock's most brilliant pop craftsman. His first major hit with Art Garfunkel was "Sounds of Silence," which hit No. 1 in 1965. The duo became superstars when four of their songs were prominently featured in the 1967 film *The Graduate*, including the catchy hit "Mrs. Robinson." After peaking with the 1970 album *Bridge over Troubled Water*, which sold 10 million copies, Simon embarked on a solo career that found him delving into gospel and R&B on well-spaced albums like 1973's *There Goes Rhymin' Simon* and *Still Crazy After All These Years* in 1975. Though his work through the late 1970s and 1980s was spotty, his career enjoyed a major resurgence in 1986 when he collaborated with the South African a capella group Ladysmith Black Mambazo on the hit album *Graceland*. (See Chapter 5, "Singer-Songwriters: Rock Grows Up.")

Singer-songwriters. The singer-songwriters comprised a genre of mostly middle-class, well-educated baby boomers who had grown up with rock music and subscribed, more or less, to the counterculture's utopian ideas. Led by **Bob**

Dylan, **Paul Simon**, and **John Lennon**, a crop of acoustic-guitar-wielding artists like **Neil Young, Joni Mitchell, James Taylor, Carly Simon, Cat Stevens**, and **Carole King** crafted tunes that broadly addressed the rock generation's struggles with maturity. The singer-songwriters reflected a post-'60s spirit that was weary of political confrontation, pondering the mysteries of love and death, and hungry for meaning and identity in a high-tech, media-saturated American culture. At the genre's peak in the early 1970s, the singer-songwriters produced music that was by turns insightful, vapid, tender, and didactic. Just when it seemed that this style would be the future of rock, it was swept aside by the eroticism of **disco** and the rage of **punk rock**. (See Chapter 5, "Singer-Songwriters: Rock Grows Up.")

Smith, Patti (b. 1946). One of the most important figures in early **punk**, Patti Smith parlayed her extensive street credibility—writing for *Creem* magazine, co-authoring a play with Sam Shepard, as well as painting and performing poetry—into a gig as leader of her own punk band in the early 1970s. After a seven-week residency at New York's **CBGB**—one of the critical moments in early punk when Smith, **Television, Blondie**, and the **Ramones** were introducing punk to New York from the club's stage—Smith released her debut *Horses* in 1975. Produced by the Velvet Underground's John Cale with a deliberately androgynous cover photo of Smith by her roommate Robert Mapplethorpe, *Horses* ranks among the all-time finest debuts, with Smith fusing rock, punk, and spoken-word into a loose but powerful collection of songs that brought a literary sophistication to punk rock. *Horses* cracked the Top 50, demonstrating that there was commercial possibility in punk, and Smith became an icon of 1970s rock, continuing to release albums through the decade and even scoring a No. 13 hit in 1978 with "Because the Night," co-written with **Bruce Springsteen**. (See Chapter 6, "Punk Rock: The Art of Noise.")

Soft Rock. Beginning in the late 1960s with bands like the Byrds, the Beach Boys, and Crosby, Stills & Nash, a style of rock known as the California sound emerged that reflected rock's growing maturity with a sound less abrasive than the psychedelic rock and hard rock of the time. In the 1970s, soft rock ruled the airwaves, with acts like the **Eagles, Linda Ronstadt, Jackson Browne**, and **Fleetwood Mac** selling massive amounts of records and packing the largest arenas. Aided by the new Adult Contemporary, Middle-of-the-Road (**MOR**), and Album-Oriented radio formats, soft-rock acts reflecting the California sound—as well as country rockers like **America** and the Marshall Tucker Band and international acts like **Elton John** and **Wings**—maintained a strong presence as the sound of the 1970s. (See Chapter 4, "The Softer Side of Rock.")

***Songs in the Key of Life* (1976).** Before releasing this ambitious double-album, child prodigy **Stevie Wonder** already had a long list of hit songs and groundbreaking albums to his credit. *Music of My Mind* and *Talking Book* in

1972 and *Innervisions* in 1973 already established Wonder as one of the most acclaimed musicians of the early '70s. On *Songs in the Key of Life*, the artist took some well-deserved creative liberties that, for the most part, do not disappoint. Pop numbers like "I Wish" and "Isn't She Lovely" display Wonder's trademark craftsmanship, while "Black Man" is a sprawling ode to racial harmony. (See Chapter 1, "Funk, Jazz-Rock, and Fusion: The Rhythm Revolution.")

Springsteen, Bruce (b. 1949). In the early '70s, record executives were desperately seeking an artist to market as "the next **Dylan**." New Jersey native Bruce Springsteen was the only one who lived up to the hype. After his first two albums in 1973, *Greetings from Asbury Park, N.J.* and *The Wild, the Innocent & the E Street Shuffle*, Springsteen released his first great album, **Born to Run**, in 1975. Songs like "Backstreets" and "Thunder Road" captured the restlessness and desperation felt by many people, especially the young working-class males who saw Springsteen as their poet laureate. Nicknamed "The Boss," Springsteen led his E Street Band on legendary three-hour concerts. His biggest album was his 1984 triumph *Born in the U.S.A.*, which sold over 10 million copies on the strength of its title song, the story of a forgotten Vietnam veteran that has been widely misinterpreted as a jingoistic anthem. (See Chapter 3, "Corporate and Mainstream Sounds: Rock Is Dead, Long Live Rock!")

Steely Dan. A popular jazz-rock group through the 1970s, Steely Dan incorporated jazz grooves into a pop format to create a number of memorable songs that would become standards on later classic rock stations, including "Deacon Blues," "Kid Charlemagne," "Hey Nineteen," "Rikki Don't Lose That Number," and "Reeling in the Years." Mainly a collaboration between singers Donald Fagen and Walter Becker, Steely Dan helped popularize the use of jazz in pop music. (See Chapter 1, "Funk, Jazz-Rock, and Fusion: The Rhythm Revolution.")

Stevens, Cat (b. 1948). The British-born Stephen Demetre Georgiou published his first song, "I Love My Dog," as Cat Stevens in 1966. He established himself in the folk singer scene with the albums *Matthew & Son* (1966) and *New Masters* (1967). That year, he was hospitalized with a near-fatal case of tuberculosis. During his recovery, he began experimenting with various world religions, a preoccupation reflected in his music throughout his career. Stevens entered his most commercially successful period with 1970's *Tea for the Tillerman*, which went to No. 8 in the United States. The 1971 follow-up, *Teaser and the Firecat*, went to No. 2 on the strength of overtly religious songs like "Morning Has Broken," "Moonshadow," and "Peace Train," which have become Stevens' most popular works. The album remains popular, reaching triple platinum status in 2001. However, in 1978, Stevens converted to Islam, changed his name to Yusuf Islam, and temporarily renounced pop music, later sparking outrage by endorsing a religious edict that put a price on the head of Salman Rushdie, author of *The Satanic Verses*, a book some Islamic fundamentalists found offensive. Though Stevens' legacy as one of the early 1970's favorite **singer-songwriters** was tainted by his later religious dogmatism, his songs have endured the test of time and remain among the decade's softer favorites. (See Chapter 5, "Singer-Songwriters: Rock Grows Up.")

Stewart, Rod (b. 1945). As singer for the Jeff Beck Group and Faces in the late 1960s and early 1970s, Rod Stewart maintained a raw, bluesy style that made him very popular in his native United Kingdom and gave him a brief splash in the United States with two Top 5 albums in 1971 and 1972. After moving to the States in 1975, however, Stewart took a decidedly pop direction that increased his fan base but disappointed critics and fans of his earlier, harsher style. His three Top 5 albums in the later 1970s—*A Night on the Town*, *Foot Loose & Fancy Free*, and *Blondes Have More Fun*—contained more shallow, sometimes **disco**-infused tunes like "Do Ya Think I'm Sexy," "Hot Legs," and "You're in My Heart," which permanently relocated the singer from the realm of hard rocker to that of pop artist. (See Chapter 4, "The Softer Side of Rock.")

Stigwood, Robert (b. 1934). One of the most powerful figures in 1970s British rock, the Australian Stigwood managed some of Britain's hottest rock acts, including the Graham Bond Organization, John Mayall's Bluesbreakers, the **Who**, and Cream. After discovering the **Bee Gees** and making the band an international success, Stigwood brought the group into film with the smash hit *Saturday Night Fever* in 1977, making a star of John Travolta along the way. Travolta would return the next year with the Stigwood-produced *Grease*, another major hit. Stigwood also produced the musicals *Tommy*, *Jesus Christ Superstar*, and *Sgt. Pepper's Lonely Hearts Club Band*, bringing himself fame in the film industry as well as in music. (See Chapter 8, "Rock on the Big Screen.")

Stranded (1974). *Stranded* is **Roxy Music's** first album recorded without synthesizer whiz-kid **Brian Eno.** Under the sole direction of Bryan Ferry, the band is less weird but no less adventurous. Ferry is alternately tortured, glamorous, and hilarious. A master of pop pastiche, he layers different styles, one on top of the other, to create sophisticated music that can be reserved ("A Song for Europe") or pure rock ("Street Life"). *Stranded* displays a sleek, glitzy veneer that shimmers over complicated songs that are self-aware but not overly serious, making this album a fairly accurate reflection of American culture in the mid-1970s.

The Stranger (1977). Musically, **Billy Joel's** *The Stranger* covers much of the same ground as *Turnstiles* in 1976—blue-collar tales set in New York, clearly influenced by **Bruce Springsteen's** working-class image. But the melodies Joel creates on the catchy "Only the Good Die Young" and the epic "Scenes from an Italian Restaurant" make *The Stranger* his best album and by far his most successful, as it would eventually sell more than 10 million copies and become one of the foundation albums of 1980s blue-collar rock.

Styx. With the lyrical gentleness of 1970s soft rockers and the full, driving sound of the decade's **progressive** acts, Styx was one of the most popular bands for young teens by the dawn of the 1980s. Though the band had been struggling in Chicago clubs for more than a decade before reaching national stardom, their break did not come until the single "Lady" slowly climbed the charts to reach No. 6 in 1975, dragging its accompanying album, *Styx II* to No. 20 on the charts two years after it was released. Subsequent albums each topped the other through the end of the decade, producing classic-rock staples such as "Fooling Yourself," "Babe," "Lorelei," "Renegade," "Come Sail Away," and perhaps their most famous tune "Mr. Roboto." (See Chapter 3, "Corporate and Mainstream Sounds: Rock Is Dead, Long Live Rock!")

Supertramp. After a false start in 1969 that yielded two poorly received albums, the prog-rock band Supertramp regrouped to release *Crime of the Century* in 1974, a surprise hit in both the United States and the United Kingdom, powered by the popular singles "Bloody Well Right" and "Dreamer." As their **progressive** sound was slowly molded into a more pop direction, the band found success among American audiences with 1975's *Crisis? What Crisis?* and 1977's *Even in the Quietest Moments*, before reaching their commercial zenith with 1979's No. 1 album *Breakfast in America*, which yielded the hit tracks "The Logical Song," "Goodbye Stranger," and "Take the Long Way Home." Supertramp was one of the forerunners of **corporate rock**—major artists who generated hit records but no easily identifiable rock stars. (See Chapter 3, "Corporate and Mainstream Sounds: Rock Is Dead, Long Live Rock!")

Talking Heads. Epitomizing the **new-wave** movement of the late 1970s—in which they were a key player—Talking Heads were intelligent, witty, ironic, often absurd, and thoroughly modern. Founded by art students David Byrne (vocals) and Chris Frantz (drums)—soon joined by Tina Weymouth on bass—the band achieved underground appreciation opening for **punk** heroes the **Ramones** at **CBGB** in New York in 1975, believed by many critics to be the beginning of both the punk and new-wave movements. After picking up keyboardist/guitarist Jerry Harrison soon after, the band released a series of groundbreaking albums through the late 1970s that earned them respect from New York's punk elite and included collaborations with glam king **David Bowie** and electronica demigod **Brian Eno**, who produced several of their albums and helped create the band's unique art-pop sound. (See Chapter 7, "A New Wave of Rock.")

Tangerine Dream. One of the few **krautrock** bands to gain (albeit limited) notice in the United States, the German outfit Tangerine Dream occupied the corner of rock music reserved for pure electronic experimentation. Described by one reviewer as the sound of "silt seeping on the ocean floor,"[5] the group produced an equivalent stage image—an antipersonality display of performers hidden behind a bank of Moog organs and synthesizers. (See Chapter 2, "Progressive Rock in the 1970s: But Is It Art?")

Taylor, James (b. 1948). A **singer-songwriter** who defined the genre in the early 1970s, James Taylor penned pensive tunes that soothed a generation of fans seeking a respite from electrified rock and the noisy tension of the 1960s. He released his breakthrough album *Sweet Baby James* in 1970. The album's hit "Fire and Rain" chronicled Taylor's stint in a mental hospital, perhaps an appropriate metaphor for a generation adrift in moral relativism. In the spring of 1971, Taylor appeared on the cover of a *Time* magazine issue devoted to singer-songwriters, and his status as king of the genre was cemented with his 1972 marriage to **Carly Simon**. With a steady string of Top 20 albums through the 1970s and on the strength of diligent touring throughout the decade, Taylor has endured as one of the era's most popular figures, helping bring the singer-songwriter movement to a large national audience. (See Chapter 5, "Singer-Songwriters: Rock Grows Up.")

Television. The band that kickstarted the New York **punk-rock** movement, the short-lived Television straddled the punk and **new-wave** scenes in the 1970s. After various incarnations, the band emerged as Television in March 1974, convincing **CBGB** owner Hilly Kristal to let them perform on Sundays, when the venue was traditionally closed. Soon other bands like the **Ramones** and the **Patti Smith** Group began playing the venue, launching the punk and new-wave movements in New York. Singer **Richard Hell** further influenced the punk genre with his fashion taste, soon making torn clothes and spiked hair the de facto look for punk fans and bands, largely thanks to **Malcolm McLaren** convincing his band, the **Sex Pistols**, to adopt the look. After Hell left in 1975, the band released the first of two albums, 1977's *Marquee Moon*, which met critical praise and was immediately recognized as a punk rock classic. (See Chapter 6, "Punk Rock: The Art of Noise.")

***Tommy* (1975).** Featuring such 1970s rock luminaries as Eric Clapton, **Elton John**, Tina Turner, and the members of the **Who**, the film musical *Tommy* has become something of a cult classic for Brit-rock fans. The movie is based on the eponymous 1969 Who album that tells the story of Tommy Walker, a boy struck deaf, dumb, and blind when he witnesses the murder of his father but later becomes a pinball champion and messiah figure. The original album is considered the first "rock opera," three versions of which—this soundtrack included—made it into the *Billboard* Top 5. (See Chapter 8, "Rock on the Big Screen.")

Tower of Power. One of the few popular jazz-rock bands that lacked direct lineage to **Miles Davis**, the Oakland-based Tower of Power lived up to its name with energetic performances that incorporated jazz, rock, and **funk** to create a unique, horn-heavy sound. Though the band spent most of the 1970s hovering around the unfashionable end of the Top 40, their sound was emblematic of the tight, complex rhythms of late 1970s **jazz-rock**. (See Chapter 1, "Funk, Jazz-Rock, and Fusion: The Rhythm Revolution.")

Van Halen. The hard-rocking group Van Halen literally changed the face of heavy metal when their self-titled debut garnered them legions of fans in 1978. The album, as well as its follow-ups *Van Halen II* (1979), *Women and Children First* (1980), and a string of increasingly popular releases in the 1980s, ignored the dark themes of heavy metal and the schmaltzy teenie-bop of light metal in favor of upbeat tempos, lightning-fast guitars, and bouncy vocals that made hard rock fun again. The group's popularity was helped by charismatic singer David Lee Roth but largely hung on the guitar wizardry of Eddie Van Halen—hailed as the new Jimi Hendrix by many—who incorporated complicated picking patters, classical influences, and blinding combinations of hammer-ons and pull-offs to be named in 1978 as *Guitar Player Magazine*'s "Best Guitarist of the Year," a title he held for the next five years. (See Chapter 3, "Corporate and Mainstream Sounds: Rock Is Dead, Long Live Rock!")

Van Halen (1978). Van Halen's 10 million–selling, self-titled debut album was to hard rock and the electric guitar at the end of the '70s (and beyond) what Jimi Hendrix's *Are You Experienced?* was to the same in the late '60s (and beyond): a heavy-metal gauntlet slapped against the face and thrown at the feet of convention. Frontman David Lee Roth was a charismatic loon of an entertainer, and the rhythm section packed a punch, but this was first and foremost a you-ain't-seen-nothing-yet introduction to guitar wunderkind Eddie Van Halen, who, like Hendrix, made his guitar sound like a heretofore-undiscovered instrument from another galaxy. An entire generation of followers would pull their teased hair out in frustration trying to learn his lightning-fast instrumental solo "Eruption."

The Voidoids. See **Hell, Richard**

Weather Report. Many of jazz legend **Miles Davis**' sidemen from the 1960s went on to create their own contributions to **fusion**, among them pianist Josef Zawinul and saxophonist Wayne Shorter. Together, the duo founded Weather Report, a percussive, experimental fusion group with heavily improvised instrumentals. Despite a constantly changing lineup, the group enjoyed at least moderate success with each album through the 1970s, an uncommon feat for a jazz-fusion band. (See Chapter 1, "Funk, Jazz-Rock, and Fusion: The Rhythm Revolution.")

The Who. One of the seminal hard-rock groups of the 1960s, the Who continued their march through the 1970s with a string of Top 10 albums, including 1973's *Quadrophenia*, 1975's *The Who by Numbers*, 1978's *Who Are You*, and 1979's *The Kids Are Alright*. While many of hard rock's surviving 1960s acts were adjusting to the times—the **Rolling Stones** delving into **disco** and **Rod Stewart** becoming a pop star—the Who just got louder and more exciting, among the first to incorporate lasers into their shows and finding a place in the *Guinness Book of World Records* in 1976 for loudest concert ever played. The party screeched to a halt, however, with drummer Keith Moon's death in late

1978, followed by a Who concert in 1979 at which eleven fans were crushed to death. The group managed to remain together for two more albums before disbanding in 1982, but their successful transition from the 1960s to the 1970s secured their place as one of hard rock's most important outfits. (See Chapter 3, "Corporate and Mainstream Sounds: Rock Is Dead, Long Live Rock!")

Wings. See **McCartney, Paul**

***Wish You Were Here* (1975).** How does a band follow up an album like 1973's *Dark Side of the Moon*, one of the most popular records in the history of rock? Rumors at the time suggested that the paranoia born of this question prompted **Pink Floyd** to wait two years before releasing *Wish You Were Here*. It plays like a postcard to former lead guitarist Syd Barrett, a sensitive soul apparently doomed by too much fame and too many drugs. One thing Floyd never fully regained after the 1968 departure of Barrett was a sense of playfulness, even though songs like "Have a Cigar" and "Welcome to the Machine" add some humor. Today, *Wish You Were Here* is mostly remembered for "Shine on You Crazy Diamond" and for its haunting title track.

Wonder, Stevie (b. 1950). Signed to Berry Gordy's Motown label at the age of eleven, "Little Stevie Wonder"—a blind piano prodigy—had his first hit at thirteen when "Fingertips-Pt. 2" became a No. 1 hit, his first of many. After a string of Top 100 albums through the 1960s, Wonder's career skyrocketed after he turned twenty-one and took creative control of his work. His highly acclaimed albums through the 1970s—1972's *Talking Book*, 1973's *Innervisions*, 1974's *Fulfillingness' First Finale*, and his 1976 opus ***Songs in the Key of Life***—made Wonder a major star and a perennial chart-topper. With influences ranging from the Beatles to Sly and the Family Stone, Wonder's melodic playing, soulful singing, and introspective lyrics established him as one of the country's great creative spirits, appealing to both traditionally black soul audiences as well as mainstream pop fans. (See Chapter 1, "Funk, Jazz-Rock, and Fusion: The Rhythm Revolution.")

Yes. With eight Top 20 albums in the United States between 1972 and 1978—including 1973's *Tales from Topographic Oceans* and 1974's *Relayer*—the elaborate **progressive** band Yes dominated the decade, riding the progressive rock roller coaster to its end with the explosion of **punk** music in the late 1970s. But in progressive's heyday through the middle of the decade, Yes stood in front of the line with successful major tours in the United States and Britain. Though critics sharply criticized the band's cerebral pomp (not an uncommon complaint with progressive bands), the group survived their detractors and even punk to remain at least a moderately successful act into the 1990s. (See Chapter 2, "Progressive Rock in the 1970s: But Is It Art?")

Young, Neil (b. 1945). Neil Young began his career playing with the group Buffalo Springfield in the late 1960s before embarking on a solo career that saw him produce both tender folk ballads and howling garage rock with the band Crazy Horse. He released his solo debut, *Neil Young*, in 1969 at the age of twenty-three. That year he played with two completely different bands. Crosby, Stills & Nash added Young to lend a gritty tone to the 1969 album *Déjà vu*, of which Young's "Helpless" is a highlight; also that year, Young released *Everybody Knows This Is Nowhere*, backed by the loud, ragged Crazy Horse. On his own, Young helped define the emerging **singer-songwriter** genre in 1970 with *After the Gold Rush*, a collection of bare acoustic songs. For the next three decades, Young would continue to cross between rock and folk boundaries, willfully hopping genres to the point that in the early 1980s Geffen Records sued Young for allegedly violating his contract by recording "unrepresentative" songs. (See Chapter 5, "Singer-Songwriters: Rock Grows Up.")

Zappa, Frank (1940–1993). While Britain produced the vast majority of the popular **progressive** acts, the United States produced Frank Zappa, not only a brilliant and original composer but also one of rock's champions in the fight against censorship that the music constantly faced. The 1970s saw Zappa take a more commercial—though still quite avant-garde—direction, disappointing some of his more particular fans but opening the door to thousands of impressionable devotees. After landing his first and only album in the Top 10—1974's *Apostrophe*—Zappa and his band the Mothers of Invention saw moderate success through the remainder of the decade with their jazz, world, and big-band experiments on albums such as 1975's *One Size Fits All*, 1975's *Bongo Fury*, and 1976's *Zoot Allures*. (See Chapter 2, "Progressive Rock in the 1970s: But Is It Art?")

NOTES

1. Vincent 1996, 183.
2. Jaan Uhelszki, "Led Zeppelin: Rock's Best Body English," *Creem*, May 1975.
3. Denisoff and Romanowski 1991, 222.
4. *Rolling Stone*, October 5, 1978.
5. Bangs 2003, 209.

APPENDICES

List of Top-Ranking Albums, 1974–1980

Shown here are the twenty-five top-ranking albums, 1974–1980, including number of weeks at No. 1, number of weeks in the Top 40, and chart debut date. These are ranked in order of total weeks spent at No. 1.

Artist	Album	At No. 1	Top 40	Chart Debut
Fleetwood Mac	*Rumours*	31	60	2/26/77
The Bee Gees	*Saturday Night Fever* (soundtrack)	24	54	11/26/77
REO Speedwagon	*Hi Infidelity*	15	50	12/13/80
Pink Floyd	*The Wall*	15	35	12/15/79
Stevie Wonder	*Songs in the Key of Life*	14	44	10/16/76
Various Artists	*Grease* (soundtrack)	12	39	5/20/78
Peter Frampton	*Frampton Comes Alive!*	10	55	1/31/76
Elton John	*Greatest Hits*	10	20	11/23/74
The Eagles	*The Long Run*	9	36	10/20/79
Billy Joel	*52nd Street*	8	34	10/28/78
The Eagles	*Hotel California*	8	32	12/25/76
John Lennon/Yoko Ono	*Double Fantasy*	8	27	12/6/80

(continued)

Artist	Album	At No. I	Top 40	Chart Debut
Led Zeppelin	*In Through the Out Door*	7	28	9/8/79
Wings	*Wings at the Speed of Sound*	7	27	4/10/76
Elton John	*Captain Fantastic and the Brown Dirt Cowboy*	7	24	6/7/75
The Rolling Stones	*Emotional Rescue*	7	20	7/19/80
Supertramp	*Breakfast in America*	6	48	3/31/79
Bob Seger and the Silver Bullet Band	*Against the Wind*	6	43	3/15/80
Billy Joel	*Glass Houses*	6	35	3/22/80
Barbra Streisand	*A Star Is Born* (soundtrack)	6	28	12/11/76
The Bee Gees	*Spirits Having Flown*	6	26	2/17/79
Donna Summer	*Bad Girls*	6	26	5/12/79
Led Zeppelin	*Physical Graffiti*	6	15	3/15/75
The Eagles	*Their Greatest Hits 1971–1975*	5	57	3/6/76
The Eagles	*One of These Nights*	5	43	6/28/75

Source: Whitburn 1987.

List of Most Significant Rock Albums, 1974–1980

James Brown
The Payback
January 1974

Roxy Music
Stranded
June 1974

Kraftwerk
Autobahn
November 1974

Bob Dylan
Blood on the Tracks
January 1975

Led Zeppelin
Physical Graffiti
February 1975

Bruce Springsteen
Born to Run
August 1975

Pink Floyd
Wish You Were Here
September 1975

Patti Smith
Horses
November 1975

Brian Eno
Discreet Music
December 1975

Queen
A Night at the Opera
December 1975

Peter Frampton
Frampton Comes Alive!
January 1976

Parliament
Mothership Connection
February 1976

Boston
Boston
September 1976

Stevie Wonder
Songs in the Key of Life
September 1976

Bob Seger and the Silver Bullet Band
Night Moves
October 1976

The Eagles
Hotel California
December 1976

Television
Marquee Moon
May 1977

Billy Joel
The Stranger
September 1977

The Sex Pistols
Never Mind the Bollocks, Here's the Sex Pistols
November 1977

Van Halen
Van Halen
February 1978

Talking Heads
More Songs about Buildings and Food
July 1978

Funkadelic
One Nation Under a Groove
September 1978

Neil Young
Rust Never Sleeps
July 1979

The Clash
London Calling
December 1979

John Lennon
Double Fantasy
November 1980

REFERENCE GUIDE

PRINT SOURCES

Aerosmith, with Stephen Davis. *Walk This Way: The Autobiography of Aerosmith*. New York: Avon Books, 1997.

Baker, Glenn A., and Stuart Coupe. *The New Music*. New York: Harmony Books, 1981.

Bangs, Lester. *Mainlines, Blood Feasts, and Bad Taste: A Lester Bangs Reader*. Edited by John Morthland. New York: Anchor Books, 2002.

———. *Psychotic Reactions and Carburetor Dung*. New York: Anchor Books, 2003.

Barnard, Stephen. *Rock: An Illustrated History*. New York: Schirmer, 1986.

Brackett, David, ed. *The Pop, Rock, and Soul Reader: History and Debates*. New York: Oxford University Press, 2005.

Breithaupt, Don, and Jeff Breithaupt. *Night Moves: Pop Music in the Late '70s*. New York: St. Martin's Griffin, 2000.

Bronson, Fred. *The Billboard Book of Number One Hits*. New York: Billboard, 1985.

Coon, Caroline. *1988: The New Wave Punk Rock Explosion*. New York: Hawthorn Books, 1978.

Copeland, Ian. *Wild Thing: The Backstage, on the Road, in the Studio, off the Charts: Memoirs of Ian Copeland*. New York: Simon & Schuster, 1995.

Crampton, Luke, and Dafydd Rees. *Rock & Roll Year by Year*. New York: DK Publishing, 2003.

Curtis, Jim. *Rock Eras: Interpretations of Music and Society, 1954–1984*. Bowling Green, OH: Bowling Green State University Popular Press, 1987.

DeCurtis, Anthony, James Henke, Holly George-Warren, and Jim Miller, eds. *The Rolling Stone Illustrated History of Rock & Roll*. New York: Random House, 1992.

Denisoff, R. Serge, and William D. Romanowski. *Risky Business: Rock in Film*. New Brunswick, NJ: Transaction Press, 1991.

Fletcher, Gordon. "Emerson Lake and Palmer." *Rolling Stone*, January 3, 1974.

Friedlander, Paul. *Rock and Roll: A Social History*. Boulder, CO: Westview, 1996.

George-Warren, Holly, and Patricia Romanowski, eds. *The Rolling Stone Encyclopedia of Rock & Roll*. 3rd ed. New York: Fireside, 2001.

Goodman, Fred. *The Mansion on the Hill: Dylan, Young, Geffen, Springsteen and the Head-on Collision of Rock and Commerce*. New York: Times Books, 1997.

Gray, Marcus. *Last Gang in Town*. New York: Henry Holt, 1995.

Green, Stanley. *Broadway Musicals Show by Show*. London: Faber and Faber, 1987.

Hassen, Barry. "Zappa: Continuity Is the Mothers' Mother." *Rolling Stone*, July 4, 1974.

Hendler, Herb. *Year by Year in the Rock Era*. Westport, CT: Greenwood Press, 1983.

Hewitt, Paolo. *The Jam: A Beat Concerto*. Omnibus Press, 1983.

Heylin, Clinton. *From the Velvets to the Voidoids: A Pre-Punk History for a Post-Punk World*. New York: Penguin, 1993.

Holden, Stephen. "Brian Ferry, *Another Time, Another Place*." *Rolling Stone*, January 2, 1974.

Holm-Hudson, Kevin, ed. *Progressive Rock Reconsidered*. New York: Routledge, 2002.

Howitt, Bernie. *Rock through History: Understanding the Modern World through Rock and Roll*. Melbourne: Longman, 1994.

The Illustrated Encyclopedia of Rock. Compiled by Nick Logan and Bob Woffinden of *New Musical Express*. New York: Harmony Books, 1977.

Jackson, John A. *A House on Fire: The Rise and Fall of Philadelphia Soul*. Oxford: Oxford University Press, 2004.

Larkin, Colin, ed. *The Virgin Encyclopedia of Popular Music*. London: Muse UK, 1997.

"L.A. Rock Uproar." *Rolling Stone*, June 5, 1975.

Macan, Edward. *Rocking the Classics: English Progressive Rock and the Counterculture*. New York: Oxford University Press, 1997.

Marsh, Dave, ed. *The Rolling Stone Record Guide*. New York: Random House, 1979.

Matlock, Glen, with Pete Silverton. *I Was a Teenage Sex Pistol*. Winchester, MA: Faber and Faber, 1991.

McMichael, Joe, and "Irish" Jack Lyons. *The Who Concert File*. New York: Omnibus Press, 1997.

McNeil, Legs, and Gillian McCain. *Please Kill Me: The Uncensored Oral History of Punk*. New York: Penguin Books, 1997.

Miles, Barry. *Zappa*. New York: Grove Press, 2004.

Miller, Jim. *Rolling Stone Illustrated History of Rock and Roll*. New York: Random House, 1980.

Monk, Noel E., and Jimmy Guterman. *12 Days on the Road: The Sex Pistols and America*. New York: William Morrow, 1991.

Moriarty, Frank. *Seventies Rock: The Decade of Creative Chaos*. New York: Taylor, 2003.

Morley, Paul. *Words and Music: A History of Pop in the Shape of a City*. Athens: University of Georgia Press, 2005.

Nichols, Mike. *About the Young Idea: The Story of the Jam 1972–1982*. New York: Proteus Publishing, 1984.

Pollock, Bruce. *Hipper Than Our Kids: A Rock and Roll Journal of the Baby Boom Generation*. New York: Schirmer Books, 1993.

Rensin, David. "Moody Blues." *Rolling Stone*, March 14, 1974.

Sarig, Roni. *The Secret History of Rock: The Most Influential Bands You've Never Heard*. New York: Billboard Books, 1998.

Savage, Jon. *England's Dreaming*. New York: St. Martin's Press, 1993.

Schinder, Scott. *Rolling Stone's Alt-Rock-a-Rama*. New York: Delta, 1996.

Shapiro, Marc. *The Story of the Eagles: The Long Run*. New York: Omnibus Press, 1995.

Sidran, Ben. "A Synthesizer Shopper." *Rolling Stone*, February 13, 1975.

———. "Tightening the Hand-Tooled, Turquoise-Encrusted Belt." *Rolling Stone*, May 22, 1975.

Sounes, Howard. *Down the Highway: The Life of Bob Dylan*. New York: Grove Press, 2001.

Trager, Oliver. *Keys to the Rain: The Definitive Bob Dylan Encyclopedia*. New York: Billboard Books, 2004.

Vincent, Rickey. *Funk: The Music, the People, and the Rhythm of the One*. New York: St. Martin's Griffin, 1996.

Welch, Chris. *Closer to the Edge: The Story of Yes*. London: Omnibus Press, 1999.

Whitburn, Joel. *Joel Whitburn's Top LPs 1979*. New York: Record Research, 1980.

———. *The Billboard Book of Top 40 Hits*. New York: Billboard, 2004.

———, ed. *The Billboard Book of Top 40 Albums*. New York: Billboard, 1987.

———, ed. *The Billboard Book of Top 40 Albums, 1955–1992*. New York: Billboard, 1993.

———, ed. *The Billboard Book of Top 40 Hits*. New York: Billboard, 1996.

———, ed. *Joel Whitburn Presents a Century of Pop Music*. New York: Billboard, 1999.

XTC and Neville Farmer. *XTC: Song Stories*. New York: Hyperion, 1998.

ALBUM LINER NOTES

Bad Company. *The "Original" Bad Company Anthology*. Notes by John McDermott. Elektra, 1999.

Clash on Broadway. Epic/Legacy, 1991.

Foreigner. *Foreigner Anthology: Juke Box Heroes*. Notes by Jerry McCulley. Atlantic Recording Corp. & Rhino Entertainment Company, 2000.

Funkodelic. *Maggot Brain*. Notes taken from Process Number Five on Fear the Process—Church of Final Judgement. Westbound, 1971.

Guterman, Jimmy. *Passion Is No Ordinary Word: The Graham Parker Anthology 1976–1991*. Rhino, 1993.

Journey. *Time3*. Notes by Joel Selvin. Columbia, 1992.

Kaye, Lenny. *Nuggets*. Rhino, 1998.

The Kinks. *Low Budget* (reissue). Notes by Fred Schruers. Konk/Velvel, 1999.

KISS. *KISS* (Box Set). Notes by Jeff Kitts. Mercury, 2001.

Led Zeppelin. *The Complete Studio Recordings*. Notes by Cameron Crowe. Atlantic Records, 1993.

McCann, Ian. *Stiff Records Box Set*. Rhino, 1992.

Osbourne, Ozzy. *Blizzard of Oz* (reissue). Notes by Phil Alexander. Epic, 2002.

Scoppa, Bud. *Hotcakes & Outtakes: 30 Years of Little Feat*. Rhino, 2000.

Townshend, Pete. *Lifehouse Chronicles*. Notes by Matt Kent and Pete Townshend. Eel Pie Productions Ltd., 2000.

The Who. *The Who by Numbers* (reissue). Notes by John Swenson. MCA, 1996.

WEB SITES

General Rock Music Sites

The All Music Guide. http://www.allmusic.com.
Reviews, biographies, and *Billboard* chart information.

Bomp! Records. http://www.bomp.com.

Creem Archive. http://www.creemmagazine.com/Pages/Archive.html.
Archives for *Creem* magazine.

Digital Dream Door's Rock & Roll Timeline 1970–1979. http://www.digitaldreamdoor
.com/pages/best_timeline-r3.html.

Fast'n'Bulbous Music Webzine: A History of Punk Rock. http://www.fastnbulbous
.com/punk.htm.

The Hyperreal Music Archive. http://music.hyperreal.org.

Make the Music Go Bang! A History of a Musical Revolution. http://pages.eidosnet
.co.uk/johnnymoped/punk/webpunk/webpunkhistorypage_introduction.html.

Official CBGB Web Site. http://www.cbgb.com.

The Old Punks Webzine. http://www.oldpunks.com/.

Punk Magazine Online. http://www.punkmagazine.com.

Punk77. http://www.punk77.co.uk.
An online history of UK punk rock from 1976 to 1979.

Recording Industry Association of America. http://www.riaa.com.

Rock on the Net. http://www.rockonthenet.com.

Rock's Back Pages. http://www.backpages.com.
Read the best writing on rock music ever.

Rolling Stone online. http://www.rollingstone.com.

The Rough Guide to Rock: Reviews and Biographies. http://www.roughguides.com/
music/rock.html.

Search & Destroy! http://www.trashsurfin.de.
Punk rock search engine.

Stiff Records. http://www.bestiff.co.uk/main.htm.

Trouser Press Magazine Online. http://www.trouserpress.com.

2 Tone Records. http://www.2-tone.info.

We Created It: Let's Take It Over! http://www.inch.com/~jessamin/.
Jessamin Swearingen's personal history of the emergence of punk rock in
America.

Performer Web Sites

Aerosmith. http://www.aerosmith.com.

B-52's. http://www.theb52s.com.

Stiv Bators. http://www.stivbators.com.
      Unofficial Web site.

Blondie. http://www.blondie.net.

Jackson Browne. http://www.jacksonbrowne.com.

Phil Collins. http://www.philcollinsfansite.com.
      Lou's Phil Collins fan site.

Elvis Costello. http://www.elviscostello.info.

The Eagles. http://www.eaglesband.com.

Emerson, Lake & Palmer. http://www.emersonlakepalmer.com.

The Kinks. http://kinks.it.rit.edu.

Led-Zeppelin.com. http://www.led-zeppelin.com.
      Comprehensive fan Web site.

Little Feat. http://www.littlefeat.com.

Patti Smith. http://www.gungho2000.com.

The Specials. http://www.thespecials.com.

Talking-Heads. Net. http://www.talking-heads.net.
      Fan Web site.

Television. http://www.marquee.demon.co.uk.
      The Wonder: "Tom Verlaine, Television & Stuff."

Pete Townshend. http://www.petetownshend.co.uk.

MUSEUMS OR SPECIAL COLLECTIONS

The Rock and Roll Hall of Fame and Museum
One Key Plaza
Cleveland, OH 44114
http://www.rockhall.com

FILMS

In chronological order:

Dont Look Back. Dir. D. A. Pennebaker. Leacock-Pennebaker, 1967.
Monterey Pop. Dir. D. A. Pennebaker. The Foundation, 1968.
Gimme Shelter. Dir. Alfred Maysles and David Maysles. Maysles Films, 1970.
Let It Be. Dir. Michael Lindsay-Hogg. Apple Corps, 1970.

Woodstock. Dir. Michael Wadleigh. Wadleigh-Maurice, 1970.

Jimi Hendrix. Dir. Joe Boyd, John Head, and Gary Weis. Warner Brothers, 1973.

Good to See You Again, Alice Cooper. Dir. Joe Gannon. Penthouse Productions, 1974.

Janis. Dir. Howard Alk. Crawley Films, 1974.

Journey through the Past. Dir. Neil Young. New Line Cinema, 1974.

Alice Cooper: Welcome to My Nightmare. Dir. David Winters. Dabill Productions, 1975.

Tommy. Dir. Ken Russell. Hemdale Films, 1975.

The Blank Generation. Dir. Ivan Kral and Amos Poe. Poe Productions, 1976.

Saturday Night Fever. Dir. John Badham. Paramount Pictures, 1977.

American Hot Wax. Dir. Floyd Mutrux. Paramount Pictures, 1978.

The Buddy Holly Story. Dir. Steve Rash. ECA, 1978.

FM. Dir. John A. Alonzo. Universal Pictures, 1978.

Grease. Dir. Randal Kleiser. Paramount Pictures, 1978.

I Wanna Hold Your Hand. Dir. Robert Zemeckis. Universal Pictures, 1978.

The Last Waltz. Dir. Martin Scorsese. FM Productions, 1978.

Punk in London. Dir. Wolfgang Büld. Stein Films (Germany), 1978.

The Punk Rock Movie. Dir. Don Letts. Notting Hill (England), 1978.

Renaldo and Clara. Dir. Bob Dylan. Lombard Street Films, 1978.

Sgt. Pepper's Lonely Hearts Club Band. Dir. Michael Shultz, 1978.

Hair. Dir. Milos Foreman. CIP Film Produktion (Germany), 1979.

The Kids Are Alright. Dir. Jeff Stein. The Who Films, 1979.

Rock 'n' Roll High School. Dir. Allan Arkush. New World Pictures, 1979.

The Rose. Dir. Mark Rydell. 20th Century Fox, 1979.

D.O.A. Dir. Lech Kowalski. 1980.

The Great Rock 'n' Roll Swindle. Dir. Julien Temple. Kendon Films (England), 1980.

Punk and Its Aftershocks. Dir. Wolfgang Büld. Stein Films (Germany), 1980.

Rude Boy. Dir. Jack Hazan and David Mingay. Buzzy Enterprises, 1980.

Jimi Plays Monterey. Dir. Chris Hegedus and D. A. Pennebaker. Pennebaker Films, 1986.

X: The Unheard Music. Dir. W. T. Morgan. Angel City, 1986.

End of the Century: The Story of The Ramones. Dir. Jim Fields and Michael Gramaglia. Gugat, Inc., 2003.

INDEX

About the Authors

CHRIS SMITH is a Vancouver-based writer and photographer who has served as music editor for *Performing Songwriter*, editor-in-chief for *Inside New York*, and associate editor for *University of Chicago Magazine*. His work has appeared in dozens of publications, including *Rolling Stone, Billboard, Time Out New York*, the *Sydney Morning Herald, Texas Music*, the *Village Voice*, and the *Journal of Visual Anthropology*. In addition to music and film journalism, Chris has worked as a combat correspondent, a festival producer, a wildlife photographer, a musician, and is the author of Volume 3 of this series.

JOHN BORGMEYER is the News Editor and Staff Writer for the *C-Ville Weekly*, an alternative newsweekly in Charlottesville, Virginia. His work has won awards from the Virginia Press Association, the Inlands Press Association, and the Association of Alternative Newsweeklies.

ROB PATTERSON has written for classic rock magazines such as *Creem, Circus, Crawdaddy, Spin*, and *Musician*. He has been a contributor to *The Rolling Stone Record Guide*, and his music writing has appeared in hundreds of daily newspapers syndicated by United Feature Syndicate and Newspaper Enterprises Association. He currently writes about music for *Harp* magazine, *Texas Music, Country Music People* in the United Kingdom, and *The Progressive Populist*. Patterson conceived of and co-produced the 1995 album *Austin Country Nights*. He sang on the Terry Allen album *Human Remains* alongside David Byrne and Lucinda Williams, has done publicity for Ozzy Osbourne, and has worked as a road manager for Don McLean.

RICHARD SKANSE is the editor of *Texas Music* magazine and a freelance writer whose features and reviews have appeared in *Rolling Stone, Tracks, Harp, Performing Songwriter, Sing Out!, The Journal of Country Music*, the *Austin American-Statesman, CMA Close Up*, and *New York Magazine*, as well as assorted Web sites such as RollingStone.com and LoneStarMusic.com. He has also contributed entries to *The Rolling Stone Encyclopedia of Rock & Roll* and *The New Rolling Stone Album Guide*.